Reading the Obscene

Post 45 Loren Glass, and Kate Marshall, Editors
Post•45 Group, Editorial Committee

Reading the Obscene

Transgressive Editors and the Class Politics of US Literature

Jordan S. Carroll

Stanford University Press
Stanford, California

STANFORD UNIVERSITY PRESS
Stanford, California

©2021 by the Board of Trustees of the Leland Stanford Junior University. All rights reserved.

"Reading Playboy for the Science Fiction" was originally published in *American Literature*, Vol. 87:2, pps. 331–358. ©2015, Duke University Press. Republished by permission. www.dukeupress.edu.

"White-Collar Masochism: Grove Press and the Death of the Managerial Subject" was originally published in *Twentieth-Century Literature*, Vol. 64:1, pps 1–23. ©2018, Hofstra University. Republished by permission of the copyright holder, and present publisher, Duke University Press. www.dukeupress.edu.

No part of this book may be reproduced or transmitted in any form or by any means, electronic or mechanical, including photocopying and recording, or in any information storage or retrieval system without the prior written permission of Stanford University Press.

Printed in the United States of America on acid-free, archival-quality paper

Library of Congress Cataloging-in-Publication Data
Names: Carroll, Jordan S., author.
Title: Reading the obscene : transgressive editors and the class politics of US literature / Jordan S. Carroll.
Other titles: Post 45.
Description: Stanford, California : Stanford University Press, 2021. | Series: Post*45 | Includes bibliographical references and index.
Identifiers: LCCN 2021007431 (print) | LCCN 2021007432 (ebook) | ISBN 9781503627482 (cloth) | ISBN 9781503629486 (paperback) | ISBN 9781503629493 (epub)
Subjects: LCSH: Censorship—United States—History—20th century. | Obscenity (Law) —United States—History—20th century. | Anticensorship activists—United States—History—20th century. | Editors—Political activity—United States—History—20th century. | Erotic literature—Publishing—United States—History—20th century. | Pornography—Social aspects—United States—History—20th century. | Middle class men—Books and reading—United States—History—20th century.
Classification: LCC Z658.U5 C37 2021 (print) | LCC Z658.U5 (ebook) | DDC 363.31097309/04—dc23
LC record available at https://lccn.loc.gov/2021007431
LC ebook record available at https://lccn.loc.gov/2021007432

Cover design: Jenny Burger

Typeset by Kevin Barrett Kane in 10/15 Minion Pro

For my family

Contents

Acknowledgments ix

    Introduction: The Naked Editor   1
1 Shocking the Middle Class   11
2 An Aristocracy of Smut   40
3 Decrypting EC Comics   71
4 Reading *Playboy* for the Science Fiction   101
5 Mad Ones, Mad Men   128
6 White-Collar Masochism   154
    Afterword: Transgression in the Post-pornographic Era   180

Notes 195

Index 255

Acknowledgments

First and foremost, I would like to express gratitude to my wife, Jenny, who gave me all the time and support I needed to complete *Reading the Obscene*. Special thanks go to her, as well, for designing the cover of this book. My son Bram was born before I completed my manuscript, and I thank him for giving me motivation to get through this project sooner rather than later. Thanks also go to my parents, Jim Carroll and Eva Smith-Carroll, and my sister, Hallie Carroll, for the encouragement they provided along the way.

I am fortunate to have worked with Loren Glass, Kate Marshall, Erica Wetter, Faith Wilson Stein, and Jessica Ling at the Stanford University Press Post*45 series. As someone who writes about editors, I appreciate all of their hard work on this project. This book was shaped by the perceptive feedback of the press's anonymous reviewers, who I thank as well.

Reading the Obscene began during my time at the University of California, Davis, where it benefited from the English department's commitment to interdisciplinarity and experimentation. I was helped immensely by Colin N. Milburn, who proved to be a careful reader and a kind friend throughout this entire process. I really could not have done this without him. I appreciate the support I received from Elizabeth Freeman, Kris Fallon, and Hsuan L. Hsu, as well, who were exceptional mentors and great allies on the job market. Additional thanks go to Ashutosh Bhagwat, Nathan Brown, Gregory Dobbins, Margaret Ferguson, Mark Jerng, John Marx, Matthew Stratton, and many other amazing faculty members who were at UC Davis. Throughout my career at UC Davis, I also received generous assistance from my colleagues, including Ian Afflerbach, Russell Backman, Molly Ball, Ashlee Bird, Mike Clearwater, Ranjodh Singh Dhaliwal, Rebecca Kling, Josef Nguyen, Magalí Rabasa, Bonnie Roy, Leilani Serafin, Marty Weiss, and Melissa Wills.

I also received thoughtful feedback from Russ Castronovo, Ivy Schweitzer, and everyone in my group at the Futures of American Studies Institute. There I met Annie McClanahan and Leah Hutchison Toth, who would go on to provide extensive advice and moral support in the later stages of my writing process.

It would have been exceedingly difficult to write several of the chapters in this project if I had not had the resources and breathing room offered by a postdoctoral position at the UC Davis ModLab. The ModLab is a partner in the IMMERSe Research Network for Video Game Immersion, which is supported by the Social Sciences and Humanities Research Council of Canada.

During the final revision stages of this project, my work was deeply enriched by my experience at the First Book Institute. I would like to thank Ben Bascom, Juliana Chow, Sean X. Goodie, Mary Kuhn, Christopher Perreira, Kathryn Walkiewicz, Sunny Xiang, and Xine Yao. Special thanks go to Priscilla Wald and Matt Tierney, who both challenged me to reconceptualize this project in significant ways. The First Book Institute turned out to be invaluable in helping me transform this into a fully formed monograph.

The English and Writing Department at the University of Tampa gave me a wonderfully supportive community to fall back on as I wrapped up this book. There I shared my writing and other troubles with Caroline Hovanec, Sucheta Kanjilal, Jeremy Lakoff, Kyle McIntosh, Ryan McIlvain, Steven Mollmann, Ashley Palmer, and Yuly Restrepo. Sarah Juliet Lauro, in particular, provided useful insights as I completed my introduction and book proposal. Thanks are due to the University of Puget Sound, as well, which has allowed me the opportunity to see this project through to the end.

I have benefited from additional comments and assistance from Lauren Berlant, Tyler Bradway, Paris Brown, Samuel Delany, Michael Barry Goodman, Jacob Lee, Benjamin O'Dell, Landon Palmer, Carrie Pitzulo, Remittance Girl, Mark Rose, Steven Ruszczycky, Whitney Strub, Sherryl Vint, Lawrence G. Walters, Amber Whittamore, and Qiana J. Whitted. I would also like to thank the EC Fan-Addict Club on Facebook, including Thommy Burns, Michael Creagen, Michael Draine, Kevin Klauber, Joe Prokes, Rob Reiner, and Gary VandenBergh, and Paul Wardle. A shout-out also goes to editor Dylan Lightfoot, who helped me clean up my writing as I prepared this for publication. Portions of two chapters appeared in *American Literature* and *Twentieth-Century Literature* in different form. I would like to thank the editors of those publications. Thanks, also, to everyone else who made this book possible.

My research would have been impoverished had I not received a number of awards, grants, and fellowships to support this project, including the UC Davis Humanities, Arts, and Cultural Studies Dean's Fellowship; the UC Davis Margrit Mondavi Summer Fellowship; the UC Davis Provost's Dissertation Year Fellowship; the UC Davis and Humanities Graduate Research Award; and multiple UC Davis English Departmental Summer Fellowships. This project also received funds from the Research Innovation and Scholarly Excellence Award from the University of Tampa.

Finally, I am deeply indebted to the libraries who helped me along the way. I thank the staff at Peter J. Shields Library at the University of California, Davis; the Macdonald-Kelce library at the University of Tampa; and the Collins Memorial Library at the University of Puget Sound. On the rare occasions when I could not find books at those libraries, I checked them out from the Sacramento Public Library, the Hillsborough County Public Library, and the Tacoma Public Library. I also appreciate the archives that have been crucial to this research, including Columbia University's Rare Book and Manuscript Library, New York University's Fales Library and Special Collections, Stanford University's Special Collections, Texas A&M University's Cushing Memorial Library and Archives, UC Berkeley's Bancroft Library, and UC Davis's Special Collections.

Reading the Obscene

INTRODUCTION
The Naked Editor

IN JANUARY OF 1966, the New York City Police Department placed Ed Sanders under arrest for possessing obscene literature with intent to sell.[1] When he was not singing for the satirical rock band the Fugs, Sanders served as the editor and publisher of a little magazine named *Fuck You / A Magazine of the Arts*, which he sold to friends and customers of his shop, the Peace Eye Bookstore. Before the bust, the state had Sanders under surveillance. Because Sanders had made a name for himself as a civil rights activist, antiwar protester, and marijuana-legalization advocate, the police sent an informant to keep tabs on him by auditioning for his band.[2] This experience made Sanders doubt the police officers when they said they stumbled on the obscene literature at Peace Eye in the process of investigating a burglary. He suspected instead that the cops had broken into the shop themselves to find a pretense to seize copies of *Fuck You* as evidence of criminal activity. Police escorted Sanders to the Ninth Precinct headquarters to be charged with a misdemeanor. What happened next, however, proved to be even more outrageous.

The incident was precipitated by a line from *Fuck You*'s contributors page. Sanders filled this front matter with dirty jokes, razzing his authors while advertising blow jobs, celebrating underage sex, and inventing editorial-board orgies. In this spirit, the editor introduced himself in his biography as a "a pacifist dopethrill psychopath & Guerilla Lovefare spaceout," boasting to the reader that "in addition to having the Ankh symbol tattooed on his penis, you will find the first 53 hieroglyphs of Akh-en-Aten's *Hymn To The Sun Disc*, on his nuts."[3] Of course, during his booking Sanders failed to record any identifying markings—the tattoos obviously did not exist—but Sergeant Charles Fetta and another officer still insisted that they needed to ascertain if he was telling the truth. The police officers marched Sanders to a bathroom, forced him to disrobe for inspection, and bent down "a bit *too* closely" to examine the editor's genitals.[4] Later, Sanders put out a press release announcing himself as "the only person in the history of American obscenity cases who has had his penis examined during station house questioning."[5] Needless to say, the authorities did not find any offending inscriptions.

On the surface, this may seem like a case of an overzealous cop with a personal vendetta. While most police rifling through the stock at Peace Eye laughed at the magazines they were confiscating, Sergeant Fetta appeared shaken by *Fuck You*'s contents. He later testified against Sanders and even shadowed him, popping up at a Fugs concert in Tompkins Square Park to search the audience's bags.[6] As unusual as Sanders's treatment in jail might have been, though, it was normal in midcentury America for an editor to be persecuted and imprisoned for publishing sexually explicit material.

From obscenity law's earliest cases to the present, editors have put their bodies on the line to publish controversial works. Public opinion and legal precedent cast editors as personifications of their publications and representatives of the audiences who read them. Fulfilling what I call the "editor function," editors served as punishable subjects responsible for the entire publishing enterprise.[7] If editors convinced the authorities that they were chaste readers, they had a better shot at escaping censorship. But, if they were shown to be impure, they were likely to face prison time. It should come as no surprise, then, that the cops examined the editor's body to search for signs of his publication's malicious intent. Although authors may sometimes take credit for transgressing censorship laws, the courts almost always tried editors and other cultural intermediaries for obscenity.

The scene between Sergeant Fetta and Sanders tells us something about the gender dynamics of these censorship struggles as well. Sanders is victimized, but it is the cop who ultimately looks shameful. In his account of the incident, Sanders hints at Sergeant Fetta's closet homosexuality: his shock upon encountering sexually explicit materials seems to betray some secret weakness or perversion, while his desire to inspect the editor's body suggests a ploy to get close to another man's naked penis. Sanders comes off as masculine by comparison. He is bold, boastful, risk taking, rule breaking, and a little contemptuous of the cop's predilections. The editor possesses masculine self-control—the censorious authority does not. Similar scenes run throughout the history of censorship in the twentieth century. Such confrontations allowed men to reassert their masculinity even in moments when disempowering circumstances appeared to place their manhood in jeopardy.

At the same time, the masculinity performed by these outlaw editors looked different from traditional or working-class notions of manliness. The circumstance around the strip search reflected the cultural hierarchies at play in many conflicts over obscenity, which often pitted well-read editors from middle-class backgrounds against opponents who they cast as uncultivated and uneducated. Sanders's narrative depicts Sergeant Fetta as a know-nothing, misreading the hieroglyphics in *Fuck You* as both sexually threatening and erotically appealing.[8] The ability to interpret and contextualize the magazine's messages and ideograms served Sanders as a signifier of formal education and literary learning. Although it is true that the editor did not have any tattoos on his person, hieroglyphics and other ancient writing systems were central to his poetics. Sanders, who considered attending a graduate program to study classical languages, learned to sight-read hieroglyphics at the New School and once taught a class on revolutionary Egyptology at the Free University. The New York State Police, perhaps detecting treason in the course title, recorded this fact in its files on criminals and subversives.[9] Sanders also named Peace Eye after the Eye of Horus, and every issue of *Fuck You* contained the editor's playful drawings of glyphs, historical or invented, alongside peace signs and cartoon hypodermic needles. Sanders's interest in hieroglyphics placed him in the same current as his two influences, Ezra Pound and Charles Olson, both of whom he had published.

Sergeant Fetta, presumably never having read Pound's *ABC of Reading* or Olson's "Projective Verse," failed to understand that the lewd hieroglyphics functioned as images suspended between graphic materiality and referential significance. Moreover, he lacked the reading skills to see that the erotic content in *Fuck You* represented "experiments with words rather than experiments with sexuality."[10] Repeating a familiar scene, the would-be censor reveals himself to be obtuse and oversexed when faced with the educated editor's publication, which he glosses in an all-too-literal way as he seeks out signs of deviance. The police officer's bad reading practices prompt him to make a fool of himself, looking for secret messages on the editor's penis. By contrast, Sanders exemplifies a middle-class manhood that takes a cerebral attitude toward sexuality, treating dirty speech as a language game in which bodies serve as signifiers.

Although Sanders was writing and editing for a coterie of poets, by 1966 the notion that graphic depictions of sex could be read as exercises in form would have been a familiar idea for mass audiences of educated readers who had made books like *Lady Chatterley's Lover* and *Naked Lunch* bestsellers. Sanders represents only a more extreme example of a type of professional-managerial masculinity that established its bona fides by showing that it could adopt a sophisticated attitude toward obscene literature. During this period, it was not unusual for a lewd hipster living in a squat to share the values and training of the professional-managerial class (PMC). As Mary Rizzo has shown, Sanders joined a wave of young people who came from middle-class backgrounds but who sought to escape their families' conformism, consumerism, and complicity with the capitalist system by adopting a lifestyle of "voluntary poverty."[11] Sanders affiliated himself with Dorothy Day's Catholic Workers—a communalist movement whose members renounced material possessions to serve the poor—until he was caught printing copies of *Fuck You* on their mimeograph machine. Later, he became a spokesperson for the counterculture of hippie dropouts who, as he told *Firing Line* host William F. Buckley, still retained their "middle-class equipment."[12] Sanders shares with his professional-managerial counterparts the view that sex is an abstraction or a symbol that can be manipulated to produce a rhetorical or aesthetic effect on his readership. No matter how scandalous Sanders and others like him may have seemed, they retained the prejudices and privileges of their class origins.

Working backward from this tableau, *Reading the Obscene* traces how obscenity became a central concern of PMC men. Chapter 1 provides a historical overview that traces how the editor became the perpetrator of obscene crimes and the PMC reader became the protagonist of censorship struggles. Together these figures conspired to initiate a middle-class sexual revolution that transformed sexuality into an abstraction. Chapter 2 shows that H. L. Mencken set the template for these professional-managerial readers at the beginning of the twentieth century by casting them as the country's unrecognized elite, a group smart enough to see through the emotionalism of censors and scolds.[13] By mid-century, this vision went mainstream as transgressive publications came to offer a kind of sentimental education for a generational cohort of affluent, white men who grew up to become engineers, lawyers, professors, and advertising executives.[14] Chapter 3 details how they spent their adolescence reading horror comic books like *Tales from the Crypt* with their friends. EC Comics editors William Gaines and Al Feldstein guided them through how to read even graphic scenes of violence as meaningless little puzzles, promulgating a game-playing attitude that prepared them for the cynical humor of *Mad* magazine and, ultimately, for the pointless rat race they would face as adults. As readers grew older, they began sneaking copies of *Playboy* under their mattresses. Chapter 4 shows how *Playboy* editor-publisher Hugh Hefner helped them become big men on campus by teaching them to take a step back from their interactions and think about how they appeared to women. By practicing this detached attitude during seduction, they learned the impression-management skills they needed to get ahead at work.

Many of these readers also found the avant-garde and counterculture during their college years. Chapter 5 reveals some of the ways undergraduate favorite Allen Ginsberg used his embodied and affective performance style to undo some of the hang-ups he experienced during his abortive career in advertising, and it seems likely that many of his readers would have found in his work an escape valve for their dissatisfaction with their own buttoned-down lives. Some, like Sanders, went further on this trip than others did, but the vast majority of Ginsberg's readers remained on upwardly mobile life paths. Chapter 6 demonstrates that many professional-managerial readers later graduated to readings from Grove Press and its house magazine, *Evergreen Review*. Expressing the idiosyncratic personality of Barney Rosset, the press used masochistic narratives to challenge its well-salaried readership to imagine what it would be like to let go completely and give up all of the power and prestige they had accrued over the course of their lives.

Some editors taught their audiences to see reading the obscene as a way of learning how to become good professional-managerial subjects, while others urged their readerships to use obscenity to heal the hidden injuries of the middle class. Either way, they all shared a belief in the power of profane speech to resolve the inner contradictions of professional-managerial masculinity.

Approaching this problem from another angle, this book is about the taming of obscenity. Whenever we think we are encountering raw, unedited obscenity, the surrounding context qualifies if not neutralizes its transgression. We see this even in the case of the editor of *Fuck You*, whose work seems furthest from the most respectable erotica purchased by white-collar readers. Sanders mocked the conceit that obscene language or images would allow the reader to transcend the page and access the real with any immediate certainty. In what may have been both a Warholian provocation and a lucrative confidence job, Sanders made a lot of money selling immodest artifacts from famous authors. For example, he hocked a jar of Ginsberg's cold cream with a signed inscription assuring the new owner that it was a "bona fide ass-wine or cock lubricant" that Ginsberg and his lover used together.[15] How can we be sure, though? We are told that the cream once held the impress of "A. G.'s cock-dent," but it has been "fluxed out."[16] Similarly, Sanders lists a fifteen-dollar "packet of pubic hair" including samples from such literary legends as Frank O'Hara and Amiri Baraka, but one imagines that a tangle of hairs from over a dozen luminaries and some unnamed donors would leave one specimen indistinguishable from another, regardless of its provenance.[17]

Sanders himself joins in this game, advertising special limited editions of *Fuck You*, each made unique by a "blotch" of the editor's sperm on the cover.[18] The overblown promotional copy that accompanies these offerings underscores the silliness of transgressive attempts to escape print mediation and enjoy direct access to the obscene body itself: indexical marks and forensic evidence fail to get us any closer. Instead, we see obscenity recast as an entrepreneurial gimmick that confirms the reader's insider status, reaffirms the editor's marketing acumen, and ultimately enriches the press. *Fuck You*'s ironic promotional strategies proved important in the obscenity trial that took place in 1967 as a result of the charges brought against Sanders during the raid of Peace Eye. Before the case against Sanders was dropped due to insufficient evidence, the prosecution's central exhibit was a parody advertisement for pornography from an imaginary subsidiary of the press, the Lady Dickhead Advertising Agency.[19] As we shall see, attempts to shock middle-class morality often converge with the salesman mentality, revealing obscenity to be elusive if not inexistent.

Obscenity is so hard to pin down because it depends entirely on context. Legal definitions will be explored at length in the next chapter, but, broadly speaking, obscenity included a complex of proscribed feelings—shame, lust, and morbid curiosity—that are usually associated with sex but sometimes connected to violence. Over the course of the twentieth century, obscenity law aspired to content neutrality: the state permitted publications depicting sex and violence so long as they did not appeal to impulses and emotions forbidden by contemporary community standards. Obscenity debates therefore often turn on legalistic versions of reception theory in which jurists try to imagine how audiences might feel about a book or periodical. Of course, obscene affects can stick to just about anything: a 1943 study of arousal in adolescent boys found that "love stories" were just one item in a long and varied list of erotic stimuli that included "punishments, examinations, sitting on warm sand, tight clothing, travelling by car, exciting sporting events."[20] To detect the diffuse and fleeting feelings associated with obscenity, judges and juries typically relied on clues from the publishing context to decide how a text or image was understood by its intended audience. This gave editors who were responsible for publishing controversial materials a strong incentive to pitch their publications to well-respected readers considered to be above suspicion. To this end, they sought out upscale audiences of professional-managerial men who supposedly had the self-possession to read transgressive literature without feeling obscene.

In this regard, *Reading the Obscene* builds on the work of Janice Radway's pathbreaking study, *Reading the Romance*. Radway suggests that the central problem facing book publishers is that they must produce ever-changing product lines for a dispersed and constantly shifting consumer base.[21] Industry profits depend on editors becoming experts in reader response as they struggle to anticipate which books will be popular with paying customers.[22] These difficulties were only compounded for transgressive editors whose publications risked running afoul of censors. On pain of imprisonment, these editors needed to predict not only how well books would sell but also how they would be read and interpreted by a readership composed of both private citizens and state actors. As such, they were forced to develop a repertoire of strategies to ensure that their books would seem to be properly received by irreproachable readers in the PMC.

Tracing the role of extreme literature in the lives of middle-class men, *Reading the Obscene* shows that editors reframed erotic and violent publications as rehearsal spaces for ambitious professionals to perfect the emotional and cognitive discipline believed necessary to manage themselves and others.[23] The PMC seems an unlikely public for borderline obscene material until one considers that, within the precincts of their occupations, professionals have often been asked to engage in unfeeling, amoral, or exceptional behavior: lawyers may say things they do not believe, doctors may gaze at nude bodies, and scientific managers may treat human beings as numbers. This abstracted attitude proves to be central to middle-class manhood as well. For the PMC, masculinity meant maintaining control over one's emotions and rejecting passive affects coded as feminine and feminizing.

Reading the Obscene argues that reading transgressive texts in normalizing or aestheticizing ways enabled white-collar workers to practice rising above private responses such as puritanical disgust and obscene desire. Through dirty books, they cultivated the self-abstraction required to carry out their official duties. Editors taught professional-managerial readers to suspend their personal judgments and impulses, an exercise in maintaining professional composure that helped them prepare to serve as functionaries in impersonal bureaucracies. By setting up carefully staged confrontations with de-censored material, editors convinced white men from the PMC that obscenity builds character. Bringing together legal history with literary sociology, *Reading the Obscene* traces the emergence of a self-disciplining middle-class sexuality over the course of the twentieth century while articulating an account of how editors constitute their own audiences by training them to adopt new reading practices.

As this brief overview suggests, *Reading the Obscene* offers an alternative theory of editorship that diverges from those of sociologists of literature who see successful editors as selecting books that reflect an audience's preexisting tastes. For Pierre Bourdieu, a strong editor knows which texts will appeal to their target audience because they share with their readers the same class background.[24] If there is no elective affinity between a text's aesthetic and an editor's readership, the result will be a misfire for the editor. According to Bourdieu, this prearranged harmony between editor, text, and audience has less to do with conscious decision-making and more to do with "practical mastery," the editor's intuitive feeling for the social rules of art.[25] The connection between editor, author, and audience ultimately derives from a common outlook conditioned by similarities in educational training, family circumstances, and socioeconomic positions.

Howard Becker arrives at a similar conclusion, albeit from a different theoretical perspective. Becker maintains that artistic activities are coordinated through conventions: spontaneous order emerges in the art world because most artistic practices, products, and institutions reflect a general agreement on how things are done.[26] In what Becker calls the "editorial moment," participants in the art world evaluate their artistic decisions with reference to these often-unspoken norms.[27] During the editorial moment, artists place themselves in the positions of others to imagine how their work will most likely be received by their peers and the public based on known conventions.[28] Of course, good artists sometimes learn to silence their inner critics, and some mavericks work to change their audience's view of what art should be. But Becker tends to cast the editorial moment as a step toward achieving consensus with the rest of the art world.[29] Like Bourdieu, Becker describes editing as the knack of choosing artworks that fall into alignment with the presumed sensibilities of an intended audience.

Unlike Becker and Bourdieu, this study emphasizes the activist and innovative side of the publishing enterprise. Simply put, *Reading the Obscene* argues that editing is a form of prefigurative reading.[30] While the majority of editors may only discern their readership's tastes, the most influential editors instill new reading habits in their readers.[31] Celebrity editors who want to invent new audiences have an array of teaching tools at their disposal. By describing an ideal reader, editors encourage their audiences to conform to its likeness. Through these reader representations, editors convey information about their target demographics and even the characterological traits of their intended audiences. Editorial pages, prefaces, and letters to the editor often present exemplary interpreters responding to the editor's publications. Whether explicitly or implicitly, these paratexts serve as manuals for reception.[32] In many cases, the ideal reader turns out to be the editor him- or herself. For example, editors such as Mencken, Hefner, and Rosset all described themselves as their own target audiences.

More subtly, editors impress on readers a shared sensibility through their manuscript selections. Readers become habituated to a publisher's house style through repeated contact with periodicals or publications in a series. Even without offering clear directives on how to read their work, editors foster new inclinations in readers simply by curating texts that elicit similar responses. By suggesting that editors help inculcate new reading habits, I am stating more than the obvious point that editors work to produce advertiser-friendly audiences who can be depended on to keep purchasing their publications—I am arguing that editors transform their published work into training regimens for developing know-how for grappling with innovative genres, styles, or modes of reading. As Radway has shown, readers can always resist these disciplining practices, but transgressive editors are quick to erase these rogue readers from the archive before the censors can detect them.[33]

The theory of editorship presented in *Reading the Obscene* allows us to avoid the false dilemma between censors who believe that pornographic readers simply reenact what they see on the page and free speech liberals who maintain that pornography has absolutely no effect on audiences. Borderline obscene publishers in midcentury America served a formative function.[34] Editors did more than simply convey certain propositional statements about sexuality to their readers: they helped readers use extreme content to build new capacities that they not only could use to negotiate with texts but also could deploy elsewhere in their own lives. Acquiring these skills and aptitudes did involve some form of desensitization; transgressive texts gradually ceased to seem so overwhelming as readers learned the protocols for dealing with them. Writing about pornographic film, Linda Williams repurposes Walter Benjamin's work on the mimetic faculty to argue that "through screening sex, our bodies are not simply shocked into states of arousal but habituated and opened up to this changing environment in newly socialized ways."[35] However, this book goes further to argue that the transferable schemas earned through persistent porn-reading can be used for surprising and creative purposes that often have little to do with autoerotic or otherwise sexual activity. Later chapters will show that the pornographic sometimes reproduces such unsexy skills and dispositions as work habits.

Although each of the figures I examine has been widely celebrated, this study resists the heroic myth of the outlaw editor and questions triumphalist histories of obscenity liberalization. As I argue in the afterword, recent events such as the weaponization of free speech have made it clear that a reconsideration of the politics of transgression is long overdue. Many of the same editors who worked to dismantle censorship also displaced obscenity onto othered audiences who they actively worked to exclude from their readerships. With this in mind, I seek to deflate some of the maximalist claims about obscenity made by theorists following Georges Bataille, who have often presented obscenity as inherently sublime and subversive.[36] When desensitization becomes a sign of distinction for PMC readers, we are forced to abandon the idea that obscenity overturns hierarchies and disrupts social order.

In the following chapter, I will begin to fill in the details of this admittedly schematic description of professional-managerial masculinity by weaving together the histories of erotic publishing, obscenity law, class formation, and gender politics in the United States. Along the way, I shall show that editors played a key role in instructing legal and lay audiences alike in how to read the obscene.

Shocking the Middle Class

PROFESSIONAL-MANAGERIAL READERS were drawn to the obscene as an opportunity to practice emotional distance and self-control. Ironically, this distancing practice promised its own pleasures: readers took satisfaction in parlaying overwhelming experiences into opportunities for intellectual mastery and skill development. For a stratum of middle managers and other young professionals, training oneself to tolerate extreme pornography proved central to subject formation and self-improvement. As we shall see, overcoming obscenity became a spiritual exercise for developing and disciplining a distinctly middle-class will to abstraction.

To understand how midcentury American editors came to market the Marquis de Sade to middle managers, we have to chart the long genealogy of obscene publishing.[1] This chapter will sketch out some of the historical context for my argument before going into greater depth about the professional-managerial sexuality that finally emerged, partly in response to this print culture, in the 1950s and 1960s. From its inception, criminal obscenity had as much to do with the person of the publisher as with the character of the book itself. Courts cracked down on publishers and distributors who marketed books that threatened to disrupt not only public morality but, just as importantly, the habits required for an aspiring middle class to achieve social mobility. Early American pornographic periodicals tried to preempt these concerns by demonstrating that the crudest of topics could be approached in a public-minded way, while late nineteenth-century publishers of erotic books attempted to position the reader as a gentleman-scholar capable of taking on an enlightened perspective on unseemly subjects. Although editors did not always succeed, they worked hard to class up pornography.

Obscenity entered into English common law through *Rex v. Curll* in 1727.[2] After Edmund Curll printed a seditious memoir, the courts used obscene libel as a pretext to convict him for republishing *Venus in the Cloister, or, The Nun in Her Smock*, a revealing dialogue between nuns, and *A Treatise for the Use of Flogging in Venereal Affairs*, an ostentatiously erudite discourse on erotic spanking.[3] Although the trial resulted in a split decision, one to two, the justices who voted to convict prevailed. According to one justice, publishing an obscene book was worse than indecent exposure because, while nudity offends only those present, a lewd publication "goes all over the kingdom."[4] Another declared that obscenity was "an offense against the peace" that tended to "weaken the bonds of civil society, virtue, and morality."[5] When the judgment came down, the court fined Curll a small sum for the newly invented crime.[6]

Blasphemous and seditious libel impugned the character of God or the monarch, while obscene libel defamed the public sphere itself.[7] Obscenity controversies concerned debates not only about the dividing line between the public and the private but also about the nature of public discourse. Whereas civil society was widely imagined as an abstract space for the circulation of ideas, pornography appeared to reintroduce unwanted embodiment, affect, and materiality into the public realm.[8] By prosecuting the crime of obscenity, courts worked in vain to shield the disinterested pursuit of reason from the promiscuous circulation of private desires.

Because the First Amendment of the US Constitution was structured around this notion of the public sphere, it has never actually protected obscenity from censorship. Early American courts adopted the crime of obscene libel, along with much of English common law.[9] According to contemporary legal thinkers, publishers and booksellers should be held legally responsible for obscenity because they transform the secret sin of a dirty manuscript into the punishable offense of a corrupting book.[10] While pornography was never officially legal in the early republic, enforcement of obscenity law remained sporadic in many parts of the United States through much of this period. New York prosecuted obscenity so rarely that one moralist, bemoaning the "flood" of pornography in 1833, observed that "one would think the devil had turned editor, and converted hell itself into a printing office."[11] Federal laws against obscenity would not arrive until Congress passed the US Tariff Act of 1842.[12]

The 1840s also marked the first moral panics over obscenity in the United States, which were kicked off by the birth of the flash press in New York City.[13]

The flash press was made up of weekly newspapers, published in New York City but disseminated widely, devoted to boxing, brothels, and blackmail. The flash press's audiences of armchair voyeurs mostly consisted of young provincial men, newly arrived in New York to fill entry-level, white-collar positions as sales clerks or secretaries.[14] This class position lent itself to the flash press's ideology, a belief system equal parts Tom Paine and the Marquis de Sade, which Cohen and others describe as "libertine republicanism."[15] To further the causes of anti-elitism, sexual freedom, and unrestrained speech, flash editors were willing to intrude on the bourgeois private sphere and disseminate their scandalous findings indiscriminately.[16] For this reason, prosecuting attorneys were galvanized to fight the flash press using the full force of obscenity law. Charges against flash editors became so frequent and successful that one noted, "An editor who has never been imprisoned for libel, may be considered a green-horn in his profession."[17]

As Michael Millner has shown, the flash press and the rest of antebellum, pornographic print culture cultivated a mode of reading that both challenged and redeployed the protocols of the public sphere.[18] The flash press, along with obscene novelettes, approached intimate matters with the same detached impersonality displayed in Habermasian rational discourse.[19] Unsentimental and unfeeling, obscene readers understood sex as bound up in a power dynamic every bit as political as slavery or the state.[20] At the same time, they also challenged existing hierarchies by presenting conventional politics as grossly corporeal: a hated politician might be depicted as retching in the street.[21] Dulled by repetitive overstimulation, the audience experienced all of this in a spirit of tedium, a jaded attitude that captured the emotional tonality of the public subject scanning the newspapers for information about the affairs of the day.[22] Through these moves, obscene publications trained readers to perform the "self-abstraction" required to speak within the public sphere even as it drew their attention to bodily experiences that must be repressed to do so.[23] As we shall see, the flash press was only the first in a long line of publishers who used pornography as a technology of the self, designed to encourage a blasé attitude to the body and its passions.

The flash press folded immediately before the rise of erotic book publishing in the US. Overseas imports and reprints largely dominated the market for literary erotica until publisher William Haines "naturalized obscene literature" in 1846 by moving from pirating pornography to publishing original works.[24] Haines's prolific and profitable business helped spark a larger trend toward American-made pornography. While editors in the twentieth century sometimes provoked censors to pump up their own public images, most pornographic editors in the nineteenth century worked hard to remain anonymous, falsifying title-page information about their books.[25] Pornographic publishers in the nineteenth century were also more likely to employ strategies of misdirection than to challenge the law. Most of them either refused to show up in court or pled guilty to their charges, and those who did fight conviction did so on narrow grounds that did not call into question obscenity law's constitutionality.[26]

Pornographers therefore put up little resistance when the federal government began to crack down on obscenity during and after the Civil War.[27] In 1865, Congress moved to stop the further demoralization of US soldiers by criminalizing the circulation of obscene materials in the federal mail. Nevertheless, the US Post Office Department enforced the ban only fitfully, and federal officials did little to restrain the interstate trade in pornography until 1873, with the passage of the Act of the Suppression of Trade in, and Circulation of, Obscene Literature and Articles of Immoral Use. Most people knew it as the Comstock Act, named after its biggest champion: Anthony Comstock, the founder the New York Society for the Suppression of Vice (NYSSV).[28] Comstock—who had been shocked by the reading habits of his fellow Union soldiers and equally dismayed at the vice he saw peddled back home—helped launch an immense moral crusade against erotic literature, sexual education pamphlets, contraceptives, and abortifacients, all of which were classified as obscene. To ensure compliance with the Comstock Act, the postmaster general made Comstock a special agent of the Post Office Department, conferring on him the power to investigate crimes and even make arrests.[29] At the end of his career, Comstock bragged, "I have convicted persons enough to fill a passenger train of sixty-one coaches, sixty coaches containing sixty passengers each and the sixty-first almost full. I have destroyed 160 tons of obscene literature."[30] He also took glee in having driven at least fifteen offenders to suicide, including abortion provider Madame Restell and feminist author Ida Craddock.[31]

Comstock's crusade brought about the case that would establish the first American test of obscenity. Comstock spent much of his career attacking sex radicals, including outspoken editors such as Victoria Woodhull, Tennessee Claflin, Lois Waisbrooker, Moses Harman, and Ezra Heywood.[32] Comstock's most lasting legal victory came with the trial of D. M. Bennett, editor of the *Truth Seeker*, for publishing a banned pamphlet arguing against marriage, *Cupid's Yokes*.[33] This case established the modern definition of obscenity, one that would be used in some courts until 1957. After striking down an appeal by Bennett, Judge Samuel Blatchford found that *Cupid's Yokes* was, in fact, obscene because it met the test laid out in the English case *Regina v. Hicklin* (1868), which held that obscenity was "the tendency . . . to deprave and corrupt those whose minds are open to such immoral influences, and into whose hands a publication of this sort may fall."[34] Typically, judges have interpreted this standard as banning any book that might debauch young children or sensitive adults.[35] The Supreme Court later affirmed the Hicklin test in 1896 when it reviewed the case of Lew Rosen, editor and publisher of *Broadway* magazine, a periodical featuring pictures of nude women, images partially obscured by a coating of lamp black that could be erased with a piece of bread.[36] Thanks to Judge Blatchford's decision, the Hicklin test would remain central to obscenity jurisprudence well into the twentieth century.

Why did censorship crusaders like Comstock suddenly come to see obscenity as such a pressing legal issue in the second half of the nineteenth century? While some suggest that obscenity law worked to contain an increasingly assertive working-class population, Nicola Beisel argues that Comstock's campaign against pornography succeeded in part because it played on elite fears about class reproduction.[37] Members of the capitalist and professional-managerial classes worried that their children would squander their inheritance of cultural and social capital by acquiring bad habits and fraternizing with the wrong crowds.[38] For example, by inducing stigmatized feelings such as lust, pornography threatened to unloose the emotional self-restraint that was increasingly becoming central to the middle-class character.[39] At a moment when remaining ensconced in the elite depended in part on marrying well and maintaining a moral reputation, Comstock argued that pornography lured well-born children into a downwardly mobile life of sin and crime. After pornography had destroyed their constitutions and characters, once-promising youths turned to gambling, prostitution, and murder. Others simply masturbated themselves to death. Factory owners, bankers, lawyers, physicians, and other white men of means supported the NYSSV to alleviate anxieties about their children's futures and reassert clear boundaries of taste, ethics, and manners between the wealthy and the poor.[40]

To combat this class ideology, erotic publishers developed their own counternarrative, turning Comstockery on its head. Although some continued to produce cheap smut for mass audiences, other pornographers tried to avoid censorship by transforming erotica into a sign of class distinction. "Fancy books"—expensive erotica—entered circulation in the US in the 1840s and became a booming trade after the Comstock Act passed.[41] Well into the twentieth century, publishers of privately printed editions of pornography outdid each other in producing ostentatiously designed books that one purchaser mocked as "furtive tomes in tasty bindings."[42] Through gold-stamped lettering and steep prices, erotic publishers signaled to both readers and police that they were writing for a select audience of affluent, intelligent men with fine sensibilities, a public that excluded such susceptible people as the young, the perverted, and the poor. A number of publishers claimed to limit their audiences to professionals who were interested in erotic classics or sexological tracts purely for research purposes.[43] Discerning readers, publishers insinuated, held themselves above the depravity and corruption that characterized obscenity.

To this end, pornographic publishing projected an imagined audience of qualified individuals who could approach erotic texts with an artistic or intellectual distance.[44] While some connoisseurs claimed to view sex with the rational detachment of doctors or anthropologists, others saw themselves as aesthetes. As Jay A. Gertzman observes, many pornographic publications cast the reader as an "aloof, uncommitted sybarite" capable of enjoying sex with a "cool, affectless sensuality."[45] Whereas the flash press abstracted sex in order to bring it into a public sphere that at least in principle any citizen could enter, the abstractions of fancy books signaled a more exclusionary print culture. Even as moral reformers warned that obscenity could undo one's middle-class upbringing, many pornographic publishers presented erotica as an opportunity to prove one's sophistication.

Obscenity as a Class Concept

Class continued to shape the terrain that censorship battles were fought upon through the first half of the twentieth century. What began in the nineteenth century as a marketing strategy for high-priced pornography became in the twentieth century a legal strategy for overturning obscenity law. Lawyers and activists strove to cement a clear connection between scandalous literature and the emergent PMC. Over the course of the twentieth century, the free speech movement succeeded in insulating questions of obscenity from popular opinion while empowering educated professionals to make determinations about censorship based on their own expertise. Meanwhile, courts became increasingly interested in how the publication context shaped whether a text triggered obscene responses from its readers. Under this heightened scrutiny, editors of borderline obscene texts began to pitch their publications to the professional-managerial audiences they knew had the most power to prevent them from being accused and convicted.

As Andrea Friedman has demonstrated, skirmishes over obscenity in the first decades of the twentieth century brought different factions within the middle class into contention.[46] White, middle-class club women and professional social workers joined forces to build voluntary organizations motivated by a progressive desire to protect children and improve urban society through cultural regulation and the extirpation of vice.[47] They were opposed in turn by legal and literary professionals from similar class positions. Procensorship forces faced a series of setbacks beginning with *United States v. Kennerley* (1913). During the trial of publisher Mitchell Kennerley, Judge Learned Hand protested that, although as judge he was bound by precedent to follow the Hicklin test, which weighed a text's effects on the most vulnerable, he believed that it would be better if obscenity was determined based on the standards of "the average conscience of the time."[48] After this victory, free speech lawyers began to push for a flexible definition of obscenity that eschewed moral absolutes so as to take into account changing social mores. Although Friedman calls this "democratic moral authority," establishing the average reader's moral limits and reading habits was a project carried out by people better paid and more educated than most citizens.[49]

The values of the PMC came to structure how sexually explicit speech was defended. Ian Hunter, David Saunders, and Dugald Williamson have rightly observed that obscenity regulation shifted "from medical policing to pedagogic management" over the course of the twentieth century.[50] Whereas nineteenth-century censors treated obscenity as a "poison" that had to be kept out of the hands of most readers, many twentieth-century jurists argued that obscenity was an aesthetic problem that could be safely confronted by anyone who had the right training.[51]

Building on this framework, I argue that obscenity gradually became a meritocratic mechanism for determining whether one was a member of the PMC. Then as now, professional-managerial workers were defined not only by their college credentials but also by the fact that they performed mental rather than manual labor.[52] Through battles over obscenity, legal and literary professionals proved that they were capable of intellectualizing anything, converting the gross material concerns of pornography into abstractions. The aestheticization of erotic images reasserted the ideological division between the clean professionals who worked with their minds and the dirty laborers who worked with their hands. Starting with the racy stories published by H. L. Mencken in the interwar period, literary obscenity moved away from interpellating the reader as an aristocrat or gentleman-scientist contemplating perversions from the safety of a study, and toward recasting audience members as managers performing the difficult conceptual labor required to ignore the concrete, sensual aspects of bodies and treat them instead as interchangeable units to be monitored and controlled.

Over the course of the 1920s, Judge Hand's pronouncements proved prescient as judges and juries became increasingly dissatisfied with the Hicklin test and unwilling to ban literary works. During this decade, a rising generation of publishers entered the field, pushing aside older and more genteel publishing houses. Many of these publishing firms were edited by first- or second-generation Jewish immigrants who had imbibed European culture, embraced modernism, and inoculated themselves against American puritanism.[53] Their cause scored a major victory when Bennett Cerf, editor at Random House, succeeded in getting *Ulysses* by James Joyce tried and acquitted in *United States v. One Book Called "Ulysses" by James Joyce* (1933).

At every step of the way, Random House's defense attorney Morris Ernst tried and succeeded to shield all deliberations about obscenity from majoritarian influences by placing it within the purview of professionals. As Ernst explains in *To the Pure*, his book-length argument against obscenity censorship coauthored with William Seagle, he took a dim view of most jurors, whom he believed to be too ignorant to appreciate fine literature and too eager to protect others from the same kinds of explicit material that they privately enjoyed.[54] Ernst made sure to eliminate jurors with vulgar tastes during selection because he believed that educated readers tended to have more liberal opinions on obscenity, but he was sometimes thwarted because "persons belonging to the book-buying public usually possess sufficient wealth or political influence to keep their names off jury panels."[55] Judges, Ernst believed, were better qualified to decide on obscenity, which may have been one reason that he waived his right to a jury trial for the *Ulysses* case.[56]

While defending *Ulysses*, Ernst continued to make the case that only experts were fit to decipher the meaning of Joyce's novel and other literary classics. *Ulysses*, he argued, was like an obscenity spoken or written in Chinese: "innocuous to anyone not acquainted with the language."[57] Because learning was equated with moral uprightness, the "style and method" of Joyce's book meant that it could not possibly be obscene because it was "incomprehensible to all but a comparatively few who are concededly immune to what the censor calls the suggestive power of words."[58] Here Ernst echoed *Little Review* coeditor Margaret Anderson who, along with Jane Heap, was prevented from serializing *Ulysses* in 1921: "Judgment on what is obscene in literature should be left to us experts."[59]

Expertise possessed obvious class dimensions. As Loren Glass suggests, the move to allow expert evidence into obscenity trials represented

> a larger shift in cultural authority in the U.S., from the fading moral hegemony of the genteel bourgeoisie to the expertise-based hegemony of the professional managerial classes represented, in the cultural sphere, by publishers, academics, critics, and authors.[60]

However public-minded the PMC might have been, they were also self-consciously elite. Ernst observed that, although *Ulysses* tended to bore the average reader, it nevertheless found a prized place at the most prestigious libraries, including Widener Library at Harvard.[61] Testimonies from academics and literary professionals suggested that censorship would do a grave disservice to Joyce's select audience of "intelligent readers."[62] While Joyce may have written a democratic novel of everyday life, one that includes voices often excluded from print, his defenders preserved the book on behalf of a distinguished minority of literary insiders.

Ernst knew that his class-based arguments against censorship were disingenuous. Elsewhere, in a discussion of the law's "apathy" toward erotica read by elites, Ernst sneered at this successful legal stratagem:

> Obscenity is also apparently a class concept. It is truly remarkable that no communist writer has yet composed a dissertation entitled: *Obscenity and the Class Struggle*. If obscenity is harmful, it is quite obvious that it will affect the physical and mental constitution of the rich and poor alike. The educated are supposed to be able to absorb a quantity of obscenity that would wreck the lives of the uneducated. Yet it has always been supposed that education made one rather

more susceptible to the influences of the passions. The upper classes lead a far more sensual life than the lower orders of society. We who live in a democracy cannot be particularly happy to recognize that there is no democracy of smut.[63]

Surveying the censor's deference to consumers of erudite or high-priced erotica, Ernst concludes that Americans live under "the rule of an aristocracy of smut."[64] The lawyer's appeal to class prejudices may have been cynical, but it worked.

Just as Ernst insisted *Ulysses* must be interpreted by literary experts, he also maintained that the community standards must be established by the well-credentialed few. In his concluding argument, Ernst states that because "people as a mass are inarticulate," they must make their moral preferences known through "newspapers, college professors, critics, educators, authors, librarians, clergymen and publishers" who "speak for the body social."[65] Judge Woolsey clearly agreed. When it came time for him to make a decision about *Ulysses*, he enlisted the help of two fellow Yale graduates: Henry Seidel Canby, a former Yale University professor who edited the *Saturday Review of Literature*, and Charles Edmund Merrill, Jr., president of a textbook publishing company.[66] Of course, it is certainly true that Woolsey, Ernst, and all the other actors in this legal drama were constrained by prevailing legal opinion that would have censored *Ulysses* if it had been found to be subversive, especially if it appealed to working-class audiences.[67] However well-intentioned their motives may have been, though, Joyce's defenders willingly or unwillingly reaffirmed obscenity as a privilege of an exclusive class stratum.[68]

One midcentury commentator would later contend that censorship was "a byproduct of class rivalry," a struggle between competing worldviews conditioned by divergent socioeconomic positions.[69] We may be used to thinking of obscenity as a populist challenge from below, suppressed by the dominant class, but the typical anti-vice activist in the twentieth century was more likely to be a "lower-middle-class censor" venting his resentment toward a transgressor who inhabited another class location that seemed to have more cultural prestige if not greater economic and political power.[70]

The US attorney appealed Judge John M. Woolsey's "not guilty" verdict, but it was ultimately affirmed by a panel of three judges, with one judge dissenting. Judge Augustus Hand, who wrote the majority opinion, recommended revising the Hicklin test so that it took into account contemporary community standards of taste and morality, evaluated the work's effect on average readers rather than prudish or puerile ones, considered the work as a whole rather than isolated passages, balanced obscenity against literary or social value, and entertained evidence from experts.[71] Nevertheless, even the influential *Ulysses* case was sometimes ignored in courtrooms where it did not set precedent, and, until the Supreme Court weighed in with *Roth v. United States* in 1957, the country followed a "patchwork" of standards in which some judges decided obscenity cases based on the Hicklin test and others decided based on Woolsey's verdict.[72]

The *Roth* decision formulated a somewhat more lenient and liberal test for obscenity, one that weighed "whether to the average person, applying contemporary community standards, the dominant theme of the material taken as a whole appeals to the prurient interest."[73] *Roth* followed the *Ulysses* decision in offering a more responsive test for censorship that took into account a shifting audience with changing mores. Obscenity was an elicited response, dependent in part on the court's appraisal of a work's readership within a social and historical context. Although *Roth* is sometimes considered a step forward toward liberalization, the Warren-led Supreme Court failed to reject obscenity law as unconstitutional or narrow in its application to only those materials that represented a clear and present danger to the public.[74] Thanks to the decision, editor and publisher Samuel Roth remained in jail for the remainder of his five-year sentence for publishing risqué books and periodicals such as his *American Aphrodite* series.[75] Once again, editors rather than authors or readers paid the price for obscenity.

Roth also confirmed that the question of obscenity hinged on the division of mental and manual labor. Quoting the *Chaplinsky v. New Hampshire* decision, *Roth* held that certain "utterances" such as obscenity or fighting words have no value protected by free speech law because they play "no essential part of any exposition of ideas."[76] *Roth* suggested that free speech law does not protect the materialities of communication, which are accidental to the central purpose of the First Amendment, namely, the protection of the free transmission of ideas between minds. The court's decision confirmed the contention of Roger Fisher, who, arguing on behalf of the United States, told the Supreme Court justices that pornographic "matter" does not have any value worth protecting because it simply does not possess enough "ideas per pound."[77]

Legal scholar Frederick Schauer later took this line of thinking to its logical conclusion when he suggested that pornography did not even count as speech for the purposes of constitutional law: writing pornography conveys bodily pleasures rather than incorporeal information. Even though erotica does not involve two people directly touching one another, writing fiction intended to produce arousal is a noncognitive "physical activity," one not unlike a "leather-clad prostitute" thrilling her client with the sound of a leather whip cracking near his ear.[78] In this view, an obscene book is no more communicative and therefore no more deserving of free speech protection than a sex toy sent by mail.[79]

Furthermore, *Roth* marked the beginning of the court's attempts to explicitly theorize the importance of the publisher's practices in determining obscenity. In a concurring opinion for *Roth*, Chief Justice Earl Warren argued that obscenity depended on the publication venue:

> It is not the book that is on trial; it is a person. The conduct of the defendant is the central issue, not the obscenity of a book or picture. The nature of the materials is, of course, relevant as an attribute of the defendant's conduct, but the materials are thus placed in context from which they draw color and character. A wholly different result might be reached in a different setting.[80]

The crime of the obscene publisher came to be known as "pandering, i.e., the purveying of publications openly advertised to appeal to the customers' erotic interest."[81] Even the most high-minded of materials could become obscene when prostituted by a smut peddler. Legal scholars supporting Warren argued that other obscenity tests relied on a fetishism that transposed the evil of pandering publishers onto the publication itself. Publisher-blind criteria risked treating the censored book like a deodand, an animal or implement sacrificed to God after causing someone's death.[82] Warren's standard meant turning from moral evaluations of inanimate objects such as print materials back to legal judgments about human guilt or innocence.

According to Warren, the pandering test rested in part on the publication's likely audience. Here, Warren borrowed from the influential 1954 *Minnesota Law Review* article by William B. Lockhart and Robert C. McClure, "Literature, the Law of Obscenity, and the Constitution." Lockhart and McClure argue that courts should take into account the channels used to disseminate publications accused of obscenity: if literature is promoted to salacious audiences, it is obscene, but if the text's publisher caters only to morally and intellectually serious readers, then it is not obscene.[83] Unsurprisingly, the criteria for making this distinction includes proxies for socioeconomic class such as the prestige of the publisher and the cost of the publication.[84] As we shall see, the courts tacitly assumed that only the knowledge workers and symbolic analysts of the PMC were capable of approaching erotic representations at the level of ideas.

Warren's position remained in the minority on the court until *Ralph Ginzburg v. United States* (1966), which held that publications could be found obscene based on the "context of their production, sale, and attendant publicity."[85] Respectable publishers could publish borderline pornographic works, but when less savory editors published comparable material, it was considered pandering. Ginzburg was convicted for publishing two periodicals—*Eros* and *Liaison*—as well as a short book, *The Housewife's Handbook on Selective Promiscuity*. As Justice William J. Brennan, Jr., admitted in his decision, publications like the *Handbook* might possess redeeming value in a "controlled, or even neutral environment," but the publishing context in which they appeared "stimulated the reader to accept them as prurient."[86] Whatever legitimacy Ginzburg had secured for his publications was undercut by the fact that he had tried to obtain mailing privileges from Intercourse, PA, and Blue Ball, PA, a dirty little joke conferring on his publications a "salacious appeal."[87] Shortly thereafter, *Edward Mishkin v. New York* (1966) underscored the importance of publishing context by stipulating that publications failed the prurient-interest test if they were "designed for and primarily disseminated to a clearly defined deviant group."[88] The decision, which concerned a publisher convicted for commissioning and selling BDSM, fetish, and gay-themed paperbacks, inspired police to renew their efforts to crack down on homoerotic media.[89]

The new standard was not without its critics: in addition to the usual civil libertarian dissenters, Justices William O. Douglas and Hugo Black, Justices John Marshall Harlan II and Potter Stewart took serious issue with the theory of pandering, which seemed to diverge significantly from previous interpretations of *Roth* by moving the focus from the text to the context. These dissents would win the day eventually, with the pandering doctrine quietly discarded.[90] Nevertheless, Warren's criteria made up part of the legal common sense, even if the courts did not always explicitly affirm them. Whatever the vicissitudes of obscenity law, publishers were pushed to present themselves to courts as representatives of decent audiences of affluent people.

Ginzburg failed in this task during the trial. In accounts from his court appearances, he seems to represent all that is wrong about his publications. Using the same terms typically applied to obscene books, an observer recounts one of Ginzburg's friends describing him as "without a single redeeming social feature. He is a lewd and obnoxious man, and the reason he is going to fail is that he acts badly in courtrooms."[91] When he showed up for trial, he wore loud clothes and a boater hat, sniping at a judge who complained about his attire. He was prickly, he made faux pas, and he somehow just "looked like a smut peddler."[92] Viewed as sorely lacking in taste, Ginzburg became a kind of living incarnation of his dirty magazines, appearing for the entire court as déclassé and therefore obscene. They did not see Ginzburg the individual—they judged Ginzburg in his role as a representative of his readership.

Ginzburg was sentenced to five years in prison and served only eight months, but he was one of the last editors to face incarceration for printing pornography. The *Roth* test had proved to be hopelessly vague and ultimately unworkable. Obscenity cases made their way up to the Supreme Court again and again, leading the justices to refine their criteria for obscenity. Drawing on the *Roth* decision, civil libertarian defense lawyers pressed for a second test, parallel to the prurient-interest test: if a work has redeeming social importance, they suggested, it is protected by the First Amendment.[93] Following the *Roth* decision, Lawrence Ferlinghetti of City Lights Books prevailed in *California v. Lawrence Ferlinghetti*, saving *Howl and Other Poems* from censorship.[94] Shortly thereafter, Grove Press under Barney Rosset fought and won a series of sensational cases, including cases defending *Lady Chatterley's Lover* by D. H. Lawrence in 1959, *Tropic of Cancer* by Henry Miller in 1964, and *Naked Lunch* by William S. Burroughs in 1966.[95] Grove succeeded in overturning longstanding bans on controversial books in part because courts readily saw that they were a "reputable publisher" backed by esteemed academics, authors, and critics, a literary press that would never "attempt to pander to the lewd and lascivious minded for profit."[96]

By 1966, Justice Brennan endorsed the social-value theory of obscenity in the *Memoirs v. Massachusetts* decision, albeit without majority approval. While courts in the late 1960s were unable to come to a consensus as to the definition of obscenity, this period saw a de facto liberalization of restrictions on erotic literature and film.[97] *Redrup v. New York* (1967) seemed to be the final nail in obscenity's coffin. A newsstand clerk, Robert Redrup, had been convicted of obscenity for selling two sex pulps from Greenleaf Classics, *Lust Pool* (1964) and *Shame Agent* (1964). The Supreme Court overturned Redrup's conviction, seeming to indicate an unspoken conclusion that even the most lowbrow pornographic literature possessed some redeeming value and must therefore be protected.

Beyond its legal significance, *Redrup* reveals a class split in the field of obscenity law under *Roth*: the courts absolved literary publications for middle-class audiences in celebrated cases before tacitly allowing sleaze to circulate freely. According to Greenleaf Classics editor Earl Kemp, when his publisher William Hamling beat federal obscenity charges of his own in Texas, he was elated: "The courtroom battle that had begun more than 30 years before in the case of *United States v. One Book Called Ulysses*, resulting in a victory for the literary elite, had now ended in 1967 with a triumph for the man in the street."[98] Obscenity, it seemed, had ceased to be a class concept.

However, the court's terse decision in *Redrup* betrayed an inability to come to a consensus on the issue, which meant that, when the court began embarking on a policy of summarily reversing obscenity convictions in the final years of the 1960s, the justices ultimately left the obscenity framework intact and unchanged for the more conservative court led by Warren E. Burger to revive in 1973 with *Marvin Miller v. California*, a case centering on a pornographic book distributor of low repute.[99] Although the *Miller* test required publications to meet stricter criteria than the *Memoirs* test—they must demonstrate "serious literary, artistic, political or scientific value"—following the decision obscenity prosecutions for text-only works became incredibly rare.[100]

We can now begin to see how some editors of borderline obscene publications succeeded in avoiding censorship by creating what Justice Brennan would call a "controlled, or even neutral environment" for erotic literature.[101] Because they determined the publishing context, editors of borderline obscene texts could encourage chaste responses to their publications while precluding prurient ones. Following the playbook laid out by Ernst, erotic publishers staved off obscenity charges by selling transgressive fiction to prestigious audiences. Evidence suggests that this was a successful marketing push. Alfred C. Kinsey's *Sexual Behavior in the Human Male* (1948) found that college-educated men were more likely to report that they read or viewed pornography compared to high school or grade school educated men, and *The Report of the Commission on Obscenity and Pornography* (1970) described average adult-bookstore patrons as predominately "white, middle aged, middle class, married, male, dressed in a business suit or neat casual attire."[102] In the process of catering to these readers, editors invented new modes of impersonal reading that both drew on and departed from the abstractive reading practices we saw in accounts of the flash press and fancy books. Erotic publishers had a pedagogical function: they cultivated new audiences capable of overcoming obscenity.

Gendering Obscenity

One reason professional-managerial men needed to grapple with obscene literature was that it helped them cope with what they thought of as a crisis of masculinity. Barbara Ehrenreich and Bill Osgerby argue that PMC men turned to racy magazines like *Esquire* and *Playboy* to negotiate with shifts in gendered patterns of reproduction and consumption.[103] Before the sexual revolution, upstanding men conformed to the "breadwinner ethic": they worked to provide for their wives, who were locked out of well-paying jobs due to the inequalities of the family wage system.[104] Although mainstream culture continued to uphold the nuclear family, male dissidents criticized this arrangement as sexually restrictive and financially draining. This argument found its way into transgressive publications, which condemned the warm feelings surrounding family togetherness and heterosexual monogamy as tools of manipulation wielded by emasculating women to trap men into paying them to stay home all day. Mencken, a lifelong bachelor, pointed out that the only reason that men shackled themselves in marriage was an unfortunate propensity for "sentimentality."[105] Women were the colder sex, he asserted, and men needed to learn the same emotional control if they wanted to avoid giving away their freedom and their hard-earned money to undeserving dependents. During the transition away from the breadwinner model, men adopted a distanced perspective on sexuality in order to escape the affective and moral attachments that bound them to what they saw as inevitable marital misery.

Putting these ideas into practice, some professional-managerial men delayed or forwent marriage and used the extra money in their paychecks to fund a lavish leisure lifestyle better suited to the booming consumption-based economy.[106] Because the old ethic construed any attempts to shirk hetero-familial commitment as symptoms of immaturity and homosexuality, the new professional-managerial bachelors reasserted their normative masculinity by making a show of enjoying sexually explicit depictions of women. Pornographic spectatorship allowed straight middle-class men to maintain their gender and sexual identities even as they shifted from the old "morality of duty" that cautioned against hedonism to "a morality of pleasure as duty" that extolled the pursuit of hetero-erotic sex as normal, healthy, and sane.[107]

Sexual objectification also helped men deal with their gender trouble at work. As masculine, homosocial offices became gender integrated, professional-managerial men turned into workplace sexual aggressors to reestablish their own masculinity while reinforcing women's subordination in low-level secretarial roles.[108] This allowed them to compensate for changes in white-collar working conditions that left them fulfilling stereotypically feminine roles.[109] Increasingly men laboring in bureaucratic organizations found themselves in positions of dependence that required them to be sensitive to the needs and feelings of their superiors, who determined whether they would succeed or fail in business. In other words, while working-class men embodied a masculine identity in physical labor and petit-bourgeois shopkeepers demonstrated the same through hard-headed practicality, the PMC frequently vied for career advancement using the same kinds of soft skills perfected by housewives. Even professional-managerial workers in the technical and academic professions found themselves unable to validate their manliness through entrepreneurial risk or backbreaking toil.

Social critics such as David Riesman saw these changes as indicative of a more fundamental shift in the nature of the self: no longer driven by steady internalized discipline, professional-managerial men followed context-specific norms that enabled them to reshape themselves continuously to fit their occupational molds.[110] Whereas older notions of manhood were said to be organized around stubborn individualism, the new masculinity involved anxiously scanning others for approval in much the same way that women had traditionally been taught to do.[111] These perceived changes became bound up in widespread worries that bureaucracy, mass culture, feminism, family togetherness, and consumerism were all sending masculinity into a terminal decline that would leave American men too "soft" to stand up against the communist threat.[112] To dispel any notion that their ingratiating behavior was somehow feminine, professional-managerial men turned to narratives about men like them who used resume-building traits such as emotional intelligence and technoscientific knowledge to seduce women. By viewing their occupations from the distanced perspective of a pornographic voyeur, men were able to see themselves as outwardly conforming but inwardly nonconforming. They might do everything the bosses wanted them to do, but they *chose* to follow the rules because this regimentation played into their kinks. Reading the obscene allowed men to achieve a perverse version of the "autonomous" personality extolled by authors such as Riesman.[113]

Although subordinating women proved central to the development of these new forms of middle-class masculinity, I want to argue that something more than a simple reassertion of patriarchal domination was going on here. Priding themselves as enlightened liberals, many midcentury male readers imagined scenarios in which they relaxed the sexual double standard and relinquished their claims to possession over women. They did not want to own women—they wanted to employ them. Bachelors dreamed of replacing the unwaged work performed by housewives with efficient waged labor they could let go at will. Mencken talked about unbundling all of the services that a housewife performed so that a man could pick and choose between them without having to commit to all of them—a bachelor could hire a housekeeper, a money manager, or a cook as needed—but by the postwar period men increasingly relied on the full treatment of office wives who performed many of the menial tasks, emotional labors, and sexual favors that legal spouses might otherwise take care of for them.[114] Although men still hyper-exploited their office wives in highly gendered ways—secretaries performed feminized labor, after all—these arrangements nevertheless represented a departure from the monogamous couple form that had heretofore prevailed under Fordism.

This fundamentally changed the character of the reproductive tasks in these men's lives. To understand how, we have to take a brief detour to look at more traditional arrangements of unpaid care work. As the Endnotes Collective points out, a housewife works in sphere of "indirect market mediation": she receives money from her husband's wage, but she does not sell her services directly to a market.[115] Although she might try to complete her household duties quickly and efficiently, a housewife does not have to face the economic compulsion to standardize her work or maximize the goods and services she provides. She may make three meals a day for her family, for example, but if she purchases a new kitchen gadget that allows her to cook everything twice as fast, nobody expects her to use the time saved to produce six meals a day. Labor-saving conveniences might have freed up housewives to spend extra time cleaning the baseboards—and, indeed, men often demanded exactly this—but they did not necessarily translate into higher productivity. Many household tasks such as childcare simply cannot be rationalized in the same way as other forms of labor: a child must be watched at all times, and multiplying the number of children under the supervision of a single individual quickly degrades the quality of care. The Endnotes Collective refers to these kinds of recalcitrant activities as "the abject," "what cannot be subsumed or is not worth subsuming" by capital.[116] In other words, abject labor can be sold to consumers for a price, but it is difficult if not impossible to reorganize the abject to extract more relative surplus value.

But professional-managerial men imagined that they could in fact carry out the real subsumption of all reproductive activities, including sex itself. This gets at the heart of why middle-class pornography seemed so disturbing—and so appealing. Sex is the ultimate abject: corporeal as well as moral, emotional, and social barriers circumscribe how much sex can be streamlined while remaining desirable. The obscene crossed these limits when transgressive literature either imagined women's bodies as modular parts in an eroticized labor process or showed those sexualized bodies rebelling against managerial control. Ultimately, men in the PMC hoped to replace direct patriarchal control over women with the "abstract impersonal domination" that governs market-disciplined work.[117]

Perpetual Spirals of Professionalism and Pleasure

By eroticizing abstractions, professional-managerial men played into some of the deepest fears and anxieties of the postwar period. Artists and intellectuals working within the American context argued that a dangerous system of abstractions held society in its grip.[118] Looking back in horror at the Holocaust, total war, and the atom bomb, some argued that personnel on both sides of World War II were able to kill without conscience because they were part of increasingly distanced and mediated chains of causal connections.[119] The sharpening division of labor, growing scale of organizations, and development of technical rationality at the expense of critical reason meant that no one followed or carried out a task from beginning to end, allowing each worker or manager to participate in the commission of crimes against humanity without ever encountering their victims face to face or, often, without even knowing they existed. Divorcing planning from implementation, abstraction seemed to boil entire populations down to numbers and symbols before liquidating them. As mass society reorganized itself along these lines, individuals found themselves isolated from others and separated from any experiences that could not be reduced to quantitative terms or standardized formulas.

The critique of abstraction was often an anti-communist as well as anti-fascist intellectual formation, and therefore it tended to oppose class-based analysis either because the system of postwar organization engulfed the worker, consumer, and capitalist alike or because classes were themselves abstractions that erased the humanity of actual individuals.[120] However, when we look closely at many of these arguments, we begin to see that what seemed to be a critique of an entire society turns out to be centered on a specific middle-class formation, one whose problems and conditions have often been misread as universal and classless.[121]

In midcentury America, the PMC embodied and oversaw a culture of abstraction. According to authors such as C. Wright Mills and Erich Fromm, members of management absorbed the values of immense, impersonal firms that treated people as functions rather than as ethical subjects.[122] Midcentury managers worked to further a larger project of forcing a system of "bureaucratic control" derived from office work onto both mental and manual labor.[123] This new regime of control replaced the arbitrary, personal decision-making of managers and foremen with the "rule of law": everything from job descriptions to dismissals was governed by fixed regulations that management could appeal to whenever they were forced to take unpopular or unpleasant actions.[124] In other words, management strove to make itself appear neutral because each employee—supervisory or nonsupervisory—was effectively interchangeable: anyone would make the same calls if they were slotted into the same position.[125] Thus, the organizational form itself maintained the hierarchy and order once governed by the personal authority of bosses. Bureaucratic control seemed to perform as if on its own, irrespective of personal wants or inclinations, and rewarded employees who bent themselves to fit the predictable routines of the system.[126] To conform to this new organizational abstraction, management imposed on itself a cool emotional style before demanding others show the same restraint.[127]

Professionals were no less pulled toward self-abstraction.[128] Under the ideology of professionalism, experts could only exercise a legitimate power or influence insofar as they presented themselves as neutral and disinterested, speaking on behalf of pure reason or public interest. Professionals therefore developed a mode of scientific or critical discourse that screened out references to the speaker's social background and private experiences, so as to become, in Alvin Gouldner's words, "disembodied, de-contextualized, and self-grounded."[129]

Theodore Roszak painted a more sinister picture of technocratic experts cursed by what he called the "myth of objective consciousness," the professional's self-conception as an alienated observer looking out onto a distant world without moral or emotional significance.[130] The indifference of technocratic experts allows them to maintain control over subservient individuals or populations without care for their autonomy or well-being:

> When they enter upon their professional capacity, they leave their personal feelings behind. Perhaps they even take pride in their capacity to do so, for indeed it requires an act of iron will to ignore the claims that person makes upon person.[131]

Although critics saw abstraction as a pervasive condition, it was best personified by professional-managerial employees.

This is not to suggest that more thoroughgoing critiques of midcentury capitalism were misdirected or wrong. At a more fundamental level, abstraction is a material process in which commodity production and exchange reduce concrete labors down to the abstract equivalence of their value measured in average, socially necessary labor time.[132] As capitalism breaks down complete tasks into a series of specialized and routinized labor activities, individual workers lose the ability to understand—much less control—the labor process as a whole. Thus, according to Marx, the "intellectual potentialities" of capitalist production come to confront the worker as an alien "power."[133] From this division between conception and execution, the PMC emerges.

As Michael Bray suggests, the knowledge worker's role under capitalism is to discipline and de-skill manual labor while reorganizing production so that it produces more relative surplus value to meet capital's ever-growing demand for abstract labor: "Capital . . . increasingly realizes its own innate tendencies through the labors of knowledge workers."[134] Professional-managerial workers are so good at tending to capitalist exploitation because they have become conditioned to think like capital and replicate its abstractive powers in their own minds. This is a mindset that subordinates the private sphere to the productive one, suspending use value as needed and ignoring intimacy, care, and other structures of feeling associated with devalued reproductive labor.[135] Successful members of the class turn this abstractive practice back on themselves as well, appearing to become impartial bearers of bureaucratic, capitalist rationality. The PMC turns out to be as much an adjunct to abstract domination as an intermediary between capital and labor.

Midcentury hip culture strove to overcome these cognitive abstractions through a return to embodied experience.[136] Cold war intellectuals, avant-garde artists, and countercultural rebels all sought to reclaim the lost sense of free spontaneity, holistic connection, and sensuous immediacy that was sacrificed to the system.[137] Norman O. Brown, for example, theorized abstraction as a process of sublimation that desexualizes life by severing mind from body and displacing denied desires onto symbols functioning as fetish substitutes.[138] Abstraction reduces the thinker to a pair of detached eyes while repressing the impulse to enter into a more tactile and erotic involvement with the world. To overcome this estranged condition, Brown looked to Dionysiac ecstasy in art, sex, and mysticism.[139] Eros obliterates the boundaries between consciousness and body, self and other, subject and object, symbol and desire. Obscenity appeared to be the only escape out of the deadening repression that Brown and others saw as central to the prevailing social order.

Although we might expect the PMC's commitment to abstraction to render them numb from the waist down, in fact middle-class men of the 1950s and 1960s underwent their own sexual revolution, sometimes parallel to and other times intersecting with the countercultural struggle for erotic liberation.[140] In Gay Talese's account of postwar sexual culture, *Thy Neighbor's Wife* (1981), the emblematic figure for this movement is John Williamson, a technician who works for defense contractors like Boeing and Lockheed before organizing the Sandstone Foundation for Community Systems Research, an elite swingers club modeled in part on the theory of social change presented in Ayn Rand's *Atlas Shrugged* (1957).[141] Williamson sees himself as practicing "sensual engineering," treating erotics as a problem that can be solved by a self-selected group of smart people, many of them successful corporate employees, operating free from government interference.[142] For some, overcoming sexual inhibitions fit perfectly well with the otherwise conventional lifestyle of a suburban professional.

The middle-class sexual revolution produced a novel discourse on sexuality, one that still dominates self-help psychology today. Rather than describing sex as a dangerous pathology or a deep inner truth, they spoke of intercourse as a communication exercise.[143] While previous generations looked to sex as a way to learn about themselves, the swingers of the fifties and sixties began to see it as a way to monitor and regulate how they impacted others.[144] Professional-managerial sexual dissidents ultimately undermined the *Roth* regime of censorship by abstracting information from sex. If sexuality functions as a feedback loop, with every erotic act a signal, dirty books, dildos, and dominatrix whips must be considered modes of communication. In this regard, the middle-class sexual revolution reflected contemporary corporate discourses that embraced cybernetic ways of thinking and reimagined organizations, employees, and the buildings that housed them as "organized patterns of data."[145] By dematerializing sexual expression, the PMC helped bring about the liberalization of obscenity law.

Of course, not every lonely insurance salesman or frustrated aerospace engineer went off to found their own polycule. Some stayed home and masturbated to the high-class fantasies of *Playboy*, which—according to Roszak—sold "well-heeled junior executives" the image of the "assembly-line seducer," the model corporate citizen whose superficial sex with strangers entails no commitments that might distract from "one's primary responsibilities—which are to the company, to one's career and social position, and to the system generally."[146] Not all of this was pure imagination, either: there was some truth to the *Mad Men* stereotype.

As Julie Berebitsky has argued, sex pervaded office culture in midcentury America.[147] At a time when comedians and cartoons often joked about secretaries being chased around their desks by their bosses, men frequently subjected women to sexual harassment. Consensual office flings were common as well, but when organizations began to take human relations seriously, managers instituted new policies to modulate and control workplace sexuality without forbidding it entirely. Managerial advice guides such as *Modern Office Procedures* took a pragmatic approach to sex between employees, allowing relationships so long as they did not interfere with productivity, morale, or company reputation.[148]

Following this advice, organizations and their employees deployed sex to achieve their business objectives. Midcentury company men plied their bosses by allowing them to have sex with their wives. Secretaries slept with potential clients at their bosses' behest. Businesses employed prostitutes as part of their public relations teams, sometimes keeping them as regular employees on the payroll, and some firms even claimed the cost of paying for sex work on their taxes. When Edward R. Murrow reported these scandals in 1959, one commentator observed that he had shown "the reach of the business spirit into sex or perhaps the reach of the sex drive into business enterprise."[149]

Even when office employees remained chaste, many young white-collar workers groomed and dressed themselves with sex appeal in mind. According to Herbert Marcuse, the new freedom to put one's body on display at work served as a form of repressive desublimation: sexiness became another way that workers advertised their marketability and offices incentivized employee success.[150] He called it "the scientific management of the libido."[151] Secretaries never worked harder than when they were romantically as well as professionally devoted to their bosses; would-be executives dreamed of what might happen once they were behind the closed doors of the corner office. Sexuality was permitted—even encouraged—as long as it did not hurt the bottom line.

At the same time, professional-managerial men proved to be reliable customers for the sex trade. They kept appointments at massage parlors attended by "refined-looking women" in "starched nurses' uniforms," "white-gowned professionals" with licenses on the walls who allowed their clientele to experience manual release as a therapeutic procedure or, at least, as an in-person service with no strings attached.[152] The emerging professional-managerial sexuality exemplified what Stevi Jackson and Sue Scott term the "Taylorisation of sex," a process that frames sexuality as a manageable process that can be rationalized through the application of "special training based on expert knowledge."[153]

Whereas countercultural sexual emancipation sought to unleash the apocalyptic orgasm, middle-class libertines treated sexuality in a more matter-of-fact manner, toying with sexual play as a hobby or healthful exercise that allowed them to optimize enjoyment by strengthening "self-control."[154] At a moment when the PMC was deeply troubled by the notion that pleasures of consumerist affluence might make the class too decadent and feminized to perform its social function, sensual engineering suggested that even perversion could be put to work.[155]

Borderline obscene print culture served a critical role in producing this new middle-class attitude. Reading a single erotic text was not enough to convert abjection into abstraction: audiences had to consume sexual images in a serialized format before such images became routine. Shocking scandals quickly become tropes or tokens when they are repeatedly rehearsed within a controlling editorial framework. Nevertheless, we should not understand familiarization as merely the deadening of pleasure. As Walter Benjamin contends, mastery through repetition has its own appeal: "The transformation of a shattering experience into habit—that is the essence of play."[156] Publishers periodically reminded PMC readers that they were capable of triumphing over moral anxieties and disruptive desires once the pornographic had become another harmless pastime.

One might counter that this "responsible hedonism" represented a substitute for a deeper and more fully authentic sex life.[157] When measured against romantic ideals that hold erotic love to be always and forever an uncontrollable force or unbreakable bond, professional-managerial sexuality might come up as deficient. Examining the middle-class sexual revolution on its own terms, however, will better allow us to see not only its specificity but also its fundamental connections to the historical circumstances in which it arose.

Professional-managerial eroticism elicits or demands a genuine enthusiasm and excitement for the rules and regulations and expresses itself in an ardent desire to see sexuality compartmentalized, buffered, and constricted. PMC men actively desired self-division, shallowness, and reserve in both their partners and themselves. They wanted friendly but formal sex with no unconscious or excessive dimensions.[158] All of American culture seemed to be begging professional-managerial men to save themselves from becoming robotic appendages of faceless corporations, and social critics across the political spectrum called for compulsory togetherness and obligatory individualism as correctives to middle-class maladies. At this moment, therefore, the most transgressive thing a professional could imagine turned out to be embracing the coldness of abstraction. Even more so than swingers clubs or massage parlors, pornography provided a secret space where middle-class men could contemplate the erotics of alienation.

Professional-managerial readers are therefore drawn to pornography because, as Susan Sontag suggests, it is a literature of abstraction. The pornographic imagination is an "affectless" process, which brings all humans and objects into generic equivalence in an operation that she likens to the reductions of "modern symbolic logic" or money circulation; erotic literature, she states, translates "everything into the one negotiable currency of the erotic imperative."[159] According to Sontag it is precisely because erotic literature treats characters in this depersonalized and detached manner that the reader has room to project themselves into various characters and elaborate on their overheated fantasies.[160] To remain abstract—to prevent the reader from filling in gaps in the text with their own desires—erotic texts have to be locked down in a controlled environment that frames them as topics of social and legal controversy. Through her essay, Sontag hoped to liberate the pornographic imagination from experts who robbed illicit speech of some of its aesthetic pleasures by translating it into the stale commonplaces of censorship debates.[161]

Sontag's approach stands in stark contrast to the professional-managerial stance toward pornography. Learning to contain oneself was a formative experience for the PMC. Obscenity controversies held a special attraction for professional-managerial men precisely because they demanded a legalistic approach to graphic depictions of sexuality that looked very much like the bureaucratic ethos. The free speech liberal is routinely asked to suspend his own judgments to defend the indefensible. Lee C. Bollinger draws a direct connection between the tolerant attitude and "the basic requirements of a functioning bureaucracy and of various social professions" where employees "must implement the orders and directives of others despite their own contrary beliefs and feelings."[162] Resisting the urge to censor extreme speech becomes a lesson in submission to official duty.[163]

These tolerant attitudes are reflected in the omnivorous cultural taste that came to be espoused by the PMC. Although Pierre Bourdieu assumes an expressive unity between classes, artworks, and aesthetics, this unity—if it ever held—began to break down during the postwar period, when the hierarchy of high and low art seemed to collapse.[164] As early as 1949, Russell Lynes observed in "Highbrow, Lowbrow, Middlebrow" that even snobs frequently consumed popular media and, increasingly, the PMC distinguished itself by its refusal to denigrate anyone else's aesthetic preferences.[165] This rising group of professionals claimed cultural distinction based on an approach to culture far more eclectic than the canons of high culture found in Bourdieu's surveys.[166] Instead of observing rigid boundaries between proper and improper cultural goods, the PMC recognized only readers with differing degrees of cultural competence, including greater or lesser degrees of tolerance.

Of course, professional-managerial readers did not merely *accept* or *endure* pornographic or offensive texts—they sought them out with enthusiasm. Even so, both the eager reader of smut and the reluctant civil libertarian found themselves obliged to restrain their inclinations. No one ever saved a publication from censorship by admitting that it appealed to prurient interest. At the same time, obscenity law's corset of restrictions helped make transgressive publications even more erotically compelling. The very fact that one had to deny one's immediate impulses and hold pornography at an intellectual distance to find social value in it only seemed to heighten the pleasure involved.

Literary pornography internalized the juridical apparatus surrounding it to become the most intense expression of this self-limiting and self-inciting dynamic. Hunter, Saunders, and Williamson argue that the genre emerged around a dialectic that sought to achieve harmony between the sensual and the moral, the sexual and the aesthetic, a dialectic that eroticized social forms even as it submitted the erotic to societal norms and formal constraints.[167] Literary pornography combined Romantic self-cultivation with confessional self-scrutiny, allowing middle-class subjects the opportunity to claim cultural distinction through ever-refined artistic explorations of their own sexualities, which are refashioned in the process of being examined.[168] I would argue, however, that in twentieth-century American culture the PMC turned away from this project of libidinal reconciliation and began instead to use this erotic machinery to manufacture new infralegal techniques of perversion. Whereas previous sexual outlaws moved to free sex from repression, the new, responsible hedonists used literary culture to produce a hypersocialized sexuality that achieved stealth gratification in its stiff formality.

All of this reflects and feeds into the broader emotional style of cold war liberalism. John Durham Peters—who sees a clear affinity between extreme speech apologetics and a "just-doing-my-job" professionalism—traces the "hard heart" and "self-abstraction" of free speech liberalism back to the Stoic tradition.[169] Defenders of freedom of expression from John Milton through Oliver Wendell Holmes, Jr., draw on a normative vision of the public sphere as a universe of discourse beyond our power to curtail or change, one that must be accepted with the same love of fate evinced by the ancient Roman philosophers for the implacable cosmic order.[170] Offensive speech is inevitable and either impossible or unwise to prevent, so the free speech defender must learn to endure it, rise above any private emotions he might feel, and respond with passive equanimity.

Free speech liberalism, then, conditions itself using masochistic techniques. Contemplating the scandalous speech act becomes akin to the Stoic's meditation on death, allowing the civil libertarian to steel himself against the unbecoming desire for state intervention on behalf of himself or another injured party. Pain from distressing speech such as violent pornography serves an educative purpose for liberals. Expression constitutes a relatively circumscribed domain where liberals supposedly perform ethical calisthenics, building the self-restraint needed to accept more consequential cultural and political differences in behavior or policy. The more extreme speech is allowed, the better it is for the liberal soul. Peters calls this the "traumatophilic streak" or the "homeopathic machismo" of First Amendment absolutism—the notion that "the tincture of poison will lift us to heights of tolerance and civic mindedness."[171] In addition to being classed, as we have seen, the ethos of abstraction is also gendered as masculine and racialized as white, presupposing a subject whose identity makes noxious speech a relatively low-stakes affair.[172]

The psychosexuality of cold war liberalism thus made a fetish out of its submission to unassailable power. Even so, must we burn Hugh Hefner? Although we can and should read middle-class literary pornography as erogenized complacency, as the sexualized smugness of midcentury white men, we can also see it as part of a futile but understandable attempt to retreat from a white-collar work culture that had already begun demanding a deeper personal commitment than many employees were willing to give.

Novels such as Sloan Wilson's *The Man in the Grey Flannel Suit* (1955) expressed a fear that the organization might readjust the worker's innermost personality and remake them to forget that they were alienated from corporate bureaucracy in the first place. An alternative to this fate can be found in another disaffected middle-class protagonist of a midcentury office novel: Frank Wheeler in Richard Yates's *Revolutionary Road* (1961). Although Wheeler is presented as a tragic sellout, when we read the novel against the grain, we begin to see why he is drawn to Knox Business Machines, which serves as an obvious stand-in for the archetypal postwar company International Business Machines (IBM):

> I want to retain my own identity. Therefore the thing I'm most anxious to avoid is any kind of work that can be considered 'interesting' in its own right. I want something that can't possibly touch me. I want some big swollen corporation.... I want to go into that kind of place and say, Look. You can have my body and my nice college-boy smile for so many hours a day, in exchange for so many dollars, and beyond that we'll leave each other strictly alone. Get the picture?[173]

Speaking the language of midcentury pornography and prostitution, Wheeler hopes to give the "big swollen corporation" his "body" while reserving for himself some private form of inviolable freedom, which he exercises through cynical critiques of "Conformity, or The Suburbs, or Madison Avenue, or American Society Today" that allow him to remain intellectually and emotionally estranged from his material circumstances.[174] Although it is easy to fault the middle-class bohemian for giving up on his wilder dreams, now that we live in a moment when firms aggressively demand enthusiastic engagement and emotional authenticity even in intolerable circumstances, it is becoming increasingly clear that the disaffection of bureaucratic time-servers is sometimes preferable to the total exhaustion of post-Fordist employees swallowed up by their careers.

The official reserve of the porn-reading professional turns out to be a more complicated attitude than it initially appears. The career employee's coldness can serve as a form of schizophrenic splitting that insulates immoral or amoral deeds from humane considerations, but it can also be the first step toward defecting from an intolerable situation. The organization man who dissociates from his work, his wife, and his family exercises the privilege of heterosexual masculinity even as he dreams of a sex radicalism that might attenuate if not abolish that power. If some critics have condemned the libertine literature of this period as objectifying women at the same moment when others have praised it as liberating sexuality, that is because both judgments must be considered as equally true. To grasp these two ideas together, we have to ground our discussion of literary transgression in the class-based print culture that produced these conjoined but conflicting tendencies.

An Aristocracy of Smut

H. L. MENCKEN is perhaps best known for his fight against puritanism. Although he struggled against censorship and prudery in all of his work as an editor, critic, and journalist, his most direct confrontation with obscenity law centered on the publication of "Hatrack" by Herbert Asbury. The story, published in the April 1926 issue of the *American Mercury*, concerns a prostitute who attempted to join a Methodist congregation only to be shunned. After being rejected, she continues to ply her trade by asking Protestants to lay with her in the Catholic graveyard and soliciting Catholics to join her in the Masonic graveyard. By publishing this controversial story, Mencken showed that he was willing to provoke a prosecution. Indeed, a fight with the censors was required to clear Mencken's character. Years before the "Hatrack" affair, Mencken had been strongly critiqued by social critic Randolph Bourne for admitting that "as a practical editor, I find that the Comstocks, near and far, are oftener in my mind's eye than my actual patrons."[1] Now that the courts were tipping in the favor of free speech rights, it was time for Mencken the editor to demonstrate that he could live up to the convictions of Mencken the critic.

To this end, Mencken published a piece that seemed calculated to pick a fight with Reverend J. Frank Chase, secretary of the New England Watch and Ward Society, an anti-vice crusader who had recently been the subject of a vicious profile in the *American Mercury* by A. L. S. Wood. Taking the bait, Chase circulated a statement condemning the "Hatrack" issue as obscene and leaned on wholesalers to pull the magazine. The Watch and Ward Society was believed to have the courts in its pocket, and, sure enough, police arrested a news dealer named Felix Caragianes for obscenity after he ignored Chase's public warning that the magazine contained illegal material.[2] Caragianes, whose stand was located in Harvard Square, defended the magazine by stating, "Fine people buy it. Professors from the college and like that."[3]

Following advice from counsel to draw Chase into open court, Mencken arrived in town to hand sell a copy to Chase in the middle of Boston Common while a scrum of fans, photographers, and police looked on. Mugging for the raucous crowd, Mencken reportedly told the censor, "I'm Mencken, please nab me," and then bit the coin the secretary handed him to test if it was "good money."[4] The provocation ended in the editor immediately being taken into custody. The *Boston Herald*, suspecting a publicity stunt, reported on the event with the headline "MR. MENCKEN CRAVES ARREST."[5]

Luckily, Mencken was sprung from jail quickly, and, the next day, the *American Mercury* had its day in court. Due to the potentially prurient nature of the proceedings, the testimony as well as the oral arguments were carried out in whispers around the judge's bench, sparing the courtroom audience the danger of obscenity.[6] Mencken testified that the readership of the *American Mercury* was "mainly persons of some education, and included many well-known men and women."[7] As if to prove this point, Mencken was followed by another defense witness, a lawyer named H. Wadsworth Sullivan, who testified that an *American Mercury* article on the topic of divorce written by attorney William Seagle had been taught at Yale Law School, where it was spoken of highly.[8] Finally, the author of "Hatrack" rounded out the testimony by asserting the veracity of the story.[9] Judge James P. Parmenter examined the magazine and dismissed Chase's complaint the next morning.

Perhaps in anticipation of this move, Chase had already headed to New York, where he convinced the postmaster general to ban the April 1926 issue. Realizing that his second-class mailing privileges were at risk, Mencken stopped the presses on the May 1926 issue and cut a potentially objectionable article from it titled "Sex and the Co-Ed."[10] Mencken's publisher, Alfred A. Knopf, eventually secured an injunction against the Watch and Ward Society, winning the right to publish the May issue, but at the end of the entire legal process they had paid out fees to the tune of $20,000.[11] Caragianes, who had been convicted of obscenity, had no desire to appeal and ended up paying a fine with help from Knopf.[12]

On the face of it, Mencken's confrontation with the law seems to be the story of a gutsy if self-serving editor standing up to censorship in the name of free speech. If we dig deeper, though, we begin to see that Mencken's tussles with so-called puritans have as much to do with race and class as they do with civil liberties. We see this clearly in the other *American Mercury* article that antagonized Chase, "Boston Twilight" by Charles Angoff. Doing a good imitation of his editor, Angoff lamented that Boston's years of glory ended in the nineteenth century. Where Boston once stood as the "undisputed literary capital" of America, now its citizens read only self-help tracts and potboilers.[13] Boston's literary landscape was desolate. Chase censored many of the superior authors that Mencken published and praised—Sherwood Anderson, Willa Cather, Theodore Dreiser, and James Branch Cabell—but no one in Boston would understand them even if they were freely available.[14] Using Mencken's term of endearment for his audience, Angoff claimed that Boston lacked the "civilized minority" required to maintain its once-high level of culture, a decline that he attributes to racial degeneration.[15] Angoff complained that the town's gene pool had been polluted by an influx of "Irish-Catholic anthropoids" who "have no more interest in ideas than a guinea-pig has in Kant's *Critique of Pure Reason* or a donkey in Goethe's *Faust*."[16] His solution was unequivocally brutal: "The invasion of these barbarians has made [Boston's] further growth impossible, and its renaissance will not take place until they are exterminated."[17]

Angoff's racist discourse on cultural capital has to be understood within the editorial context established by Mencken. Anti-egalitarian ideas were central to Mencken's publishing venture. Like Angoff, Mencken regularly reminded readers that he wrote for an intellectual class perpetually beleaguered by the dullard masses. The title of the first magazine Mencken edited along with George Jean Nathan hails his elect as the *Smart Set*, with smartness standing in for both intelligence and sophistication. Although Mencken designates this readership as a natural aristocracy, Sharon Hamilton points out that the *Smart Set* subscribers were typically college students or recent graduates preparing to enter into the professional-managerial class.[18] An early appraisal of Mencken describes his readership as "embattled highbrows," a group consisting

> mostly of artists and writers, professional people, the intellectually restless element in the college towns, and such members of the college-educated business class as could digest more complicated literature than was to be found in the *Saturday Evening Post* and *McCall's Magazine*.[19]

This audience was not as disparate as it may now seem: doctors, professors, artists, and managers during this period all shared the same material interest in professionalization. As Erik Olin Wright argues, the middle classes achieve their relative affluence and autonomy largely because they are able to hoard job opportunities for themselves through "social closure," that is, by erecting occupational barriers including "mechanisms of exclusion over the acquisition of education and skills."[20] Mencken targeted an audience of ascending professional-managerial readers, anxious in their class status and eager to distance themselves from their subordinates. Although Mencken himself had very little formal education beyond high school, his work served to shore up the monopoly on expertise that the PMC necessarily depended on. To better restrict its membership and ensure class reproduction, the PMC set itself up as a cultural elite.

Mencken furthered this project by rooting class inequality in innate, biological distinctions between individuals. Like many racialist thinkers, he temporalized the differences between social groups, representing those he imagined to be his inferiors as throwbacks to a prior moment in natural history. While the puritan Neanderthals remained hopelessly archaic, the civilized minority emerged as the forward dawning of the future. Its superiority manifested itself in what Peter Osborne would call the "self-transcending temporality" of modernity: the right to dominance, for Mencken, was predicated on the ability and willingness to abandon old values and develop better ones.[21]

Mencken's intellectual aristocrats were entrepreneurs, creative and attuned to novelty. The editor praised the organizational innovations of Henry Ford and the advertising expertise of Edward Bernays in much the same terms he used to laud authors such as Joseph Conrad and Theodore Dreiser. These figures invented new ideas and imposed them on the masses who, even in their best moments, could only carry out the plans of their betters. Whenever the "anthropoid rabble" broke free from domination, though, it threatened to topple its resented superiors and to drag civilization back into its superstitious past.[22] Mencken's modernizing readers were therefore inevitably opposed by "the eternal mob" that had remained virtually the same throughout all of history, cleaving to old superstitions and opposing all innovations.[23]

The key test for a reader's place in this hierarchy was their response to obscene modernism, the sexual and formal transgressions of early twentieth-century literature.[24] Those who sought to censor Mencken's more daring publications relegated themselves to the more genteel era of the nineteenth century if not the Stone Age.[25] Translating legal thinkers such as Theodore Schroeder and Judge

Learned Hand into Nietzschean terms, Mencken's magazines suggested that the criteria for obscenity would always be inadequate because even the most fundamental norms and standards were subject to historical change. What was obscene yesterday cannot bind artists and intellectuals today, who have already moved on. To prevent itself from falling behind, the civilized minority must learn to view its own ethical stance from the perspective of a later moment in history in which it is already outmoded.

Combining his admiration for Fordist management with his commitment to moral modernism, Mencken conditions readers to consider women's bodies from the thoroughly disenchanted vantage point of a management scientist carrying out a time-motion study. By resisting the temptation of obscenity, Mencken's readers are able to decompose moving flesh into a series of static images that can be reconfigured and modified at their will. Not everyone can carry out this perspectival shift. According to Mencken, only the civilized minority has the genetic predisposition to overcome its irrational attachments and see the world from the distanced and secularized perspective of the future.

To help establish this sense of class distinction, the *Smart Set* introduced readers to modernist authors by publishing their works alongside more popular fare. Mencken's magazines constitute an early precursor to the shift toward cultural omnivorism, demonstrating a wide range of cultural tastes from the lowbrow to the highbrow.[26] This middle-class dilettantism was also reflected in the magazine's business model, which combined the independence of a literary review with the mass appeal of a commercial magazine. Like an editor of a little magazine, Mencken insisted that he would never sacrifice the quality of the publication to obtain a greater number of readers. Anticipating the editorial visions of publishers such as *Playboy* and Grove Press, Mencken wrote in "A Word about *Smart Set*," "We have run our magazines as we have written our books—primarily to please ourselves, and secondarily to entertain those Americans who happen, in general, to be of our minds."[27] One of the magazine's slogans put it more bluntly: "One Civilized Reader is Worth a Thousand Boneheads."[28] Even as the *Smart Set* avoided threats to the magazine's editorial integrity by minimizing the number of advertisements it carried, it also rejected the patronage strategies that made the modernist little magazine sustainable in the absence of sufficient sales or advertising revenue.[29] Much like his politics, Mencken's editorial project was driven by a fierce individualism disciplined and affirmed by market competition.

Or so he claimed. In fact, the *Smart Set*'s profitability depended on subsidies from the so-called louse magazines that Mencken and Nathan edited.[30] These popular periodicals, which often printed rejected *Smart Set* submissions, included *Parisienne*, a magazine that catered to the public's wartime fascination with French bohemia and, more notably, *Black Mask*, the influential detective pulp magazine that came to define the hard-boiled crime genre. Although the *Smart Set* sometimes published pulp stories itself, the louse magazines generally dealt with more lowbrow and risqué material. *Parisienne* was accused of obscenity by John S. Sumner of the NYSSV, a charge that the publisher beat thanks to a hefty bribe to one of the case's three presiding judges.[31] Later, in his memoirs, Mencken panned other pulp editors as "broken down hacks" and called their target audiences "morons," despite the fact that the *Smart Set* often turned out to be a parasite to the louse magazines, which paid their own way and then some.[32] The editors eventually sold off the louse magazines for a substantial sum that put them on sound financial footing for the rest of their careers.[33] As we shall see, Mencken's editorial ethos relied on the disavowed exploitation of the vulgar and the obscene.

Feeling constrained at the *Smart Set*, Mencken left the magazine in 1923 to found the *American Mercury*.[34] The *American Mercury* better expressed Mencken's "editorial personality": he published the review through his book publisher Knopf and, although his *Smart Set* partner Nathan served as coeditor for the first two years, after that Mencken retained sole editorial control.[35] The new magazine won over a broader audience—the *Smart Set* tended to limit itself to urbanites, while the *American Mercury* also reached readers across the country—but it maintained the same class basis.[36] The review proved to be even more popular with college undergraduates than the *Smart Set*, but Mencken also claimed to be editing for "the leading men of science and learning, the best artists, in all the arts" along with "such men of business as have got any imagination."[37] Calling these forward-thinking readers "the middle minority," Mencken believed that this superior caste stood up against the backwards masses, who constantly threatened to undo all forms of progress.[38]

By casting the debate over censorship as a conflict between two hierarchically ordered and temporally disjunct species, Mencken breaks apart the already tenuous bonds between free speech liberalism and democratic politics. From Zechariah Chafee to Alexander Meiklejohn, civil libertarians have often defended freedom of expression on the grounds that it enables democratic deliberation.[39] Mencken, on the other hand, views public debate as foolish and futile. Always the contrarian, Mencken seeks to protect free speech from obscenity law through a sustained attack on the very notion of the public sphere that undergirds most other free speech arguments. Anthropologist Johannes Fabian argues that intersubjective communication depends on a prior assumption of coevalness, the sense that the speaker shares the same moment in time with their interlocutor.[40] Mencken, however, splits the obscenity controversy into a puritan past and a civilized present, with each side of the debate inhabiting a different epoch. Because of this rift in time, he suggests, forward-thinking individuals cannot be beholden to the rules and values promoted by the residual masses. Mencken does not care to convince the public: he just wants to chuck those he disagrees with into the dustbin of history.

Methodologically, this chapter differs from the subsequent ones in this book insofar as it tracks an editorial persona across a network of print publications rather than focusing on a single periodical or publishing company. Nevertheless, this discrepancy reveals what is specific to editorship as a training mechanism for forms of life and modes of reading. Hemingway is right when he suggests in *The Sun Also Rises* (1926) that "so many young men get their likes and dislikes from Mencken."[41] More fundamentally, though, Mencken's readers received from him an orientation toward their own historical moment. By keeping up with Mencken, professional-managerial readers developed a reflective mode of reading that allowed them to see themselves as productively estranged from their own time.

The Incommunicability of One Stratum of Life and Another

Mencken's fight for free expression differs dramatically from modernist projects of de-censorship—exemplified by D. H. Lawrence—that saw the obscene as a way of freeing westerners from alienating abstractions and recapturing the supposedly primitive experience of immediacy in the sensuous present. Mencken certainly would have agreed with Lawrence's contention that prudish responses to erotic material were the inauthentic "mob reaction" of mass men.[42] However, while Lawrence condemns both scientists and modern artists for inadvertently promoting what he called "mentalized sex," Mencken seems to have enthusiastically sought to "kill dynamic sex altogether, and leave only the scientific and deliberate mechanism."⁴³ For Mencken, the obscene is an opportunity to rise above the mob by showing that one is civilized, a state he equates with the inborn ability to maintain a sense of spatiotemporal distance from lived experience in the here and now.

We see this clearly in Mencken's essay on Joseph Conrad in *A Book of Prefaces* (1917). Here as elsewhere, Mencken uses criticism as an occasion to reflect on his own sensibilities and to ventriloquize his viewpoints through other authors. Quoting from Arthur Symons, Mencken argues that Conrad exposes the "bare side of every virtue," he reveals all "dreams and illusions" and "lays them mockingly naked," looking upon these debunked myths with perfect indifference.⁴⁴ The author's philosophical burlesque strips the world of emotional or ethical significance, displaying a value nihilism that serves as "proof of the greater maturity of his personal culture, his essential superiority as a civilized man."⁴⁵ According to Mencken, Conrad's inherited disposition toward detachment derived from his racial makeup, which combined Polish nobility with an "Asiatic" tendency toward brooding self-examination that finds expression in "Nirvana, the desire for nothingness, the will to not-will."⁴⁶ Distancing, Mencken suggested, was genetically determined.

Mencken's racialized spectator seems to hover outside of the universe, observing without personal interest. In this regard, Mencken's aesthetics parallel Edward Bullough's influential essay "'Psychical Distance' as a Factor in Art and as an Aesthetic Principle," which appeared just a few years before Mencken's preface. Bullough characterizes aesthetic appreciation as based on greater or lesser degrees of "Distance," a psychological state achieved when the perceiver inhibits all practical attitudes and responses.⁴⁷ Somewhat similar to Kantian disinterestedness, Distance allows the subject to attend to emotions or impressions without reducing them to those aspects relevant to their particular wants or interests. Bullough measures distancing ability through what he calls the "Distance-limit," the degree of psychic proximity at which it becomes impossible to remain impassive.⁴⁸ The stuff of obscenity—"explicit references to organic affections, to the material existence of the body, especially to sexual matters"—lies very close at hand to most spectators and therefore often becomes a test determining the range of one's Distance-limit.⁴⁹ This feature of Distance proves especially salient during censorship cases:

> The difference in the Distance-limit between artists and the public has been the

source of much misunderstanding and injustice. Many an artist has seen his work condemned and himself ostracized for the sake of so-called 'immoralities' which to him were bona fide aesthetic objects.... In fact, the whole censorship problem, as far as it does not turn upon purely economic questions, may be said to hinge on Distance; if every member of the public could be trusted to keep it, there would be no sense whatever in the existence of a censor of plays.[50]

The concept of Distance—which now structures both expert and vernacular art discourse—developed through an engagement with the problem of obscenity. Artists extend their Distance-limits by daring to aestheticize what would otherwise be considered obscene, and, in the process, they risk what Bullough calls "under-distancing" (a failure to maintain a minimal distance) or "over-distancing" (a state of excessive remoteness).[51] The most advanced modern art thus often proves closest to erotic transgression.

Mencken's Conrad is a master of Distance. He proves to be so far beyond experiencing prurient desire that he considers the "petty jousts of sex" too trivial and ridiculous to write a novel around.[52] Similarly, Conrad's fiction dispels all romantic sentiments, casting love as a "feeble phosphorescence or a gigantic grotesquerie."[53] Mencken's version of Conrad shares his scorn for sex, a derision that would often set Mencken at odds with contemporary moralists. According to Mencken, his puritanical critics bear an innate defect that leaves them incapable of checking their ethical concerns and sensual reactions long enough to appreciate art from a proper distance. Just as Conrad's aesthetic distance springs forth from his noble heritage, the puritan's under-distancing is a product of "the whole mental sluggishness of the lower orders of men."[54]

While Bullough's aesthetics tend toward spatial metaphors, he also observes that "temporal remoteness" helps facilitate psychical distance.[55] The urgencies that once compelled ancient artworks no longer grip us in the contemporary moment, allowing audiences to hold them at a remove. The category of the pornographic was formulated around this effect. Curators coined the term "pornography" to describe the Secret Museum, an archeological collection at the National Museum of Naples, which held a treasure trove of artifacts from Pompeii ranging from murals of Bacchanalian orgies to sculptures of Priapus.[56] The museum is said to have restricted access to learned men capable of appreciating the evidentiary value of the artworks. However, M. L. Barré's illustrated catalog of the Secret

Museum had a wider and more uncontrolled circulation, which meant the author was forced to take steps to safeguard readers from prurience through paratextual and representational strategies:

> We have endeavored to make [this collection] inaccessible, so to speak, to poorly educated persons, as well as to those whose sex and age forbid any exception to the laws of decency and modesty. With this end in mind, we have done our best to regard each of the objects we have had to describe from an exclusively archaeological and scientific point of view. It has been our intention to remain calm and serious throughout. In the exercise of his holy office, the man of science must neither blush nor smile. We have looked upon our statues as an anatomist contemplates his cadavers.[57]

Pornography only becomes safe and inert when it is viewed from a specialist's point of view, whether that is the perspective of a medical doctor or a classicist. Barré's engravings, surrounded by untranslated Greek and Latin and enclosed within an expensive eight-volume set, thus commend themselves to an audience of antiquarians capable of treating pornographic images as so many forensic clues to a lost civilization. Bodies painted on the brothel walls are no different from the skeletons immured within volcanic ash.

Mencken's cohort takes a similar approach to pornography, a strategy best exemplified by Willa Cather's "Coming, Eden Bower!" Cather's novelette appeared in the August 1920 issue of the *Smart Set* in bowdlerized form before being reedited and de-censored for Cather's short-fiction collection *Youth and the Bright Medusa* (1920), where it was printed under the more suggestive title "Coming, Aphrodite!" The narrative centers on Don Hedger, a modern painter living in a Greenwich Village apartment. A reclusive man, Hedger's solitude is disturbed when aspiring singer Eden Bower moves into the adjoining unit. The artist's initial irritation with his new neighbor quickly turns to voyeurism when he happens to look through a knothole in the back of his closet and accidentally spies her doing gymnastics in a negligee. The "Aphrodite" version of the story has Eden fully nude, but even in the *Smart Set* variation barely concealed eroticism nevertheless ghosts through.

The peeping artist's response to what he sees captures the alchemy that modernism so often performs on the obscene. As Hedger gazes on, Eden's flesh seems to evaporate into an airy cloud:

The soft flush of exercise and the gold of the afternoon sun played over her together, enveloped her in a luminous mist which, as she turned and twisted, made now an arm, now a shoulder, dissolve in pure light and instantly recover its outline with a next gesture.[58]

Like so many artistic nudes before her, Eden's framing precludes obscenity; her naked body dematerializes to become an abstract and incorporeal pattern. Because of Hedger's artistic training—"A woman in negligée was not an improper object to a man who had worked so much with unclad models"—he views her intimate dance as an occasion for aesthetic appreciation, concentrating entirely on the form of her movements, their "energy" and "motion."[59]

In this scene, Cather figures a classic problem in censorship history. During the final years of the nineteenth century, censors led by Anthony Comstock fought against portraits, photographs, and reproductions depicting nude models.[60] Despite initial successes in suppressing nudes, Comstock was challenged and bested by artists who claimed that their expert judgment gave them the warrant to determine the difference between art and obscenity. In 1890, a controversial play, *The Clemenceau Case*, crystallized the argument leveled against the censor by an emerging artistic profession.[61] Based on Alexandre Dumas's recently translated novel *L'Affaire Clémenceau*, the play brought the artist's studio to the Broadway stage, depicting an apprenticed sculptor named Pierre Clemenceau. In the play's pivotal moment, Pierre's master asks him to sculpt a nude woman from life, a test that allows the sculptor to prove that he is able to rise above his base inclinations and become a true artist. The play scandalized and titillated audiences—the lead actress appeared on stage in nothing but tights, joining a wave of semipornographic, semi-artistic images of nude models—and indeed even in the play Pierre does not maintain his self-control for long before becoming a dissipated criminal himself.[62] The play was banned in Boston and its source material was censored by the New York Society for the Enforcement of Criminal Law.[63] Nevertheless, this scene reveals the female nude as the crucial dividing line between art and obscenity.[64] Through the nude figure, the artist makes social as well as cultural distinctions: how one approaches the model determines not only the genre of the artwork but also the aesthetic refinement of the spectator.

Hedger lays claim to high culture, but, at the same time, he betrays an intense pleasure in the very process of aestheticizing her body. In what one critic views as a masturbatory gesture,[65] Hedger imagines drawing Eden's dance:

Hedger's fingers curved as if he were holding a crayon; mentally he was doing the whole figure in a single running line, and the charcoal seemed to explode in his hand at the point where the energy of each gesture was discharged into the whirling disc of light.[66]

Obscenity escapes from its Kantian containment, form gives way to formlessness, and chaste beauty terminates in the orgasmic sublime as Hedger's little pencil bursts and expends itself in his sweaty grip.

Even in the breakdown of aesthetic norms, however, we see another technique for regulating obscenity. As Allison Pease argues, modernists as diverse as Aubrey Beardsley and James Joyce sought to transcend the pornographic by submitting it to "an ironic distancing that focuses not on sexual representation itself, but on how that representation is mediated and received."[67] The same holds true in Cather's story. When Hedger renders his model as a figure in the air that leaves no material trace, he suddenly realizes that she has "disappeared," leaving only the medium that illuminated her, "the golden shower which poured through the west windows," which in turn gives way to "a vision . . . out of the remote pagan past."[68] While taking readers from prurient voyeurism to classical art, Cather moves her audience from the obscene image to its refined reception. The body is gone, but the hallucination remains. Meanwhile, Cather's language switches from prosaic realism to fantastical reverie, leaving behind the closet filled with Hedger's dirty laundry to arrive at an "enchanted" place "bathed . . . in Helianthine fire."[69] The clipped reportage of the rest of the scene is interrupted by rhythmic, sinuous, and self-consciously stylized sentences. Smut dissolves into literary craft.

This passage applies one of Mencken's characteristic methods for regulating the obscene: Eden's movements cease, and she becomes frozen in time, like the figure on Hedger's page. As she is relegated to art history—if not Edenic myth— the text denies her contemporaneity with Hedger, who, we later learn, is so modern that he refuses to paint in the same period's style twice. The couple can never inhabit the same space-time, breaking the immediacy required by the obscene. Like the fish in a bowl Hedger observes in an earlier scene, Eden demonstrates "the incommunicability of one stratum of life and another."[70] Indeed, the gulf between them seems so great that Eden enacts the conventions of ancient Greek statuary and painting even as Hedger draws her following the avant-garde canon of nonrepresentational art. Apotheosized into an antiquated Aphrodite, Eden becomes safely inaccessible, more the subject of literary ekphrasis than prurient interest. Once this structure is in place, even the most unspeakable images can be neutralized: Hedger later recounts to Eden's horror and our bemusement a tale of lust and murder set in the mummifying time of ancient Aztec pseudomyth. The text's temporal distancing allows Cather's readers to see themselves as smart in their capacity to move beyond the erotic obsessions of previous generations.

As we shall see with other middle-class voyeurs, Hedger responds to this spectacle by turning self-conscious shame into class-conscious self-improvement. He immediately notices the filth in his apartment and hires out a maid to make it presentable. His thoughts quickly turn from domestic squalor to social status. For Hedger, Eden represents both bourgeois culture and mass commercialism. He associates her with the chic women he sees emerging from high-end shops, the kind of "girls" he imagines as "artificial and, in an aesthetic sense, perverted": "he saw them enslaved by desire of merchandise and manufactured articles."[71] Hedger therefore finds himself troubled when Eden seems to ascend to his platonic notion of femininity, shedding her classed nature and all other determinations to become "the immortal conception, the perennial theme."[72] After they become lovers, Eden will once more betray this ideal, asking him to compromise to achieve popular success, but even then Hedger ultimately remains drawn to her so long as he can contemplate her from afar as a memory, locked in his own autobiographical past. Hedger can only tolerate Eden by rescuing her from time—and from the rapid turnover of fashion, fame, and consumer goods—so as to reproduce her as a static image.

Here it may seem strange to associate a lumpen painter with the middle class. Although Hedger sometimes makes money as a commercial draughtsman—seemingly without time or effort—his primary occupation is as a self-employed artist, taking in very little income. While Hedger inhabits a different political-economic position from his professional-managerial readers, his class ambivalence still would have resonated with this audience. Hedger moves through working class environs, consorting with dockworkers and factory women. At the same time, however, he is resolutely *not* proletarian; like the PMC, Hedger proposes "to live by the sweat of the brow rather than of the hand."[73] What binds Hedger to the civilized minority, then, is that his livelihood depends on specialized education and training. Rejecting the bourgeoisie but hovering above the proletariat, Hedger's contradictory class location depends on the store of cultural capital that allows him to remain on the mental side of the division between mental and manual labor. Hedger proves his class identity by simultaneously resisting the bourgeois by engaging with the pornographic and refusing the working class by aestheticizing the erotic body, whose vigorous labors and excessive corporeality were so often classed as proletarian. According to Mark McGurl, a similar dynamic motivated much of modernist fiction, which displayed an intellectualizing attitude toward forbidding and obscene topics as a way of establishing an ethos of literary professionalism while also differentiating its audience of PMC readers from other middle-class audiences accustomed to easy reading.[74]

Cather, of course, was not as cynical as her editor Mencken, and we see a great deal more ambivalence in the text than this reading admits. At some moments, Eden does seem to be the conformist that Hedger sees her as. She follows the dictates of her dancing instructor, worries about the whims of popular success, and pursues a marriage of convenience with a wealthy suitor as a way of bankrolling what will turn out to be a successful career as a vocalist. Nevertheless, Eden finds small opportunities for resistance by manipulating men, evading her future by hanging out in Greenwich Village for a summer, and even stealing a moment of danger and pleasure with a lady trapeze artist to whom she is introduced by Hedger. Importantly, the narrative also gives us Eden's perspective, passing between the two characters before finally ending with Eden looking backward on her time with Hedger. Within the context of the *Smart Set*, however, these possibilities were downplayed to privilege the bohemian man's point of view. Mencken, writing a review of *Youth and the Bright Medusa*, commends Cather for depicting the artist's consciousness: "She does not look *at* him through a peep-hole in the studio door, but looks *with* him."[75] Although Mencken is far more open to women authors than many of the later anti-censorship editors, in the final instance he sides with the masculine artist whose gaze seems to freeze everything he looks upon. Women serve as constitutive others in Mencken's narratives, confirming men's transcendence by allowing them to overcome excessive heterosexual desire and reject the feminine lure of primitivism, emotionalism, and fanaticism.

We see the same temporal structure repeatedly in the pages of the *Smart Set*. Sometimes it appears in a critical mode: Dorothy Parker's "Such a Pretty Little Picture" opposes the sweet snapshot of the family on their lawn to the festering discontent of a failed marriage that it conceals.[76] More often, though, temporal distancing serves as a way to manage the unmanageable. In F. Scott Fitzgerald's "Benediction," the protagonist Lois's outdated image of her estranged brother

Kieth, captured in an old photograph, melts into the charming man before her whose liveliness elicits the clear and present danger of her own incestuous longing. Fitzgerald captures this illicit lust with the image of the candle flame, burning and transitory. Her brother, who has taken monastic vows, seems to reciprocate the feeling even as he successfully represses it. He now faces such worldly temptations with the everlasting rituals of his faith and the self-mortification of his order. As the sister grows frantic, losing her mind in the midst of a benediction, she looks at her brother and a fellow monastic and notices "a certain coldness in both their profiles . . . a pallor about the mouth and a curious set expression in their eyes"— "they were like dead men."[77] The brother escapes the lure of perishable flesh and hot blood by becoming as timeless and lifeless as a still image. Commenting on the story's republication in *Flappers and Philosophers* (1920), Mencken notes with obvious pleasure that its appearance in the *Smart Set* "brought down the maledictions of the Jesuits and came near getting the magazine barred from the Knights of Columbus camp-libraries."[78] Nevertheless, Mencken suggests, this story offers the "intelligent Catholic" no grounds for offense.[79]

The temporal distancing we find in the fiction Mencken published recalls his own cynical musings on love. Frederick Lewis Allen attributes to the civilized minority a disappointment in sexual romance, which had seemed to depreciate as it became a "quantity production."[80] While it seems highly doubtful that Victorian monogamy made sex any hotter, as Allen suggests, Mencken did make a concerted effort to deflate the idea that one's sexuality contains some essential truth or exciting mystery. In the *Smart Set* essay "Osculation Anatomized," Mencken takes on what he calls "the labial infamy," that is to say, kissing.[81] Perhaps saying more about his own experience than anyone else's, Mencken reflects that kissing does not resemble the "mush" that has been written about it: "An instantaneous photograph of such a maneuver, taken at the moment of incidence, would probably turn the stomach of even the most romantic man."[82] Unmoved, Mencken complains of the "pseudo-asthmatic spasm" and "leaden pallor" that comes from breathless embrace.[83] By all accounts, Mencken was somewhat of a cold fish. Like Brother Kieth, the editor kills eroticism and deadens obscenity by fixing them in some superseded split-second as though through the art of postmortem photography. For Mencken's audience, the obscene was always something experienced retrospectively, from a temporal distance, which means that anyone who continues to experience sexual under-distancing in the modern era must be suffering from psychological regression or evolutionary degeneration. The puritan is a man or woman in the wrong time.

The Disenchantment of the Word

One of Mencken's more controversial publications turns on precisely the idea that the obscene is always something superannuated. James Branch Cabell's *Jurgen, A Comedy of Justice* (1919) began as a short story in the *Smart Set* titled "Some Ladies and Jurgen." The narrative follows Jurgen, a poet turned pawnbroker, who wins the favor of a deity named Koshchei the Deathless after he is overheard defending the devil. By way of reward, Koshchei abducts Jurgen's nagging wife and offers to give him a new helpmate in her stead, conjuring up three women from history: Queen Guinevere, Queen Anaïtis, and Helen of Troy. Jurgen, however, rejects the hand of each in turn. Once an inveterate playboy and besotted romantic, Jurgen now no longer has any use for divine love, carnal lust, or poetic longing. When Queen Anaïtis entices him with "monstrous pleasures," detailed only in ellipses, Jurgen speaks about his past affairs in the third person:

> Such escapades were pleasant enough; but they were not very serious, after all. For these things concerned his body alone: and I am more than an edifice of viands reared by my teeth. To pretend what my body does or endures is of importance, seems rather silly nowadays. I prefer to regard it as a necessary beast of burden which I maintain, at considerable expense and trouble.... You come a good deal too late, my lass, so that all this to-do over nameless sins and unspeakable caresses and other anonymous antics seems rather naïve.[84]

The novel version of this narrative dramatizes Jurgen's world-weariness by sending him back into his own past, where he reencounters his lost conquests. Jaded by the years, he is pained to realize that the women he loved were nothing like he imagined or remembered.

After Jurgen encounters the banal reality of his first love, one of his guides, a centaur, explains to him,

> My poor Jurgen, who were once a poet! She was your masterpiece. For there was only a shallow, stupid and airy, high-nosed and light-haired miss, with no remarkable good looks,—and consider what your ingenuity made from such poor material! You should be proud of yourself.[85]

The perspective of time allows Jurgen to see that women possess no value of their own until they are imbued with meaning by the gaze of the masculine spectator; men supply everything that is erotic, romantic, or otherwise significant about them beyond their worthless bodies. Indeed, the text underscores this point by presenting Jurgen with a row of all the women with which he has ever had sex. Their corpses lead him to reflect on the "insanity" of love that once gave life to this assembly line of "dead flesh."[86]

Running precisely counter to later fantasies of middle-class self-renewal such as Sinclair Lewis's Menckenian novel *Babbitt* (1922), Jurgen flees from reenchantment. He spends the narrative looking for an exit from the increasingly fantastical erotic cosmologies that keep him from his loveless marriage and his humdrum profession, which, however prosaic, nevertheless allow him freedom from the irritation that things might be otherwise. When he contemplates the possibility of returning to rapturous youth, he reaffirms the "virtue of preserving a cool heart" and, with only a little tearful regret, decides he would prefer to remain an older and wiser man.[87] As in so many pornographic books that came before him, Jurgen's achievement of dull respectability at the end of the novel redeems all of the dalliances that precede it.

Although Cabell writes in an antique pseudomedieval style, *Jurgen* is actually at the forefront of the emotional reorganization of the middle class that was underway in the 1920s. As Peter N. Stearns argues, during this period the Victorian vision of spiritual love gave way to a more subdued and secularized version of love that replaced soul communion with sexuality.[88] Even marital experts no longer drew on religious language to preach about the otherworldly ecstasies of heterosexual monogamy. Banishing the angel from the household, the new scientific marriage manuals reframed matrimony as a mutually beneficial socioeconomic relationship governed by rational cooperation that, ideally, included satisfying orgasms.[89] Jurgen, however, has even more in common with the playboy figure featured in later upscale men's magazines such as *Esquire* and *Playboy*, which presented middle-class bachelors as levelheaded pragmatists whose reasonable expectations about erotic pleasure brought them dangerously close to becoming trapped inside the childish fantasies of hysterical women who masked their machinations in the delusion of true love.[90] Getting too carried away, allowing oneself to be transported by love, was the quickest way to end up snared by the marriage trap. In both bachelorhood and marriage, all emotional excess became suspect if not outright forbidden.[91] Overcoming Victorian sexual repression, Stearns suggests, actually required middle-class men to take on even greater degrees of self-control as they tried to close themselves off from a whole host of romantic jealousies, passions, and dreams.[92]

By presenting itself as a narrative of disillusionment with eroticism, *Jurgen* allows audiences to read about sexual escapades even as they are disavowed. Cabell's novel displays a distinctly de Man–ian irony: the text splits its protagonist between mystified and knowing selves, past and present perspectives, and in so doing it enables readers to enjoy his many affairs even as they simultaneously understand them as meaningless when reviewed with the wisdom of later years.[93]

Free speech advocate Schroeder took up precisely this position when he criticized censorship in *"Obscene" Literature and Constitutional Law: A Forensic Defense of Freedom of the Press* (1911):

> When, from the vantage ground of an age of true enlightenment, future generations shall look back on our vaunted age of (contemptible?) civilization, they will be moved by mingled feelings of pity and scorn, even as we are so moved when looking back upon the 'Dark Ages.' As now we see the monstrosities of the witch-craft superstition, so some future generation will look back in wonderment at our present sex-superstition.[94]

Temporal doubleness—seeing oneself from the dispassionate view of the future—allowed readers to free themselves of both the passion and shame associated with obscenity.

Schroeder's history of the end of obscenity is Jurgen's life blown up into a metanarrative. Anti-censorship advocacy depended on the same modernist narrative of secularization found in Cabell's fantasy. On his adventures, Jurgen overcomes a series of mythological figures before finally seeing that God and heaven are nothing more than virtual realities generated by a rationalistic creator to satisfy Jurgen's grandmother, who upon death refuses to accept a godless universe.[95] Praising Cabell's novel by anticipating the offense it will cause, Mencken calls the author "a Scoffer, and, worse, he scoffs at Sacred Things."[96] Obscenity, the novel suggests, belongs not only to foolish youth but also a mist-shrouded religious era long left behind by secular modernity.

Puritanical censors are obviously motivated by religious faith, but I want to suggest that Mencken saw a more fundamental difference in worldview standing between him and his opponents. Distance was impossible in presecular cultures because, as Charles Taylor argues, they understood the self as "porous."[97] In this enchanted worldview, qualities that secularists think of as subjective or psychological could exist independently of the mind as properties of nonhuman objects, agents, or forces. Forest spirits were said to emanate force fields of panic, for example, while certain relics were holy regardless of what any individual might think of them. Because thoughts, moods, and meanings moved freely between mind and world, the porous self was always in danger of being overcome by alien powers. Just as a devil might take over a demoniac's body, an immoral image exerts a malefic influence on the mind of its viewer.

Within the secular order, however, there is a strict separation between interiority and exteriority. Concepts and affects reside exclusively in the inner realm of the mind or what Taylor calls the "buffered self."[98] An observation might make someone sad, or a psychoactive drug might render its user euphoric, but sadness and euphoria do not exist separately from the perceiving or partaking subject. This new, secular way of splitting facts from feelings makes possible the disengaged and ironical attitude that Mencken promoted in his discussions of sexuality.

Policing the boundaries between subject and object, free speech advocates like Schroeder make the case that "'obscenity' is not a quality inherent in a book or picture, but wholly and exclusively a contribution of the contemplating mind."[99] He proves this point through an ethnographic survey of decency customs—in cultures from ancient Greeks to indigenous Mexicans—that shows that there has never been any general agreement on what counts as obscene.[100] In fact, psychological and legal evidence suggests that obscenity varies not only by nation but also by individual: Schroeder recounts how *Uncle Tom's Cabin* (1852) placed one man on his path to becoming a "sex-pervert."[101] Meanwhile, evolutionary biology has disproven the literal historicity of Adam and Eve, figures often cited by judicial opinions as proof that modest shame follows as a universal consequence of eating from the tree of knowledge.[102] Schroeder argues that obscenity is wholly subjective and has nothing to do with the inherent properties of the books on trial, making it impossible to establish a stable definition or reliable test for determining purity in print. Just as Jurgen can gaze upon the bodies of old lovers and feel absolutely nothing, modern readers are bound by no compulsion to feel or want anything when they encounter an explicit sexual representation. To put it another way, critics of obscenity law argued for the arbitrariness of the signifier: because reception was always contingent on the reader's variable responses, nothing could considered be inherently obscene.

Nevertheless, without siding with the censors, we should be skeptical of any ideology that suggests that only enlightened secularists are capable of approaching texts from a reflective and historicist perspective. Nearly a century later, Mencken's intellectual heirs—the New Atheists—revived the notion that religionists are incapable of achieving distance when they argued that so-called Islamic terrorists are overpowered by a text—the Qur'an—that automatically compels unquestioning obedience.[103] These nonsecular readers, we are told, are so dangerous because they cannot differentiate the modern present from the Qur'anic past, a hermeneutic failure that indicates, in the words of one report, "backwardness and underdevelopment."[104] It is only against this racialized caricature of the "fanatical literalist mentality" that both Mencken and the New Atheists are able to position themselves as singularly sovereign subjects fully in control of how they interpret and internalize what they read.[105]

Mencken does not shy away from this imperial view of literary interpretation: the disenchantment of the word makes way for an active nihilism that refashions language to its own purposes. Mencken's "Footnote on Criticism" presents the critic as an artist in his own right, one who simply uses commentary on literature as an occasion to impose his own thoughts and feelings on the work of art to relieve his inner impulses:

> It is the pressing yearning of every man who has ideas in him to empty them upon the world, to hammer them into plausible and ingratiating shapes, to compel the attention and respect of his equals, to lord it over his inferiors.[106]

The authors the critic writes about, then, become "mere raw material for his work of art," a social fact that pits the critic against all other artists who, naturally, do not want to serve as someone else's art supplies.[107] Mencken is moved by a literary-critical will to power that seeks to put him above all other authors, especially the "pedagogue" who debases himself by evangelizing the ideas of others or stooping to improve the world of letters.[108] Because Mencken does not see language as possessing essential value or meaning, let alone inherent obscenity, he can treat it as an instrument that can be bent to his will. Literary interpretation becomes another weapon for achieving domination.

Mencken, as ever, remained in the minority on this view. Cabell's book escaped prosecution until Walter J. Kingsley, a theatrical press agent, sent a letter to the *New York Tribune*, published on January 3, 1920, tipping the readers off to the fact that a dirty book had made a "clean getaway" from the censors by allegorizing "all the perversities, abnormalities, and damn-foolishness of sex": "There is an undercurrent of extreme sensuality throughout [*Jurgen*], and once the trick of transposing the key is mastered one can dip into this tepid stream on every page."[109] Rumor had it that *Jurgen* was circulating as a lewd puzzle for the cognoscenti, and, according to one columnist, the book had even become a hit among New York chorus girls who vied with one another to see who could decipher the most *double entendres*.[110] Kingsley's letter brought *Jurgen* to the attention of Sumner, who on January 14, 1920, appeared at Cabell's publisher, Robert M. McBride & Company, with a summons and a warrant to shut down production of the book and seize all remaining copies.[111] The next day, Sumner cited publisher Robert McBride and editor Guy Holt, who, fearing prosecution, immediately pulled the book from shelves.[112] Thanks to their lawyer's political influence, the *Jurgen* case was transferred to a notoriously backlogged court where it sat untried for more than two years. As is often the case, the trial only brought fame to the censored work, which became a prized item among used booksellers and pirate bookleggers.

In the meantime, an unrepentant Cabell wrote a satire dedicated to Sumner called *Taboo*, a pamphlet-length text that strongly hinted that would-be censors opposed *Jurgen* because they were suffering from geriatric erectile dysfunction. The pamphlet employs the same distancing strategy later used by Alex Comfort when he framed his sex manual—*The Joy of Sex* (1972)—as a cookbook. In a thinly veiled allegory, Cabell tells the story of the land of Philistia, where literary references to meals are outlawed but everyone can be seen eating. The censor appears in this story as a man of law who declares all talk of gastronomy "lewd" on account of the fact that "age [has] impaired his digestive organs."[113] Cabell's cause was also championed by an emergency committee, which gathered over 160 signatures and letters in his support, including a note from Mencken. These were collected in a 1920 book, *Jurgen and the Censor*.[114]

Ultimately, the *Jurgen* case came down to the question of allegory. Although the book is filled with remarkably large staffs, "manful" excursions into caves, and lances piercing pink veils, one of its many forged epigraphs presents us with an imaginary scholar—E. Noel Codman—commenting that "if readers of *The High History of Jurgen* do not meddle with the allegory, the allegory will not meddle with them. Without minding it at all, the whole is as plain as a pikestaff."[115] Cabell composed this quotation by repurposing William Hazlitt's lines describing *The Faerie Queen*, a poem the English critic thought stood on its own without the need to search for a connection between its characters and historical personages, but in this instance the final image of the pikestaff dares the reader to see it as a phallus. Juvenile as this strategy might seem, it succeeded in 1922 with Judge Charles C. Nott, who wrote in his opinion for *People vs. Holt, McBride & Co., Et Al.* that *Jurgen* was not obscene because, although certain passages "may be considered suggestive in a veiled and subtle way of immorality," the work as a whole was a harmless work of fantasy, and, anyway, "it is doubtful if the book could be read or understood at all by more than a very limited number of readers."[116] Because he believed only a civilized minority could ever decode the book, it was safe for public circulation. Morris Ernst and William Seagle would later complain that the *Jurgen* trial and similar decisions set up an "aristocracy of smut," an elite audience unbound by obscenity law.[117]

A Religious Orgy in Tennessee

Mencken was outraged by the *Jurgen* trial, fuming that "in any civilized country such a book would be received with enthusiasm by every educated man; here it is exposed forthwith to the stupid attack of persons without either intelligence or taste."[118] Despite his near-constant exasperation with his country's wowsers, Mencken refused to retreat to bohemian Paris or some other heterotopic space where he could enjoy artistic and critical autonomy. As his critics complained, Mencken remained in the US writing and editing for a middlebrow public because he was driven by an impulse toward domination that meant that he required an audience of rubes to harangue and humiliate.[119]

This will to power can be found in Mencken's most famous polemic, his coverage of *Tennessee v. John Thomas Scopes*, widely known as the "Scopes Monkey Trial," in the *Baltimore Evening Sun*. Although the trial has come to be known as a fight between progressive enlightenment and benighted religion, Mencken proved less interested in saving Scopes or restoring science to the schools than he was in knocking down William Jennings Bryan's biblical populism in vindication of his own doctrine of social Darwinism.[120] Although Mencken was often skeptical of scientific experts, he placed his faith in evolutionary biology because it seemed to readily comport with his political philosophy.[121] As Chip Rhodes puts it, "He is a realist, but the object of his steady realist gaze is not material reality; it is the fact of the distinction between superior and inferior subjects."[122] The Scopes trial was as much a struggle over community self-government as a struggle over science education: Bryan argued that democratically elected officials should set the school curriculum, while Mencken pushed a vision of a professional-managerial elite dictating what was best for a subordinate population.[123] As Clarence Darrow gathered witness statements from academic experts, Mencken wrote in the *Baltimore Evening Sun* that the Tennessee creationists were Neanderthals hostile to modern science because of their "congenital hatred of knowledge": "The intellectual heritage of the race belongs to the minority, and the minority only."[124] The scientific principle proved only incidental to Mencken's reassertion of rank.

The Scopes trial is especially important for the history of free speech because it was a crucial turning point for the American Civil Liberties Union (ACLU), which took up the case. As Laura Weinrib has shown, the ACLU was founded as part of a struggle for "the right of agitation."[125] During the organization's early years, ACLU activists and lawyers fought for free speech protections for radical labor organizers to strike, boycott, and picket in order to help further the cause of revolution. Their position quickly began to shift with the Scopes trial. Instead of using free speech as an instrument of class warfare, the ACLU built alliances with conservatives and liberals alike while repositioning itself as championing the politically neutral cause of civil libertarianism: they might fight for the right to teach evolution during one trial, but in another they would ally with the religious right by working to overturn a ban on private schools directed at Catholics. By presenting themselves as impartial advocates for civil liberties, the ACLU could avoid the stink of radicalism even as it defended communist revolutionaries.[126]

Part of this shift, however, meant that the ACLU had to abandon its commitment to popular sovereignty and embrace the same legalism that conservatives had once used to strike down labor legislation on constitutional grounds.[127] As it moved from supporting the right to worker self-organization to supporting the right to individual free expression, the ACLU embraced the courts as a countermajoritarian institution that would protect minority opinions from the will of the people. In the Scopes trial, this manifests in a brief on behalf of professionalism:

the ACLU argued that Scopes should be allowed to perform his job duties to the best of his abilities regardless of what the populace might think.[128] To shield Scopes from public censure, the ACLU appealed to what one lawyer called the "men of the Supreme Court Bench, conscientiously avoiding emotion or passion, removed by training and thought from the influence of popular demands."[129] The ACLU would use similar arguments as it began litigating against obscenity laws, which also allowed the organization to broaden its ideological base of support and distance itself from charges of left-wing partisanship.[130]

Mencken was precisely one of those allies who would not have gotten on board with the ACLU when its primary mission was to provide legal support for anarchists, socialists, and union organizers. Instead, he was drawn to what he saw as the ACLU's defiance of public opinion and religious dogma. We can see this in the disdain with which he describes the ACLU's opponents. Repeatedly, Mencken portrays the creationist's crusade using the language of obscenity.[131] In his journalistic accounts of the trial, Mencken captures a local Pentecostal group, the Church of God, using the same voyeuristic chronotope seen in Cather's short story. Mencken describes creeping up on a church revival in the middle of a forest where he finds congregants praying in tongues, kneeling together in an "obscene heap," their bodies intermingling with one another as they call for the forgiveness of an attractive penitent woman who convulses and moans like "a tomcat at a petting party": "It was like peeping through a knothole at the writhings of a people in pain."[132] So inspired, the churchgoers peel off from the service, disappearing into the woods in pairs for secret assignations. Despite hinting at the believers' desublimated eroticism, Mencken reintroduces discretion to the scene by positioning himself as a "strict behaviorist."[133] The faithfuls' feelings are not his concern. Wavering between professional decorum and salacious objectification, Mencken records their animalistic movements and incomprehensible sounds with all the dispassion of a zoologist.

More often, however, Mencken draws on the jargon of anthropology to chasten his enemies in Dayton, Tennessee. The editor repeats this move frequently throughout his work. His influential diagnosis of Southern cultural pathology, "The Sahara of the Bozart," calls on anthropologists to take their craniometers to the region's white rural poor to confirm their degeneracy, while his observations on national character taxonomize the average American specimen as a member of another species of hominids, *Boobus Americanus*.[134] Thus, covering the Scopes trial, Mencken classifies evolution's opponents as anthropoids or Neanderthals, equating their religious officiates with pagan sorcerers and designating their way of life a relic or recrudescence of an archaic past.

Mencken's observations find parallels within a longer tradition that associated pornography, exoticism, and anthropology. Throughout the first half of the twentieth century, mail-order erotica dealers in the United States, including imprints such as the Anthropological Library, the American Ethnological Press, and the Eugenics Publishing Company, sold studies of sexual customs to a mixed audience of humanists and heavy breathers.[135] These anti-censorship strategies probably found their inspiration in a group of Victorian scholars and libertines. As Lisa Z. Sigel observes, an anthropological trend within literary pornography in England from the 1860s through the 1880s emerged out of a clique of writers, bibliographers, and explorers in the Anthropological Society of London who called themselves the Cannibal Club.[136] Insulated from censure by their superior social standing, members of the Cannibal Club drew on the "distancing mechanisms" of ethnographic and scientific discourse to write and publish openly on nonnormative sexualities in colonized non-European populations.[137]

Despite their public personae, Cannibal Club members were not the unbiased sexologists and anthropologists they claimed to be. Most club members were elite Tories whose belief in innate hierarchy led them to support the Confederacy in the US Civil War and espouse the theory of polygenesis, which posited the independent origins of human races, long after it had fallen out of favor in the scientific community.[138] Deeply racist, the Cannibal Club took a ghoulish attitude toward imperial subjects: club member Sir Richard Burton tried in vain to find a fresh human skin in Dahomey, Africa, with the intention of returning to England with binding for an anthropodermic edition of the Marquis de Sade for a fellow Cannibal.[139] While Cannibal Club members were able to speak more freely because they claimed the neutrality of academic inquiry, their pornographic studies of other cultures only served to reify imperial power and white supremacy by hypersexualizing and dehumanizing subjugated peoples.[140] When Mencken cast his enemies in the hinterlands as an orgiastic cult of obscene savages, he knowingly or unknowingly exploited conventions established by imperialist pornographers.

Even when Mencken does not explicitly describe his enemies or inferiors as anachronistic, he often succeeds in fixing them in time by writing about them in the ethnographic present. By speaking about past ways and traditions in the present tense, anthropologists present non-Western cultures as if they have never undergone contact or any other historical change: the society being studied *is* matriarchal, animistic, or totemistic.[141] Through the ethnographic present, the anthropologist abstracts away the complexities and contradictions of colonial and postcolonial life. This move ostensibly allows the expert to avoid getting caught in a series of inelegant qualifiers and caveats—including reminders to the reader that time has passed between fieldwork and publication—but it also serves to dehistoricize the target culture. Mencken used the ethnographic present precisely for this purpose. Mencken describes Appalachian anthropoids and American "booboisie" as eternal types because, for him, they are fixed once and for all. The masses' purported obstinacy, incorrigibility, and ineducability make it easy for Mencken to generalize about them without considering the time dimension.

Mencken even called on the anthropological community to join him in this project. Rounding out a review of Margaret Mead's *Coming of Age in Samoa: A Psychological Study of Primitive Youth for Western Civilisation* (1928), Mencken asks the readers of the *American Mercury*,

> Why doesn't some ethnologist go to a village in Tennessee (or Vermont, or Ohio, or Kansas), and describe its people as [Mead] describes her Samoans? . . . All sorts of delusions and superstitions survive from a less critical day—for example, the belief that American yokels are more moral than city folk. Confronted by such palpable nonsense, one goes to the sources for light, and finds that there are none. We know far more about the daily life of the Pueblo Indians than we know about the life of Mississippi Baptists. Whenever, by some accident, light is let into the subject, there is gasping surprise, and even horror. This happened, typically, when a gang of slick city jakes descended upon the primitive mountain village of Dayton, Tenn., at the time of the Scopes trial, and found it full of Aurignacian [i.e., Paleolithic] men clad in dressy mail-order suits, with Bibles under their arms. But science is never horrified. It has no more moral scruples than a movie critic or a beauty doctor. It simply sets forth the facts. I herewith summons [sic] it to proceed to business.[142]

When Robert S. Lynd and Helen Merrell Lynd subsequently carried out a similar project in *Middletown: A Study in Modern American Culture* (1929), Mencken cheered their results while excoriating their research subjects in a review titled,

"A City in Moronia."[143] As in the passage exposing the Pentecostal orgy, Mencken places himself beyond righteous outrage and prurient interest by claiming the neutral objectivity and impersonal reserve of the educated expert. Social evolutionism substitutes temporal ordering for moral or preferential valuation, holding the modern to be superior to the primitive, and thus it allows Mencken to pass judgment on his enemies free from the embarrassment of articulating alternative standards. The audacious humor of devolving a courtroom of creationists into a pack of extinct primates turns out to be only an added bonus.

When Bryan died not long after the Scopes trial, Mencken placed the trial's prosecutors safely behind him: "Heave an egg out of a Pullman window, and you will hit a Fundamentalist almost everywhere in the United States today. They swarm in the country towns, inflamed by their *shamans*, and with a saint, now, to venerate."[144] Because he spatializes time, Mencken conceives of the civilized minority as hurtling forward toward the city of the future while the rural masses stand still. Dayton, and wherever else the mob dwells, becomes an anachronistic space, backwards and unchanging. Expelled from the reader's contemporaneity, sealed off in another discursive universe, the uncivilized majority becomes a mute target of obscene insult and invective, dripping in yolk. While this image may simply capture the insecure self-assertion of Mencken's audience of upwardly striving collegians, looking back with newly disdainful eyes at their childhood homes, it also comes to encapsulate the domineering attitude of an ascendant class of managers and professionals.

The Aristocracy of Efficiency

As we have seen, Mencken's elitism structured his thinking on questions of art and obscenity. Although his class ideology is often articulated in almost feudal terms, it is a product of twentieth-century developments in mass production. Writing in his notebooks near the end of his life, Mencken summed up his social philosophy in his characteristically blunt manner:

> The existence of most human beings is of absolutely no significance to history or to human progress. . . . They are, at best, undifferentiated slaves upon an endless assembly line, and at worst they are robots who leave their mark upon time only by occasionally falling into the machinery, and so incommoding their betters.[145]

According to Mencken, most people are entirely superfluous and only a small number of naturally gifted thinkers from superior populations contribute anything to the management or improvement of "civilization."[146] Mencken's crude view of the world as an eternal struggle between the exceptional minority and the ignorant masses emerged in part out of his own early work as a popularizer of Friedrich Nietzsche. According to Mencken's strangely Americanizing interpretation in *The Philosophy of Friedrich Nietzsche* (1908), the German philosopher calls for an "aristocracy of efficiency."[147] Nietzsche, he suggests, rejects the old aristocracy as outmoded and decadent, envisioning instead an aristocracy based on an inborn capacity for revolutionary new ideas. Mencken's Übermensch is a Schumpeterian entrepreneur who introduces novel values and methods into the world by imposing them through sheer strength of his will.[148] The aristocracy of efficiency deserves to be served by the proletariat, who have earned their lowly places by being born conformists. Borrowing an image from publishing, Mencken quotes Nietzsche as condemning these inferiors "as blurred copies of their betters, printed on bad paper and from worn out plates."[149] Unlike the aristocrats, these workers are only good at carrying out the commands of their betters. The "ideal ploughman," Mencken writes, "is one who has no thought of anything higher and better than ploughing."[150] Only Mencken's civilized minority should be capable of transcending their present circumstances.

Mencken's Nietzsche naturalizes the split between conception and execution introduced by Taylorist and Fordist management. As Harry Braverman argues, workers prior to Taylorism drew on tradecraft and professional experience to make their own ad hoc decisions about how to carry out their work.[151] This knowledge gave workers a significant amount of autonomy, allowing them to slow down, stop, or sabotage production at will. To combat proletarian unrest, Frederick Winslow Taylor's so-called scientific management sought to strip control from workers by planning out every step in the labor process in advance. Leaving nothing up to the worker's discretion, Taylor and other management experts prescribed the exact motions for each and every labor task. With this regime in place, Taylorism could subdivide production into the smallest tasks possible. Instead of paying skilled craftsmen to carry out an entire manufacturing process from beginning to end, Taylorist managers hired high-priced, skilled workers for difficult or complicated steps in the process while assigning cheaper unskilled or semi-skilled labor to complete the rest of the job, driving down total wages. Because capital always seeks to maximize surplus value by reducing the cost of labor power, Taylorism set off a race to the bottom as management found new ways of de-skilling more and more occupations. Always in service of capital, Taylorism produces and holds open the split between the brow and the hand.

The Taylorizing process depends on managerial methods of abstraction.[152] Like Hedger gazing upon Eden's gymnastics and seeing only the graphic traces made by his crayon, management science reduces complex bodily movements to simple diagrammatic instructions. Hedger's voyeuristic record of Eden most resembles Frank Gilbreth's cycle graphs, studies produced by attaching a light to a worker's hand and asking them to perform a task while a researcher captures them with a time-exposed photograph.[153] The resultant image reduces their actions to the continuous, bright line made by the bulb and collapses a series of successive actions into one synchronous moment arrested in time, allowing the management scientist to analyze them for inefficiencies. Like Eden dissolving into mist while Hedger tracks her motion, the worker's body appears in Gilbreth's photographs as a blurred ghost disappearing behind their repeatable techniques.

Although many critics complained scientific management was dehumanizing for the workers, Mencken welcomed this new system of worker control. In a *Smart Set* review of Henry Ford's *My Life and Work* (1922), Mencken expresses some skepticism about the role of industrial psychologists and other management scientists before launching into an encomium to Taylorism: "Ford's capital discovery in manufacturing was this: that very few of the operations in an ordinary plant require any intelligence in the operator—in brief, that a moron is quite as useful in industry as a Socrates."[154] Erasing the class struggle between management and labor, Mencken argues that Ford treats his workers like "slaves" because they are by their very nature "machines," mindless drudges made so by God.[155] We find the same theme in *Friedrich Nietzsche* as well. Echoing Taylor's comparison of workers to oxen or dray horses, Mencken tells us that the aristocracy of efficiency "regard[s] the proletariat merely as a conglomeration of draft animals made to be driven, enslaved and exploited."[156] Bosses and workers appear in his writings as two separate species.

In this regard, Mencken stands at the end of a long tradition of what David R. Roediger and Elizabeth D. Esch term "whiteness-as-management."[157] Although Mencken's relationship to race was not always overt or straightforward, a strong current of racism and racial thinking runs through his work. In *Friedrich*

Nietzsche, Mencken informs us that so long as Black people constitute a separate race they will be subordinate to whites, regardless of improvements in education or social condition.[158] One perverse passage fantasizes about a public project to forcibly vaccinate Black populations to prevent the spread of disease, a medical procedure he claims they could never understand.[159] In Mencken's mind, Black bodies, like the bodies of all proletarian workers, exist only as tools for the aristocracy of efficiency. Management stands as a biological type apart from workers, chosen by natural selection to be the civilized minority. Although Mencken in his later years would reject eugenics as collectivist—the freak successes in every race should be allowed to rise to the top—he persisted in viewing superiority as an inborn, biological property.[160]

A pattern runs through all of Mencken's work: a disenchanted figure wrests the future from the inertia of the past. Mencken, a kind of authoritarian Richard Florida, looks forward to a world in which the creative class commands routine workers, brilliant minds manage docile bodies, distanced readers master obscene texts, the moderns topple the old puritans, and the genetically superior overcome subhuman anthropoids. It is easy to see why Mencken's vision chimed well with the ambitions and insecurities of young professionals looking to distinguish themselves from the lower classes and make their mark on the world.

Dominance has its costs. Mencken's readers secured their managerial positions by becoming alienated from their bodies and other workers. The end result of Mencken's strategy against censorship is the automation of sex. Overcoming pornographic impulses prepares readers to view the body from the bloodless perspective of an efficiency expert. Fordism transforms the proletariat into human motors, machines with no psychic or physical energy to waste on the pleasures of idleness.[161] From the class standpoint of management, these workers are always lagging behind, and, because the workers are incapable of anything beyond mechanical repetition of the same, it falls to management to invent newer, faster methods of organizing labor.

The manager, then, is always a debunker of old customs and traditional ways of doing things. The term "debunk" was coined by William Woodward less than a decade after Henry Ford offered the *Chicago Tribune* his most famous interview response: "History is more or less bunk. It is traditional. We don't want tradition. We want to live in the present, and the only history that is worth a tinker's dam is the history we make today."[162] Nothing is sacred to the Fordist manager: the moral order of workers, alongside any sense of enjoyment in their own bodies, must be swept aside to make space for the assembly line.[163]

Mencken's ideal of liberty without democracy, first tested in the realm of free speech, quickly became an ideology governing management and markets. Outraged by the New Deal, Mencken turned ever harder to the right during the 1930s. During this time, he became a key influence on Ayn Rand, whose transgressive novels about professional-managerial rebels struggling against the masses inspired middle-class swingers and Satanists before joining the canon of Republican party politicos.[164] We can see Mencken's spirit in the present moment not only in Randian sermons on makers and takers, job creators and welfare sponges, but also in the cultural style of the alt-right. Like Mencken's civilized minority, the alt-right advertises itself as a group of impious provocateurs whose commitment to unfettered inquiry and merciless reason leads them to reject equality and elevate themselves above the hyperemotional scolds who try to censor them. Hate's embrace of free speech is one of the ultimate consequences of a First Amendment doctrine unmoored from any commitment to democratic self-government. Indeed, in the afterword I will suggest that the transgressive cultural style that marked the ascendency of the PMC mutated into the alt-right as the style's practitioners became downwardly mobile. Mencken, who even in his most progressive moments represented the antinomianism of elites, now lends his name to the H. L. Mencken Club, a white nationalist association. The Mencken Club's most prominent cofounder is Richard Spencer, the dandified Nazi who croons to his critics, "tomorrow belongs to us."[165]

Decrypting EC Comics

H. L. MENCKEN set the type for controversial editors who came after him. As we shall see, editors of borderline obscene material after World War II followed his lead in constructing audiences of professional-managerial readers who prided themselves on being more cool, rational, and self-possessed than audiences susceptible to obscenity. Mencken also helped popularize the powerful image of the persecuted editor daring to publish what the censors could not handle. Although not all outlaw editors succeeded in achieving the same symbolic and social capital as Mencken, they often drew on the same repertoire of postures and strategies to negotiate their way through an increasingly arbitrary and unpredictable censorship regime.

The obscenity scare of the 1950s began not with sex but with violence. The first major censorship campaign of the decade focused on horror and crime comic books rather than on pornography.[1] Fearing that comic books corrupted the morals of the youth, community organizations across the country encouraged children to collect and burn them in public bonfires.[2] Comic book censors were on shaky legal ground: when the Supreme Court overturned *Winters v. New York* in 1948, it held that laws against obscenity did not extend to depictions of violence.[3] Nevertheless, this did not stop cities and states from outlawing horror and crime comics. One of the procensorship movement's prime targets was Entertaining Comics (EC), which published gory and irreverent comic books for adolescent audiences. Like many controversial publications, EC's *Panic* magazine was banned in Massachusetts in 1953.[4] When word of the ban reached New York, where EC's offices were located, two police officers were dispatched to purchase a copy of *Panic* directly from the editor so that they could make an arrest. Upon arrival, they bought the issue from EC's receptionist, Shirley Norris. EC editor and publisher William Gaines hid in his office, while his business manager Lyle

Stuart told the cops that "it'll kill him if you take that man."[5] Stuart volunteered to be arrested instead, but because Norris actually committed the alleged crime, she was taken into custody and charged for selling "indecent literature."[6] Luckily the judge immediately dismissed the case.[7]

Although EC largely avoided legal trouble, many parents and experts worked hard to drive them out of business. Psychologist Fredric Wertham spearheaded the anti-comic book movement, and, thanks in part to Wertham's efforts, the United States Senate Subcommittee on Juvenile Delinquency held a widely publicized series of hearings in 1954, allowing senators to grill comic book publishers on their influence on children. Gaines volunteered to speak at the hearing, hoping to vindicate the comic book industry, but his testimony proved to be especially disastrous and stoked the outrage of censors.[8] Responding to the uproar following the hearings, Gaines helped organize the Comics Magazine Association of America to coordinate an industry-wide response.[9] This, however, proved to be his undoing. The association decided to avoid further controversy by regulating the industry through the Comics Code Authority, which, like Hollywood's Hays Code, attempted to avoid government censorship through voluntary self-censorship.[10] Titles with Comics Code Authority approval could not feature sex, bloodshed, excessive violence, unpunished criminality, profanity, disrespect for police authority, or the undead. Words like "horror" and "terror" could not even appear in the titles of code-sanctioned comic books.[11]

In effect, these restrictions brought an end to the crime and horror comic book trend among code-approved publishers, and those who sought to buck the code quickly found themselves thwarted by distributors who did not want to face pushback from procensorship groups. EC Comics was forced to immediately cancel its horror and suspense titles, including popular lines such as *Tales from the Crypt* and *Crime SuspenStories*.[12] When the publisher's science fiction comic books also faced trouble with Comics Code administrators and distributors alike, EC gave up on all of its New Trend series with the exception of *Mad* magazine, the humor publication that would eventually become the publisher's main focus.

Nevertheless, the Comics Code failed to prevent a wave of legislation tightening restrictions on comic books. Over a dozen states passed laws regulating the distribution and sale of comic books.[13] Wertham's victory over the comic book industry only emboldened later censorship advocates who targeted pornographic literature. As Whitney Strub argues, the crusade against comic books anticipated the strategies of later anti-obscenity campaigns while "establishing an analytic framework that would shape responses to pornography."[14] Understanding Wertham, then, will help us grasp the larger stakes for the battle over obscenity.

Censorship debates ultimately came down to conflicts between competing methods of reading. While Wertham saw reading as a process of empathetically identifying with literary characters, EC cast its readers as "fan-addicts," members of an imagined community with its own rituals and watchwords that had little to do with moral uplift.[15] Throughout the EC comic lines, the fan-addict does not appear as embodied in any one character. Even in the many second-person stories found in the pages of EC comic books, the perspectival character often appears as a generic, masculine cipher. What bound fan-addicts together instead was a shared approach to the comics, including a commonly held capacity to respond to the texts as a game of prediction. Whoever anticipated what happened next in an EC comic won.

Fan-addicts did not identify with the scabrous creatures in the pages of EC because such sympathy was not necessary to beat the game. EC readers had only to observe and extrapolate from the monsters' previous actions to guess their next moves. By taking a strategic and almost cybernetic orientation toward comic narratives, EC fans followed the lead of editors Gaines and Al Feldstein, whose production workflow treated fiction as abstract puzzles. The editorship of Gaines and Feldstein transformed horror and crime periodicals into a series of repetitive training exercises that allowed readers to become better and better at recognizing patterns and extrapolating from them. To do this, the publisher taught readers to see characters not as unique persons but as game pieces that could be easily sacrificed. The frightful scenes featured in many EC comics served as a repulsive force that kept readers from overidentifying with particular characters, as a shock that disrupted rigid habits, and as an erotic stimulus that rewarded creative foresight. All of this provided EC readers with an entrée into a white-collar way of life that approached social organizations as gamelike. EC readers learned not only how to predict the uncertain and respond to the unexpected—they also learned to take a playful stance toward serious matters.

Censorship and National Character

Wertham intervened in a larger debate raging about reading and character formation. Many midcentury social critics worried that mass media seemed to have taken over cultural reproduction for the bourgeois family, infiltrating the private home to transmit new values to impressionable young children.[16] Channeling these anxieties, Wertham testified to the Subcommittee on Juvenile Delinquency: "Formerly the child wanted to be like daddy or mommy. Now they skip you, they bypass you. They want to be like Superman, not like the hard working, prosaic mother and father."[17] As consumer society expanded, children and adolescents became just another market to be manipulated, enticed, and molded in the image of the commodity.[18] New structures of character formation produced new kinds of subjects. Escaping the confines of their parents' Protestant work ethic, children seemed to become increasingly receptive to messages from the outside. David Riesman described the new postwar subject as a human "radar," scanning the crowd for subtle cues on how to be.[19] Whereas the "inner-directed" person internalized the guiding principles of their parents, the "other-directed" personality changed in response to external feedback.[20] Midcentury moral panics had as much to do with alarm at the nation's apparent loss of private interiority as they had to do with Judeo-Christian morality.

Censors agreed that subjectivity was increasingly superficial. Wertham scoffed at the very word "deep" whenever it was invoked to describe the causes of juvenile crime: "The team-experts like the word *deep*. . . . They use this word as an answer to any objection that is raised. The reply that things are 'deep' or 'deeper' or 'far deeper' is supposed to answer everything" (emphasis original).[21] Wertham discounted psychoanalysis's obsession with the hidden recesses of early childhood along with popular culture's belief in innate character dispositions as explanations for juvenile delinquency. Wertham's research trajectory led him to focus on exterior and social causation. His first published essay, "The Catathymic Crisis: A Clinical Entity," argued that a patient's experience of a traumatic event could provoke in them unconscious and unresolvable emotional tensions that would later compel them to erupt in uncharacteristic and seemingly unmotivated bursts of violence.[22] A single horrific sight might lead an otherwise sane person to murder someone out of the blue and then return to apparent normality. For Wertham, the self proved fragile indeed.

Wertham's interest in tracing the roots of antisocial behavior persisted through his work at the Lafargue Clinic, a psychiatric treatment center founded in Harlem in 1946 that provided inexpensive care to a predominately Black patient population. Wertham's work reflected his commitment to seeing the psyche not as an isolated "unit" but as part of a larger network of social ties.[23] All too often, Wertham suggested, the courts blamed individuals for what were in fact reflections of larger cultural and political problems. Wertham's belief in social psychiatry pushed him to speak out against racial segregation, which he and his staff determined to be even more psychologically damaging than the kinds of sexual problems treated in Freudian psychoanalysis.[24]

Most famously, Wertham directed his attention to another stimulus to juvenile delinquency: comic books. While pursuing studies on adolescent crime, Wertham organized a therapy group he called the "Hookey Club."[25] In these group settings, Wertham observed that children at play often acted out disturbing tropes from comic books. Many young patients even claimed that comic books inspired them to perpetrate crimes. The Hookey Club functioned not only as a form of psychological treatment but also as a research method to explore the cultural and social dimensions of delinquency. Drawing from newspaper accounts as well as firsthand case studies, Wertham gathered shocking tales of depravity in which comic books purportedly drove child readers to commit rape, burglary, armed robbery, and assault.

Wertham continued to pursue this line of inquiry while at Lafargue, but it was his role as an expert witness in a censorship case in 1948 that propelled him into an anti-comics crusade. When *Sunshine and Health*, a nudist magazine, was accused of obscenity, Wertham testified on its behalf, asserting that not only was the periodical above reproach but far more scandalous material could be found in comics marketed to children.[26] Wertham's speech, which he delivered while brandishing a spray of gruesome titles purchased earlier that day, received a write-up in the *New York Herald Tribune* that caught the attention of the editor of the *Saturday Review of Literature*, who solicited an article from him on the topic. Wertham quickly became the public face of opposition to crime and horror comics, featured in pieces in *Reader's Digest* and *Collier's*. Going beyond the more reserved condemnations of other comic critics, Wertham's anti-comic screeds seemed to imitate the same pulp crime structure of the comics he condemned. The *Collier's* article—"Horror in the Nursery" by Judith Crist—begins with a photograph reenacting a purported crime inspired by comics. A boy and a girl hold down their victim, a well-dressed youth whose lips peel back in what must be either agony or satisfaction while his body is penetrated by the fountain pen that his comic-crazed assailants are pressing into his arm "like a hypodermic."[27]

As the ink spurts out onto his skin, the prone boy is graphically violated. With material like this, it should come as no surprise that Wertham soon proved himself as a successful moral crusader.

Wertham's 1954 book *Seduction of the Innocent* crystallizes the moral panic surrounding crime and horror comic books. Underneath the meandering professional anecdotes and sensational, tabloid-style melodramas, the book offers a surprisingly simplistic model of media influence. According to Wertham, the monsters and criminals inhabiting comic books function as direct examples for impressionable young readers to follow. The reader identifies with comic book brutes and thereby degrades their "ethical image," a preconscious self-understanding that Wertham likens to body image.[28] Comics thus bring about "moral disarmament": "It is an influence on character, on attitude, on the higher functions of social responsibility, on super-ego formation and on the intuitive feeling for right and wrong."[29] Comic books reshape their audiences in fundamental ways, Wertham argues, and they do so by retraining reader emotions and desires through bad role models.

Leslie Fiedler argues that Wertham vilifies comic books because they transgress against middlebrow literary values. In his 1955 essay, "The Middle Against Both Ends," Fiedler explains that middlebrow thinkers have opened up a "two-front class war" against highbrow modernism and lowbrow mass culture: "the sentimental-egalitarian conscience [of the middlebrow] against the ironical-aristocratic sensibility on the one hand and the brutal-populist mentality on the other."[30] What Fiedler dubs the "genteel middling mind" opposes the poetry of Ezra Pound no less than it does the pulp novels of Mickey Spillane because both fail to carry forward the middlebrow project of healing class divisions through a universally shared literary culture.[31] This endeavor fails because highbrow culture proves skeptical of all universalisms—including, in the Pound affair, liberal democracy and racial equality—while lowbrow culture rejects the middle class's condescending attempts to improve the morals of their social inferiors.

However, I would argue that middlebrow reading practices were more than just methods by which the middle class strove to achieve, in Fiedler's words, "cultural hegemony."[32] Middlebrow reading habits provided some small relief from the hidden injuries of the professional-managerial class. In her study on the Book-of-the-Month Club, Janice Radway argues that the club's editors nurtured reading habits such as empathizing and identifying with literary characters. This "middlebrow personalism" allowed professional-managerial readers respite from the coldhearted rationalism that came from seeing the world like a technocrat.[33] By emotionally engaging with the lived experience of others, middlebrow readers countered their class tendency to reduce individuals to abstract categories or instrumental functions. In the pages of these novels, the populations administered by the PMC turn out to be just folks. Although this affectively charged reading practice encouraged a form of tolerant humanism, Book-of-the-Month Club judges rejected novels that elicited unacceptable emotional responses, including responses to the obscene such as revulsion or prurient interest. Famously, the club convinced Richard Wright to censor sexual passages from *Native Son* (1940).[34] Middlebrow modes of reading afforded readers the opportunity to imaginatively blur the line between classes or identity categories and to commune with unfamiliar others while still maintaining the reader's sense of distinction and self-possession.

Wertham operates under this theory of reading. A professional expert with a penchant for easy moralizing, Wertham was a thoroughly middlebrow figure. Indeed, the Book-of-the-Month Club selected Wertham's collaboration with Mary Louise Aswell—*The World Within: Fiction Illuminating Neuroses of Our Time* (1947)—and, later, the club's judges considered *The Seduction of the Innocent* as an alternate selection. (Wertham claims that comic book publishers successfully pressured the Book-of-the-Month Club into dropping the book.)[35] Throughout his work, Wertham denounces comic books because they fail to account for the full complexity of their characters, who often appear as stereotyped or subhuman, and promote identification with morally objectionable figures. This, Wertham suggests, poses a serious threat to middle-class children, leading them down a path of criminal dissipation.[36] Wertham never considers the possibility that comic books might be inducing other kinds of reading habits.

Of course, Wertham and other progressive-minded censors were not alone in seeing obscene literature as a moral problem. Although Wertham cast himself as a liberal fighting off the depredations of the market on children's minds, his underlying theory of speech regulation anticipates what would eventually become the neoconservative orthodoxy, which also called for the state to wield pastoral power. Walter Berns, who cites Wertham with approval, makes this ideology explicit in *Freedom, Virtue, and the First Amendment* (1957).[37] According to Berns, the overriding principle governing First Amendment debates should be the government's duty to protect republican virtue.[38] Censorship is critical to preserving the moral character of a "self-governing" citizenry, by which he means not only a nation of citizens able to engage in deliberative debate but also a nation of citizens able to control their own impulses.[39] For this reason, Berns rejects the notion that censorship should be limited to media that fail the clear-and-present-danger test.[40] Although free speech liberalism protects citizens from immediate incitements to criminal action, it shirks the law's responsibility to form and protect the characters of its subjects. Pornography—along with flag-burning and communist propaganda—offers a dangerous moral education in evil.

Because regimes depend on the character of their citizens, Berns argued, de-censorship works to dissolve the nation through the corrosive influences of disloyalty and depravity. Paradoxically, this state of civil anarchy ends in authoritarian rule. As Berns spells out in "Pornography vs. Democracy: The Case for Censorship," liberalism's promotion of "shamelessness and the fullest self-expression or indulgence" quickly lead to "tyranny": "To live together requires rules and a governing of the passions, and those who are without shame will be unruly and unrulable; having lost the ability to restrain themselves by observing the rules they collectively give themselves, they will have to be ruled by others."[41] If citizens want to preserve *any* of their liberties, Berns argues, they will have to restrict some of them.

While Wertham does not think in quite these terms—as a psychologist, he is concerned with mental hygiene rather than civic virtue—he nevertheless makes a similar argument about the politics of obscenity. Like many of his contemporaries, Wertham worried about the American character's susceptibility to totalitarian influence. Other, more sophisticated thinkers took this as an opportunity to produce artworks that trained spectators in the habits and attitudes they associated with the democratic personality.[42] Wertham, however, trained his eye on restricting media that appeared to instill fascist principles such as racial superiority, violence for the sake of violence, and the glorification of the superman. Wertham saw society as a gardener watching over growing children, cultivating their characters while protecting them from blighting influences.[43]

Reading like a Maniac

It is easy to dismiss Wertham. Many have cast him as a fanatical killjoy, while others have picked apart his methods as failing to follow the now-prevailing standards of positivistic research. It has even been revealed that many of the case studies he draws out in his work were conflated and stylized if not outright falsified.[44] At the same time, it seems strange how much vitriol goes into rebuking or refuting a man who turned out to be an incredibly minor and largely forgotten figure in criminal psychology. This animosity toward Wertham seems even more curious when placed alongside fan accounts of EC's impact on them. Fans often joke that EC warped their sensibilities and ruined their lives. Although fan-addicts are clearly poking fun at the Wertham scare—these tongue-in-cheek biographies quickly turn into success stories—their accounts also reinforce a larger narrative about EC's enduring influence. EC, we are told, launched the underground comix movement, the counterculture of the 1960s, and even the New Left.[45] EC comic books are subversive, somehow, but not in the brutal way that Wertham suggests. Despite EC readers' mockery of Wertham's work, they nevertheless admit that the comic books changed their characters. Wertham's challenge, then, has to be met head-on with an alternate explanation of reading and character formation.

Middlebrow censors like Wertham promote reading as an exemplary and affective practice: fiction shapes readers' characters by pushing them to emotionally identify with moral or immoral models for behavior. EC comics, however, elicit a very different reading style. EC's editorial framing presents horror and suspense stories as intellectual puzzles that improve readers' abilities to decode, replicate, and respond to patterns. By deadening his feelings through repeated viewings of violent or grotesque scenes, the fan-addict distances himself from what he sees as overly emotional or identificatory readings. In effect, EC turns obscenity into a formal device for resisting the reader's desire to invest in characters, and it does so in order to transform high-stress fantasies into practice zones for a form of reading that, as we shall see, orients the reader toward strategic pattern recognition.

Gaines served not only as the figurehead of EC but as its ideal reader, what his biographer called "the total audience."[46] EC's formative model of reading emerges out of Gaines's editorial reading practices. Gaines followed a routine when he collaborated with coeditor Feldstein. Every night, Gaines wolfed doses of Dexedrine and "read like a maniac," flipping through science fiction and horror stories until early in the morning.[47] Taking notes, he boiled these narratives down to premises that he would then subvert or simply plagiarize to produce "springboards," which he would pitch to Feldstein the next day.[48] On a typical morning,

Feldstein rejected springboards until Gaines got "hysterical," and then, finally, they would hit on a story seed worthy of a script, which Feldstein banged out during the remaining hours of the workday.[49] Once they had a script, Feldstein created an armature for the comic by placing the narration boxes and dialogue bubbles on the page using Leroy lettering, a very blocky and uniform font many fans experienced as "cold and detached."[50] The editors then assigned artists to illustrate the stories, following the narration as guidelines for their cartoons. The entire workflow at EC depended on an editorial approach that standardized cartooning by seeing stories as manipulable and repeatable structures.

During the editorial process, the Feldstein method often changed its horror or science fiction source material completely. We see this quite clearly in "Jellyfish," the EC knockoff version of Ray Bradbury's "Skeleton." EC adapted many of Bradbury's short stories, which were published without acknowledgment until Bradbury nicely asked to be compensated and credited for his ideas.[51] Bradbury's story follows Mr. Harris, a man tormented by the uncomfortable and uncanny awareness of his own skeleton. The story turns around this ghoulish figuration for Harris's alienation from himself, a psychic malady that ultimately drives him to see a creepy bone specialist who solves the problem by dissolving his skeletal structure. In the final scene, his wife Clarisse comes home to a seemingly empty house only to squash Harris like a beached "jellyfish."[52] Very little of this narrative survives the Feldstein method. As "Skeleton" becomes "Jellyfish," the translation process leaves Bradbury's story almost unrecognizable except for the final image of the gelatinous victim. Instead, we get a story about a pharmaceutical company whose corrupt business manager Charles Norton tries and fails to convince his fellow employee Howard Norton, a biochemist, to adulterate insulin shots for greater profits. When the biochemist refuses, his colleague calls him a "spineless jellyfish ... with no backbone."[53] The business manager goes ahead with his plan without the biochemist, but, when drug users start dying from insulin shock, he ends up framing him. In jail, the biochemist continues his experiments, discovering a chemical compound that dissolves calcium and phosphorus salts. Upon release, the biochemist ingratiates himself with his old employer again and tricks Charles into drinking the potion. Quickly, the business manager collapses into a blob on the floor ("UUUGGNNN! GLLAGHH!"), and the last panel shows us the grinning face of the biochemist as he prepares to stomp: "Now *you* are the jellyfish!"[54]

Where Bradbury's story sets up a series of dialectical tensions—between one aspect of the self and another, between exterior life and interior life, between the supernatural metaphor and its psychic referent—the EC adaptation squishes everything flat. Even the story's central image seems to work on only one level. One never even gets the sense that the biochemist is weak willed or yielding like a jellyfish at all—in fact, he is standing up to the business manager in the very first panel. The business manager's unsubstantiated insult serves as nothing more than a flimsy pretext for the narrative's trick ending. EC's editorial process literalizes Bradbury's metaphors and evacuates them of any psychological depth.

Here and elsewhere, EC characters tend to possess very little in the way of history or psychological complexity—what you see is what you get. When they do have some quirk or derangement, it manifests in the most obvious and caricatured of ways—the neat freak arranges the organs of his victim into carefully labeled jars, for example. While "Skeleton" gives us a rich sense of Harris's inner experience, often shifting into free indirect discourse, "Jellyfish" only offers a few thought bubbles in which the biochemist repeats to himself his rival's insults: "So he said I had no backbone, eh? Well . . . we'll see! We'll see!"[55] Disinvested from the characters, readers are left to admire the cleverness of the devices that hold up the story, including the wordplay around jellyfishes and the vivid splash page centering on the image of the biochemist's boot rising up to crush the reader along with an actual sea creature. The Feldstein method rips the skeletal structure out of Bradbury's narrative while leaving the heart and guts on the cutting-room floor.

The Games Fan-Addicts Play

One could condemn the shallowness of EC's characters as a deficiency. Critics such as Irving Howe rejected the flat characters found in most comic books as the latest manifestation of mass culture's "depersonalization of the individual."[56] Cribbing from Theodor Adorno and Max Horkheimer, Howe argues that comic books served as a mirror of the industrial processes that reduced both workers and commodities to their exchange values. However, the mass culture critique assumes an aesthetic purpose that few comic books attempted to achieve. As Riesman observes, comic books stood at the leading edge of a cultural shift from inner-directed reading to other-directed reading. Inner-directed reading allowed bourgeois readers to internalize aspirational norms by emulating characters depicted as rising above their class stations to higher occupations.[57] Because these Horatio Alger protagonists longed for something greater, their personalities necessarily exceeded their social roles. Through its representations of self-determining characters, inner-directed print encouraged readers to break away from traditional or communal demands. This regime of reading was therefore solitary and private. Other-directed reading, however, often took place in crowds. Riesman describes children "lying on the floor, reading and trading comics and preferences among comics."[58]

Indeed, EC comics were written so that fan-addicts could read them out loud to their friends.[59] Instead of losing themselves in the characters, comic book readers treated the narrative as a kind of competitive game. Constantly aware of the presence of others, comic book fans tried to best their peers by showing off their trivia knowledge or guessing the outcome of fantasy and crime stories before they flipped to the end.[60] This is why comic books tended to be filled with stereotyped figures: a deep attachment to any given character would only hinder the other-directed reader's rapid acquisition of media knowledge and predictive ability.

Whether or not we buy the full historical argument offered by Riesman, it offers us far better insight into EC fandom than the moralistic arguments leveled by mass culture critics. Many EC readers gained a knack for what George Evans called "the old picture-puzzle bit":

> [Feldstein] always presented the reader with a challenge: Can you outguess me? And they'd often develop the same story and have three different endings for it, saying to the reader, now, can you top me with another one.[61]

When Gaines defended his comic books in front of the US Senate, he testified that this idea was central to his test of whether a story was strong: if a child liked the story and could not guess the twist ending, he knew that it was good enough to publish.[62] As he told his questioners, he did not bother to ascertain any long-term moral effects on the reader.

We catch a glimpse of the fan-addict's puzzle-solving in "Concerto for Violin and Werewolf." The story follows a violinist visiting his former teacher in Brudja, a village in Transylvania. As the narrative unfolds, it becomes clear that the entire town is infested with werewolves. The violinist, however, comes prepared. Surrounded in the central square by slavering wolf-men, he reaches down into his violin case as he explains how he discovered the werewolf plague and planned for it in advance. While touring in America, he recounts, the violinist read a story about a "townful of vampires," a story called "Midnight Mess" in *Tales from the Crypt* that gave him the solution to his current predicament.[63] Analogizing from this example, he intuited that Brudja was a "townful of werewolves" and prepared by stowing a Thompson submachine gun full of silver bullets in his case.[64] Unfortunately, his former teacher has already gamed out this response, swapping out the werewolf hunter's weapon for a violin. The musician gambles and loses, eaten by shapeshifters.

EC narratives thus often resemble game-theoretical scenarios, each with their own moves and countermoves. Although the revenge plot provides the most common occasion for competitive strategy, Wallace Wood's science fiction stories in *Weird Science* and *Weird Fantasy* often take the form of dilemmas that force characters to act with deadly consequences based on imperfect information. "Deadlock!," a typical Wood offering, opens with space travelers making first contact with an alien vessel. Using universal translators, the two crews parlay with one another by radio. The comic flashes back and forth between crews as they debate what move to make next. Both sides follow the exact same step-by-step logic: although the two parties declare themselves peaceful, neither side can trust the other, and both are unwilling to set a course away for fear of being followed to their home worlds by hostile invaders, so, unfortunately, one of the ships must be destroyed. "It is too bad!" the alien tells his human counterpart.[65] Polite to the end, the spokespeople for both ships agree to describe themselves, and they each respond by remarking to their fellow crewmates, "They sound ghastly!"[66] Evenly matched in every way, the two ships destroy one another using self-guiding missiles.

Wood's speculative standoffs serve not only as parables of mutually assured destruction but also as allegories of what Peter Galison would call the "Enemy Other."[67] This sinister but rational figure emerged out of operations research, cybernetics, and game theory during World War II. Each of these research fields treated the enemy's intentions as a black box, focusing instead on their observable behavior. While developing anti-aircraft fire controls that could automatically predict the future trajectories of Nazi bombers, cybernetics scholar Norbert Wiener realized that what was going on in the cockpit interior did not matter: he could calculate the next maneuver of the enemy plane based entirely on the prior flight patterns of the aircraft. It made no difference whether it was the reflexes of the pilot or the mechanism of the bomber that determined a bomber's idiosyncratic path. The outcomes were the same. When viewed from the perspective of an anti-aircraft predictor, both human and machine collapsed together to form a single servomechanism. From his research on mechanized warfare, Wiener developed a "quasi-solipsistic" theory of communication and control that sought to predict human actions without any reference to the minds of others.[68] As he worked on military projects alongside Wiener, John von Neumann developed a theory of games that formally described the strategies of players whose intentions are unknowable and whose rationality makes them operationally equivalent to calculating machines.[69] Together, these sciences endeavored to produce a complete conceptual picture of agents that bracketed any question of psychological interiority.

Wood's bugeyed monsters slither out of the same national fantasy as the seemingly robotic Luftwaffe pilots. The inscrutable yet intelligent mutants and aliens in Wood's comics seem to be locked into strategies that require a constant escalation of bloodshed. Even when the human space-farers cannot know or, in the case of "Deadlock!," even see their opponents, they can still extrapolate what they are going to do next. This is also the attitude of the fan-addict who views the comic book as a game. Unable to empathize with the Enemy Other, the EC reader takes up the position of Wiener's anti-aircraft predictor to forecast the alien's projected course based solely on inputs about their past performance.

EC therefore joins what Marianna Torgovnick calls "the war complex."[70] Rather than directly confront the firebombing of Dresden or the nuclear devastation wrought in Hiroshima and Nagasaki, postwar American culture rewrote these traumas by projecting them into a potential future that might be thwarted only if the hero appears in the nick of time. Popular culture's obsession with doomsday scenarios reflected not only cold war fears but also a collective coping mechanism for reworking unbearable cultural memories by playing them out differently in alternative scenarios: "The pattern seems like a controlled experiment in simulated loss, a complicated, adult instance of the toddler's game Freud called *Fort/Da*."[71] Past atrocities could be made to seem manageable when they were displaced into futuristic science fiction scenarios that could be anticipated if not averted by a shrewd reader.

Beyond these contemporary influences, we can see structural affinities with older violent narratives—the novels of the Marquis de Sade. As Frances Ferguson argues, de Sade projects enclosed worlds in which characters are valued based on nothing more than their publicly observable actions.[72] Beliefs, emotions, histories, and ascriptive status disappear in Sadistic narratives, which rank characters by their sexual performances. Who you are does not matter so long as you can pull off the erotic gymnastics demanded by the sadistic masters. Using cybernetic language, Ferguson suggests that "pornography . . . accustomed us to evaluate actions in a relative way and to see them as the output of a system rather than of an individual intention or agent."[73] In this regard, de Sade anticipates the logic of utilitarian social systems such as classrooms that order students by their test scores.[74] Transgressive narratives would continue to capture the performance-based subjectivity of the meritocratic elite through the postwar period.

Readers not only competed with one another to win prestige; they also used the comic books to become better players. EC's brainteasers habituate readers to pattern recognition. Gaines often tells a story of an encounter with an archetypal fan-addict that illustrates this point: a boy walks into the EC offices, and, speaking in a halting and "simple" way, tells the editor, "All ya stories, dey gimme da same idea. You sharpen a pencil, a pencil sharpens ya head."[75] Gaines thought this was as apt as it was hilarious: "The EC way was he got it the same way he gave it. . . . You broil live lobsters; you end up getting broiled alive."[76] Although this is sometimes cast as a lesson in poetic justice, I would argue that what these stories really teach is a form of structural thinking. The fan-addict's lex talionis is a repeating formula that treats all particulars indifferently. This often-retold story defines the fan-addict as a reader who can reproduce the rules for constructing a good EC story. The terms that get plugged into this algorithm have no inherent value or importance, allowing EC readers to develop a purely functional perspective on what are often quite horrendous images.

This is the view taken in two of the most notorious stories ever published by EC—"Foul Play!," which appeared in *The Haunt of Fear* and "In Each and Every Package," which appeared in *Crime SuspenStories*. Both were excoriated during the 1954 Subcommittee on Juvenile Delinquency hearing where Wertham testified. Panels from "Foul Play!" appeared as bad examples in *Seduction of the Innocent*. Gaines regretted publishing "Foul Play!," and even the artist Jack Davis later expressed discomfort at having drawn such a thing.[77] Davis would later tell an interviewer, "I wanted to bury my head. I wished I never did it."[78] The story begins with what appears to be an ordinary game of night baseball before flashing back to the career of a dirty pitcher, who kills one of his opponents by kicking him with poisoned cleats. In classic EC fashion, the bereaved baseball players get their revenge by luring him back to the stadium on the eve of the new season to kill him. The final panels—which Wertham used as evidence against crime comics—return us to the night baseball scene. Each piece of equipment is revealed in turn to be another body part ripped from the murderous player. We are asked to look upon the "long strings of white pulpy intestines that mark the baselines" and to note the "heart that is home plate."[79] In the most infamous image, the pitcher holds the man's severed head, with one eye bulging out of its socket and the other eye drooling down his cheek. All in good fun!

"Foul Play!" comes so close to obscenity because it takes such ghoulish delight in resisting the kinds of affective and identificatory moves that characterize middlebrow readings. The story systematically destroys any hope of identifying with the characters on an emotional level beyond a kind of gleeful sadism. The baseball team is an anonymous mob, and even the felonious pitcher is almost as thinly characterized. All of these players function as what Evans would call "straw people," stock characters serving as a pretext for frights.[80] Like the dismembered ballplayer, the figures in these comics turn out to be play equipment. Cartoonist Gahan Wilson, reflecting on the influence EC had on his life, recalls the images in "Foul Play!" but not the details of the narrative: the dead player becomes a "hated coach or umpire or some other feared father figure."[81] Ultimately, "Foul Play!" reduces its cast of unlovable characters to interchangeable game tokens and empty player positions.

EC's ludic formalism is mirrored in the language of its narrators, the Ghoulunatics. Introducing and concluding each comic, the Crypt-Keeper (*Tales from the Crypt*), the Old Witch (*The Haunt of Fear*), and the Vault-Keeper (*The Vault of Horror*) speak in a show business cant peppered with awful puns on morbid themes. For example, in the Jack Davis–illustrated vampire cabdriver story "Fare Tonight, Followed by Increasing Clottyness," the Crypt-Keeper begins this "blood-curdling yarn" with the now-classic greeting: "Welcome, boils and ghouls."[82] Like the stories they narrate, the horror hosts place a series of ghastly yet arbitrary signifiers into a conventional syntax that effectively predetermines their meaning in spite of their loathsome resonances. These gamelike structures frame and contain the borderline obscene elements of the narrative. As Gaines pointed out, the Ghoulunatics' "black humor" serves to defuse built-up tension or fear from the stories.[83] EC comic books use the Ghoulunatics' ridiculously macabre patter to signal to readers that they are about to enter a game world, one distinct from our own and not to be taken too seriously.

Even EC's more realistic suspense stories engage in this play of equivalences. From clones to body-hopping witches, characters in EC comic books constantly switch positions with one another.[84] This is the basic premise of "In Each and Every Package." A man kills his wife and buries her chopped-up remains in a series of parcels in the backyard, scheming to have his mistress take her identity. Although this seems like the perfect crime—his lover perfects an imitation of the dead wife and even recreates the deceased's face through plastic surgery—their plan falls apart when they are chosen at random to be part of a game show called "Treasure Hunt."[85] At first they play like any other contestants—the host cannot even keep their names straight—but by the end things take a turn for the worst when the game show segues into an actual hunt for buried treasure—"Choke... gasp..."—in the contestants' backyard.[86] The game flips, winning turns to losing everything, and the unearthed corpse becomes the prize in each and every package. The reversible symmetry we see in "In Each and Every Package" acts as the central organizing principle in so many EC narratives. Murders and victims, winners and losers, all turn and swap places.

We can now begin to see why Gaines got into so much trouble when he was called to testify before the Senate on horror and suspense comics. Gaines testified on April 21, 1954, immediately after Wertham. Gaines began the hearings strongly. He had spent the entire night with Stuart perfecting his opening speech, taking Dexedrine and NoDoz to stay awake.[87] This left Gaines nervous and exhausted once he had finished his prepared remarks. He seemed especially rattled when Senator Estes Kefauver began to question him about the cover of *Crime SuspenStories* featuring an image from "In Each of Every Package" that depicted the protagonist wielding a blood-spattered ax and holding the dead-eyed head of his wife by the hair. Senator Kefauver asked Gaines, "Do you think that is in good taste?" To this, he replied,

> Yes, sir; I do, for the cover of a horror comic. A cover in bad taste, for example, might be defined as holding the head a little higher so that the neck could be seen dripping blood from it and moving the body over a little further so that the neck of the body could be seen to be bloody.[88]

Gaines's testimony precluded any identificatory reading of the image. Whereas the Senator referred to "her body," Gaines spoke of "the body," "the head," "the neck," severing the corpse from any possessive personhood.[89] The senators objected to the subject matter, while Gaines focused entirely on the manner of presentation.

Gaines's observations draw on the comic publisher's longstanding editorial policy. As Feldstein pointed out, EC had two "standards" for two different types of violence. One was "ordinary violence" (true-to-life murders) and the other was "the violence of fantasy"—"unrealistic schizophrenic violence" that would include crimes such as "dropping a guy into a pot of hot fat and making him into a French fry."[90] EC assigned scenes of fantasy violence to its most outré artists—Graham ("Ghastly") Ingels and Jack Davis—as if to make the carnage seem like "the punch line of a joke."[91] Ordinary violence, however, was assigned to more realist or illustrative artists such as Jack Kamen or George Evans. EC Comics often held back from directly depicting ordinary violence by blocking the killings from full view or banishing them to somewhere in the comic book gutter. By these criteria, then, the *Crime SuspenStories* cover was in perfectly good taste because it followed the formal principles for ordinary violence by obscuring the stump of the neck. The editor was concerned more with playing by the rules of his own game than with obeying the moral precepts the congressmen claimed to uphold.

Gaines's testimony turned out to be an absolute failure, in part because he failed to perform a sentimentalizing emotional response to the cover image of the slain woman. *Newsday* excoriated him as demonstrating "the detached manner of a surgeon after a hard day at the autopsy table."[92] Of course, it would be a mistake to suggest that EC comic books are totally flat and bereft of emotion. Although the entire format militates against attachment to characters—who are typically introduced and killed off in fewer than eight pages—it nevertheless offers more impersonal sensations and thrills. EC comic narratives follow the same dramatic structure as masculine heterosexual pornography. As Feldstein observes, the EC stories "build up" until they reach a "shock" or "sudden lapse of taste," a narrative tension and release that is "parallel to the orgasm ... all the foreplay up to the climax."[93] For fantasy violence stories, the final panel offers not only the satisfaction of an answer to the story's guessing game but also what appears to be a total breakdown of representational limits. As in "Foul Play!," anything held back or obscured in the rest of the story comes to light on the last page. The puzzle solutions at the end of EC tales take on the intensity of the money shot, another visual device that promises perfect visibility and absolute, uncensored truth.[94]

At the same time, the twist ending functions as a shock to the reader. One could argue, following Walter Benjamin, that shock serves to break through the psychic defenses of the blasé reader, who has become so adapted to repeated scenes of violence that he does not experience them at all.[95] Even those most horrific of images quickly become just another trope in EC comic books—here is *another* story about the pain of having one's veins filled with embalming fluid. The shock, then, wakes readers from their unthinking and habitual responses by introducing an unexpected discontinuity into otherwise predictable stories.

More fundamentally, though, the shock endings offer feedback to fan-addicts. The formulaic nature of pulp fiction and the repetitiveness of the periodical allow fans to return to the same kinds of narratives again and again, helping them to develop a better predictive model of the comic book over time by adjusting their reading expectations based on past issues.[96] The shock allows readers to become like one of Wiener's targeting mechanisms. Here my point is not that EC's editors or readers were directly influenced by cybernetics. Instead, I want to suggest that cybernetics discourse simply offers one of the most clearly formulated examples of a broader turn toward a way of being and knowing characterized by an improvisational relationship toward an open future. As Orit Halpern argues, cybernetics reconstituted perception as "the ability to respond": instead of describing objects, the new cybernetic vision scanned the world for abstract outlines that provided cues for future actions while filtering out all irrelevant information.[97] Other cultural documents, such as the avant-garde productions of the Bauhaus school, capture this epistemological and aesthetic shift by designing new pedagogical practices and interactive environments.[98] EC Comics, however, formally represents this new ethos by dramatizing the process of pattern sensing under conditions of risk and uncertainty.

EC's most memorable shock appears at the end of "Judgment Day!," a science fiction story about an astronaut from Earth who disqualifies a planet from entry into a galactic federation because its inhabitants still maintain racial segregation and domination. In the final panel, the space-traveling protagonist lifts off his helmet to reveal that he is a Black man: "Beads of perspiration twinkle on his dark skin like distant stars."[99] As in many EC stories, Blackness appears as an eruption into a presumed-white universe.[100] This story was nearly censored by the Comics Magazine Association's Comics Code Authority. The Code Authority objected to a Black man appearing in the story, and, when it met resistance, it compromised by asking the publisher to remove the sweat from his face. Gaines responded to these complaints with a firm "Fuck you!"[101]

More often, though, EC science fiction terminates in an atomic apocalypse. The bomb drops, or the entire planet explodes as a punch line. EC's adaptation of Ray Bradbury's "There Will Come Soft Rains" encapsulates the dread expressed by these stories. The story takes place in an automated smart home still standing amid irradiated rubble. Although nothing is left of its inhabitants except a flash-burned shadow on the side of the house, the smart home continues to follow its predetermined schedule—cooking, cleaning, drawing baths, and setting out card tables. The only living creature we encounter is a dog, which starves to death in front of a locked kitchen door as the house robots on the other side prepare and then discard food at every mealtime. Cheerfully announcing daily activities for the long dead—"Off to school! Off to work!"—the smart home evokes the blithe automaticity of cold war consumers who prepared for every creature comfort but were blindsided by nuclear war.[102] By the end of the story, this holocaust is replayed again in miniature when a storm knocks a tree through the window, shattering the self-contained, self-perpetuating world of the smart home. A branch strikes a container of cleaning solvent, which explodes, engulfing the house in flames. The house screams to no avail, and even the automated sprinklers and firefighting drones fail to smother the blaze, which razes the building to the ground. In the end, all that remains is a single scorched wall, whose built-in speaker intones the date forever.

The Strangelovian climaxes at the close of so many EC entries represent more than just warnings of nuclear peril. Procensorship critic Gershon Legman claimed that comic books enrolled readers in a "Universal Military Training of the Mind," and, although he clearly exaggerates the danger and efficacy of comic books, it is nevertheless true that EC helped many fan-addicts face their fears with greater calm and assuredness.[103] In many ways, these narratives play out in the same way as the war games staged by the defense community throughout the 1950s and 1960s. According to nuclear specialists such as Herman Kahn, strategic foresight depends on an imaginative and spontaneous attitude equipped to deal with seemingly improbable or impossible scenarios. As Kahn put it, "To be fully aware of the shape of reality it is necessary to glance beyond its boundaries on all sides."[104] One way military strategists developed this facility was through roleplaying games and military simulations that provided a feel for encounters with radical uncertainty.[105] EC comic books operate in a similar fashion, whether they are surprising readers with the resurrection of the vengeful dead or the extinction of the human race. From "In Each and Every Package" to "Concerto for Violin and Werewolf," EC stories feature meticulous plans that go awry because of some freak accident. In short, EC comics use the unspeakable to drill readers in the unforeseeable.

Desensitization Is Fun

Paradoxically, fan-addicts emerge from these narratives of abjection with an even greater sense of self-mastery. Like hot sauce and heavy metal, extreme horror constitutes an endurance aesthetic in which the spectator finds pleasure in transforming agonizing or difficult experiences into technical expertise. In our own moment, spicy-food fanatics obsess over climbing up the Scoville scale, and metalheads train themselves to find the beauty in brutal blast beats. Horror movie maniacs graduate from marathoning creature features to scouring *Famous Monsters of Filmland* or *Fangoria* for details about fake-blood squibs and latex prosthetics. Even BDSM practitioners are wont to brag about their leatherworking skills or home-construction projects in their dungeon play spaces. There is an intense pleasure to be found in pushing the limits of one's tolerance for the once unbearable as an object of disinterested contemplation or skillful manipulation. What middlebrow censors so often miss is that desensitization is fun.

One way that fan-addicts learn to surmount the feelings of horror or revulsion elicited by these images is by figuring out how they work and how they are made. As Robert Warshow notes in "Paul, the Horror Comics, and Dr. Wertham" (1954), this was the strategy his son took:

> I think that [my son] Paul's desire to put himself directly in touch with the processes by which the comic books are produced may be the expression of a fundamental detachment which helps to protect him from them; the comic books are not a "universe" to him, but simply objects produced for his entertainment.[106]

Fan-addicts therefore immerse themselves in the inside baseball of comic book publishing, or they learn how to make comics themselves.

As Jared Gardner argues, comics helped foster participatory culture because they constantly reminded readers of their status as "*made* things," foregrounding the labor involved in their own creation while inviting the reader to join in.[107] Cartoonists who loved EC growing up often describe their responses as shock followed by obsession and then finally mastery once they have learned how to draw pictures like the comics themselves. Cartoonist Paul Mavrides recalls this process: "I read them. I studied them. I copied them. I memorized them. I integrated them into my psyche. I fused them with my atomic structure."[108] By learning to cartoon, they transformed the originals from incomprehensible horrors into 2D images they could fully grasp. Even fan-addicts who could not draw showed off their ability to reproduce the EC form. Fan letters to the magazine frequently lapse into Ghoulunatic puns or spin out horror fantasies to scare and amuse the editorial staff. Meanwhile, EC inspired a prolific community of fanzine creators, who demonstrated their connoisseurship and erudition in the pages of titles such as *Squa Tront*.

The fan-addict thus escapes obscenity by translating shocking affects into cognitive know-how, moving from helpless terror to competent understanding. This is what Wertham misses in his crude exemplary model. Wertham believed that EC turned fan-addicts into criminals by showing them violent scenes. In reality, EC offered an exercise regimen that used media violence as a tool for seeing the world as a series of artificially constructed codes. EC's horror comics thus help develop the kinds of interpretive competencies demanded by its later *Mad* magazine issues. Many fan-addicts raised on earlier EC comics would later prove ready to keep up with the magazine's rapid relay of allusions, all nested within multiple representational frames and several levels of irony.[109] EC's science fiction stories anticipate the *Mad* reader's savvy by offering countless examples of characters resisting or failing to resist mass media conspiracies from another planet. By breaking readers of their sentimental attachments and sympathetic identifications, EC cleared the way for fan-addicts to become not only shrewd comic consumers and underground comic artists but also junior semioticians.

At the same time, however, EC's interpretive methods are a far cry from the hermeneutics of suspicion. Outside of the preachies—EC's didactic stories, usually found in the suspense lines—EC editors resisted any imputation of a deeper meaning to their work. During his testimony, Gaines rejects the idea that EC comic books contain any message that is not "spelled out carefully in the captions."¹¹⁰ EC stories tend to mock anyone who imagines they can see hidden meaning beyond surface appearances. In Feldstein's "The Flying Saucer Invasion," readers follow reporters and radio personalities as they work to make sense of a rash of UFO sightings. Along the way, they ask a crazy-eyed Wertham caricature what it all means: "The flying saucer is mass hysteria brought about by post-war insecurity and economic anxiety! It is obviously a pathological illusion aggravated by continuous publicity given it by press, radio, and *comic books*."¹¹¹ The secretary of defense more or less agrees, calling all the witnesses into his office and convincing each one of them that they hallucinated the spacecraft. However, on the same day the newspapers dismiss the UFO scare as "psychological," an observatory catches sight of a stream of saucers, which in the punch line panel we see hurtling toward planet Earth.¹¹² Time and again, EC comic books insist that, although the world may be unpredictable, it is not indeterminate or unknowable. Demystification only distracts the reader from strategic pattern recognition.

In fact, EC comics rule out the spectral entirely. Nothing haunts the EC comic book—there is no phantom nonpresence or uncanny history lingering behind its images. Like most editors resistant to overarching theories of their careers, Feldstein scoffed at the idea that EC comics could be psychoanalyzed, but he does seem to be onto something.¹¹³ In an advertisement for submissions in *Writer's Digest*, EC informed prospective writers that it adored "walking corpse stories," but it refused to entertain "ghosts, devils, goblins or the like."¹¹⁴ EC relied on the supernatural to move its stories along now and then, but virtually all of its monsters, magical or mundane, appeared as flesh-and-blood creatures. In these self-contained game worlds, there is no hint of a hidden dimension behind the figures on the page.

Would-be censors were offered this lesson when they attempted to read ulterior motives into EC comic books. Gaines and Stuart responded with a parody editorial advertisement titled, "Are You a Red Dupe?" It begins with a comic strip depicting a Soviet censor hanging a Russified version of the editorial mascot Melvin (Melvin Blizunken-Skovitchsky) and warming his hands on a bonfire fueled with issues of *Panisky Comicskys*, a Slavic stand-in for EC's *Panic* comic magazine. According to the caption, "The group most anxious to destroy comics are the communists!"¹¹⁵ The overheated editorial then presents a snippet of anti–comic book criticism from the *Daily Worker* while insinuating that the

Communist Party USA somehow has connections to Legman and Wertham. This comic parody of McCarthyism cautions readers to be suspicious of anyone they meet who publicly opposes comic books: "We're not saying he *is* a Communist! He may be innocent of the whole thing! He may not even read the 'Daily Worker'! It's just that he swallowed the red bait . . . hook, line, and sinker!"[116] Gaines admits that the editorial was "pretty dopey": "I made up the ad out of devilishness. It was supposed to be a spoof, but it didn't come off that way."[117] The editorial succeeded only in irking the congressmen in charge of the juvenile delinquency hearings.[118]

Through "Are You a Red Dupe?" EC displays its contempt for paranoid reading. The seed idea for the advertisement came from Paul Kast, an EC staff member. According to Gaines, Kast watched a fascist soapbox speaker come undone when someone in the crowd called him a communist.[119] All of the interpretive frenzy of anti-communist hysteria is turned back on itself with a flippant and sophistical retort. Censorship advocates, who dug deep to unearth fascist subtexts buried inside horror and crime comics, turn out to be in the thrall of an even more occult totalitarianism. Here as elsewhere depth readings in EC appear to be deceptive or delusional.

Organization Wolfman

The abstractive abilities fostered by EC would serve its reader well in bureaucracies that treated employees as so many slots in an organization chart. As the president of IBM Tom Watson warned in a widely quoted 1957 commencement speech, the "organization man" has become "as depersonalized as a jellyfish wrapped in cellophane."[120] Although EC does not teach its readers to peer behind the veil of ideology, it does provide a no-tears guide to the kind of quick-wittedness that will hold them in good stead in their future careers as managers and professionals.

In a 1962 sociological survey of *Mad*'s teenage readers, Charles Winnick found that the magazine allowed teenagers to learn about the adult world of "business customs" while laughing at it at the same time.[121] As Winnick puts it,

> The teenager may feel that he is learning to emulate "gamesmanship" while laughing at it. He can be an inside "dopester" while chivying inside dopesters. It would be analogous [sic] to, for example, a reader of Ovid's *Art of Love* or Castiglione's *Book of the Courtier* studying them for the apparent purpose of

ridiculing love-making and the courtier's life, respectively, but actually sopping up much "how to" information on these subjects.[122]

This attitude, I would argue, runs throughout EC's history. Even in the days of horror and crime comics, EC presented itself to readers first and foremost as a business enterprise. EC's in-house fanzine, the *National EC Fan-Addict Club Bulletin*, immersed readers in the office life of the publisher, spreading jokey gossip about the artists, editors, and staff. Perhaps inspired by these bulletins, many fan-addicts actually made pilgrimages to the EC office building. Sometimes the editorial crew performed gags for adoring visitors—on one drop-in everyone at EC put on a show of executing an elaborate ritual of obeisance before William Gaines—but even on more uneventful visits there was an element of pretend.[123]

Warshow's account of his son's EC fandom describes his semi-ironic "exaltation" upon meeting Johnny Craig and Gaines: "I am sure the children's enthusiasm contained some element of self-parody, or at any rate an effort to live up to the situation—after all, a child is often very uncertain about what is exciting, and how much."[124] Here, the children were acting more adult than Warshow thought. As contemporary social critics often pointed out, the new middle-class subject was defined by their ability to maintain appearances while also treating them as an artificial performance.

EC even offered actual experience in the rat race. In one issue of the *Fan-Addict Club Bulletin*, the reader is even asked to volunteer to become a "roadman" for EC: "How would you like to have a hand in increasing our sales, and insuring our continued success?"[125] Dedicated fan-addicts can help the press, we are told, by moving EC comics to the front of the newsstand display whenever they see them hidden from view and by asking newsdealers to carry EC comics if they do not already. Nevertheless, even as it hails readers as junior sales representatives, the editorial voice maintains its mock-ghoulish tone, admonishing any overeager roadmen: "BUT PLEASE, YOU MONSTERS, DO IT POLITELY."[126] The same half-kidding salesmanship runs throughout EC's paratexts, which cast its publications and its editorial staff as exceptionally bad. When the EC Fan-Addict Club is first introduced, the Vault-Keeper describes it as a scam run by the "mercenary idiot editors": the organization is just "their latest insidious money-grabbing scheme to 'con' a few more coins from your . . . or your old man's . . . grimy little piggy bank."[127] By anticipating censorious responses and satirizing them in advance, EC hopes to counteract its critics.

For example, when Gaines presents himself in a capsule biography in *Mad*, he responds to recent censorship controversies by describing himself as the illiterate son of an "international communist banker" and claiming that he amassed his capital for "Evil Comics" by selling drugs, running a brothel, and distributing pornographic Tijuana Bibles.[128] The "Publisher of the Issue" feature then quotes his editorial mantra:

> I don' care if it don't gotta plot! I don' care if it don't got grammar. I don' care if the pitchers ain't from talent! All I care is get inta every story *sadism, snakes, masochism, pyromania, snakes, fetishes, snakes, necrophilia, phallic symbols, snakes,* and all the rest of that *esoterica* what I can't think of this minute.[129]

The accompanying illustration is of Gaines topped with a halo and wearing a beatific smile. By inverting the normal rules of self-presentation in business life, EC not only avoids sounding corny but also trains its readers to see the rules governing white-collar work as flexible and ungrounded in any value beyond themselves.

In so doing, EC inducts readers into what Mark Seltzer calls "the official world."[130] Drawing on Niklas Luhmann, Seltzer describes the characteristic institution of the postwar period—the bureaucratic office—as a "gamelike" structure that generates itself by reporting on its own actions.[131] Viewed from the bureaucracy's perspective, anything that is not registered in internal memos or measured by proprietary metrics does not exist. This self-referentiality, according to Seltzer, lends the official world the same self-standing quality as late modernist art, suspense novels, and parlor games, and, like these genres, the official world trains those who participate in it to respond in its own terms.[132]

The official world is an operationally closed system. As EC grew increasingly successful with *Mad*, Gaines strove to transform his office into an air-conditioned microcosm. Even while he presented work life as a long-running put-on, Gaines ran a perfectly neat and organized office that was only occasionally disordered by practical jokes. In this cartoonists' terrarium, Gaines appointed himself as patriarch and his employees as family.[133] As such, Gaines refused to justify his business decisions by any logic beyond his own eccentricity. When EC came under the control of conglomerate Warner Communications, Gaines reasserted his prerogative by having a highly unusual clause inserted into every contract: "The proprietor's (Gaines's) right to withhold consent shall be absolute and shall not be subject to any criterion of reasonableness."[134] Even after the merger between *Time* and Warner Communications, Gaines kept his rebellious streak as editor of *Mad*: "My technique is to be such a maniac that [my parent corporation is] afraid to deal with me.... We publish for ourselves. Fortunately, what we like the readers like."[135] Gaines's editorial control allowed him to remain unmoored from external norms or standards. Wholly autonomous, the official world's primary business is representing itself to itself.[136]

EC sells so many comics in part because of its constant reflexive discourse on EC comics. EC comic books present their own editorial process in a winking fashion, transforming the publisher's self-advertisement into entertainment and its crass cynicism into arch knowingness. We find one of EC's many self-models in "Kamen's Kalamity." The story takes place in the EC offices, where Feldstein and Gaines have recently hired Jack Kamen to work on their romance comics. Unfortunately, the market for love collapses, and the editors are forced to shift their attentions to the more profitable horror comics. Kamen, however, is slower on the uptake than fellow cartoonists, Ingels, Craig, and Davis, who respond to the new trend by torturing voodoo dolls modeled on their boss Gaines. Thwarted from getting ahead, Kamen shouts, "Okay! Okay! I'm gonna be horrible! You'll see! YOU'LL SEE!"[137] Kamen storms back to his suburban home, where he harangues his wife for keeping the house so pleasant. Secluding himself in the studio, Kamen roughs his hair up and chews on a soap bar to get into the spirit, but, as he starts working, he begins to transform into an actual raging werewolf. As he closes in on his wife and children, who shriek with terror at the growling cartoonist, Kamen wakes up to hear the sound of his wife screaming at a mouse. Although it was all a dream, Kamen has remade his personality to better fit the new line of horror comics.

Just as in the suburban antipastorals that the comic travesties, the business firm subordinates the intimate sphere while colonizing the unconscious. This fantasy proved so powerful that the very first fan fiction about EC—written as a radio play by fanzine writer Larry Stark—turned out to be a Mary Sue office romance in which the author-protagonist wins the heart of an EC secretary before, of course, turning into a lycanthrope.[138] Once the comic book publisher's aesthetic imperatives swallow up the cartoonists' and fan-addict's dreams, nothing seems to exist outside of the EC office. Whereas middlebrow reading practices lead professional-managerial workers into a warmer world beyond the instrumental rationality of white-collar labor, EC allows readers to make a game of managerial monstrosity.

To this end, EC's foul play serves as an emotional buffer that allows readers to cope with the inane miseries of midcentury work life. As Winnick observes, EC allows its readers "an opportunity to 'go away a little closer' to some important American institutions."[139] Building on Erving Goffman, Seltzer declares this recessive stance to be the characteristic attitude of the official world.[140] As we increasingly spend our everyday lives in simulated realities, it becomes easier to tell ourselves that it is all just a game and everyone we meet is just a player, separated from us by a board and counters. Fan-addicts start to look like the asylum inmates Goffman describes in *Behavior in Public Places*. In this study, Goffman details the techniques for civil inattention required to maintain composure in the distressing spaces of Central Hospital, where another patient might be masturbating or ranting just a few feet away. To negotiate these moments of unbearable proximity, the patients would retreat into what he calls "inward emigration" or "awayness," a retreat into a "playlike world in which [the subject] alone participates."[141] During this state, interpersonal relationships are momentarily suspended. Although this usually takes place during harmless pastimes such as drawing in the dust or cutting paper shapes, the state of awayness sometimes causes patients to forget themselves entirely: "An angry elderly male patient would cough up phlegm and then play with it abstractedly on the table before eventually wiping it off."[142]

If they had been captured in comic book form, Goffman's observations on the asylum might easily have been illustrated by someone like Ingels, the reclusive artist who was entrusted with what Gaines called EC's "ooky monsters, slobbering blobs of protoplasm, and messed up old people."[143] Often, Ingels's artwork looked as if he had traced little caricatures in human waste, as if these figures were rendered in dripping saliva and suppurating meat. EC's repellant doodlings, its constant gloating in nastiness: all of this works to keep others at bay. The fan-addict's involvement in the obscene allows him to drop out of the world while still participating in it.

In this regard, the fan-addict's most prominent successor is Patrick Bateman, the affluent yuppie in Bret Easton Ellis's *American Psycho*, who maintains all the outward social graces even as he recedes into real or imagined scenes of serial killing. Following a linguistic strategy that would have made the Crypt-Keeper proud, he evades notice by using the syntax of banal business exchanges to confess his bloody crimes: he tells one date that he is into "murders and executions, mostly," and she assumes that he means "mergers and acquisitions."[144] Ellis would later admit that he wrote the controversial novel as an homage to EC comics such as *The Vault of Horror* and *Tales from the Crypt*.[145]

Even as EC offers a glimpse into office life, it affords readers all the pleasures of teenage alienation. The bonds of love dissolve quickly in EC comics. As one fan-addict put it, "Husbands killed wives; wives killed husbands; both killed and were killed by each others' lovers. Parents killed children, and children killed parents, nannies, kindly old neighbors, and each other. Brothers killed sisters, and sisters killed brothers."[146] EC horror and crime comics tend to start off claustrophobic and then collapse inward until all characters are dead save a single one, who, more often than not, ends up trapped in a coffin. In at least one story, even the first-person narrator turns out to be a corpse, his story taken down verbatim and repeated by one of the hosts. EC's many crypts and vaults symbolize not only the horror of the grave but also a desire to withdraw from others and take up the wickedly antisocial attitude of the Ghoulunatics.

This is a moment of real negativity. At a deeply conservative historical moment of compulsory domestic togetherness, fan-addicts seemed to reject the bourgeois heterosexual family and flee from the sentimentalism of middlebrow culture. Although there may be nothing really revolutionary about EC comics, they nevertheless express an intense disgust with cold war America that manifests itself paradoxically in the ferocious longing to remain lonely even in the crowd.

And yet this negative desire is in turn pressed back into the service of the official world. This is the loathing on which possessive individualism thrives. The same impulse that pushed fan-addicts to fantasize about being buried alive or stranded on deserted spaceships led to the hermetic idiolects of comix culture and the masturbatory microworlds of cartoonists like R. Crumb, but it also manifested as the architecture of suburban atomization.[147] The game-playing attitude and the pattern-seeking perspective would be employed by hippie gurus and hawkish technocrats alike. Here is another thing that the censors missed: literary transgression develops open-ended capacities rather than automatic responses, which means that what is so dangerous and exciting about obscenity is that it helps implant in readers abilities and dispositions that can manifest in wildly contradictory ways.

Fans played games with horror, learning to take a superficial attitude toward their deepest fears. When they got older, however, they used this approach as a coping mechanism for the everyday drama of office life and even, we shall see, the travails of love and sex. At this point, as Gaines observed, many of *Mad*'s readers graduated to a very different kind of game, one created by *Playboy* founder Hugh Hefner.[148]

Reading *Playboy* for the Science Fiction

"**I ONLY READ *PLAYBOY* FOR THE ARTICLES**" often appears as the punch line to a joke—an excuse too farfetched to be taken seriously. Nevertheless, this alibi is not as implausible as it sounds. During its heyday, *Playboy* served as a significant cultural, political, and literary venue, featuring interviews with public figures from Ayn Rand to Fidel Castro while publishing authors as divergent as Vladimir Nabokov and Jack Kerouac. Most readers and critics forget, however, that in the 1950s and 1960s *Playboy* was also the most visible mainstream publisher of science fiction short stories. For many years, *Playboy* printed a science fiction story in nearly every issue and produced a number of speculative fiction–themed anthologies. Futuristic narratives of progress proved to be integral to the overall *Playboy* sensibility, an attitude exemplified by editor and publisher Hugh Hefner. Hefner's lifestyle, heavily covered by the magazine, promised an end to both sexual repression and onerous labor in a controlled environment filled with state-of-the-art gadgets. This vision of another world so impressed Norman Mailer that he went so far as to describe Hefner's Playboy mansion as "a spaceship wandering down the galaxy along a night whose duration was a year."[1] If Hefner and his Playmates were like astronauts, the magazine appeared as a message from the future. Espousing an ideology of youthful optimism, *Playboy* positioned itself at the forefront of social and technological change.

One of *Playboy*'s earliest science fiction offerings was a serialization of *Fahrenheit 451* by Ray Bradbury. Within the context of *Playboy*, *Fahrenheit 451* becomes a reflection on the magazine's publishing strategies. While many read Bradbury's narrative as a warning against state censorship, one of the principal book-burners, fire captain Beatty, explains that it was "technology, mass exploitation, and minority pressure" that led to the immolations in the novel.[2] Laying out the novel's reactionary premise, he explains that, as the market for books and other media expanded, it ran into an increasing diversity of "minor minor minorities," who, regardless of authorial intentions, took offense: "Colored people don't like *Little Black Sambo*. Burn it. White people don't feel good about *Uncle Tom's Cabin*. Burn it."[3] Unable to write for a particular public outside of the indistinguishable mass, authors in the novel's world are left to the mercy of their unintended readers, who, in the end, decide to destroy all books.

This audience trouble parallels *Playboy*'s own problem with censors, an obstacle the magazine framed as an attempt by a "minority" to impose its views and attitudes on others.[4] While courts never convicted Hefner or his publishing company, *Playboy* was forced to fight a legal battle with the United States Post Office Department to obtain second-class mailing privileges in 1955 and, in 1963, faced prosecution in Chicago for printing a nude pictorial of Jayne Mansfield.[5] The nature and exclusivity of *Playboy*'s audience are important here because determining obscenity was a question of reception. Since at least the Comstock era, censors in the US presented obscenity law as a way of shielding women, children, the working class, and people of color from the baneful influence of pornography, portraying these groups to be particularly vulnerable or susceptible to obscene suggestions.[6] As a result, publications that appealed to white, wealthy, educated heterosexual men—the kind of readers *Playboy* claimed as its audience—were much more likely to escape obscenity prosecutions. By defining its target demographic in this way, the magazine claimed to avoid the crossed signals alluded to in *Fahrenheit 451*. Carefully policing its readership, *Playboy* transformed risqué pictures into another sign of its distinction, signifying the iconoclastic tastes of a young professional-managerial cohort.

However, publication proves to be the last moment a publisher has full power over a document.[7] Manuscripts can be kept in lockboxes, and letters have clearly marked addresses, but books, periodicals, and other publications are dispersed into the world with no way of knowing what their final destinations will be.[8] Walter Kendrick argues that publishing is inextricably linked to problem of obscenity. Describing published works as "promiscuously available," he maintains that "any book or picture will give itself equally to all comers," regardless of what the author or editor intends.[9] No matter how carefully Hefner and his staff tried to program its readership and its responses, uninvited readers acquired *Playboy*s and did what they wanted with them. For example, memoirist Joe Westmoreland recalls flipping straight to *Playboy*'s Sex in Cinema section in seventh grade to look at stills of nude men, turning the magazine into makeshift homosexual pornography.[10] The moment that *Playboy* magazine was released into the hands of unknown readers, it risked obscene reappropriations.

Media producers in the world of *Fahrenheit 451* deal with unpredictable audience reactions by appealing to the lowest common denominator without challenging, upsetting, or excluding anyone. Bradbury and Hefner, however, offer another solution. After the novel's protagonist flees the book-burning firemen, he escapes into the countryside where he finds the "odd minority" of exclusively male readers who live as transients outside of society.[11] These renegades have dispensed with media entirely—instead of reading books, they memorize them and now go by their titles: "I am Plato's *Republic*."[12] Despite its beginnings as a short story in *Galaxy Science Fiction* and its end as a Ballantine paperback, *Fahrenheit 451* is, as Evan Brier suggests, "a version of mass culture used to respond to the threat of mass culture."[13] Whereas the media landscape described in the rest of the book produces a culture populated by violent thugs, hypnotized spectators, and juvenile delinquents, the community of scholars depicted in this bestseller represents a logocentric, pastoral force akin to the one in the *Phaedrus*.[14] In this utopian realm, all of the undependable intermediaries between texts and their readers disappear, while the audience is narrowed down to a select and discriminating few. Here, reading becomes safe again. Surprisingly, *Playboy* frames its reception in much the same way. Even though *Playboy* reached a mass public, the magazine claimed to be Hefner's private form of self-expression, a notion expressed in the tautology, "Hugh Hefner is *Playboy*, and *Playboy* is Hugh Hefner."[15] Fighting against the anarchy of publication, Hefner reduces his audience to the one person he might claim to have complete, private control over—himself.

How did *Playboy* come to be viewed as the brainchild of just one editor? In other words, how do we account for the Hefnerization of *Playboy*? To answer this question, this chapter will examine the first twenty years of *Playboy* (1953–1973), the magazine's most influential period. During this time, Hefner served not only as the magazine's editor but also as its spokesperson, its animating spirit, and even its ideal reader, setting the tone for the publication. When Hefner fills the editorial position, the heterogeneous network of readers, employees, institutions, and media technologies that make up the publishing process seem to become passive and obedient intermediaries for the decisive vision of a single individual. We can think of this fictive identity as the editor function. In order to pry open some of the contradictions in this subject position, I will explore science fiction, a component of the magazine that has been edited out of critical discussion by the governing *Playboy* narrative.

Playboy's editorial policies worked to solidify the magazine's identity, suggesting that Hefner, the publication, and his readership were all one and the same. This account of *Playboy*'s readers proved vital to winning over reluctant advertisers and avoiding censorship. Using the figure of Hefner as a normative model of its audiences' reading practices and emotional sensibilities, the magazine was able to skirt charges that it appealed to prurient interest. Like Hefner, readers were described as cool—capable of examining and thereby restraining their own bodily and emotional impulses. Within this fantasy, *Playboy*'s seduction narratives become training regimens for masculine self-discipline: by providing responsive feedback to men's courtship strategies, women enable them to reflect on themselves for the purposes of self-improvement. Science fiction facilitates this pedagogical process by empowering *Playboy* readers to distance, confront, and overcome potentially disturbing emotions and frightening thoughts. Science fiction estrangement allows *Playboy* readers to imagine their private lives as technical or administrative problems, projecting a future in which sexuality is another form of human capital to be cultivated and controlled. Here, the figure of Hefner provides the perfect example of an entrepreneur whose intimate life has become a business venture. As Hefner suggested, "*Playboy* exists, in part, as a motivation for men to expend greater effort in their work, develop their capabilities further and climb higher on the ladder of success."[16] At the same time, however, the editor's dream of fusing with his media empire threatens to become a nightmare in which he risks being overcome and absorbed by the network he has created. As Hefner put it, "I found that I had built this marvelous machine, but far from being master of that machine, the machine was ruling me."[17]

Instead of intervening at the level of representation or ideology, then, I begin my analysis with the politics of publishing. The primary question is not "How does *Playboy* depict gender and sexuality?" Instead, I will consider "Who is included as a recognized reader?," "What counts as sanctioned reader practice?," and, most importantly, "Who is authorized to decide?" Moving away from the ethics of cultural consumption and toward the structural logic of bibliographic production grounds this discussion in the material infrastructure of publication while avoiding the more popular approach to *Playboy*, the liberal humanist problematic of sexual objectification. Regardless of whether readers feel that a nude Playmate is an end in herself, she always appears in the *Playboy* network as a mediator for the editor, processing his messages without reading them. In this respect, *Playboy* differs from most other contemporary periodical and book publishers only in the fact that it makes an erotic spectacle out of the male-dominated conditions of media ownership and control. The magazine's explicitness makes it a telling case study in the gendered and sexual dimensions of editorship.

The Fully Automated Love Life of Hugh Hefner

Many editors claim to be fans of their own published material and pride themselves in their ability to anticipate their readers' desires. For example, Anna Gough-Yates's study of British women's magazines in the 1980s and 1990s finds that editors frequently boasted about their intuitive understanding of their magazine's readership, an understanding derived from membership in a shared culture. They made statements like "All of us on the staff . . . are [the] target audience" and "I *am Marie Claire*."[18] At *Playboy*, editor A. C. Spectorsky expressed a similar sentiment when he described Hefner as "schizophrenic," capable of moving among the mindsets of publisher, editor, and reader.[19] What makes Hefner extraordinary, though, is his insistence that he is the sole, intended reader, a narrative that runs throughout *Playboy*. Asserting that he edited for himself, Hefner directed the magazine at the man he aspired to be.[20] A prolific diarist, scrapbooker, and archivist, Hefner conceived of *Playboy* not so much as a public, money-making enterprise as a document of private self-expression.

This fiction proved to be very useful when the magazine marketed itself to advertisers. While high circulation was certainly important to the advertising industry, what they really wanted was a "carefully-screened, homogeneous group of buyers."[21] For many magazines, it was not enough to produce saleable content to make a profit—they also needed to constitute, maintain, and document a target audience with marketable demographics and consumer habits.[22] Following this logic, *Playboy* signaled its intense focus on a particular market segment from the very first issue, asking any female readers to "please pass us along to the man in your life and get back to your *Ladies Home Companion*."[23] Actively excluding women from the magazine's purchasers, *Playboy* made clear that its intended audience was generally affluent and uniformly male, a claim it reinforced with published survey data and in-house advertisements. The *Playboy* persona serves as an exemplar of a rising class of managers and professionals that Hefner liked to call the "Upbeat Generation." Although *Playboy* presented this group as nonconformist, pleasure seeking, and intellectual, they were also described as competitive, individualistic, entrepreneurial, and deeply invested in capitalism.[24] In other words, they were just like Hefner.

As Hefner becomes both sender and receiver of its message, the magazine moves from an intimate public to an internal monologue. However, book historians such as Adrian Johns, D. F. McKenzie, and Robert Darnton remind us that publishing is above all a social process.[25] Darnton's communication circuit model illustrates how print commodities become involved with a wide-ranging cast of printers, suppliers, shippers, booksellers, and other functionaries from the moment the author submits the manuscript to the moment the reader acquires the finished product.[26] For *Playboy*, though, this circuit becomes a self-referential loop, cutting out all of the unpredictable social actors beyond the publisher and collapsing the organization of the publishing company into a single figure. In addition to defining its target audience (Hefner and those like him), this strategy allows *Playboy* to neutralize the contributions of models and secretarial staff while establishing an authorized editorial tone precluding obscene or prurient interest. These simplifications help the magazine to downplay or hide the crises of meaning, use value, and capital that always attend publishing. This is important because it helps Hefner dispel accusations of obscenity. The editor has total control over the magazine because he is inseparable from it, calling himself the "living personification of the magazine."[27] This is the same future predicted in Arthur C. Clarke's futurological article, "Machina Ex Deux [sic]," which predicts that cyborg unions will allow users not merely "to control but to *become* a spaceship or a submarine or a TV network."[28] For Hefner, though, this future has already arrived.

Rather than communicating with readers, then, Hefner offers himself up as their example. Whereas other pinup magazines presented readers with nudes in a vacuum, the *Playboy* Playmates and other features of the magazine signified the achievement of an exalted lifestyle. Readers did not simply want the girl next door—they wanted to become Hefner, the kind of man who could acquire the girl next door. Through the editor's cool character, *Playboy* instructed readers on how they should receive the magazine's contents, foreclosing on the possibility of hotter and therefore more obscene responses. While the magazine does not always use the term directly, *Playboy*'s favorite characters make up a who's who of coolness in the 1950s and 1960s: Miles Davis and a host of other jazz musicians, James Bond, Lenny Bruce, Frank Sinatra, and Hefner himself.[29]

Coolness is notoriously difficult to define, but most accounts of it include technical competence, narcissism, hedonism, and the careful management of emotions.[30] What these traits share is their detachment and reflexivity: coolness approaches first-person emotional and bodily experiences through a third-person, limited perspective. As Helmut Lethen argues, the "cool persona" denies his psychological interiority, focusing instead on observable behaviors and outward appearances.[31] The promise is that, as long as the cool persona obeys his superior officer during combat, wears the right patch on his motorcycle jacket, or plays his instrument well, it does not matter what he is secretly feeling. In this regard, coolness serves as a "performative armor," shielding its wearer from having to disclose unpredictable or embarrassing affects.[32]

Although coolness has largely been associated with Black masculinity, it possesses multiple genealogies, moving from subculture to subculture, from subculture to mainstream, and back again. According to Alan Liu, coolness became increasingly pervasive after the rise of Taylorism and Fordism, after what he terms the "age of automation."[33] During this period the workplace grew chill as management science suppressed anger, celebration, socializing, and other forms of unproductive expression in order to render workers more docile and reduce labor strife.[34] To carry out these managerial duties, as we have seen, white-collar workers were forced to take on the same emotional distance and restrain themselves. As a result, many managers and professionals reported feeling alienated from their own personalities and emotions. Through industrial psychology and self-help literature, white-collar affect became another project to administer. At the same time, these developments pointed to a more utopian dimension of coolness. As affective life underwent rationalization, it lost any appearance of necessity. The cool persona becomes an object, the product of external, social forces, and yet this condition reveals the contingent and conventional nature of subjectivity, thereby opening up the prospect of self-transformation.[35] Coolness suggests that persona is determined by an artificial code of conduct as opposed to any spontaneous intuition or inner judgment, by ways of doing things rather than ways of being. No longer governed by the dictates of the soul, these forms of behavior can be acted on and changed. Technique replaces essence, enabling the cool character to modify himself for his own end.

Following this ethos, *Playboy* collapses the distinction between work and leisure, administering pleasure with cool calculation in its endless sex advice and self-improvement columns while treating the office as a venue for nonconformist self-expression and even as an erotic playground. Remixing the protocols of sex and work life, the playboy wines and dines clients during business hours and seals deals with his mistresses during off-hours. Coolness, then, is in part a response to the moving dialectic of the intimate and the professional. As work time expands and becomes indistinguishable from play time, workers must adapt by treating their personalities and intimate lives as part of the capital machinery of the firm. To this end, Hefner kept an apartment next to his office during the early years of *Playboy* and later moved his workspace into the Playboy mansion, where he labored for days without stopping, allegedly taking Dexedrine to keep awake, all the while doing most of his job in bed or on the bedroom floor and occasionally taking breaks to have sex with models and staff.[36] In "Shel Silverstein's History of *Playboy*," the cartoonist pokes fun at this by depicting Hefner and a woman standing on a comically oversized version of his famous motorized, circular bed, complete with a multimedia console: "Well . . . *Good Housekeeping* has its test kitchen. . . . *Popular Mechanics* has its mechanical lab. . . . *Sports Cars Illustrated* has its test track and shop."[37] Mixing business with pleasure, Hefner's intimate life became part of the means of production for *Playboy*, with sex functioning as just another editorial duty.

Other than Hefner, Ian Fleming's Bond character is the *Playboy* fixture who best exemplifies the 24/7 lifestyle promoted by the magazine. Following *Playboy*'s publication of "The Hildebrand Rarity" in March 1960, Bond and Hefner became closely connected with one another.[38] The magazine serialized Fleming's last three Bond novels—*On Her Majesty's Secret Service* (1963), *You Only Live Twice* (1964), and *The Man with the Golden Gun* (1965)—while also providing extensive coverage of the Bond films. In a quotation often reprinted by the magazine, Fleming announced, "I'm sure James Bond, if he were an actual person, would be a registered reader of *Playboy*."[39] The superspy certainly shared the same concerns as the magazine's ideal audience: most of the Bond narratives revolve around his inability to maintain work-life boundaries.[40] A typical novel starts with Bond venturing to some vacation spot—a casino, a beach, a ski resort—where he pursues the villain while undercover as a pleasure seeker. Even when Bond genuinely tries to get away from his stressful job, he immediately finds himself embroiled in another espionage plot. Bond stories hinge on leisure that becomes labor, playful games that turn out to be dangerous business, and erotic relationships that transform into professional rivalries or allegiances. Like Hefner, Agent 007 lives to work.[41] This imbalance takes on a tragic note when Bond tries to extricate himself from his official duties long enough to go on a honeymoon in *On Her Majesty's Secret Service*. As Bond rides off with his new bride, Contessa Teresa "Tracy" di Vicenzo, they are attacked by his old foes from the terrorist organization SPECTRE, Ernst Stavro Blofeld and Irma Bunt. His wife is killed, and he ends the serialized novel in denial about her death, looking down at her corpse while saying, "There's no hurry, you see . . . . We've got all the time in the world."[42] Harried professionals will certainly sympathize on more than one level with this scene.

All of this takes a toll on Bond, who, over the course of the *Playboy* serializations, goes from cool to cold. Fleming told *Playboy* that the essence of Bond is that he is "detached" and "disengaged."[43] However, as the figure of Bond's archnemesis Blofeld suggests, indifference is always liable to slide into "accidie," a listless boredom that can only be aroused—if at all—by the most extreme forms of sadism.[44] Bond begins *On Her Majesty's Secret Service* as a well-functioning operative—his brain is as efficient as "an IBM machine"—but he becomes progressively more blank and inhuman.[45] To avoid the pain of mourning his murdered wife, Bond throws himself into a mission in Japan where circumstances force him to take on a new identity by putting on yellowface, a conceit that allows him to adopt the racialized unfeeling ascribed to the Orientalist stereotype.[46] After playing at being a stoic samurai, Bond receives a head injury that erases all of his memories and renders him almost catatonic. *The Man with the Golden Gun* gives us a Bond completely divorced from attachment, sensation, or emotion when the amnesiac agent is brainwashed by the Soviets and sent off as a Manchurian candidate programmed to kill his former boss, M. At his lowest, Bond embodies Hefner's fear that his all-consuming job will transform him into an automaton.[47]

Despite printing these allegories of overwork, Hefner seemed to see Bond as a role model. In Hefner's highly publicized homelife, he took on an aloof, managerial pose, orchestrating revels but never completely losing himself in them. Early during his tenure as editor, Hefner's first wife, Millie Hefner, recognized another split within his personality: Hefner had become a distant "viewer of life," watching the "fantasy character" he had created.[48] Adopting a series of props and mannerisms, Hefner presented his private life as both a job and a theatrical performance. *Playboy* literature reflects Hefner's cool practice of autosurveillance. Paradoxically, even the most heated sexual language allows readers and authors to grow cooler. In a meditation in *Playboy* on literature and obscenity, "Literati of the Four-Letter Word," literary critic Leslie Fiedler likens allegedly obscene authors such as D. H. Lawrence, James Joyce, Edmund Wilson, and Norman Mailer to a boy scrawling dirty graffiti:

> Until he has written for his own sake and that of the little girl he fears and desires the four-letter name of desire, the small boy has no sense of owning what racks him, his own sex; and until the writers of a society have written their versions of the four-letter words, that society has no sense of controlling its deepest torments and pleasures.[49]

Literature is increasingly focused on sexuality, Fiedler argues, because it offers the "dangerous joy of self-knowledge" central to the literary.[50] By holding up a mirror, literature allows readers to externalize themselves as objects of knowledge so as to manage their more troubling impulses.

Here Fiedler echoes the management techniques detailed by Eva Illouz in *Cold Intimacies: The Making of Emotional Capitalism*. During the midcentury period, middle-class professionals developed new strategies to discipline emotions using communication. Management science prompted supervisors and employees to verbalize their troubling or disruptive feelings as a way of intellectualizing and neutralizing them.[51] At the same time, therapeutic culture began to push middle-class couples to treat their intimate problems as communication breakdowns that could be solved only through endless rounds of highly scripted and therefore emotionally controlled conversation.[52] While all of this may sound like the incitement to discourse on sex described by Foucault, the playboy differs in important ways from the confessional subject.[53] Confession calls up deep and obscure secrets that must be interpreted to understand oneself; communication offers instantaneous feedback on impression management. For the playboy, sexuality is not so much an intense revelation or an impenetrable mystery as it is a source of actionable information. Communication, no less than confession, serves as a practice of self-disciplining. Nevertheless, for Fiedler and *Playboy*, who remained under the repressive hypothesis, this new transparency sounded like progress. Heavily influenced by pop Freudianism and, above all,

Alfred Kinsey, *Playboy* sought to liberate readers by revealing to them their own secret lives.

Whereas Fiedler lists more highbrow authors as examples of self-scrutiny, *Playboy* often turned to paraliterary genres like science fiction to encourage this reader response. *Playboy* was known in the science fiction community for offering respectability, extraordinarily high payment rates, and a national audience to its authors, including major figures such as Arthur C. Clarke, Ray Bradbury, Richard Matheson, Harlan Ellison, and Ursula K. Le Guin. In effect, *Playboy* offered the genre a stepping-stone between the pulps and the more prestigious slick magazines.[54] Although *Playboy* has been all but excluded from science fiction criticism, appearing only as a brief mention in a few publication histories, fans in the 1950s and 1960s held the magazine in higher esteem than many of the dedicated genre publications. Even to this day it is common for science fiction author blurbs to boast of publication in *Playboy*.

Some of the reasons for science fiction's strong presence in *Playboy* are purely biographical. Growing up, Hefner was a science fiction fan and a member of the *Weird Tales* Club.[55] Ray Russell—who began as an associate editor in 1954 and rose to executive editor between 1955 and 1960, remaining a contributing editor into the 1970s—wrote science fiction himself and was involved in the Group, a circle of authors centering on Charles Beaumont and Bradbury who often contributed to the magazine.[56] Spectorsky proved amenable to genre stories, while fiction editor Robie Macauley would go on to write *A Secret History of a Time to Come*, a novel set in the postapocalyptic future. And, famously, Robert Anton Wilson and Robert Shea drew on conspiracy theories found in letters they received while editing "The *Playboy* Forum" feature to produce the 1975 science fiction cult classic *The Illuminatus! Trilogy*.

Science fiction also contributed to the magazine's masculine self-image. In *The Playboy Book of Science Fiction and Fantasy*, Ray Russell, writing as the "editors of *Playboy*," reiterates that *Playboy* is "edited by men, for men" (and for women interested in finding out "what their men care about") before observing that the magazine's gendered editorial perspective "ties in quite happily with the indisputable fact that [science fiction is] enjoyed and written by far more men than women."[57] Science fiction joined well-cut suits and soft-core pornography in the province of the *Playboy* man. True to its word, *Playboy* published almost exclusively male science fiction authors during the 1950s and 1960s. When Ursula

K. Le Guin sold "Nine Lives" to the magazine, fiction editor Macauley requested that she use only an initial instead of her full first name, obscuring her gender because "their readers would be frightened if they saw a female byline on the story."[58] After toying with a fanciful author biography for "U. K. Le Guin," and musing over submitting "He is a housewife and the mother of three children," Le Guin wrote the following for the magazine: "It is widely suspected that the writings of U. K. Le Guin are not actually written by U. K. Le Guin, but by another person of the same name."[59]

Just as importantly, though, *Playboy* borrowed science fiction's reflexive structure to reconfirm its own coolness. In Darko Suvin's often-cited definition, science fiction is "the literature of cognitive estrangement."[60] By presenting readers with places that vary wildly from their own, science fiction makes the familiar seem unfamiliar, encouraging readers to reevaluate their own worlds. Like Brecht's alienation effect, science fiction suggests that the status quo is historically contingent and therefore malleable. Far from representing total otherness, then, the alien beings of science fiction offer the reader a looking glass that both "reflects" and "transforms," like a "virgin womb and alchemical dynamo: the mirror is a crucible."[61] This formal structure fits well with the Fiedler model of literary self-examination. However, although Suvin seems to suggest that science fiction is inherently critical, if not revolutionary, the image of the virgin womb hints at another possibility. Instead of marking a leap into another future, science fiction can just as easily become a mere reproduction of the present. *Playboy* transforms speculative fiction into specular fiction, transplanting the present into the future in order to subject it to technocratic modification. For example, Bond lives in a world much like our own, only with cooler gadgets. In this regard, *Playboy* science fiction shares a kinship with management and self-improvement literature, from Taylor's scientific management to the tech industry's life hacks, discourses that defamiliarize routine concerns by framing them as engineering problems. Like management science, these stories suggest that the future will be a playback of the present, manipulable but ultimately the same.

Given *Playboy*'s focus on sex, many of the *Playboy* science fiction stories feature male protagonists duping or dominating their lovers through technological wizardry or preternatural powers. As Liu notes, one of the hallmarks of coolness in the age of automation is the redeployment of Fordist-Taylorist "rationality" for aesthetic and leisure pursuits.[62] Just as underground car culture poached from the assembly line to build drag-racing hot rods, *Playboy* mated the scientific rationalism of golden age speculative fiction with the sensualism of the *Playboy* bachelor. For example, we see this in "The Fully Automated Love Life of Henry Keanridge" by Stan Dryer. In this short story, the titular character stumbles through a series of events that force him to marry and take on three mistresses, one by one. To keep them all straight, Henry surreptitiously uses a computer, the Electronic Logistics Systems Analyzer (ELSA), owned by his employer Acme Trucking, to store all of their data and plot a route between them. Everything goes as planned until ELSA—who registers him a truck—decides he needs a week of automotive maintenance, and Henry is compelled to come out with his secret to his company's systems analyst or watch his dating scheme fall apart.[63] In the end, Henry's private woes become transformed into business opportunities as he and the systems analyst decide to start Femme-Share Incorporated, offering ELSA to paying clients.[64]

While Henry is the one who is automated in the story, his movements dictated by computer programming, the accompanying illustration by Hy Roth suggests otherwise. ELSA is pictured as an enormous reclining nude, her body opening up to expose a forest of wires, ducts, gauges, and tape machines. Punch cards spill out of the giantess's backside, and, somewhere in her midriff, she contains chambers displaying a small harem of identical, naked women, posing in front of what appears to be a peepshow or prostitution window. A male figure in a suit (presumably Henry) sits in front of the console, and, smiling, examines a printout while jerking a phallic lever positioned near his lap. Significantly, Henry faces away from his mistresses, who are located behind and below him; instead he chooses to watch their schematics.

This image recalls an exchange between Arthur C. Clarke and Spectorsky, who joked in correspondence about feeding the formula for the perfect feminine form into a computer to produce a Playmate using the curve-tracer.[65] The illustration takes that fantasy one step further by depicting the playboy's joy not in women's data but in his system for managing that data—the cool eros of metadata. Here we see the same reversal that took place in *Playboy* offices, which channeled libido into work life while administering love life like a job. The story and illustration extrapolate from the same impulse that led to Hefner's little black book of coded information about women and the later data sheets that appeared next to *Playboy* centerfolds: the desire to control and observe intimacy under the cold light of reason, submitting both emotion and sex to management science.

By the end of the 1960s, psychologist Rollo May worried that this attitude toward sex had spread throughout the culture. Self-conscious couples consulted how-to manuals and sexological reports to improve their performances in bed, and, as a result, they found their sex governed by "bookkeeping and timetables" that determined how often they should sleep together.[66] Anxious to not fall behind the Kinsey statistics, they came to treat sex as an obligation that could not be turned down, an approach that tended to rob the act of any spontaneity or intimacy. Even the orgasm became an opportunity for feedback and score-keeping rather than a shared experience: men ruined the mood by insistently asking women whether it was good for them, too.[67] In what May calls "the new puritanism," playboys prove to be as alienated from their own bodies as their strict Protestant forebears: the expert seducer is a "latter-day Baconian" who develops knowledge of the body only to gain power over it, allowing them to treat sex like a fine-tuned "machine."[68] In an image that very much recalls the *Playboy* narrative, May warns that "the lover, with his age-old art, tends to be superseded by the computer operator with his modern efficiency."[69]

As alienated as he might be, though, Henry Keanridge's machine would fall apart if the women disappear from its viewing chamber, and he turns out to be masturbating to his own user profile. As Gayle Rubin and Eve Kosofsky Sedgwick point out, women are made to act as mediators between men, cementing homosocial masculine relationships while serving as an apotropaic against overt homosexuality.[70] When men come together as a group to watch a strip show, the body of the woman serves to reconfirm the spectators' heterosexual masculinity.[71] Playmates give *Playboy* editors and readers the license to engage in what Hefner called a "monthly 'conversation,'" scrutinizing their own intimate lives together with an eye toward improving them in order to better appeal to women.[72] Playmates therefore act as vehicles for masculine self-discovery, allowing men to uncover the truth about themselves.

The Girl next Door

The same dynamic is at work in *Fahrenheit 451*. Early in the novel, Montag encounters a young woman, Clarisse McClellan, setting off the chain of events that leads to his rebellion and ultimate defection from the dystopian society of the novel. Until he meets Clarisse, Montag lives an unexamined life, taking the violent media culture and oppressive police state of the future as given. His relationship with Clarisse, however, gives him a new perspective, forcing him to see his home and his wife as "strange."[73] Clarisse achieves this perceptual shift not through logical argumentation but simply by paying close attention to him. After remarking on the "beauty" of her face, the protagonist marvels,

> How like a mirror, too, her face. Impossible; for how many people did you know that refracted your own light to you. . . . How rarely did other people's faces take you and throw back to you your own expression, your own innermost trembling thought?[74]

Clarisse's regard—as much as her Socratic questioning—enables him to strip away the routinized responses inculcated by education and professional training and view himself without prejudice. There seems to be little else to Clarisse beyond her ability to awaken Montag to himself. As the novel notes, she possesses an "incredible power of identification," anticipating his slightest movement so that "he [feels] that if his eye itched, she might blink."[75] Like Fiedler's four-letter graffiti, Clarisse allows Montag to observe his experience as if from the outside, offering him an alienated perspective on his own life. Revealing Montag, Clarisse becomes his speculum.

Clarisse contrasts sharply with Montag's wife, Mildred. Mildred spends her days engrossed in interactive television on the wall screens of their living room, and, at night, she blocks out everything with an audio Seashell plugged into her ear. Utterly distracted, she ignores Montag, who fantasizes about taking control of the Seashell broadcasting station to get through to his wife. Whereas Clarisse is receptive, Mildred is forgetful and opaque. She cannot remember where she first met her husband, nor does she recall that he saved her from attempted suicide. When medical technicians arrive to detoxify her body and replace her blood after too many pills, they peer inside her with an optical device—the Eye—that discovers only "emptiness."[76] While Clarisse provides a circulatory system for Montag's experiences, Mildred proves to be a noisy and unfaithful medium. The novel likens Mildred to "a hard stratum of marble" that might be found at the bottom of "a trench in one's yard"; stony, sterile, dull, and intractable, no meaningful or lasting impressions of Montag are recorded upon her surface.[77] Ultimately, Clarisse's estranging point of view allows Montag to see this and shows Mildred to be anything but a girl next door. We learn that her hair has been "burnt by chemicals to a brittle straw" and her "body [is] as thin as a praying mantis from dieting."⁷⁸ Not only does she fail to conform to Playmate beauty standards, but she also lacks the untouched and naturalistic quality of the classic *Playboy* model. Unlike the Playmates, she is not a young woman ready to be molded and shaped.

The novel's opposition between the dull housewife and the pliable young woman is telling given Clarisse's place in *Playboy* history. The first time the phrase "the girl next door" appeared in *Playboy* was not a reference to a Playmate—it was Bradbury's description of Clarisse.⁷⁹ As a kind of medium, Clarisse shares a kinship with the first girl-next-door model, Janet Pilgrim, who would later appear in the July 1955 issue. Pilgrim, described as "Playboy's Office Playmate," supervised subscriptions in Playboy's circulation department while also modeling as a Playmate. In her initial photograph, Pilgrim sits at her typewriter, looking eagerly at the camera as if waiting to take dictation, while in a later picture Pilgrim leans over Hefner's shoulder, reading from a sheet of paper in his hands; a caption informs us that they are "[discussing] the magazine's rising circulation."⁸⁰ She is eager to receive and transmit the words of the editor and, by extension, the reader. In addition to overseeing subscriptions, Pilgrim embodies the means of circulation itself, with her seminude body stamped on popular holiday gift-subscription cards.⁸¹ Like her namesake, this Playmate is a long-distance traveler, journeying through the mail in the buff. Identifying wholly with her employer's interests, what convinces Pilgrim to pose nude for the camera is not a yearning for fame and recognition but, rather, the irresistible temptation of a new Addressograph machine.⁸²

Unlike Mildred, *Playboy* Playmates always appear to be enthralled by the voices of their men. The telephone appears as a prop in about a dozen photo shoots during this period, allowing Playmates to "cheerfully [while] away phone-filled hours talking to and about men."⁸³ Mere adjuncts to male suitors, the Playmates have nothing to say about themselves—like Clarisse, their "favorite subject . . . is everyone else"—and many of their photo spreads end with the Playmate stripping down, choosing an outfit, and putting on makeup to prepare for a night out with the male caller on the other end of the line.⁸⁴ Phonographs are also a regular feature in the background and copy-text of pictorials, with Sinatra almost always ending up on the platter. The "titillative tones" of Sinatra—a singer Hefner identified with—sent some Playmates into ecstasy and abandon, clutching records to their bare chests.⁸⁵ These tableaus allow *Playboy* to maintain a strictly homosocial communications schema: women appear in the magazine but never as senders or receivers of messages about themselves.

The magazine enters the realm of science fiction when it transforms women into anthropomorphic representations of media technology.[86] *Playboy* metaphorizes Playmates as hi-fi stereos, office equipment, television signals, and books.[87] One *Playboy* issue even features photographs of nude women modeling as typefaces. Borrowing from a typographic company's controversial trade ads, the pictorial includes "Hellenic," half-clad in a toga and striking a stately pose next to a vase, and "Railroad Gothic," who is tied up and slung over a toy railroad track.[88] Beyond the punning and wink-wink euphemism, the magazine suggests that Playmates act as the media apparatus for men, storing and transmitting data about them.[89] In the narratives accompanying most pictorials, Playmates continuously report back to men on their performances, wavering back and forth in response to different stratagems before finally agreeing to take their clothes off for the camera.

This feedback is crucial to the cool persona, who is defined by public appearance and behavior. As with Clarisse, the Playmate defamiliarizes the masculine spectator, allowing him to see his actions from a third-person point of view and adjust them accordingly. Thus, in nearly every "What Sort of Man Reads Playboy?" ad, a woman stands nearby, watching the *Playboy* male with interest or adoration, confirming his material and romantic success.[90] *Playboy* offers an eroticized exercise in the role-taking moves counseled by authors such as Dale Carnegie, who taught managers to tailor their words and actions based on how they imagined their clients and colleagues would receive them.[91] The *Playboy* persona therefore examined his appearance and behavior with the kind of acute self-awareness normally associated with femininity.[92] Following this impulse, Hefner announced that he had constructed his elaborate public character, with his pipe and rotating bed, "all because of wanting to be a sex object in the best sense of the word."[93] Although Playmates are instrumentalized in the process, the editor is the target of objectification.

Based on these descriptions *Playboy* might seem incredibly cold, but Hefner described himself and his target audience as "sentimental."[94] At first this seems paradoxical and even contradictory to what I have argued so far. Even Hefner's biographer Steven Watts sees a tension between the editor's romantic streak and his detached persona.[95] However, if we follow Tania Modleski, we begin to see that, despite the magazine's rejection of femininized emotions, it embodies a characteristically masculine mode of sentimentality. Modleski points out that the most hyperemotional of male melodramas center on hardboiled figures like Clint Eastwood who refuse to let their feelings show.[96] While white men in male-oriented melodramas remain steely and controlled, women and people of color in these narratives act as emotional surrogates, performing suffering and other extreme emotions that conventionally masculine men struggle to keep under wraps. By the same token, *Playboy* women are encouraged to gush, cling, and feel even when men recede into themselves, allowing *Playboy*'s male addressees to come into close proximity with stereotypically feminine affects while still maintaining a subdued, masculine demeanor. Sending a woman head over heels with candlelight schmaltz becomes just another confirmation of the man's savoir faire. By presenting women as instruments of masculine self-revelation, *Playboy* promises a kind of sentimentalism without the stain of effeminacy.

Silencing Women

While later pornographic magazines boast about offering raw or amateur material, *Playboy* fetishizes the process of turning a reluctant girl next door into a glamorous, polished model, taking the readers behind the scenes with images of the makeup session and photo shoot.[97] The consequences of this project were made explicit when Hefner's Playmate and one-time "special girl," Cynthia Maddox, complained to Diana Lurie of *Life* magazine that she had been cast "as a living, breathing embodiment" of *Playboy* femininity: "Sometimes—God, I don't feel like I have any identity of my own."[98] Meanwhile, defending his propensity to look for "innocence and sweetness" in his young girlfriends, Hefner responded that "most of the girls I have gone with have benefited because I give them an identity and, when they come out of the machine, they are better for it."[99]

In Hefner's metaphor, women become the raw material for his labor process, receiving value through his work without conferring any of their own. Here the editor functions like an author, taking on the privileges of literary property. As "author" and proprietor of *Playboy*, Hefner devalues the work of other cultural intermediaries involved in the production of the magazine and downplays the autonomy of the medium itself.[100] In this authorial regime, the paper, ink, binding, and (I would add) models are "merely accidents," "vehicles" for conveying what is truly essential—"the author's invention and labour."[101] The Playmate's alleged absence of worth allows the editor to remain self-reliant. Just as manuscript or a photograph selected and prepared for publication supposedly takes on the character of the magazine while also demonstrating the discernment of the editor, the Playmate is subsumed by the editor function.

Hefner's reach even extends to the Playboy clubs, which offered members and customers the experience of being personally served by waitresses in bunny costumes. When Gloria Steinem went undercover to become a Bunny at the New York City Playboy Club in 1963, she found that the clubs were not as glamorous as their public image suggested.[102] Steinem discovered that the clubs paid wages lower than the job advertisements promised, and they often forced Bunnies to perform unpaid labor as part of their training and to split their tips with the house.[103] On the job, Bunnies suffered swollen feet, lost circulation, and endured other strains from walking on high heels in tight-fitting costumes for long hours.[104] According to Steinem, staff training taught Bunnies to accept sexual harassment from customers as a matter of course but hired plainclothes detectives monitored them to make sure that they did not go home with any of the customers, which would spoil the company's reputation and risk legal action.[105] Nevertheless, the clubs invited Bunnies to attend private *Playboy* parties—bringing male dates to these events was strongly discouraged—and allegedly fired one Bunny for rejecting an important club member using strong language.[106] Hinting that the Bunnies were obligated to entertain their employers in private, Steinem points out that the prehire screening included a gynecological exam with a test for sexually transmitted diseases.[107] She submitted to this procedure only under protest.

Through all of this, though, the clubs monitored Bunnies to make sure that they projected the girl-next-door image while on the floor: the *Playboy Bunny Club Manual* or *Bunny Bible* told recent recruits that "we depend on our Bunnies to express the personality of the magazine."[108] Bunnies nevertheless complained in private. Steinem found it especially degrading that they were required to respond to the guests' incessant, lewd comments with flirty, pre-scripted deflections: "I was an IBM machine and I was being programmed."[109] Reduced to automatons, the Bunnies could not speak for themselves.

Here *Playboy* seems to scream out for the kind of antipornography feminism championed by Catharine MacKinnon and Andrea Dworkin. Throughout this book, I have made a point of setting aside the question of whether pornography should be censored. Debates such as these degrade the analytical powers of their participants by disallowing the kind of fine-grained aesthetic and political distinctions that cannot be expressed in juridical verdicts. Even when they avoid legalism, arguments that set out to evaluate pornography as a genre often appear equally impoverished. The most plausible argument about pornography's value also proves to be the least interesting one: it depends. Porn studies abandoned this judgmental problematic for very good reasons.[110]

Nevertheless, *Playboy* does seem to confirm second-wave feminism's suspicions about pornography, a fact that suggests that some elements of its conceptual apparatus might still be useful if only in this limited case. *Playboy* comports well with the ideas of feminist philosopher Rae Langton, who presents the most convincing reformulation of MacKinnon's case against pornography.[111] Langton argues that pornography brings about the gender inequalities that it depicts. Drawing on J. L. Austin, she describes pornography as a performative utterance, a speech act that does what it says. One way that it accomplishes this is by declaring women incompetent to speak authoritatively about their sexual preferences and experiences. Pornography intimates that women enjoy whatever is done to them, which means that even when they say "no," they really mean "yes." The genre thereby nullifies women's rights to withhold sexual consent, testify against abusers, or speak out about sexual domination. She calls this form of silencing "illocutionary disablement"—women might make locutions, they might say things, but their words have no force because they do not count as speech acts.[112] Pornography cannot be defended on First Amendment grounds because it silences women, violating their right to free speech.

Crucially, Langton's argument depends on the idea that pornography holds authority over the erotic domain.[113] Just as a judge's jurisdiction enables them to perform speech acts such as passing judgement, pornographers must be seen as authoritative speakers about women's sexuality in order for them to subordinate women to men's desires. If pornography were taken to be fictive, fallible, or otherwise counterfactual, it would not be understood to performatively preempt women's protests. I would argue that these felicitous conditions do not hold for many examples of pornography, which clearly inhabit the realm of fantasy.

In *Playboy*, however, the editorial context encourages readers to think of the magazine as an authority on sexual matters. Playmates were supposed to be women from everyday life whom *Playboy* readers could conceivably meet and seduce if they followed the prescriptions laid out in the rest of the magazine. Although erotic images do not possess either rhetorical power or illocutionary effects on their own, they can be made to signify as sexual imperatives by a persuasive editorial figure. Early *Playboy* issues presented women as deceitful or ambivalent about their sexual desires, encouraging men to ignore them when they cried after sex: "The unvarnished truth in most cases is that the lady is willing, but wants to go on record as protesting and regretting."[114] When the *Playboy* women say something that a man does not want to hear, their utterances register only as meaningless emotionalism.

We see this quite clearly on an episode of *Playboy's Penthouse*, Hefner's short-lived television talk show. The show features Rona Jaffe promoting her popular novel, *The Best of Everything* (1958), which had recently been adapted for film. The novel follows the lives and loves of five women working in a New York publishing house. Jaffe wrote the book after a stint as an associate editor at Fawcett Publications and based the novel's narrative on the life experiences of working women.[115] One of the villains of the piece is an editor past his prime, Mr. Shalimar, who exploits his editorial authority and perceived prestige to woo his secretaries. Mr. Shalimar serves as an editor of an imprint featuring pulpy women's fiction, and so he transforms these seductions into market research, integrating probing questions about his secretaries' past exploits and desires into his pickup lines. These scenes reveal him to be an out-of-touch and incompetent editor who depends entirely on the underpaid women in his office for insight into their demographic. With its unflattering portrait of the editorial figure, the novel serves as a mild critique of the masculinity of the publishing industry even as it celebrates the prospect of women finding love and marriage in the office.

When Jaffe appears on *Playboy's Penthouse*, however, she is given a dressing-down by Hefner and Spectorsky. The *Playboy* editors both tease her for writing what they see as a frothy "soap opera," and Spectorsky pointedly implies in his interview questions that the novel was ephemeral entertainment rather than real "literature."[116] When Jaffe defends herself by arguing that women have reported seeing their lives in the novel, one of the interviewers laughs dismissively and says, "Oh, I see," scoffing at the authority of women's experience.[117] At the end of the interview, Hefner explains to a consternated Jaffe that their barbed questions reflect *Playboy*'s editorial line, which objects to what they see as the "over-feminization" of American culture.[118] Throughout this period, *Playboy* published essays by Philip Wylie, author of *Generation of Vipers*, arguing that the growing consumer power of mothers and housewives had transformed men into their castrated subordinates.[119] *Playboy* hoped to reverse this supposed gender imbalance. Over the course of the whole exchange, it becomes clear that women cannot level even a small complaint against abusive or caddish male editors in the precincts of *Playboy*, where Hefner holds dominion.

Playboy often placed its Playmates in demeaning and subservient positions. At the same time, we should not concede to Hefner all the influence that he pretended to possess. As Jennifer Saul argues in her critique of Langton, pornographic works have only as much authority as the audience is willing to grant them.[120] Their illocutionary effects depend a great deal on their reception, including the context in which they are viewed. An issue of *Playboy* examined in private does something different from one interpreted in an academic seminar or displayed in a feminist lecture against pornography. As we have seen, editors have no final say over what their audiences do with their publications. Judith Butler is therefore right to warn against seeing pornography as a "divine performative," an utterance that transforms desire into reality by making women into its image.[121] If pornographic speech acts possessed the sovereign power granted to it by MacKinnon and other antipornography feminists, it would be impossible to re-signify or contest them.

A Fly in the Ointment

Indeed, even within its pages we see hints that *Playboy* might not be as effective in maintaining gender inequality as we might think. Hefner's fantasy of impressing his identity onto a feminized communication medium at times threatens to destabilize the very gender boundaries that underwrite it. Frederik Pohl reflects on this problem in the "The Fiend," which follows Dandish, a criminal sentenced to pilot a spaceship with his brain while his body is locked away on Mercury—the ultimate in cool detachment. Dandish's ship is carrying seven hundred hibernating colonists to a new planet, and he spends the long, lonely journey fantasizing about taking one of the female colonists out of stasis. After years of plotting, Dandish becomes "a connoisseur of victims . . . leafing through the microfile photographs that accompanied each colonist's dossier like a hi-fi hobbyist shopping through a catalog."[122] In addition to commenting on *Playboy*'s Playmate media, this scene alludes to the often-depicted labor of the editor—selecting potential models from their headshots. Commanding his environment much like Hefner at the Playboy mansion, Dandish seems assured to snare his chosen victim, Sylvie.

However, Dandish is immediately thrown off balance by the woman's plastic-looking hair—damaged by the liquid helium bath that preserved her during hibernation—which reminds Dandish of a painful scene in which he obliquely revealed to his psychology instructor his dream of owning a woman as a slave. The instructor informed him that this fantasy "was a repressed wish to play with dolls," telling the class that "this fellow is role playing . . . acting out a wish to be a woman. These clear-cut cases of repressed homosexuality can take many forms."[123] Sylvie underscores this point by protesting that she is "not a doll," and Dandish's heterosexual masculinity is further called into question when we learn that, as a teenager, he wore "long permanented hair and the lacquered fingernails that were the fashion for kids that year."[124] Following an inversion model of homosexuality, the narrative suggests that the *Playboy* dream of perfect control over women allows men to vicariously become them. The Playmate is shown to be the dandyish editor in drag. Here Pohl's story echoes the critiques of *Playboy* leveled by working-class men's magazines, which implied that Hefner's magazine used sex to overcompensate for its insecure masculinity or latent homosexuality.[125]

Gender panic also surfaces in George Langelaan's "The Fly," published in the June 1957 issue, centered on a scientist—André Delambre—developing teleportation technology. As Bruce Clarke argues in his brilliant analysis of "The Fly" and its adaptations, André is not broadcasting to the world but is instead sending a "message of himself to himself."[126] I would argue that the teleporter, when appearing in *Playboy*, becomes as an allegory for the magazine's communication circuit so that, like Hefner, André serves as both the analytic subject and the analyzed object. Within this media system for one, however, another entity appears—a fly sneaks into the teleportation chamber with him, and, in the process of transmission, mixes its particles with his. On the other side, he comes out with an insectoid head and arm, while a fly buzzes off with his body parts. The fly, according to Clarke, symbolizes the demonic return of the material medium as noise.[127] The media apparatus and all of its contingencies interpose between André and himself, causing him to come out not as he intended, a perfect copy of himself, but instead as something obscene, the fly-human hybrid. André's predicament is beautifully expressed by the page design. The overleaf of the first page of the story is an almost empty page, its blankness interrupted only by a picture of a life-sized fly. This image disrupts the textual idealism of conventional reading, forcing the audience to attend not only to the material exigencies of viewing the page, including an unimpeded line of sight, but also to the physicality of the page itself.[128] When stripped of printed words, the cream-colored background, normally invisible, becomes foregrounded, while the trompe l'oeil of the fly reminds us of the paper's two-dimensionality. Just as the fly represents the uncanny reappearance of the repressed medium, this page jars the audience out of their fantasy of unmediated communication, demanding that they remember that they are reading a physical, print publication.

Given that media are gendered for *Playboy*, it is no accident that the connection between the story's frame narrator, Francois, and his departed brother André (a name derived from the Greek for "man") is a woman—André's wife Hélène, whose narrative voice and typewritten confession relate almost all that we know about André. "The Fly" is therefore as much about Francois's quest to determine Hélène's fidelity as it is about André's unfaithful transmission. Indeed, it is Hélène who, in the end, ruins André's chances of reversing the teleportation mistake. After beaming himself across the room six times, he is unable to extract the fly parts from himself, but Hélène insists that he try once more. When he does, the lost particles of another failed teleportation test subject, those of their cat Dandelo, recombine with his own. André's hopes to find the corrupting fly and take the trip with it once more to undo the mutation are rendered impossible. He ends the story an abject and monstrous feminine creature, with the "pink and moist" nose of a cat and a mouth that has become "a long hairy vertical slit from which hung a black quivering trunk that widened at the end, trumpet-like, and from which saliva kept dripping."[129] Not only has he been crossed with a pussy, but also his voice has been taken away from him, replaced by oozing genitalia. Bereft of direct speech, he must type out his messages and give them to his wife-cum-secretary, on whom he is now dependent to help carry out his assisted suicide. André the man dies, and his secretary betrays him by divulging his obscene secrets to others. But even this betrayal is undone again by the unpredictability of communication: Francois shows the confession to the police investigator who, claiming it to be mere ravings, throws it into the fire. Unlike Clarisse and Janet Pilgrim, Hélène fails in her role as medium, allowing her hysteria to interrupt and contaminate exchanges between men.

Even more disturbingly, however, "The Fly" hints at the precariousness of the editor function. Hefner is not simply a biographical individual—he is also, among other things, a media representation, an editorial perspective, an array of publications, a lifestyle, and a managerial position. Far from simply being *Playboy*, Hefner is an effect produced by the *Playboy* network, and, as this narrative suggests, that network could rebel against him at any moment. As the individualization of a collective assemblage, the editor function is always in danger of dispersing into its component parts. Just as André cannot control the circulation of his atoms as they beam across the room, the figure of Hefner remains at the mercy of the people, images, texts, and technologies that work together to produce the editorial persona for popular consumption. While Hefner claims to be editing for himself, he can only do so through others.

But a boy can dream. Hefner still aspired to the self-contained media network hinted at in *Fahrenheit 451*. Just as Montag settles in with his fellow readers in the countryside, another conflagration destroys the dystopian city. The fire of nuclear war acts as a purifying flame, burning away not only the censors but also the minorities and the mass media that catered to them. In *Fahrenheit 451*, as in "The Fly," fire signifies entropy and noise—the antithesis of cool—but here it appears as a deus ex machina. Now, the all-male group can be sure that no interlopers will come between them. Granger, the leader of the readers, comforts Montag on his lost wife in a rousing speech, which insists that, before the rebuild, they will pause and reflect: "Come on now, we're going to build a mirror factory first and put out nothing but mirrors for the next year and take a long look in them."[130] With Clarisse dead along with Mildred, Montag no longer even needs a girl next door to reflect on him.

Although Hefner would never dispense with his Playmates, *Playboy*'s editor function is also predicated on censorship and exclusion. Despite its proclaimed libertarianism, *Playboy* rejected material that called into question the identity of its readers and the editor, constituting an audience sharing same tastes, dispositions, and demographic characteristics. At the same time, *Playboy*'s intimate public risked allegations of homosexuality, so it was forced to include women as intermediaries between men. The magazine's depiction of women as media devices made it possible for the editor to appear as the final author of the publication, erasing the labor of other employees such as models and secretaries by transforming them into mere inscription surfaces. To borrow a phrase Boris

Kachka used to describe publisher Roger Straus, the Playmate fiction allows the editor to speak with the "Royal 'I,'" taking credit for the actions and work of others.[131] When this narrative fell into danger, though, the cool detachment of science fiction allowed the *Playboy* reader to supervise and regulate his responses, facing the horrors of communication failure and gender confusion without succumbing to obscenity. Like a game of chicken run or five-finger fillet, *Playboy* science fiction becomes another opportunity for the cool persona to maintain composure in the face of emotionally fraught uncertainty.

Even *Playboy* science fiction has its limits. Material the magazine rejected tells us what *Playboy*'s editorial philosophy would not permit. According to Harlan Ellison, the magazine thought his supernatural short story "Pretty Maggie Moneyeyes" was "a knockout piece of writing, but it could not possibly be published in *Playboy* because the male character was weaker than the female," explaining that the fact that "the woman was dominant in the philosophy and action of the story . . . would seriously unsettle *Playboy*'s 'young urban male readership.'"[132] The woman in question is Maggie, a beautiful prostitute who maintains an icy distance from her clients and her own body, presenting herself as "a chromium instrument, something never pitted by rust and corrosion."[133] By the story's conclusion, however, it is the protagonist who becomes a mechanism, his soul trapped inside a haunted slot machine thanks to Maggie's guile. This is the magazine's worst fear realized. *Playboy* is replete with cautions against scheming gold diggers and marriage-minded seductresses, but it could not accept a story in which a woman so coolly indifferent to men gets away with it. For *Playboy*, coolness must remain a privilege of masculinity.

Coda: Lenna, the First Lady of the Internet

Even as *Playboy* magazine declined in influence, Playboy Enterprises expanded into media ranging from computer games to satellite radio. Although the golden bunny logo is perhaps the magazine's most well-known image—leaping from the pages of *Playboy* to adorn a wide variety of licensed products—a photograph of playmate Lena Forsén (formerly Lena Söderberg and Lena Sjööblom) turned out to be even more important for visual culture. Forsén, who *Playboy* dubbed "Lenna," posed for the magazine in a nude pictorial in November of 1972. The magazine plays up her Swedish origins: she supposedly left her home country because the government's steep tax rate and generous welfare provisions were "too socialistic."¹³⁴

Whatever her origins, a head crop from Miss November's centerfold would soon become radically detached from any national or biographical context. During the summer of 1973, a team working at the University of Southern California's Signal and Image Processing Institute tore the magazine's photograph of "Lenna" from an issue they had lying around the lab and scanned the section of her face peeking over her nude shoulder to use as a test image.¹³⁵ Unbeknownst to the model, her likeness circulated throughout the computing field and soon became the industry standard for testing digital-image processing and compression algorithms, including the Signal and Image Processing Institute's newly developed JPEG format.¹³⁶ Despite *Playboy*'s later objections on intellectual property grounds, countless scholarly journals reprinted the Lenna image.¹³⁷ Forsén, who came to be known as "the first lady of the Internet," did not find out that she was featured in one of the most shared images of all time until she was invited to speak at the conference of the Society for Imaging Science and Technology in 1997.¹³⁸ Forsén considered the Lenna image to be a strange honor but came to regret the fact that she was never compensated for the ubiquitous use of her media-historical picture.¹³⁹ At the moment Forsén was finally obtaining recognition, many in the engineering community had begun to speak out against the image, which, they argued, alienated women engineers by casting the profession as a misogynistic boys' club.¹⁴⁰ As Marie Hicks points out, the Lenna image became the standard at precisely the moment men were taking over computing occupations and forcing women programmers out.¹⁴¹

Once more, men treated a woman from *Playboy* as a media technology for transmitting data between men. Once more, a playmate's body allowed men to refine their own images. Only after four decades did a significant number of science and technology journals stop accepting the test image in published articles.¹⁴²

Mad Ones, Mad Men

"GINSBERG WORE KHAKIS," according to a Gap print advertisement from 1994. In the captioned photograph, the Beat poet sits on the ground wearing a rumpled suit jacket and a sloppy necktie, his khakied legs bent into a meditation position. Although his hands, resting on his lap, come together to form a mudra, his face seems more smirking than serene. Behind him we see a Buddhist shrine. Beside him sits his own camera. Ginsberg seems self-consciously staged: his foot slips off the seat cushion because he has been angled toward the photographer. We are being offered a glimpse into his private life, maybe, but everything here is for show. The rest of the advertisement looks like every other entry in the campaign—the celebrity shot, the Gap logo, and a single terse slogan, all in monochrome—except for the fact that, over to the left of the image, we read, "All fees for Mr. Ginsberg's image are donations to Jack Kerouac's School of Poetics, The Naropa Institute, Boulder, CO."

This image joined a spate of Beat-themed advertisements: Jack Kerouac appeared posthumously in the same campaign in 1993, and William S. Burroughs bounced between looping video monitors in a 1994 Nike television spot. While Kerouac was helpless to withhold his product endorsement, and Burroughs seemed happy to be paid as a pitchman, Ginsberg sought to undermine his role in the advertising industry by presenting the full-page ad as an exercise in charity, devotion, and the advancement of poetry. The notice preserving Ginsberg's opposition to crass marketing strains the eye: its white letters fade into a light gray background, legible mostly to those already in the know. As one might guess from this image, throughout his life Ginsberg maintained an uneasy and uncertain relationship with the field of advertising.

In 1951, just a few years after graduating from Columbia University, Allen Ginsberg began a career in market research and public opinion polling. He started out coding questionnaires part-time for Doherty, Clifford and Shenfield before quickly moving to National Opinion Research Center (NORC), an organization run out of the University of Chicago with an office in New York City.[1] Working alongside Carl Solomon and John Clellon Holmes at NORC, Ginsberg helped gather information on Americans' reactions to issues ranging from atomic energy to socialized medicine in order to help lawmakers, government officials, and academic researchers better understand public opinion.[2] One of NORC's central projects was an ongoing series of surveys on race relations—the first of its kind—which frequently revealed the depths of white racism, discovering that many white respondents considered Black Americans more likely to be unpatriotic and communistic.[3]

In an October 1960 journal entry titled "Subliminal," Ginsberg reflects on his past career as part of a broader indictment of 1950s containment culture: "I was working in Market Research. / Who threw poison onion Germs in Korea? / Do big fat American people know their Seoul from a hole in the ground?"[4] Ginsberg's writings on this period reveal American respondents to be blind to their own interior lives as well as their nation's imperial adventures. In this largely forgotten entry, Ginsberg's voice as the market researcher quickly comes to resemble the interrogator in his poem "America," who asks questions such as "America when will we end the human war?" before finally receiving a series of caveman responses: "The Russia wants to eat us alive. . . . Her wants to Grab Chicago. Her needs a Red *Reader's Digest*. Her wants our auto plants in Siberia. Him big bureaucracy running our filling stations."[5] The America queried in "Subliminal," "America," and Ginsberg's research offers answers that prove to be as paranoid as they are insensitive and obtuse. The American respondent's fatal flaw lies in their inability to imagine that others might desire something different from what they want. The average American of the poem fears that the Bolsheviks envy all the familiar things the smug provincial knows and loves: midwestern towns, middlebrow magazines, and middle-class jobs. Like many of his contemporaries, Ginsberg associated the average American that emerged from social data such as survey responses and polling numbers with a stultified and atomized mass society.[6]

American public opinion got that way, Ginsberg suggests, through media brainwashing. The advertising industry produces the very ignorance its market research departments work to diagnose and capitalize on. Ginsberg should know, he argues, because he helped "pick people's brains" in the advertising field, where he learned "the technology of brainwashing for Ipana toothpaste."[7] Although his most notable achievement was working on the "Brusha, Brusha, Brusha" campaign, he had grander ideas about what he could do with his advertising acumen.[8] Ginsberg, like Burroughs, imagined that he could turn the tricks of the hidden persuaders against themselves, subverting a mass communication system that threatened individuality, self-expression, and poetry itself.[9]

Ginsberg's rejection of advertising in favor of poetry serves to buttress one of the foundational myths of his poetic career. Ginsberg spent the first half of his twenties bouncing between market research jobs. He worked on toothpaste advertisements for Doherty, Clifford and Shenfield in the spring of 1951, and, after coding for NORC, he moved on to George Fine Market Research in 1952, where he focused on cosmetics and deodorant.[10] Unsurprisingly, Ginsberg found himself unhappy among the Madison Avenue men he would later smear as "the fairies of advertising."[11] After Ginsberg moved in with a girlfriend and began a job in San Francisco at the market research firm Towne-Oller and Associates in 1954, he became deeply depressed and looked to the psychiatrist Philip Hicks for answers.[12]

During one of their sessions, Hicks asked Ginsberg to reveal what he really wanted in life, and the poet responded that he yearned to quit his job, find an apartment with his lover Peter Orlovsky, and spend his time writing poetry.[13] Unlike the market research respondents, Ginsberg knew himself. Hicks gave Ginsberg permission to follow his desires, precipitating an epiphany that would lead Ginsberg to give up the straight life of squares entirely. Ginsberg, the story goes, wrote up a report for his employers showing that he could be replaced by a computer, rendering his entire branch office in San Francisco obsolete. When Towne-Oller offered him a promotion and a position in the New York office, Ginsberg is said to have demurred, preferring to follow his muse while taking in unemployment benefits.[14] This narrative, which Ginsberg recounted in an interview, presents the poet as beating the professional-managerial class at their own game while also revealing much of their work to be rote, mindless, and ultimately dispensable.[15]

But this story does not appear to be true. Ginsberg remained at Towne-Oller for months after he followed Hicks's advice and shacked up with Orlovsky.[16] A letter from Towne-Oller to Ginsberg shows that Ginsberg and several women coworkers were terminated because the company's expenses were so high that it could not continue paying for the overhead on the San Francisco office.[17] Ginsberg, upset, tells Kerouac that he is "being replaced by an IBM mechanical brain," but there is no evidence that Ginsberg planned his own obsolescence.[18] Journal entries from this period suggest instead that he only sank deeper into despair.[19]

While the accepted history shows us Ginsberg making an absolute break with advertising, I would argue that Ginsberg's professional dissatisfaction neatly parallels many of the concerns that motivated contemporary advertising men. It is easy to see why Ginsberg and many other admen became jaded. Thomas Frank shows that the advertising industry in the early 1950s viewed itself as a scientific enterprise governed by quantitative research that yielded strict, step-by-step formulas for producing effective advertisements.[20] The advertising employee was not an artist: according to industry discourse, intuitive leaps only impeded the market researcher's systematic search for a product's unique selling proposition, the quality differentiating a commodity from its competitors, while flights of imagination hindered the copywriter's task of drilling that selling point into the minds of consumers through repetition.[21] As Ginsberg's reminiscences on his work history suggest, this often meant leveraging surveys and polling research to uncover what was already obvious, all the while treating customers as mindless marks.

Such hard-sell advertising methods soon came to seem stale. By the end of the decade, the Doyle Dane Bernbach agency (DDB) would lead a new trend in advertising by overturning marketing's rules and norms with unconventional advertising campaigns for Volkswagen and Avis. Bill Bernbach, cofounder and creative director of DDB, wrote that "the real giants have always been poets, men who jumped from facts into the realm of imagination and ideas."[22]

In what came to be known as the creative revolution, the advertising industry opened its doors to nonconformists who ignored statistics entirely. As an author in *Madison Avenue* magazine put it, "Don't let the pie-charts and research mumbo-jumbo fool you. An advertisement is a seduction. . . . There are no objective standards against which the efficacy of a seduction can be measured in advance."[23] Scientism only created more distance between advertisers and consumers, whereas the new creatives valued "sensitivity," an openness to feeling out consumer impulses and desires that some "Mad Men" would later try to chemically enhance through psychedelic drugs.[24]

Marketers in this era began to adopt countercultural ideas about the self. Mary Rizzo details how lifestyle marketing research over the course of the 1960s and 1970s convinced industry professionals that consumers could move between class identities through cultural performances.[25] While the old guard slotted consumers into rigid socioeconomic hierarchies, lifestyle marketers believed that consumers defined themselves through their stylistic preferences. Many in marketing therefore came to believe that consumer choices had to be understood as expressive acts of self-making rather than reflections of the consumer's preexisting background. Although they may have gone in different directions, the Beats and the lifestyle marketers both espoused a dramaturgical perspective that saw identities as roles. Blue collar, white collar: these were all costumes that could be shed by changing shirts.

Given the elective affinities between business and Beats, we might imagine a Ginsberg in an alternate universe continuing to pursue his career in advertising, dumping Towne-Oller for DDB, and making a name for himself by tweaking consumers in commercials for Quaker Oats. Ginsberg's contemporaries often critiqued this side of him: Mel Weisburd called Ginsberg a "vulgar salesman for himself," while Denise Levertov complained that he was "conducting a regular propaganda campaign" after she saw his photograph in *Mademoiselle*.[26] Beyond Ginsberg's self-promotion, we find him taking up a parallel literary project that addresses the same problem faced by the advertising creatives. If Ginsberg's waged work represented a technical, abstracted, and ultimately imperceptive way of knowing other people, his poetic performances promise a way to resensitize the poet and his audience.

Once Ginsberg published his work in *Howl and Other Poems*, he found it harder to awaken readers to the emotions of others than he had realized. Ginsberg invited queer sociality through his oral poetry, bringing men together to physically feel one another's rhythms. His editor, Lawrence Ferlinghetti, defended *Howl* from obscenity charges by reinterpreting it using a fundamentally different reading method. Reflecting the homophobic legal culture of the 1950s, Ferlinghetti's defense argued that Ginsberg's poems cautioned against the invasiveness of sociality: sodomy became a paranoid metaphor for the intrusions of society on an imperiled, masculine individual. Through this strategy, the defense drew on a stock of images found in bestselling sociological paperbacks that argued that professional-managerial subjects were adopting an ethos that evacuated the self of any stable authenticity in order to treat everyday life as a kind of theatrical performance in which one adopted whatever role seemed most effective. Over the course of the trial, it became clear that this was a facile argument made solely to win over the judge, and, indeed, the defense itself came to look like opportunistic playactors. The moral outrage manufactured by the defense team in *California v. Ferlinghetti* turned out to be the kind of posturing that the Beats dragged in their more slapstick moments.

Blown by Human Seraphim

Writing about "Howl," Ginsberg suggests that its value resided in the embodied communication of "true feelings."[27] Hoping to get closer to his readers, Ginsberg presents the poem as a script for a vocal performance before a live audience rather than as a document to be read in solitary silence. Ginsberg claimed that these poetry readings bypassed what he called "the system of academic poetry, official reviews, New York publishing machinery, national sobriety and generally accepted standards of good taste," allowing his feelings to circulate free from editorial constraint.[28] In other words, reciting poetry in person allowed Ginsberg to situate the text as an intimate and unmediated communion. While we might look askance at Ginsberg's phonocentrism, he nevertheless draws on a long tradition of seeing oral performance as a more live and embodied way of experiencing literature. Reading aloud, Michel de Certeau suggests, has a distance-canceling effect. The premodern reader, who found silent reading so strange, "interiorized the text" by adopting its rhythm, allowing him to make "his voice the body of the other."[29] Ginsberg hoped to achieve a similar incorporation of the word.

Vocalizing the poem, he later asserted, functioned as a yogic exercise: the "rhythmic units" or breath-based lines of poems such as "Howl" "were basically breathing exercise forms which if anybody else repeated would catalyze in them the same *pranic* breathing physiological spasm that I was going through and so would presumably catalyze in them the same *affects* or emotions" (emphases original).[30] Whereas normative reading practices suspend and subdue the body, treating the reader as an invisible pair of eyes, Ginsberg trains the reader to approach the poem as respiratory, muscular, and sensational.[31] As Daniel Belgrad argues, the corporeal discipline of "Howl" and the physical changes it induces in the reader serve a larger project to defeat Moloch, the poem's symbol of corporate liberalism's alienation and self-estrangement.[32] By breathing someone else's breaths one could feel their feelings, overcoming the detached disposition toward others that characterized the midcentury PMC.

In some respects, Ginsberg's poetics appear to be an especially radical form of middlebrow personalism. As we have seen, middlebrow personalism presents reading as an empathy-inducing therapy for cerebral technocrats who feel like their work estranges them from others.[33] Through literature and culture, the PMC strives to erase the differences between themselves and the people they normally monitor and manage.[34] Thus, in Ginsberg's "Howl," there is always a slippage between witnessing the predicaments of the poem's hipsters and actually becoming them. For example, the speaker in "*Howl*" claims to be with Solomon in Rockland State Hospital, receiving shock therapy alongside him, offering a "gesture of wild solidarity" to the asylum inmate in a move that actually made the historical Solomon uncomfortable.[35] Here and throughout his work, Ginsberg theatricalizes the life-aesthetics of oppressed populations, translating them into posture that anyone including straight, white, middle-class readers might take up with the same ease as slipping into a yogic pose. Ginsberg cannibalizes Solomon's life especially, appropriating his phrases and metaphorizing him as Christ, an empty cipher for vicarious experience. Ginsberg's psychiatric history, marginalized sexual identity, and ethnic background all complicate this picture, certainly, but they do not undermine the fact that the poet shares with middle-class liberals the notion that material differences in power, wealth, and privilege can be resolved through artistically produced shifts in affect or consciousness.[36]

Once we begin to read Ginsberg's work as a protest internal to the PMC, we begin to see connections between his poetry and contemporary management fads such as sensitivity training. Drawing on Luc Boltanski and Eve Chiapello, Jasper Bernes argues that management science absorbed and acted on poetic critiques of its labor practices and organizational forms in the 1960s and 1970s. Management science provided capitalists with the impetus and justification to produce a more open, flexible, and participatory workplace that succeeded in blunting systemic opposition even as it demanded greater self-management and personal commitment from workers to increase productivity amid frequent layoffs and falling profits.[37] As we have seen, though, management did not always have to wait to coopt artistic critique because they often developed along parallel lines. During this period, artists and managers were both grappling with the same concerns.

Like the Beats, management scientists saw the value of greater openness to others. Training groups or "t-groups" were initially developed by National Training Laboratories in 1947 to offer group therapy focusing on interpersonal dynamics, but business managers soon turned to sensitivity-training methods to improve human relations.[38] T-group sessions used role reversal and other dramaturgical conceits—as well as an ethos of complete candor—to elicit deep, buried emotions from buttoned-down employees, who sobbed and raged among subordinates and colleagues. This shared experience allowed t-group members to forget that they were ranked in a bureaucratic hierarchy back at the office and to see each other instead as equals in the here and now. Although top-down orders were replaced with instantaneous feedback from fellow group members, power imbalances remained, and, in the cultlike atmosphere of these weekend retreats, managers achieved more control over employees than they ever could through more formalized, rational means. These results led William H. Whyte to hold up sensitivity training as a prime example of the conformist social ethic critiqued in *The Organization Man* (1956).[39]

Proponents of sensitivity training, on the other hand, emphasized what they saw as t-groups' more liberatory aspects. Popular sensitivity-training manuals such as *Behind the Executive Mask* stressed the technique's ability to foster greater "intimacy" between men even as it helped train more democratic managers.[40] *Playboy* magazine went as far as to contextualize sensitivity sessions for businessmen within a broader cultural shift "from the cerebral to spontaneous sensuality" that included orgasmic bioenergetic workshops, erotic massage, Norman O. Brown's philosophical hedonism, and tantric sex.[41] Some psychoanalytic critics feared the training had gone too far, arguing that trainers encouraged participants to give vent to sadistic and masochistic impulses while violating the privacy of other trainees.[42] Part of the appeal of sensitivity training was that it was bordering on transgressive, reenacting something like raw and improvisational performance art for use in the boardroom. Unbeknownst to Ginsberg, the business world already possessed its own culture of spontaneity.

When Ginsberg begins to talk about the reading body, however, he departs from managerial best practices and the Book-of-the-Month Club model of readerly identification. For Ginsberg, reading is an erotic and mystical commingling that crescendos in orgasm. In a coauthored essay, Ginsberg and Gregory Corso describe the famous first reading of "Howl" at Six Gallery in 1955 as reaching a "rhythmic crisis" and a "high peak of ecstatic elongation of the line structure," a formal and physical climax that leaves the audience weeping.[43] The audience's convulsions bring them into affective resonance with Ginsberg's body in part because they reenact the Beat poet's own composition process: Ginsberg is said to have incorporated masturbation and autoerotic fantasy into his writing routines.[44] Ginsberg's culmination would have arrived in the final lines of the poem, which describe the speaker as locked in an amorous embrace with Solomon that ends with an explosion of euphoria, which wakes them from their insulin comas, demolishes the hospital walls, and allows them to escape naked into the night. Beat reading becomes an orgiastic process, tearing down all of the emotional barriers thrown up by institutions to produce the same nondual experience described in mystical visions.

Ginsberg's orgiastic breath-poetics fall in line with the acting methods invented by Solomon's guiding light, Antonin Artaud.[45] Using a series of exercises Artaud terms "affective athleticism," actors are supposed to be able to reproduce the thoughts and feelings of their characters through controlled respiration.[46] According to the author of *The Theater and Its Double*, this works because "the soul can be physiologically reduced to a skein of vibrations."[47] When your vocal system reverberates with someone else's frequency, you become filled with their soul. Like Hefner's playmate, the Beat's body serves as a medium passing along the messages of others.

Despite inhabiting the feminine position in Hefner's schema, the Beat might have more in common with the playboy than it might seem. As Rachel Blau DuPlessis has pointed out, while Ginsberg offers a more unconstrained vision of what it means to be a man, he does so within an exclusively masculine intimate sphere. The "homosocial wildness" of the Beats allowed them greater freedom at the expense of those they imitated in their performances: "To have maleness shift to absorb feminization, sexual 'deviance,' and otherness is a very large social gain in ranges of subjectivity—for men."[48] The Beats scorned effeminate homosexuals and relegated women to stereotyped roles such as scold or sex object even as they laid claim to unconventionally gendered forms of emotional receptivity.

Not all of the Beats were enraptured with the possibility of becoming media technology. For Burroughs, this often means imagining the body as a protoplasmic gel, whose colloidal properties allow it to be imprinted with information patterns—engrams and language viruses—that overwrite the subject's own personality in a form of possession.[49] Burroughs therefore tended to figure this form of total union with others in abject terms: he often imaged one body absorbing another in what he called "schlupping": "a blind worm hunger to enter the other's body, to breathe with his lungs, see with his eyes, learn the feel of his viscera and genitals."[50]

Although this language was usually reserved for penetrative sexual encounters, the Beats also applied it to editors who might violate the integrity of their famously unrevised manuscripts. While working as an editor for Ace Books, Solomon betrayed the intended meaning of Burroughs's manuscript of *Junkie* by combining it in a tête-bêche edition with *Narcotic Agent* by Maurice Helbrant, a true-life memoir of a retired Federal Bureau of Narcotics operative, and by prefacing the main text with a moralizing statement that recast Burroughs's novel as an antidrug screed.[51] In a later edition of the book, published by Penguin under the name *Junky*, Ginsberg describes this violation as the work of the "schlupp publishing industry."[52] The editor threatens to become an obscene textual parasite invading the authorial host.

More typically, though, Ginsberg prefers to describe communication channels using the language of "angelology," a discourse that envisions a perfect media system composed of faithful and selfless intermediaries, whose sole purpose is to provide a channel for someone else's messages.[53] While the angels of orthodox religion tend to dematerialize to assure noiseless transmissions, Ginsberg's "angelheaded hipsters ... who blew and were blown by human seraphim" form a spiritual daisy chain that allows each angel to pass along breath and other fluids.[54] Ultimately, Ginsberg's poetic project comes down to the image of two or more bodies coinciding in the same space in "unlimited intimacy," as when the protagonists of his poem "let themselves be fucked in the ass by saintly motorcyclists."[55] Although this may sound like base materialism, Ginsberg sees queer sociality as an inspired exchange that overcomes all of the distortions of linguistic, technical, and even corporeal mediation.[56]

Ginsberg's performance at Six Gallery would put him into close contact with another angel and, ultimately, launch him into stardom. Although Ferlinghetti had already been planning to publish a collection of Ginsberg's work, this reading is often recounted as his breakthrough moment: cast as the Emerson to Ginsberg's Whitman, Ferlinghetti is said to have written him by telegram the day afterward: "I greet you at the beginning of a great career—When do I get manuscript of *Howl*?"⁵⁷ While this story may have been apocryphal, it is nevertheless true that the Six Gallery reading accelerated the publishing timeline for Ginsberg's poetry.⁵⁸

Ferlinghetti became so crucial to spreading Ginsberg's words to others that the poet later took time out of a psychedelic trip to send him a letter bearing this invocation:

> O what a great working seraph you are to be there in the faraway, holding your faith 3000 miles for years waiting for me to send message, book, I wanted to send you something sublime—naked mama or trumpet of divinity—anything beyond materialist illusions—and I wish I could thank you for when I envision you like that so kind a messenger, making secure [sic] the communication gets sent across cold Atlantics and vast empty voids so men can know someone is guarding the signal and the great impulses of being are really sent back and forth by the specters of this dimension who are gathering to decide what to do with the cosmos, whether to recognize the vast image of being and publish it to all gathered consciousness.⁵⁹

This passage points to a common trope among other San Francisco Renaissance authors such as Robert Duncan and Jack Spicer, for whom the angel functions as a symbol of hovering between "multiple worlds," an experience of "physical and metaphysical in-between-ness."⁶⁰ Ferlinghetti must cross over between queer and straight, Beat and square, author and audience, aesthetic disinterest and economic interest.⁶¹ In this journey, the editor must live up to the promise of evangelizing on behalf of the author while risking a descent into the noise of the surveilled market. When *Howl and Other Poems* was initially published, however, Ferlinghetti did not always seem like a perfect go-between for the poet's words. To get past censors, Ferlinghetti was forced to reinterpret Ginsberg's book in ways that often departed from the author's poetic aspirations, including his vision of angelic communion through spoken poetry.

A Legal Defense of Poetry

Ferlinghetti anticipated early on that *Howl* would have trouble with the law.⁶² Before publishing *Howl and Other Poems*, the editor asked the American Civil Liberties Union to represent him gratis and convinced Ginsberg to replace some of the profanities in "Howl" with ellipses. As they expected, the San Francisco

Collector of Customs confiscated copies from the second run of *Howl*, shipped from their English printer. When the ACLU announced that it would contest the seizure, however, the US attorney in San Francisco decided against filing condemnation proceedings. This was only a short reprieve. A few days after the books were released, two investigators from the San Francisco Police Department's juvenile bureau visited City Lights Books to buy a copy of *Howl* from store manager Shigeyoshi "Shig" Murao. Ferlinghetti and Murao were charged with obscenity and taken into custody. After posting bail, the ACLU arranged for lawyers Lawrence Speiser and Albert Bendich, along with celebrity trial lawyer Jacob W. Ehrlich, to represent Ferlinghetti and Murao pro bono. The court quickly dropped Murao's case because the prosecution could not establish that he was aware of *Howl*'s contents before he sold it. Ferlinghetti, however, went on to be tried by Judge Clayton W. Horn.

More than free speech was at stake in the *Howl* trial: *California v. Ferlinghetti* represents just one battle in a long campaign of state surveillance and repression of homosexuality.[63] Judging homosexuality a crime, censors subjected publications addressing gay and lesbian audiences or themes to greater scrutiny than their heterosexual counterparts. This legal double standard can be seen most clearly in *One, Inc. v. Oleson* (1958), a case fought by the homophile magazine, *One*. Delayed by lengthy postal inspections and cognizant of the risk they faced, *One* asked attorney Eric Julber to formulate a list of guidelines that editors could follow to avoid prosecution.[64] When readers protested the magazine's new reticence, *One* published an explanation of the rules in the October 1954 issue, under the headline "You Can't Print It!" Noting that "what is permissible in heterosexual literature is not permissible in *One*'s context," the magazine stated that it could no longer publish personal ads, "cheesecake" art, direct descriptions or indirect allusions to homosexual acts, endorsements of homosexuality, and even "fiction with too much physical contact between characters."[65]

Even these stringent precautions did not save the magazine from obscenity charges: Los Angeles postmaster Otto K. Oleson seized that very issue and *One* spent nearly four years in court.[66] Although the magazine boasted nothing more salacious than a short story featuring a lesbian kiss and a doggerel poem with jokes about being "goosed" in the public toilet, *One* was initially found guilty of obscenity.[67] They narrowly succeeded in winning the case only when the Supreme Court overturned the ruling under *Roth* in a per curiam decision. While the justices never recorded their thinking on this topic—the case was not argued in court, and the ruling took up all of a sentence—their clerks' notes reflect mixed opinions, acknowledging that many straight-oriented magazines were far more explicit than *One* while also expressing discomfort with its contents.[68] This decision heartened the homophile community, but it passed largely unnoticed elsewhere and did little to stop continuing prosecutions of gay and lesbian media.[69]

The *Howl* trial must be read against this background. While many accounts present the *Howl* trial as a triumph of poets over philistines, separated from broader questions of sexual politics, *One* magazine columnist Dal McIntire put the prosecution in the context of a crackdown on homosexuals in San Francisco, including the suspension of the liquor license of the Black Cat bar, the dismissal of school and other state employees on moral grounds, and a series of vagrancy charges targeting homosexuals.[70] In all likelihood, *Howl* was seized not merely because it depicted sex but because it depicted queer sex.

Ferlinghetti ultimately won his case, and the judge handed down a decision widely celebrated as an unambiguous victory for free expression. Legal scholar William Eskridge writes that "*Howl* was a raucous, sodomy-saturated, mocking attack on conformity in general and closeted sexuality in particular, and Horn's opinion said this was precisely what the first amendment protects."[71] However, the trial transcripts and the decision itself reveal something very different. The poem's defenders skirt the issue of sodomy while ignoring the erotic reading practices advocated by its author. In *California v. Ferlinghetti*, the defense succeeded because they were able to downplay its queerness and enlist *Howl and Other Poems* into the service of a paranoid reading style that was fast becoming the dominant literary-reading method of university English departments.

From the beginning, Ferlinghetti's lawyer Ehrlich emphasizes that he is discussing the book itself and not the poems' oral renditions. Ehrlich first draws on the book's paratexts in his opening statement, when he reads the entirety of its cover to the court:

> Let us stop with the cover. Is there anything about this book that indicates that there is something in it that will destroy the moral tenor of the community or do anything which would lead to a moral breakdown of the people of this City, to say nothing of Police Officer Woods?[72]

It is true: no one could mistake the book jacket of *Howl* for smut. As salacious as a cold shower, the cover reads as forbidding and austere. City Lights Books clearly lifted its design aesthetic from Berthold Wolpe, who worked at Faber and Faber under T. S. Eliot. The cover features a stark, unadorned, black-and-white design with the title set in Wolpe's Albertus font, a typeface based on rubbings of bronze memorial tablets.[73] A handwritten or typewritten document can easily be changed, but a metal inscription is not so readily effaced or emended, lending the typeface a sense of permanence and monumentality. Albertus's history and connotations run counter to Beat poetics: whereas Albertus derives from eternal epitaphs for the dead, Ginsberg of course claims to model his work on jazz, a spontaneous performance outside of any accepted institution. By pointing to the cover, Ehrlich bracketed the sensational poetry events where Ginsberg first presented "Howl," disassociating the book from Ginsberg's Dionysiac oral renditions and resituating it within a more august and academic literary tradition.

The book, the defense suggests, demands to be read in a different way from its oral performances. To salvage *Howl* from the censors, Ferlinghetti and his team reinterpreted the text using paranoid reading protocols. Freud argues that paranoia functions a mechanism for repressing homosexual desire. The paranoid, unable to come to terms with his forbidden fantasies, transforms his unconscious love for the same-sex object into hate, a feeling that is then projected back onto the object of desire. By externalizing his aggression, the paranoid rationalizes his inordinate hostility toward the man who has elicited these conflicted responses in him: "I do not *love* him—I *hate* him, because HE PERSECUTES ME."[74] Guy Hocquenghem reconfigures Freud's analysis to argue that antihomosexual paranoia constitutes a social structure rather than an individual pathology. As Freud observes, sociality itself possesses a libidinal dimension: there is an "erotic factor to friendship and comradeship, to *esprit de corps* and to the love of mankind in general."[75] To prevent male homosocial relations from becoming desublimated as homoerotic love, repressive institutions such as the police and the state mobilize paranoia to attack homosexuals as members of a nefarious "conspiracy" dedicated to destroying society itself.[76] In both cases, we see paranoia as a strategy for neutralizing obscene desires.

Working within a somewhat different theoretical framework, Eve Kosofsky Sedgwick also theorizes paranoia as a response that avoids positive affects to focus on negative ones.[77] Sedgwick's paranoid turns out to be the literary critic who spends their time undermining any text that might appear to afford the reader pleasure by revealing it to be the product of vast, totalizing systems built on power and violence. By disavowing all hope and anticipating every risk, the paranoid reader avoids being caught unawares. The literary critic is thus able to maintain the pretense of knowing everything in advance, albeit at the expense of actually enjoying or learning anything.

We see both of these senses of paranoia operating in tandem in the defense team's attempts to desexualize Ginsberg's poetry during the *Howl* trial. While Ginsberg's poetics began from a commitment to recognizing and fostering queer sociality, Ferlinghetti was forced to preempt the homoeroticism of "Howl" by recasting the entire text as a persecution fantasy and undercutting the text's sensualism using the hermeneutics of suspicion.[78] During the trial, the Moloch passages in the second section served as the key to retroactively understanding the poem's more sexually explicit images in the first section. As a result, while Ginsberg presented his poetry as a reparative gesture that would undo the cold mental abstraction of postwar culture, Ferlinghetti reframed "Howl" as a morbid symptom of bureaucratic, capitalist alienation.

In a statement to the *San Francisco Chronicle* following the seizure of copies of *Howl*, the editor writes that the poem is "a gestalt, an archetypal configuration of the mass culture that produced it."[79] According to this gloss, Ginsberg correlates and combines the fragments of a degraded society to convey the disorder of "official culture," and this is precisely what so outrages "officials":

> In condemning ["Howl"] . . . they are condemning their own American world. For it is not the poet but what he observes which is revealed as obscene. The great obscene wastes of "Howl" are the sad wastes of the mechanized world, lost among atom bombs and insane nationalisms, billboards and TV antennae.[80]

Ferlinghetti initially seems to equivocate between affirming and rejecting the poem's homoeroticism. At first it appears that he could be suggesting that the poem's representations of violence should be considered far more objectionable, far more obscene, than any representation of sexuality. City Lights author Kenneth Patchen says as much when he suggests that words like "hate" and "bomb" are "the really obscene four-letter words."[81] As Ferlinghetti's defense of Ginsberg unfolds, however, it becomes clear that the editor is reading the poem's homoeroticism as another symptom of social illness. He likens Ginsberg's explicitness to Walt Whitman's sexual candor but then lumps them together along with Francisco Goya's bloody war prints in a category of works that reflect "a world . . . you wouldn't want your children to come across."[82]

Legally and socially discouraged from making a case for queer liberation, the poem's defenders reinterpret the pleasure in the poem as a sign of some deeper social trauma, steadfastly ignoring the possibility that Ginsberg's poem could bring readers into homoerotic communion with one another.[83] Joining Ferlinghetti in speaking on behalf of Ginsberg, William Carlos Williams argues that the poem's aim is to expose shameful secrets to the well-known disinfecting properties of "air and sun"—"the only thing in our lives to which the young can look to keep virtuous."[84] Without saying it outright, Ferlinghetti's defense makes a play for redeeming social value by casting homosexual desire as an indictment of the bankrupt society from which it emerges.

The implicit connection between homosexuality and social dysfunction would have been clear to readers at the time. Throughout the 1950s, popular sociologists wrote bestsellers warning that conformity threatened American heterosexual masculinity. Whether they called this phenomenon the social ethic or the other-directed personality, critics agreed that oversocialization rendered men too pliable and ingratiating to others. Now that middle-class American men had given up the tough independence of small-business ownership to work for someone else in offices where they were required to be increasingly responsive to social signals, they had abandoned their rugged individualism and had become "soft" in stereotypically feminine or emasculated ways.[85] Sensitivity training was making men *too* sensitive.

As Timothy Melley has argued, critics responded to this imagined predicament with increasing paranoia.[86] Despite growing scientific and empirical evidence of social influences on human behavior, cold war liberals remained ideologically committed to the idea that they were rational, free individuals. Unable to abandon their belief in the liberal subject, critics were backed into an "all-or-nothing conception of agency" that placed control in either individual sovereignty or all-powerful totalitarian systems.[87] If individuals were not rational agents with complete freedom to choose for themselves, the only alternative was that every thought and action must be preprogrammed by a single, seamless, all-pervasive organization—a Moloch. Because liberal individualism had always been coded as masculine, these conspiracy theories read dominant social structures as "*feminizing* forces, domesticating powers that violate the borders of the autonomous self, penetrating, inhabiting and controlling it from within."[88]

If Ginsberg presents an obscene vision of queer sociality in "Howl," Ferlinghetti's defense must counter with the paranoid theory that society itself is a dangerous threat to the individual. The liberal subject, compromised by mass society and anal sex, loses its integrity, making it unable to consent or refuse. In his analysis of the trial of *Naked Lunch* by Burroughs, Tyler Bradway shows that presenting queer sexuality as an involuntary fantasy or hallucination worked as a powerful defense against obscenity charges.[89] Homosexuality therefore becomes in the *Howl* trial a violation forced on the poem's speaker by Moloch rather than something that he takes part in willingly: society made me do it!

Needless to say, Ginsberg would have disagreed with this reading of his poem. He complained that critical response to his and Kerouac's work consisted of "nothing but lame sociological bullshit."[90] But by this point Ginsberg was thousands of miles away, traveling Tangiers, Morocco, and he never took the stand on behalf of his publisher. While the attorneys and witnesses sometimes speculated on Ginsberg's intentions, his authorial voice remained absent from the proceedings.

During the trial, Ferlinghetti's defense continued to follow the editor in reading the entire poem as a high-minded social critique, one that, according to the defense witnesses, proceeds through a modern retelling of Dante's *Inferno*. Here the defense seems to be inspired by the book's preface by Williams, which ends with a playful warning: "Hold back the edges of your gowns, Ladies, we are going through hell."[91] By speaking in the hidden scare quotes of camp, Williams's warning enacts a common queer anti-censorship strategy: one can read him as either condemning Ginsberg's queer themes as hellish or teasing the readership for considering it as such.

We see very similar moves in contemporary gay-themed periodicals, such as physique magazines, which were edited to appeal to readers in an ambiguous and doubled way. Rather than simply suppressing or bowdlerizing illicit materials, editors placed them within ironic interpretive contexts that allowed for both obscene and chaste readings by queer and straight audiences.[92] Through editorial paratexts, even pornographic images were made to elicit divergent reading practices from multiple audiences, providing queer readers the plausible deniability of straight readings.

However, upon taking the stand the defense's star witness—English professor Mark Schorer—ignored the campiness of Williams's statement and instead accepted it as a literal appraisal of the novel. When confronted with the poem's homoerotic images, he suggested that they reflected the poem's "impression of a world in which all sexuality is confused and corrupted"—"modern life as a state of hell."[93] Author Vincent McHugh echoed Williams and Schorer in his testimony, reading the poem as "a vision of a modern hell" with a literary genealogy that extends from Dante and the *Odyssey* through Ezra Pound's fourteenth and fifteenth *Cantos*.[94] While Ginsberg's work did show a greater affinity for the modernists than he would often admit, the difference between "Howl" and Pound's Dante pastiche would have seemed immediately obvious to many readers. In the *Cantos*, as in the *Inferno*, Pound consigns his enemies to eternal torment, placing hated politicians, publishers, usurers, and philologists underneath a "great arse-hole" that rains filth down on them until they are ultimately submerged.[95] Pound's hell fails to disturb his readers because, as Eliot averred, it is reserved "for the *other people*, the people we read about in the newspapers, not for oneself and one's friends."[96] Nothing could be further from Ginsberg's professions of adhesive love for Solomon and the other sufferers in his poems.

Regardless of what the author might think, the defense persisted in reading the poem as a rendition of the *Inferno* because Dante's poem represents an architectonic structure in which even individual moments of extreme depravity are subsumed under its overarching theological and formal designs. Midcentury obscenity law depended on evaluating publications based on the work as a whole rather than on isolated passages, a legal doctrine that encouraged strong theories with pretensions to totalizing, explanatory power. The paranoid style of literary interpretation allowed the defense to justify otherwise offensive or controversial lines in the poem by subordinating them to the rest of the text, and, ultimately, to the broader social and historical context. After all, as Sedgwick suggested, the paranoid armed with a theory of everything cannot be shocked by anything.[97]

Indeed, this paranoid method of literary criticism arose out of historical conditions of censorship. Susan Sontag later argued that what would come to be known as the hermeneutics of suspicion emerged as a technique for salvaging canceled texts: when a text's literal meaning becomes objectionable, interpreters revise the text by inventing for it a new hidden meaning located below its embarrassing surface features.[98] The erotic images of the Song of Songs become the vehicles of spiritual metaphor.[99] In the process, interpretation intellectualizes artwork, drawing the reader away from art's sensual properties toward its otherworldly ideas.[100] While Sontag deplores interpretation's deadening influence on the senses, the defense promoted this effect to counteract the homoeroticism of Ginsberg's poems, lift them out of the bohemian underworld of the Beats, and install them safely in the literature seminar room.

Perhaps the most paranoid interpretation of the poem was delivered by Leo Lowenthal, a Berkeley literary sociologist who studied at the Frankfurt School. In his testimony Lowenthal draws ideas from his book *Literature and the Image of Man*, which traces the history of the individual from its emergence in the early modern period through its decline in the modern era. The individual, formed in the wake of feudalism, now faces liquidation by an increasingly totalitarian social system.[101] His reading of Ginsberg's "Howl" placed the poem near the end of this historical process: the speaker of the poem sets off on a doomed quest for "self-identification," striving but failing to find himself and to achieve "fulfillment by friendship and love."[102]

Although Ginsberg would have undoubtedly endorsed Lowenthal's dark predictions concerning the crisis of the individual—his reading practices seek to rectify this problem—the notion that the individual was a vanishing social construct completely contradicted Ginsberg's anthropology, which championed what he called "unconditioned individuality."[103] Lowenthal and Ginsberg's views on literature are shaped by fundamentally different approaches. Whereas Ginsberg seeks to reground poetry in the particularity of concrete experience and face-to-face community, the defense encourages a typological reading that sees each of the poem's figures as a token representative of vast sociological categories. Ferlinghetti's witnesses save Ginsberg's poetry by reproducing through it the same invidious abstractions that the poet had worked so hard to counteract.

Judge Horn's decision ratified the defense team's literary interpretations. According to Judge Horn, the ramblings of the hipsters in part I of the poem paint a "picture of a nightmare world."[104] Like most paranoid interpretations, the Moloch reading of "Howl" precludes upsetting surprises but only at the expense of any possibility of pleasure or joy. As disappointing as these feats of interpretation might be, they were legally necessary because they provided coverage for Ginsberg's illicit sexuality. Paranoid interpretation allowed the defense to deny what often seems obvious and blatant in *Howl and Other Poems*. When Ehrlich was faced with questions about "America," a poem that designates its speaker as "queer," he leaned on witnesses' readings of "Howl." Quoting lines that suggest the speaker suffers from some unnamed and perhaps unspeakable malady, Ehrlich emphasizes his abject state at "the bottom of the pit," arguing that

> your Honor can't feel that anguished cry nor can I. We cannot understand it. We have never lived his life. A man doesn't know the pain of a toothache unless he has a toothache. In love with your life and devoted to her, you still cannot share or feel her toothache.[105]

Although the "zone of privacy" surrounding heterosexual intimacy would not be established until *Griswold v. Connecticut* in 1965, the principle here is much the same: the court's later privacy doctrine allowed greater autonomy for heteronormative sex while maintaining state regulations of homosexuality.[106] Following a similar reasoning, Ehrlich attempts to save Ginsberg's implicit homosexual tendencies from charges of obscenity through a comparison to the inviolable personality of a man's long-suffering wife. In other words, Ehrlich represents the love that dares not speak its name through an analogy with the problem that has no name.

This argument suggests that homosexuality is permissible only if it remains closeted and subtextual—a private and inexpressible disease that presents in public as straight as June Cleaver. Even the paranoid reader—who presumes to know everything in advance—cannot gaze into the closet in Ehrlich's reading. The erotic communion Ginsberg officiated over in his poetry readings is dismissed as impossible. In short, Ferlinghetti's defense team saved *Howl* by completely discounting its poetics.

Did the Liberals Believe in Their Myths?

Ferlinghetti's defense reinterpreted "Howl" as a case study in how even the most intimate aspects of the self could be permeated and colonized by the social system represented by Moloch. As we begin to look carefully at the trial, however, it becomes clear that the defense team is part of the same paranoid system its members are critiquing. Far from presenting their own individualized interpretations of the text, the defense lawyers and witnesses converge on a consensus that comports fully with existing sexual and legal norms. Like the other-directed personalities and organization men of popular sociology, the defense conforms to the expectations of those in power. They follow along perfectly with the editorial paratexts that framed the book—and yet it is clear that they do not fully believe what they are saying.

Despite the self-seriousness of Ferlinghetti's defense witnesses, the trial transpired amid a circus atmosphere. Laughter sporadically erupted from the gallery while witness testimony took on an unreal tenor. At one point, Judge Horn was forced to admonish spectators that "we are not playing games."[107] This mood was due in no small part to the influence of Ferlinghetti's star lawyer, Ehrlich, who was given to showboating and grandstanding. Journalists described Ehrlich as a flamboyant lawyer: he led a glamorous career, defending celebrities such as Errol Flynn, Howard Hughes, and Billie Holliday with a success rate that earned him the nickname "The Master." A consummate actor, Ehrlich had a penchant for histrionic speeches—often moving jurors to laughter and tears—and this helped him achieve local fame and later national recognition as the inspiration for television courtroom dramas such as *Sam Benedict*. Even before *Howl*, Ehrlich had demonstrated his flair for the dramatic in the obscenity trial of nude fan-dancer Sally Rand, in which he invited the court to watch her burlesque performance at a nightclub, an act that convinced the court she was not guilty. For Ehrlich, the trial was not just theater—it was show business. With his oversized reputation, Ehrlich became something of a playboy, often seen wearing flashy jewelry and entertaining women on lunch dates.[108] A creature of his own publicity, Ehrlich reveled in the changeable and contradictory personae he projected. As he wrote in *A Life in My Hands: An Autobiography*, "I am content to let the public images, like changing wraiths in a spectral fantasy, assume whatever form they will. As long as there *is* an image, I know that I am alive and effective and a part of this town and the life I love."[109]

In this regard, Ehrlich shared the same ethos as many cold war liberals who, as Michael Trask has shown, pursued an "epistemology of make-believe."[110] Refusing all foundations and firm, fixed ideologies, liberalism chose instead to engage in "collusive play-acting," pretending to hold whatever positions their roles required.[111] According to Andrea Most, liberalism casts the ideal individual as "theatrical, anti-essentialist, mobile, focused on exterior modes of self-presentation, capable of shucking off history and tradition and being repeatedly born anew."[112] Privileging performative expediency over permanent commitment, cold war liberals held that only communists were true believers. Liberalism's show-stopping theatricality shines brightest during obscenity trials. As a matter of course, free speech libertarians were called on to feign adherence to very traditional ideas about art, opportunistically exploiting the language of high culture and moral propriety. In *California v. Ferlinghetti* and other obscenity trials, the absurdity of this situation often comes through, with defense witnesses acting in exceedingly ironic and facile ways.

Given the pervasiveness of cynicism among witnesses and jurists, it is obvious that this is not simply a matter of individual bad faith. Citizens in court must don what Milner S. Ball calls the "persona juris," the mask of the law, a role that allows them to engage in the public drama of the legal system while protecting their own privacy.[113] This social and legal fiction gives lawyers like Ehrlich the license to present arguments on behalf of their clients even if they do not personally believe in the relevant law or their own arguments.

Paul Goodman argues that this kind of cynicism was endemic to postwar culture. American society had become "a rat race" in "an apparently closed room," a frantic but self-contained world that permitted no values, goals, or perspectives beyond it.[114] The paranoid subjects that he called "hipsters" played along with this game without believing it.[115] They were masters at making themselves over to whatever the organization or institution required at the moment even if they prided themselves in knowing that it was all merely a performance. The hip attitude taken up by the disaffected middle classes further allows them to resign themselves to the disappointments of a sterile and inauthentic existence, which, at the very least, come as no surprise to them.

The obscenity trial—which forced its participants to take up positions at variance with their private beliefs—therefore became an exercise at the kind of roleplaying that was inescapable in professional-managerial occupations. These skills would only become more important for the workforce that, according to Paolo Virno, now negotiates the economic turbulence of post-Fordism by relying on opportunism (the capacity to respond nimbly to ever-shifting possibilities) and cynicism (the capacity to treat these varying situations as so many arbitrary games).[116] Realizing the goal of sensitivity training, the virtuosic worker must rapidly modulate their social performances based on instantaneous feedback.[117] Ferlinghetti's protean lawyer turns out to prefigure a way of being that would come to dominate the PMC.

The defense's commanding performances win the court over but only at the cost of evacuating its own arguments of any real substance. Nobody in the court seemed to believe that obscenity was real in the first place. Co-counsel Bendich later characterized the prevailing obscenity doctrine of the time as "silliness," favoring instead a clear-and-present-danger test.[118] Bendich was not alone: during his closing arguments, Ehrlich expressed open skepticism about obscenity law. Even the prosecutor, Ralph McIntosh, seemed uninvested in the trial's outcome.[119] In this and many other obscenity trials, there is a sense that both sides are going through the motions, pretending to believe in the idea that a book might represent a grave threat to the individual and the community even as they read excerpts of the book aloud again and again. As Ehrlich put it, "It is interesting that the person applying such standards in censorship never feels his own physical or moral health in jeopardy."[120] Obscenity prosecutions could never work if obscenity actually caused any harm.

The *Roth* test that they used to determine if *Howl* was obscene betrays liberalism's depthless deference to accepted norms. Obscenity law has proved so slippery in part because some of its key terms ("average person" and "contemporary community standards") remain empty, reflecting cold war liberals' desire to uphold public decency without positing firm, foundational morals. The *Roth* test is not a fixed list of prohibited words, images, or messages but, rather, a flexible procedure that asks judges and juries to interpret literature as if they were "average" citizens applying to media whatever mores their community maintains at that place and time—regardless of their own aesthetic sensibilities or moral convictions. The Warren court thereby replaced an outmoded and unresponsive Comstockery with a thoroughly tolerant and pluralistic form of state censorship capable of taking into account divergent and ever-evolving notions of decency to repress relative sexual deviance.[121]

When obscenity ceases to reflect any innate essence, it becomes purely performative. Given the rarity of actually offended parties in the courtroom, obscenity trials tend to take place almost entirely in this subjunctive or speculative mode, with the prosecution donning the face of an imagined victim and the defense playing the part of the author, editor, and ideal reader. Neither Ginsberg nor Ferlinghetti ever needed to take the stand because Ehrlich could do their voices. Even the existence of obscenity itself required a willing suspension of disbelief: judges, lawyers, and commentators frequently admitted that there was little or no concrete evidence for a causal connection between pornography and antisocial conduct, and yet they proceeded to support censorship under the presumption that a link could conceivably exist. If obscenity trials did not carry the threat of jail time, they would seem like an elaborate game of "let's pretend."

Obviously, the Beats and the mainstream liberals differ in their acting techniques. While liberals maintain what Richard Rorty terms a "private irony" or a disjuncture between inner doubts and outer speech acts, the Beats work to cancel the difference between the public and private spheres through the group bibliotherapy of the poetry performance.[122] Despite any personal misgivings, liberals were willing to sacrifice sexual minorities to achieve free speech policy goals. Indeed, throughout the Warren years, liberal legal strategists chose to make precedents that carved out narrow exceptions to laws restricting sexuality and reproductive rights while also acceding to the primacy of the heteronormative family.[123] But, when the Beats and their allies seem to be playing along with the logic of state homophobia, they make it known that they do so under duress.

We see this clearly in Ginsberg's testimony in the 1966 trial of *Naked Lunch*. An amused commentator observed afterward that Ginsberg seemed to be "'camping' to some extent, putting the court on by answering questions in precisely the sort of school-marmish, bad-Arnoldian jargon the court obviously requires."[124] Embracing the artifice of camp, Ginsberg registers his protest by embarrassing the court with the hip kind of put-on that Jacob Brackman would call "relentless agreement": he reveals the pretentiousness of the proceedings by parroting back the court's stereotyped assumptions using the phoniest language possible.[125]

We might understand Ginsberg's self-canceling testimony as a specific example of a larger strategy of emotional-labor sabotage. Goodman complained that Beats often adopted an "expressionless mask-face," performing social roles in such a way that clearly demonstrated they were emotionally and mentally checked out.[126] We might compare this move to what flight attendants call "going into robot," a state of occupational alienation in which emotional workers allow their smiles to grow vacant and cease to hide the fact that they are merely pretending to like their customers.[127] While some Beat performances established relations of queer intimacy, others travestied the inauthenticity of straight society.

We see this same refusal to pretend not to pretend in Ginsberg's poetry. The speaker in "America" begins the poem as a dope-smoking pink, but he becomes "obsessed" with *Time* magazine, and, following the Beat habit of becoming what they read, he realizes that he, too, is America.[128] At this point, the poem shifts, and he begins channeling the voices of America, speaking in a more frantic tone. Moving past parody, Ginsberg protests America by making unavoidable the exhausting affective labor required to mimic and maintain normalcy. He may not be employable in the army or the factory, but he is still forced to put his "queer shoulder to the wheel."[129] As in "Howl," Ginsberg's protagonist takes on the same zany quality that Sianne Ngai so aptly describes.[130] If Hefner's playboys registered the personal cost of labor-time's subsumption of leisure by collapsing into immobility, Ginsberg protests the same through frenetic overexertion. At first Ginsberg shows off his virtuosity—like Ehrlich he is an expert at impression management, capable of becoming anyone—but he quickly becomes exasperated by the demands of a post-Fordist regime that requires him to quick-change between discrepant roles and to mass-produce strophes like an automobile assembly line.[131] Whereas cold war liberals prided themselves on the effortlessness of their personal transformations, Ginsberg's poetry makes clear that he is drained—beat—by the "deep acting" required by emotional labor.[132]

We can see this same sense of dejection in Ginsberg's personal correspondence. Publication left Ginsberg feeling "more depressed than pleased": "*Howl* seems like a drop in the bucket-void and literary furor illusory—seems like its [sic] happening in otherland—outside me, nothing to do with me or anything."[133] The censorship of his work in San Francisco "seemed faraway."[134] Ginsberg's melancholic detachment from the publication persisted while his writing career took an almost Burroughsian turn, overwhelming and consuming the author. As Ginsberg later told Ferlinghetti, "Fame or notoriety seems to invade my personality like a cancer, I develop an alternate self as author of *Howl*, and that's an absolute bringdown—you have no idea."[135] For the Beats, publication spelled the death of the author, the moment in which their personas and writing were plucked from the semiprivate circuits of letters, journals, and poetry reading and were thrown into a publishing world where they circulated beyond their control.[136] The published work becomes a simulation of the author's manuscript, the same but somehow subtly alien.

It is no wonder, then, that Ginsberg viewed mainstream publishing as implicated in self-censorship and subterfuge, practices considered anathema to the Beat sensibility. He saw this in one of his key visions, which he experienced while reading William Blake's "The Human Abstract" at the Columbia University bookstore. Looking around, he felt that everyone in the store was privy to the open secret of the "great unconscious" connecting all people, and yet they hid that knowledge by donning "fixed expressions" like "masks" and performing conventional "roles."[137]

Most notable among these dissemblers was a previously unremarkable clerk, who appears in Ginsberg's hallucination as a "great, tormented soul" with a hidden love life.[138] Bookselling becomes a kind of cosmic passing: "The position that everybody was in was *ridiculous*, everybody running around peddling books to each other."[139] Here, dealing in books becomes a symbol for "a vast antinatural psyche," "a shutting off of the perception of desire and tenderness which everybody *knows*," motivated by "fear" and "self-consciousness."[140] While Ginsberg ties this experience to cold war paranoia, the poet's vision seems to be an indictment of a publishing industry governed by the epistemology of the closet.[141] Ginsberg's prophecy came true. Censorship law and public censure would push many publishers to reject the Beats' manuscripts out of hand while forcing those who did publish their books to perform straightness for their audiences, dissimulating what they knew and felt about their publications. This proves to be a specific example of a larger problem in the publishing industry, which relied on appealing to more mainstream audiences even when they were printing transgressive texts. As we shall see when we turn to Grove Press, these circumstances sometimes compelled even the most avant-garde of trade book publishers to compromise their political ideals.

6 White-Collar Masochism

BETWEEN ITS FOUNDING in 1947 and its labor crisis in 1970, Grove Press became the epicenter of radical politics and culture. A major translator of late modernism and the avant-garde, Grove introduced US audiences to the theater of the absurd and the Nouveau Roman, publishing authors as important and far ranging as Samuel Beckett and Jorge Luis Borges. During the same period, the press served as a vehicle for revolutionary thought, printing Frantz Fanon, Malcolm X, Fidel Castro, and Ho Chi Minh. Meanwhile, Grove made its mark on domestic policy, championing freedom of expression in a series of obscenity court cases defending its publication of *Lady Chatterley's Lover* by D. H. Lawrence (1959), *Tropic of Cancer* by Henry Miller (1961), and *Naked Lunch* by William S. Burroughs (1962). Grove's legal success allowed it to become a premiere publishing house of philosophical and not-so-philosophical pornography, coming out with landmark editions of the Marquis de Sade's work. Under editor and owner Barney Rosset, who purchased the press in 1951, Grove constituted a nexus of aesthetic experimentation, left-wing politics, and literary erotica, a configuration unthinkable in mainstream publishing today.

Many of Grove's most famous works were reprints or translations of books published overseas—legally or illegally—but it brought them together in a new constellation that appealed to a different American audience.[1] Although, like most publishers, Grove did not track its readers, it did carry out a readership survey for the press's house magazine, *Evergreen Review*.[2] The magazine and press shared editorial staff—Rosset topped the masthead—and the magazine featured excerpts and selections from virtually all major Grove authors. As Rosset states, he "wanted to tie *Evergreen Review* to Grove Press as much as possible."[3] The editorial discourse in *Evergreen Review* therefore reflects how the press saw itself. Using research from Marketing Data Inc., the press described the average subscriber in 1966 as "a 39-year-old male, married, two children, a college graduate who holds a managerial position in business or industry, and has a median family income of $12,875," which is $102,115.44 in 2020 US dollars.[4] An astounding 90 percent of *Evergreen*'s subscribers were men, and, while the survey does not state it outright, their high salaries and supervisory roles suggest that Grove's readership was also predominately white.[5] Surprisingly, the survey revealed the average Grove reader as a member of the professional-managerial class, "'sold out' types" who hardly fit the image of the austere militant or hedonistic youth projected by the magazine's contents.[6] Although the press undoubtedly published for readers from many different backgrounds, it described its audience as the very class it so vehemently opposed.[7]

Rosset shared this tension. The editor was radicalized at a wealthy private school, the Francis Parker School, where he and several classmates produced a newspaper titled *Sommunist* (a portmanteau of Socialist-Communist) and, later, the *Anti-Everything*.[8] Rosset entered the book business with the help of his father, a midwestern banker, and, when his father died, he merged his father's bank with the press in order to pay for the court battles over *Lady Chatterley's Lover*.[9] This combination of affluence and radicalism would come under fire during feminist and worker protests at the press in later years. Throwing Rosset's wealth back in his face, the activists' list of demands read, "No more mansions on Long Island for boss-man Rosset and his executive yes-men flunkies."[10] Nevertheless, Rosset seemed to believe he could inhabit the position of moneyed revolutionary, claiming "that most progressive, left-wing enterprises have come out of small-business entrepreneurship."[11] "Small-time capitalists" like himself could get away with promoting avant-garde or even anti-capitalist causes because they had certain "advantages," including "a certain flexibility" that comes with financial security.[12] According to Rosset, Grove Press and other risk-taking publishers depended on "middle-class people with money to lose."[13]

When Grove profiled its audience in the *Evergreen Review*, it was in a sense examining itself. This is very much in keeping with the overall editorial strategy of the press. As Grove editor Gilbert Sorrentino suggested, "Grove flourished because it considered the tastes and prejudices and opinions of—NOT some amorphous audience whose desires had to be satisfied—its editors. And above all, Barney's tastes and opinions."[14] In other words, Rosset *was* the press's target audience. He personified the publishing enterprise so that his conflicts and paradoxes were its conflicts and paradoxes. As a result, Grove's self-reflexive discourse along with its publications became a way of attempting to work through what it meant to be a white-collar radical. Although Grove's professional-managerial readers might not have owned as much property as Rosset, they shared with him the experience of being forced to reconcile their material conditions with their ideological aspirations.

How did the press resolve this contradiction? It did so by presenting the Grove audience with a fantasy of masochistic selflessness. Masochism, or what Leo Bersani terms "self-shattering," allowed Grove's white-collar radical to disabuse himself of middle-class egoism while imaginatively sacrificing his own power.[15] Bersani's formulation is particularly apt for describing Grove because, as Janet Halley suggests, his work provides an ideal-typical example of "abjection-supremacist" thought, which maintains that masochism totally undermines power by gesturing "to a state of being in which the self/other structure of social life is suspended and the political will to dominate rendered inarticulate and helpless."[16] By undercutting mastery over the body, this form of political masochism appears to destabilize mastery over the world. Erotic depersonalization therefore seemed to offer a way for Grove's affluent, white, masculine persona to leave behind class and identity categories, throwing off the stigma of its privilege. Moments of sublime and obscene abnegation in Grove literature thus serve to suspend the problem of the professional-managerial radical's particular interests and perspective. Grove empowers them to say, along with Beckett's ravaged and disintegrating figures, "What matter who's speaking."[17] The midcentury middle class often presented itself as classless and universal by promoting doctrines of the human and the individual, but, through Grove, it succeeded in the same project by opposing those very terms.

Grove's attempt to resolve its class contradictions would have larger implications for literary culture. The press published major works in the literary and artistic movement that Susan Sontag called the "new sensibility," a sensibility that rejected the notion of "individual personal expression," favoring instead "the impersonal" and "transpersonal."[18] This was, in effect, an aesthetic of antihumanism; the new sensibility militated against the agency and coherence of individuals by promoting sensations and experiences that exceeded the limits of conscious control or rational thought, including interpretive criticism.[19] Even before the advent of poststructuralism, Grove published many of the primary texts featured in antihumanist critique, works that rejected the sovereignty of the ego while welcoming the ecstasy of self-dissolution.[20] The press did not always espouse the philosophy it enacted—Grove was not a main translator as such of French theory. Instead, Grove functioned as a mediator between one set of literary values and another, dismantling the old humanist consensus while printing the canon of antihumanism even before these developments could be explicitly formulated in American literary criticism.

In fact, Grove heralded the eclipse of the individual in the most minor and denigrated of genres—pornography. The press was drawn to obscenity in part because it constituted the fracture point between humanism and antihumanism, dramatizing both the terror and the allure of erotic nonsovereignty through its depictions of objectified, fragmented, or otherwise compromised selves. More often than not, though, the workaday life of the managerial subject returned in his erotic literature, albeit in refracted forms. Many of the greatest scenes of transgression in Grove literature hinge on a breakdown of educational training or managerial discipline—the naughtiest thing a white-collar worker can countenance is professional failure, a crisis in the production and reproduction of human capital. In these narratives, the death of the subject appears so scandalous and so enticing because it represents a squandering of personnel or future earning potential, épater le bourgeois as a human resources nightmare.[21]

Grove's publications represented a break with midcentury literary culture. After the de-Marxification of the intellectual and artistic scene in the US, many turned to individualism as a central critical value, displacing the struggle against capitalism into an artistic struggle against quantitative abstraction and mass man.[22] This transposition allowed thinkers to chart a way between the capitalist organization man and the communist true believer, maintaining a private and uncommitted skepticism that the *Partisan Review* termed "critical nonconformism."[23] Although this narrative is best recognized in the New York Intellectuals, who championed the autonomy of art against a homogeneous and all-consuming mass culture, we can see parallels in other critical schools: literary Americanists called for Emersonian self-reliance, press-ganging the newly canonized American Renaissance into the fight against totalitarianism, while New Critics attended to the qualitative particularity of the literary object, shielding it from the instrumental rationality of northern industrial capitalism.[24] For cold war critics, literature helped preserve individual identity in the age of Fordist standardization and

Soviet leveling, producing a nation of Huck Finns and Holden Caulfields.[25] In short, literary culture fostered rebellion through private expression and the appreciation of idiosyncrasy, the kind of rebellion that rarely caught the attention of the House Un-American Activities Committee.

This commitment to literary self-cultivation had a clear class basis. As literary individualism rose to prominence, popular works such as *White Collar* by C. Wright Mills, *The Organization Man* by William H. Whyte, *The Lonely Crowd* by David Riesman, and *The Man in the Gray Flannel Suit* by Sloan Wilson all bemoaned the loss of the entrepreneurial individual after the rise of large corporations. Andrew Hoberek points out that this narrative of decline derived from the history of the PMC: the old middle class of small-business owners gave way to the new middle class of white-collar workers, leaving the new class formation without capital and therefore vulnerable to proletarianization.[26] Although the ideology of American individualism originated in the eighteenth century, its postwar articulation responded to the worries of workers whose livelihoods depended not on ownership of capital or productive labor power but instead on more subjective properties. Professionals were hired for their mental acumen, their education and experience, and their winning personalities. Alienated from economic capital, the PMC relied on what would come to be known as human capital. If they could not run an actual business, they could run their lives like a firm. While industrial workers strove to seize of the means of production, professional-managerial workers longed to take back control over themselves by asserting their individuality in their private lives.

As one might expect, literary individualism prized works that helped to develop individuality while devaluing works that seemed to threaten it. Critics therefore placed pornography, along with more common bête noires such as kitsch or mass culture, in direct opposition to the literary. We can see why in *Obscenity and Public Morality* (1969) by Harry Clor, perhaps the most sophisticated defense of censorship under *Roth v. United States*. Clor equates obscenity with antihumanism: the obscene transforms private, meaningful human events into a public spectacle that degrades them to "a sub-human or merely physical level."[27] Obscenity takes the purely external view of the onlooker, the outsider who sees anatomy rather than love. Pornography thus divorces the object of this "depersonalized sexual desire" from any human context, turning them into a soulless body and disintegrating that body into its constituent parts, rendering it "a thing or a collection of things, completely controlled and manipulated by another."[28] Clor presents obscenity as a danger to the subject's organic wholeness, simplifying and repurposing a Marxist, humanist notion of alienation for conservative ends. This notion of pornographic self-estrangement would become the commonsense understanding of obscenity, reappearing in thinkers as divergent as neoconservative Irving Kristol and radical feminist Catharine MacKinnon.[29]

During this period, however, other critical views began to emerge. "The Pornographic Imagination" by Susan Sontag concedes everything to pornography's opponents—we learn, for example, that "pornography is a theatre of types, never of individuals"—and yet comes to radically different conclusions.[30] Sontag argues that pornography offers an exploration of "extreme forms of consciousness that transcend social personality and psychological individuality," modes of experience systematically denied by secular modernity.[31] Sontag's essay, undoubtedly informed by French structuralism, indexes a movement away from individualist ideology and toward what would come to be called "the death of the subject."

This break in US literary values, however, was not simply the product of a new, critical trend or a change in literary fashion. If you examine the titles cited in the death-of-the-subject narratives, a trend emerges. Sontag's essay references *Madame Edwarda* by Georges Bataille (published in excerpt by *Evergreen Review* in 1964), *Story of O* by Pauline Réage (1965), and *The Image* by Jean de Berg (1966).[32] Leslie Fiedler offers remarks on the oeuvres of Burroughs, Jean Genet, and Edward Albee.[33] Foucault alludes to "Texts for Nothing" by Beckett (1967).[34] Deleuze and Guattari draw on *Molloy* and *The Unnameable* by Beckett (1959), *Naked Lunch* by Burroughs (1962), and *Sexus* by Miller (1965).[35] Bersani carefully reads *Funeral Rites* by Genet (1969).[36] And, of course, countless antihumanists invoke the name of de Sade.[37] Here it becomes clear that Grove translated, published, or republished many of the key works in the antihumanist canon. In effect, as Loren Glass argues, Grove's "vulgar modernism" functioned as a "transitional formation," bridging the gap between high modernism and postmodernism.[38] While it is true that Grove's publications of French antihumanists were limited—the press published Barthes's essay on Grove author Alain Robbe-Grillet, as well as Maurice Blanchot's influential Beckett review, "Where Now? Who Now?"—these examples suggest that Grove established the preconditions for the philosophy's emergence in the US, making the subject's death imaginable, even desirable, in literature.[39]

Rumors of Their Demise Are Greatly Exaggerated

We see the emergence of the death-of-the-subject narrative in Miller's *Tropic of Cancer*, which Rosset considered one of Grove's most important books. Miller's project, along with Grove's, is to recover everything that has been previously edited out of literature. His work therefore dwells on material deemed worthless, subjects falling outside of the canons of taste and propriety, including images and concepts that fail to conform to the prevailing standards of humanism. Whereas petit-bourgeois individualists saw personal life as a utopian space outside of the ravages of capitalism, a place where they could transcend their social situation through intimate life or private thought, Miller rejects personal life as an escapist reverie tolerated only insofar as it does not interfere with capitalist production.[40] He therefore moves to cancel the difference between thought and life, fusing the two together through obscenity. Obscenity not only works to collapse the private and the public but also stands in the ambiguous zone between action and expression. Legal theorists argue that obscenity conveys physical effects rather than mental or emotional ones, making it more akin to conduct than speech.[41] As Miller suggests in the opening pages of *Cancer*, "This is not a book. . . . No, this is a prolonged insult, a gob of spit in the face of Art, a kick in the pants to God, Man, Destiny, Time, Love, Beauty."[42] Eschewing the paradoxical stance of the New Critics or the ironic one of the New York Intellectuals, Miller constructs a literature of corporeal engagement, the kind of aesthetic that later would be championed by Artaud in *The Theater and Its Double* (1958) and Sontag in her *Evergreen Review* essay "Against Interpretation" (1964). More than just a mental worker's overvaluation of the body, these passages display a desire to close the fissure between the personal realm and capitalist labor, to overcome the "discrepancy . . . between ideas and living."[43]

Rather than carve out a space away from the depredations of capitalism, as bourgeois individualism sought to do, Miller's method is to mirror these processes, pushing them to the point of intolerability. With "cool scientific detachment," Miller observes white-collar labor expanding to colonize intimate life so that sex becomes interminable work abstracted from any purpose or end; for example, as he watches a friend coupling with a prostitute, he can only think of the printing presses at his job, endlessly spitting out newspapers.[44] Passages like these led Kate Millett to condemn Miller's sex scenes as a "gray abstraction of 'organ grinding.'"[45] Characters become broken down into sets of organs, which are then combined and recombined with other sets.[46] Here obscenity directly opposes the humanist aesthetics of midcentury critics. Lionel Trilling lobbied for a literature of "variousness, possibility, complexity, and difficulty,"[47] while John Crowe Ransom confronted utilitarian rationality with a poetics of particularity, one in which the "poem celebrates the object which is real, individual, and qualitatively infinite."[48] Pornography, however, boils all of those differences down until there is nothing but undifferentiated sex—Miller's prostitutes and friends appear as fungible as labor, money, and newspaper copy.[49]

As George Orwell's review of the book's initial publication by French publisher Obelisk Press suggests, Miller demonstrates total "acceptance" of the world regardless of criteria such as utility or virtue, an attitude that leads him to become "passive to experience."[50] While Orwell presents this as a critique, Miller's refusal to act, negate, or resist proves integral to the author's politics and aesthetics. Miller explains in "Obscenity and the Law of Reflection" that, when the entire world has become obscene, the reproduced image of obscenity allows the artist to bring that fact into awareness and move beyond it.[51] Rather than flinch from the degradations of white-collar and lumpen existence, Miller affirms and even luxuriates in them. This accelerationist strategy derives masochistic pleasure from taking capitalism through to its logical and ultimately self-destructive conclusions, finding a way out through its gleeful pursuit of the worst.[52] Obscenity, according to Miller, unleashes forces outside of the artist's control, leading to his transformation: it is both "the agony of death" and "the preconscious writhing in the face of a life to be."[53] Miller's antihumanism promises transcendence through debasement.

For all of his sadistic outbursts in *Cancer*, then, Miller's most characteristic posture is that of a stricken spectator, enduring and enjoying some shocking scene from a rapidly shrinking distance. His encounters with the traumatic begin with detachment and end with absorption and identification so that, when he observes a woman's vulva, he comes to imagine himself as broken in two: "A glance at that dark, unstitched wound and a deep fissure in my brain opens up."[54] In this moment of misogyny, Miller claims to experience the psychic disintegration procensorship authors have long warned about.

Tellingly, he figures this breakdown as the undoing of clerical labor. The "fissure" that opens up in Miller empties out a sort of mental filing system, allowing repressed thoughts to burst out: "All the images and memories that had been laboriously or absent-mindedly assorted, labeled, documented, filed, sealed and stamped break forth."[55] This hallucination, which echoes an earlier moment in which Miller wonders what it would be like to be a woman and be entered by a man, leads Miller to entertain a "suicidal wish," a desire "to flow on, one with time, to merge the great image of the beyond with the here and now."[56] He names this yearning for death "the obscenity that is ecstasy."[57] Miller's masochism is bound up with the desire to relinquish power and the active, agential self that power helps call into being. Abandoning a white-collar ethic of distanced, critical nonconformism, Miller gives up his independent perspective to merge with the other.

Obscenity threatens the self through both its formalism and its formlessness. Pornographic abstraction vacates the self of particularity while pornographic abjection dissolves its boundaries. The novel levels a critique against humanism—that much is obvious—and yet it does so in the service of a covert universalism with the potential to become nearly as mystifying. Published by a press that printed so few women authors, Miller's masochistic martyrdom purportedly allows him to inhabit the body of a woman, giving up his own masculine position. Fiedler enjoys a similar fantasy in the 1965 essay "The New Mutants," which asserts that the prevalence of pornography points to the beginning of a "post-human" era and the extinction of the rational ego found in the mythology of white, bourgeois, Protestant men.[58] Recycling and revalorizing the old tropes of masculinity in crisis literature, Fiedler claims that the explosion of obscenity signals white men's collapse into passive and irrational alterity, a state in which they are rendered feminized, homosexual, childish, mad, and Black. Obscenity allows these men to seem to move beyond their social positions, escaping their partial and limiting standpoints. In other words, obscenity promises entry into a condition not fundamentally different from the naturalized private sphere of bourgeois individualism.[59] The lash of the whip leaves an unmarked subject.

The white-collar masochist had good reason to want to become other. We find in one Grove advertisement a *Mad* magazine–style cartoon of a young IBM executive slumming it in a beatnik café. He wears a polka-dotted bowtie and complains about the price of coffee, but what really marks him as a square is his taste in literature. When he joins a group of hipsters chatting about books, he interjects, "Boy, that Edna Ferber is one hell of a writer!"[60] Laughed out of the coffee house, he returns to an apartment filled with markers of uncool taste—a "Walter

Keane" painting, Glen Miller records, a collection of old *National Geographic* magazines—where he sits and stews: "What's wrong with me? Well built! Nail down 15 thou a year!"[61] That's when he has an epiphany: he can buy an *Evergreen Review* subscription! When he returns to the café, he rattles off a list of Grove authors that floors all of the hipsters. The strip ends with a curvy woman in a black turtleneck hanging around his neck while he brags, "I'm hip!"[62] The ad, modeling its pitch on self-improvement programs like Charles Atlas's, promises that a subscription will lead to a "vital and more interesting you."[63]

Although obviously a parody—a goofy caricature of Sartre looms over the panels—the ad nevertheless plays to the audience's real concerns. One contemporary advertiser reported that businessmen who had "grown weary of singing company songs at I.B.M. picnics" liked to imagine themselves escaping their morally compromised and erotically unfulfilling lives by joining the counterculture of young middle-class dropouts.[64] The white-collar masochist, it seems, longed to be someone else. Shedding the sappy, middlebrow sentimentalism represented by Ferber, the managerial subject can aspire to pass as a down-and-out bohemian despite his class position.

But escaping sentimentalism does not prove so easy. As Lauren Berlant points out, the whole point of Ferber's work is to promote a universalist ideology that sees "recognition of common suffering as the basis of human solidarity."[65] By locating movement-building in emotional and physical pain, white-collar masochists seem to follow the same path taken by privileged but progressive white women who believed they could bypass political struggles to change material inequalities simply by feeling the misery of Black and working-class others as echoes of their own personal problems. Berlant calls this sentimental culture of liberalism "a kind of soft supremacy rooted in compassion and coercive identification [that] wants to dissolve all that structure through the work of good intentionality."[66] And yet again and again edgy readers resist the obvious overlaps between their own reading practices and the ones cultivated by feminine, sentimental genres. In addition to abjecting or objectifying women, Grove authors achieved distance from sentiment by framing anguish in normatively masculine terms. Women protagonists of sentimental fiction responded to hardships through anxious and hopeful striving for a better life in which they finally become "somebody."[67] Even when nothing seems right, they try to work things out and remain committed to conventional narratives of fulfillment and belonging.

White-collar masochists, on the other hand, allow their lives to slide until they can become nobody at all, a posture only possible for men who know someone will ultimately take care of them.

Here there is a difference in degree but not in kind between Miller's fuck-up protagonist and the bad-boy characters who have come to dominate popular film and prestige television. Whereas sentimental narratives furnish readers with utopian dreams of living a quietly conventional life, the readers of transgressive literature take their pleasure in characters who possess potential but let it go in ostentatious displays of abdication and irresponsibility. Writing about David Fincher's *Fight Club* (1999), Claire Sisco King shows that in the postpornographic era white men continue to exert an "abject hegemony," in which the destabilization of the boundaries of the masculine self allows white men to "absorb" feminine and other identities in a blob-like fashion.[68] Claiming to be out of control and irresponsible for one's actions becomes a way to covertly wield influence over marginalized subjects while avoiding the critique of power. Miller's masochistic self-negation therefore poses no contradiction to his hyperbolic assertions of sexual dominance over women.

Revolutionary Suicides

Beyond an aspiration toward manly hipness, Grove's motives for killing the subject derive from the politics of its implied readership. From the *Port Huron Statement* to the Weather Underground organization, the radical middle class displayed a profound ambivalence about its own class position. Barbara Ehrenreich and John Ehrenreich describe a "guilty self-effacement on the part of PMC radicals," while Catherine Liu goes even further to call it "radical self-loathing."[69] It is no surprise why the middle class might hate itself: authors, sociologists, and political thinkers cast the midcentury middle stratum as a class of bloodsuckers, toadies, and fascists-in-waiting or as a fuzzy social group of feckless rubes and arch-philistines exemplified by such literary unfortunates as Willy Loman and George F. Babbitt.[70] Burroughs, to take just one example, announced that he was "all for eliminating the whole stupid middle-class."[71] Many Marxist and New Left radicals considered the middle class a phantom, a temporary aberration that would disappear with the sharpening of class contradictions, or a purely ideological category upheld by anti-communists as proof of Marxism's irrelevance. For example, former Grove Press editor Harry Braverman argued in *Labor and*

Monopoly Capital that "middle layer" employees were liable to experience the same proletarianization as many of the office clerks of previous generations.[72] With this tentative prediction, Braverman disposes of the lower half of the middle class and all of the conceptual and political problems that came with it. And many radicals would have been happy to see them go. Whereas the immiseration of the proletariat could be dialectically transformed into its revolutionary strength, the psychological misery of the desk jockeys was derided as a distraction from more objective concerns. If the PMC was not an external enemy or an ideological construct, it was, at least, something to be overcome.

This explains at least part of the reason why the Cuban Revolution loomed so large at Grove: at a moment in which the middle class posed a problem for left-wing politics, the Fidelistas showed that doctors and lawyers could disappear into the mountains and return as hardened revolutionary cadres. As Van Gosse shows, many artists and intellectuals in the US first received Fidel Castro as a kind of hipster, a hypermasculine figure whose beatnik beard and seemingly ambiguous revolution—initially allied with neither Washington nor Moscow—made him a "rebel without a cause."[73] When US citizens looked south, what they saw often had more to do with their own fantasies and desires than with Cuban politics. LeRoi Jones's (Amiri Baraka's) *Evergreen Review* essay "Cuba Libre" quickly became a meditation on the author's class anxieties and his place within literary culture. Upon arriving in Cuba in 1960, Jones finds himself branded a "cowardly bourgeois individualist" by revolutionary poets who ask him, "In that ugliness you live in, you want to cultivate your soul?"[74] Prodded by their questioning, Jones rejects the private rebellions of the Beats and other bohemians, which have come to represent quietism at best and complicity at worst. Cuba offers a clear way out of this predicament for artists and other professionals: they can join the revolution. Thus, in Grove's *Revolution in the Revolution?* by Régis Debray (1967), we find that

> the first rule of guerrilla life is that no one survives alone. The group's interest is the interest of each one, and vice versa. To live and conquer is to live and conquer all together. . . . Under these conditions class egoism does not long endure. Petty bourgeois psychology melts like snow under the summer sun, undermining the ideology of the same stratum.[75]

If the labor process fails to dissolve the PMC, then military praxis will do just as well.

Here I want to be careful to underscore that I am not making the facile and patronizing argument that Grove was radical chic.[76] Although affluent, white men made up a significant demographic for Grove, it was by no means its only readership. Many of the press's young Black readers *did* take up arms in insurrectionary action based on Grove books. They were especially drawn to Fanon's *Wretched of the Earth* (1963), which begins with a preface by Sartre warning white audiences that Fanon is not writing for them and continues with the author laying out a new vision of humanism that exceeds the hypocritical slogans of Western colonizers.[77] Whereas many Grove authors promoted the masochism I have been detailing, Fanon presents a training manual for subjectivation.[78] Rejecting the respectable politics of the Black, middle-class organizers who led the civil rights movement, the Black Panther Party saw in Fanon a prescription for channeling spontaneous riots into organized militant violence, a transformation that would allow the Black *lumpenproletariat* to become the new revolutionary actor on the world stage.[79] Fanon's work—which was required reading for party members—empowered Black radicals and encouraged them to become disciplined cadres.[80] When a Black Panther leader, David Hilliard, shot wildly at police in an act of reckless transgression, one of his comrades restrained him by reminding him of passages from Fanon that counseled strategic action based on a careful and educated analysis of the revolutionary situation.[81] While some readers may have seen in Grove an invitation to uncontrolled self-abandonment, many Black people read books by Fanon and other authors such as Malcolm X as a call to conscious self-assertion. More than any of the other presses examined in this study, Grove was multifarious in its impacts.

Nevertheless, the path of armed resistance was unavailable to many of Grove's more comfortable readers. Barring revolution, then, the only way out for the managerial subject was to narrate its own demise. Grove accomplished this trick by imagining the PMC's failure to accomplish its job duties or to achieve cultural reproduction. Grove's works are filled with scenes of botched management or sabotaged pedagogy. The managerial subject, representing a class that finds its ideological justification as well as its livelihood in education, dreams of unteachable students forever in need of rough discipline. Self-sabotage thus becomes a means of rebellion and refusal. At Grove, the managerial subject finds power in its absorption into the corporate world and its masochistic passivity. For example, parodying Napoleon Hill's *Think and Grow Rich* (1937), Burroughs in *The Ticket*

That Exploded advises office employees to use audio-suggestion techniques to get ahead, such as splicing the sounds of coworkers with their own to achieve subconscious identification: "Become the breathing word and the beating heart of that organization become that organization."[82] Having hooked the audience, Burroughs quickly turns from giving tips to up-and-comers ("Suppose you are some creep in a grey flannel suit you want to present a new concept of advertising to the old man") to promulgating methods for inciting riots and subverting ideological messages.[83]

To grasp the political import of these language breakdowns, we must understand the PMC as a mediating agency that uses its facility with communications to prevent open conflict between dominant and subordinate groups.[84] The Burroughsian project of cutting up received texts and introducing noise into mass media signals takes on a new class character in Grove as the misuse of work equipment if not an outright dereliction of duty. This class bias also sheds new light on Grove's dramas, which often turn at key moments to an aesthetics of unspeakability and incommunicability. We see this communication failure in Grove's published scripts by Eugène Ionesco, Beckett, Harold Pinter, and Jones (Baraka), playwrights whose dialogue devolves into nonsense or violence that only confirms the irreducible alienation of their characters. Scenes of shared incomprehension turn out to represent a cultural method for defecting from the middle-class mission of fostering civil cross-class conversation as a strategy for surveilling and subduing social inferiors.

By the same token, we also see in Grove fictions a rejection of the PMC's erotics of communication. Tommy Dukes in *Lady Chatterley's Lover* represents this position when he explains that Clifford Chatterley thinks that "sex is a sort of communication like speech," an arid, intellectualized view of sexuality that the novel proceeds to disprove by presenting a deeper form of wordless bodily communion as an alternative.[85] Sadean pornography goes even further in rejecting this idea. Even as many midcentury lotharios thought of making love as a mutually pleasurable exchange governed by continuous feedback between partners, de Sade argues for a sexual egoism in which it is impossible to apprehend let alone find satisfaction in another person's erotic fulfillment.[86] As Simone de Beauvoir suggests in "Must We Burn Sade?"—which appears as a preface to the Grove edition of *120 Days of Sodom and Other Writings* (1966)—the Sadistic master is trapped in his own alienated subjectivity while he abuses his object, and he can only experience how his object might feel by allowing himself to be beaten and tortured in the same way.[87] Needless to say, the Sadean ideology violates the PMC's burgeoning ethics of informed, consensual sexuality while also negating its purpose of encouraging comity between fundamentally opposed and unequal class formations. Tasked with maintaining capitalist hegemony, these professionals dream of naked aggression.

The class charged with maintaining capitalist relations also holds the potential to bring everything down, not because of its independence but because it is so implicated in capitalism that even its private life has become integrated into its workings. While other white-collar employees dream of retreating into the suburban pastoral, Grove's organization men fantasize about falling down on the job. Working as a hiring manager at a telegraph company in *Tropic of Capricorn* (1961), Miller brings the system to a halt by hiring the most incompetent of workers: "I laughed all day thinking what a fine stinking mess I was making of it."[88] These novels offer us a kind of managerial potlatch, a lavishly wasteful expenditure of company resources that also characterized its publisher.

Although Grove employees never set out to wreck the business, they often placed pleasure over profits. Rather than demanding financial reports predicting how well prospective books would sell, the editorial staff ignored publishing best practices to rely instead on their own tastes or preferences. Rosset, according to S. E. Gontarski, "personalized publishing, made it an extension of his will, psyche, and libido."[89] Often, Rosset would approve books based only on a meeting of a few minutes, demonstrating an impulsiveness that brooked no interference and disregarded financial consequences.[90] Indeed, Grove's catalog was filled with books that all of the other publishers rejected, not only controversial or obscene ones but also books that seemed like commercial losers to everyone else. Grove's dealings did often involve some economic calculation: because some authors were desperate and many had already published their books overseas, their publication rights could be acquired at rock-bottom prices or, in the case of works without copyright protection, for free.[91] Nevertheless, as *Newsweek* reported, Rosset had "no intention of making each [book] pay its own way."[92] This policy remained in place throughout Rosset's tenure, forcing the editor to subsidize the company with his own private wealth as it hemorrhaged money.

Grove's extreme disinterestedness won the company cultural capital, which it leveraged to cement long-lasting business relationships with authors who might otherwise have moved on to bigger and better-paying publishers as their literary fortunes improved, and its pursuit of banned books stirred up free publicity that made Grove publications like *Lady Chatterley's Lover* instant bestsellers.[93] Nevertheless, this strategy also led to its eventual downfall. Defying conventional aesthetic values and holding market ones in abeyance, Grove became such an artistic and political force because it allowed itself to fail. *Screw* magazine publisher Al Goldstein, speaking with characteristic delicacy, called Rosset "the worst, most fucked-up businessman in America."[94] It turns out that a truly subversive entrepreneur must also be a failed capitalist, a self-liquidating one.

This dynamic animates Burroughs's mastermind, Dr. Benway, who appears in *Naked Lunch*. When he is not acting as a scientist or medical doctor, Dr. Benway works as a "manipulator and coordinator of symbol systems," a description that echoes *Playboy* editor A. C. Spectorsky's term for the PMC.[95] Dr. Benway attempts to engineer entire societies, but these hyperbolic scenes of total control only serve to unleash anarchy. Burroughs's gloriously failed professionals tell us something about the nature of sadism. As Foucault has shown, power works to make itself invisible and efficient, such that subordinates internalize its strictures and follow them even in the absence of a master.[96] Sadism, however, makes for the most overt and energy-intensive mode of domination possible, requiring the dominator to stand over the submissive to micromanage their every move. The aristocrats in de Sade's *120 Days of Sodom* spend an inordinate amount of time fussing about their charges' bathroom habits. If power is the ability to govern a body's or population's actions without direct physical contact, sadism often falls short of even this basic criterion. Unlike disciplinary power, sadistic mastery flirts with its own reversal through its sensationalism and extravagancy, an ostentatiousness that exhausts the dominator while emboldening the submissive. "Torture locates the opponent and mobilizes resistance," as Dr. Benway puts it.[97] Grove's sadism expresses a more fundamental masochism.[98]

Grove was, in many ways, a masochistic company, giving itself over to organizational failure with reckless abandon. We can see this reflected in its numerous sadomasochistic (SM) novels, which run counter to liberal narratives of self-development and success. Elizabeth Freeman points out that SM works to undo chrononormative models of progress and maturation, destabilizing both historical and biographical temporalities.[99] In Grove's scenarios, the submissive often remains in perpetual training, never quite obtaining mastery over themselves or their world. Travestying bildungsroman novels and conversion narratives, the masochistic character moves from enlightened autonomy to Gothic subjugation, returning to obsolete disciplinary technologies that replace more subtle forms of power with overt and spectacular domination. As in Beckett's novels and plays, the masochist is drawn toward absolute helplessness, confinement, and constraint, a reduction in circumstances running precisely counter to the normalized coming-of-age-story.[100] Unable or unwilling to internalize norms, the masochistic subject veers off from conventional life paths to remain under tutelage.

Tropic of Cancer, for example, features an author-protagonist who enjoys being an unappreciated starving artist, arrested in a preparatory stage for his career under the patronage of the cold and distant figure of Mona. This masochistic dynamic structures the novel's form. We see Miller's preparation to become a great author but never the moment of his artistic success, while Miller as a personality remains in a state of becoming, half-formed and self-refuting, reinventing himself over and over again.[101] Fragmented, episodic, and unpolished, *Cancer* follows no clearly recognizable biographical or narrative development. Miller's refusal to edit his work to produce a more finished form duplicates the author's rejection of self-improvement: "I have made a compact with myself not to change a line of what I write. I am not interested in perfecting my thoughts, nor my actions."[102] More than just a novel about the author's failure to launch, *Cancer* depicts Miller's pleasure in betraying his own unreachable standards and his wallowing in his own ineptness. Thus, what sets out to be a hymn of praise for Mona only ends in her disappointment and disgrace, as if inviting her to punish its author.

Miller's masochism resists life trajectories ordered by linear, teleological progression toward competent, professional adulthood; it is a rejection of chrononormativity that holds a specific political import for the PMC. Although all workers might be governed by the timeline of the resumé, white-collar workers especially acquire and explain economic power through an ever-increasing accumulation of human capital, one that begins with schooling and continues through ascending job positions. A mathematized update of the Horatio Alger narrative, the concept of human capital justified income inequality as a function of differences in investments in education, training, or experience: greater earnings accrue to more-skilled employees and positions. Grove's masochistic novels, however, feature downwardly mobile characters whose rigorous discipline only serves to waste their potential under the service of arbitrary masters. The schools of misrule found in so many of these texts work to disrupt transmissions of cultural inheritance predicated on generational continuity and social reproduction.[103]

In de Sade's *Philosophy in the Bedroom* (1965), a dramatic dialogue featuring a young virgin's miseducation by libertines, the author exhorts his readers "to destroy, to spurn all those ridiculous precepts inculcated in you by imbecile parents."[104] The submissive forgets more than she learns, becoming increasingly unfit for socially or economically productive life. Even subjects who begin their masochistic training as capable professionals typically end by retreating into hapless servitude: the protagonist of *Story of O* begins the novel as a skilled, self-assured professional, but, by the end of her SM training, she has thrown away her career and, in one of the book's endings, her life. Masochism negates human capital analysis point for point, stripping the entrepreneurial self of rational choice, disrupting the process of cumulative skill building, and halting the subject's movement along a path toward more remunerative prospects. Grove yearns for, as the title of one Jones (Baraka) short story put it, "The Death of Horatio Alger."[105]

PMC Radicalism and the Obscenity of War

Nevertheless, the fantasy that middle managers could absolve themselves of their guilt through masochistic self-sacrifice collapsed with the waning of the 1960s. The Vietnam War made many conscientious middle-class youths drop the professional-managerial postures we have been examining throughout this study—passivity, detachment, cynicism, mediation, abstraction—and take up a stance that insisted on its authentic commitment to immediate, concrete action. To understand why that was the case, one must consider the shifting politics of the radical middle class during this period. Barbara Ehrenreich and John Ehrenreich argue that during the early 1960s the PMC radicals of the New Left framed their protests as an extension of their class project.[106] Some campus leftists imagined that if well-informed professionals were given full autonomy, they could make the world more rational, peaceful, and sane. However, as the Vietnam War progressed and the military-industrial complex tapped the nation's brain trust, it became obvious to many middle-class protesters that the university system—the key site for middle-class social reproduction—no longer served as a reservoir of alternative values because it had become so deeply complicit in imperialist bloodshed.[107] PMC radicals ceased to see their class formation as a force for good when they learned their members were performing weapons research and recruiting for the war machine.

Even more damningly, the war served as an indictment of scientific management. The war was prosecuted by a class of elite managers headed by Robert McNamara, a Harvard Business School graduate who ran the Ford Motor Company before becoming secretary of defense.[108] McNamara's team was composed of the smartest experts, but in the end they used their advanced knowledge of Fordist managerial techniques to create a system that rewarded soldiers and superiors for maximizing the number of dead bodies while minimizing their own costs.[109] Vietnam became a killing ground for fatal abstractions: influenced by game theory, the war's managers pursued a strategy of attrition, seeking to inflict enough damage on the enemy that they would see it was rational to give up their sovereignty and submit to American demands.[110] Under this scheme, missiles became a media technology for communicating messages to the enemy.[111] Despite the state-of-the-art research that went into the war planning, however, all of these abstractions ran aground. Soldiers gamed the system by falsifying body counts, career-minded officers knowingly sent their subordinates to die in ambushes so that they could improve their kill ratios by calling in retaliatory airstrikes, and the Viet Cong guerrillas refused to surrender based on the logic of a cost-benefit analysis.[112] As military accountancy provoked civilian atrocities and planes tried to bomb the Vietnamese landscape until it matched the flat, visible grid of the gameboard, the managerial elite revealed themselves as monstrously evil as well as monstrously incompetent.[113]

Other social changes forced the question of middle-class collaborationism. An influx of Black and working-class students into the university encouraged professionals to abandon their paternalistic mission to oversee and improve the conditions of marginalized populations and prepared them instead for direct confrontation with the capitalist state. PMC radicals came to see their previous political work as "a pale abstraction compared to this militance which came from 'the streets.'"[114] While the affluent rebels of the late 1950s and early 1960s found corporate life to be massified, alienating, and conformist—unpleasant and unfulfilling but maybe not unconscionable—the antiwar activists in the late 1960s and early 1970s faced a fundamentally violent system that might send them overseas to kill and be killed. Middle-class dissatisfaction sharpened into deep moral repugnance. While the thirtysomething IBM manager might still turn to transgressive literature to cope with his despair, young men were forced to resort to direct action to resolve the problem of the draft.[115]

These shifts resulted in corresponding shifts in how college-aged aspirants to the PMC thought about free speech and obscenity. Activists in the Berkeley Free Speech Movement and the antiwar protests rallied around the radical-leftist right to collective agitation rather than the liberal right to individual free expression.[116] The New Left therefore held a view of speech antithetical to the libertarianism of cold war liberals. As Michael Trask makes clear, cold war liberals promoted a free speech doctrine that safeguarded ineffectual speech, "the free floating and disembodied circulation of discourse," while the Free Speech Movement saw authentic and unconstrained language as bringing together "a community of persons organized around intimate contact and utterances that serve as vows or bonds."[117]

This colored how the Free Speech Movement responded to sex censorship. In 1965 the poet John Thomson kicked off the short-lived Filthy Speech Movement by stationing himself at the edge of the University of California Berkeley campus with a sign with the word "fuck" on it, amending it only to specify that it was a verb.[118] When Thomson was arrested, Mario Savio reluctantly called for obscene-speech protections on a procedural basis, but the civil rights and antiwar activists of Berkeley considered this issue to be "too abstract" to get behind.[119] The movement fought for speech directed toward specific political goals—for example, Paul Robert Cohen's "Fuck the Draft" jacket—not for freedom of speech in general.[120] Whereas free speech libertarians were often equivocal or evasive about the relationship between pornographic literature and real-world behavior, the New Left valued "explicitness" only when it showed that the speaker was being direct and emphatic about achieving practical changes in line with their actual beliefs and intentions.[121]

The Filthy Speech Movement did not receive too much support from civil libertarians at Berkeley, either. When a member of the fund created to support Thomson, the Fuck Defense Fund, read aloud from *Lady Chatterley's Lover* to protest his arrest for obscenity, professor Mark Schorer—who wrote the introduction to the Grove edition and defended it in court—told a crowd of students that the Filthy Speech Movement's antics alienated many faculty members who otherwise would support free speech and complained that a substantive difference stood between encountering the four-letter word in a print copy and having it "thrust upon one's attention in a public place": "One is a matter of private edification or indulgence; the other can easily become a public nuisance."[122] Most of his audience expressed agreement through acclamation. Hal Draper's *Berkeley: The New Student Revolt* (1965) dismissed the protesters as "sophomoric" and chided them for attacking the linguistic symptoms of sexual repression rather than the root causes.[123]

Even within the Filthy Speech Movement, we see a shift away from the kind of socially acceptable obscenities that characterized cold war liberalism. The other obscene target of administrative repression at UC Berkeley was *Spider*, the student-run magazine which stood for "Sex, Politics, International Communism, Drugs, Extremism, and Rock 'n Roll." When Thomson was busted for his sign, *Spider* pointed out that administrators cracked down on honest and open uses of the word "fuck" while willfully overlooking the groups of frat boys who walked around campus wearing "I Love Pussy" buttons that were supposedly in reference to a contestant in the campus Ugly Man contest named after the Bond girl Pussy Galore from the recent film *Goldfinger* (1964).[124] The same issue continues this line of attack through a remarkably sophisticated critique of the popularity of Ian Fleming's James Bond novels on campus, arguing that Bond constituted "a response to the Bomb and the post-modern technocratic society" that had stripped American citizens of their ethical decision-making capabilities:

> Americans are enamored with James Bond for many of the same reasons they idolized John F. Kennedy. The highly successful Kennedy administration was a regime of pure technicians; it was neither moral nor immoral by design, but often immoral because the technicians had failed to include morality in their list of important variables.[125]

Citing the failures of cold war liberalism ranging from its inadequate legislative response to anti-Black racism to its support for Ngo Dinh Diem's puppet regime, the *Spider* author draws a connection between the cold efficiency of *Playboy* magazine's favorite superspy and the state's willingness to do anything—even commit mass murder—on the basis of "tactical necessity."[126] Shifting political circumstances made this kind of ruthless professionalism impossible to defend, and even Hefner would become radicalized for a time after being roughed up by police during the protests surrounding the 1968 Democratic National Convention in Chicago.[127]

EC Comics had fared a little better among campus activists: Tom Hayden, president of Students for a Democratic Society, credited *Mad* magazine with forming his radical sensibility, and it remained the favorite magazine of a majority of college students well into the sixties.[128] However, many on the left were split as to whether *Mad* remained as relevant as it had been in the 1950s, when poking fun at corporate advertisements still seemed subversive. *Esquire* magazine suggested that *Mad* played it safe by avoiding substantive issues such as segregation, while other readers such as Robert Anton Wilson countered that the magazine had in fact become *too* preachy, dealing with issues that its fans did not care about in a style more didactic than funny.[129] Either way, the cynical gamesmanship found in its pages did not seem adequate to the politics of the day and eventually gave way to the cult of authenticity which became the cultural dominant for many middle-class adolescents. Because he resonated with these ideals, Allen Ginsberg made a more or less seamless transition between 1950s hipsters and 1960s hippies.

While the Vietnam War changed the significance of the PMC's cool detachment, it also undermined its support for the aesthetics of abjection. New Left figures such as Savio rejected the bureaucratic depersonalization that transformed students into raw material for the machine, a notion that Berkeley students expressed by pinning IBM punch cards to their clothes that read "I am a student: Do Not Fold, Spindle or Mutilate."[130] The violence implicit in this injunction would become brutally manifest as the numbers of dead rose in southeast Asia. Anti-censorship advocates had long argued that war was the *real* obscenity, but it was not until the data-driven escalation of bloodshed in Vietnam that this slogan became a lived reality for many on the left. Sylvia Shin Huey Chong argues that photographic and televised images of military atrocities in southeast Asia—including but not limited to *Saigon Execution* (1968), *Massacre at My Lai* (1969), and *Napalm Girl* (1972)—cemented in the psyches of many American viewers what she called the "Oriental obscene," a spectacular display of Asian bodies transformed by brutal violence into traumatized and traumatizing objects.[131] As images of civilian casualties circulated through the antiwar movement, and as the Third World, gay, and women's liberation movements fought to achieve self-determination, the voyeuristic pleasures surrounding sadistic violence and masochistic disempowerment would became increasingly suspect in activist and literary milieus.

The cultural politics of obscenity shifted at the same historical moment when the PMC had been exposed as integral to the capitalist and imperialist system. These conditions left Grove vulnerable to another challenge: the rise of second-wave feminism. After a group of feminists took over the underground newspaper *Rat Subterranean News*, radical feminist Robin Morgan called for women and other oppressed people to destroy and supplant the publishing scene dominated by white male editors who printed lewd images of women alongside counter-cultural content and anti-capitalist calls to action. These men, she argued, were merely "the liberal co-optative masks on the face of sexist hate and fear."[132] The unstable mixture of smut and socialism found in their publications was antithetical to the ideals they claimed to uphold: "A genuine Left doesn't consider anyone's suffering irrelevant or titillating; nor does it function as a microcosm of capitalist economy, with men competing for power and status at the top, and women doing all the work at the bottom (and functioning as objectified prizes or "coin" as well). Goodbye to all that."[133] In Morgan's farewell, Hefner and Ed Sanders were both effectively the same—partners in patriarchy—regardless of their political and aesthetic differences.[134] Morgan would soon call out Rosset, as well. No longer enduring state censorship or holding itself aloof from the prevailing power structure, the white-collar masochist could no longer pretend to be powerless.

Goodbye to All That

In April of 1970, Morgan and several other Grove employees were terminated after they reached out to the Furriers, Leather, Machinists Joint Board (AFL-CIO) to organize a union. Although the company claimed that the firings were not retaliatory, Morgan reports that they were precipitated by Rosset's discovery of an article by feminist Ellen Smith Mendocino detailing the press's exploitation of women both as employees and as sex objects.[135] Morgan pled innocent to any connection with the piece, but it clearly anticipates her later criticism of the press. Mendocino's "A Feminist Takes on the Evergreen," reprinted in *Rat*, hits Grove right where it hurts, ruthlessly laying bare the press's humiliating contradiction: "While putting down the ethos of middle class commercialism in its articles and fiction, Evergreen [sic] turns around and sells itself by the worst sort of pandering to that ethos."[136] Although this takedown might not have held true in its earliest issues, in recent years *Evergreen Review* had begun publishing nude pictorials and erotic comics as well as a growing flood of low-grade pornographic literature that had been liberalized in part by Grove's efforts. With this new editorial line, Glass points out, *Evergreen Review* "had gained a reputation of being the *Playboy* of the counterculture."[137] In keeping with this critique, the article casts Grove's demographic as grasping salesmen, grubby backroom dealers, and dirty old men in a moment when countercultural radicals refused to trust anyone over the age of thirty.

After the firings, Morgan and a group of feminists including Ti-Grace Atkinson occupied the press's offices, issuing an extensive list of demands. The statement condemns Rosset and other staff members as "wealthy capitalist dirty old straight white men" before excoriating *Evergreen* authors for selling a "hypocritical radicalism" to fund their "cushy life-styles": "No more wearing of a radical mask by these exploiters to cover the sexist leer, the racist smirk, the boss-man's frown!"[138] Morgan would make clear her thoughts on the contents of Grove fiction in a later essay, which discounted the notion that men can achieve "woman-identification" through masochism:

> He who has power can do what he likes, *including playing at powerlessness* in a manner never available to the powerless. For him it can be an experiment, a game, a fad, a fake (or even genuine) attempt to divest himself of his power, or a mere kicky new experience. It can be whatever he likes or imagines to be, because it is his *choice*, by nature temporary and dismissible the instant it no longer amuses him. (emphasis original)[139]

According to Morgan, this masochism is just another masculine prerogative; no amount of vicarious suffering can produce real solidarity between oppressor and oppressed.[140]

Nevertheless, radical feminists faced a class problem of their own, one that looked remarkably like Grove's. Grappling with economic inequality, many feminist organizations shed members, fostered seething resentments, or simply foundered and split.[141] Morgan, looking back on this period, decried its "failure vanguardism," a "suicidal" impulse that finds radicalism only in personal and political dysfunction.[142] Even as they rejected Grove, many feminists took up and reworked its characteristic postures. With the fragmentation of early radical feminism, anti-pornography campaigns seemed to offer a way out of this self-defeating impasse. Whereas Grove deployed antihumanist obscenity to blur the distinction between its imagined audience and their others, cultural feminists transformed it into a supervening shared injury that would allow them to take up the fallen mantle of radical feminism, erase the histories of other feminisms, and profess to speak for women everywhere regardless of class, race, gender expression, or sexuality in the name of a new feminist humanism.[143] Although radical feminists like Morgan may have been correct in criticizing Grove's facile attempt at becoming-woman, the unified and essentialist conception of feminine identity they proposed as an alternative turned out to be just as problematic. Morgan's transphobic remarks, especially, reveal the bankruptcy of this position.[144]

Political masochism proves to be no substitute for the often-unsexy work of redistributing and renegotiating power to build cross-class and cross-identity coalitions. As long as Grove stayed exclusively under the control of white, middle-class men, its radicalism would remain a problem. Grove's management betrayed this fact when it called the police to cart the feminist occupiers away in handcuffs, and, although the unionization drive ultimately failed, the company soon slipped into financial ruin, limping along until Rosset sold the company in 1985 before being fired himself.[145]

Nevertheless, by dismantling the subject Grove cleared the way for an examination of the structures that penetrate and determine intimate as well as professional life. We see this quite clearly in Kathy Acker, who published most of her major works with the press. Senior editor Fred Jordan found Acker's novels in Rosset's slush pile in 1983 and bought them all, publishing the books with the same light editorial touch that he offered to experimental authors such as Beckett.[146] By Acker's account, Grove treated her very well up until the point when Rosset was fired and the press's new owners began interfering with Jordan's editorial decisions.[147] Acker's writing was deeply engaged with the thematic and aesthetic concerns of Grove authors, including Genet, de Sade, and Burroughs. As Glass puts it, "the entire Grove Press backlist is Acker's archive."[148]

Indebted to Grove, Acker takes the press's obsession with erotic self-negation in a very different direction. In both fiction and daily practice, Acker used masochism to deconstruct the feminine subject and self-fashion a body more resistant to the disciplining fictions of identity. Acker's depictions of women enjoying their abjection reveal and critique how patriarchy shapes and controls the feminine psyche in fundamental ways.[149] These narratives, which sometimes rely on Acker's own autobiography, came to inspire the vital genre of autofiction developed by

Chris Kraus and the Native Agents series she edited for Semiotext(e).[150] While political masochism served as an indulgence when used to exculpate powerful men, it became a tool for interrogating and altering intimate life when taken up by feminist thinkers. In a statement that would have shocked Grove's feminist occupiers in 1970, Acker showed that "masochism is now rebellion."[151] Masochism takes on a very different valence when it is being carried out by marginalized subjects for whom the achievement of self-possession in the present system only means taking personal responsibility for forced choices that are often inimical to their flourishing.

Although antihumanism provided far more insights into the politics of subjectivity than the individualism that preceded it, at Grove the doctrine's articulation through white-collar masochism often obscured the political-economic positions of its devotees. Obscenity disburdened the managerial subject: Miller surrenders to flux, and Lawrence's lovers serve as avatars of masculine and feminine principles, while Burroughs's agents and addicts devolve into soft machines operated by cosmic conspiracies. Through Grove publications, the white-collar masochist could cease to be an individual member of a dominant class and become instead a victim or a conduit for forces outside of his control, even as he reaps private rewards. White-collar masochism turns out to be an eroticized version of the exculpatory narratives promulgated by contemporary members of the PMC, who claimed that they were merely "slaves" to the capitalist social relations they helped reproduce and reinforce.[152] Although this masochistic pose proposes a more sophisticated theory of power, it can just as easily become a justification for it. The boss always reminds us, "My hands are tied."

AFTERWORD
Transgression in the Post-pornographic Era

FOLLOWING *MILLER V. CALIFORNIA* (1973), the Supreme Court case that established our current definition of obscene speech, the written word became all but exempt from obscenity. After 1973, only a single successful obscenity prosecution went forward: *Fletcher v. United States*.[1] In 2006, US attorney Mary Beth Buchanan prosecuted Karen Fletcher for publishing graphic stories about sexual violence against children on her website. The zealous George W. Bush appointee clearly brought the case to court for political reasons, and the court's decision did not set any precedents. Missing an opportunity to overturn *Miller*, the case's agoraphobic defendant accepted a plea deal to avoid going to trial.[2]

Outside of anomalous cases such as these, purely textual obscenity is now basically a dead letter. Bolstered by changing social mores and a new media landscape, Fletcher's lawyers argue that nonvisual print media cannot be obscene because reading requires voluntary participation.[3] While visual pornography might surprise a spectator, it is impossible to inadvertently read a book: the reader must actively imagine the scene depicted and consent to continue scanning the page. As Fletcher's defense points out, literary obscenity effectively prohibits certain mental imagery, it is unconstitutional insofar as it creates a category of thought crime.[4] As with many sex laws, literary obscenity remains on the books only because it is almost never enforced, effectively stigmatizing explicit speech without actually prohibiting it. While obscenity still does not receive full First Amendment protection, we have effectively entered what Walter Kendrick terms the "post-pornographic era."[5]

Theorists such as Sylvère Lotringer and Jean Baudrillard expressed ambivalence about the end of obscenity prohibition because it also means an end to the possibility of transgression.[6] While their arguments may be overstated, it is true that obscenity law prior to 1973 enabled a form of cultural politics that is no longer possible. Faced with the threat of censorship, transgressive editors rose to public prominence and spoke on behalf of audiences they described as straight, white men from the professional-managerial class. The controlled environment of this editorial context transformed erotic literature into teaching texts for an emotional distant but cognitively powerful form of middle-class subjectivity. It was easy to keep one's cool while reading some bland, middlebrow fare, but only the most self-possessed professionals could take an abstract view of pornography and other obscene material. While some professional-managerial readers looked to transgressive literature as a way of finding pleasure in their own alienation, others discovered in obscenity an anticipation of workplace reforms that would only come into full fruition in the post-Fordist era. Through violent or sexually explicit content, they learned to enjoy the rigid impersonality of bureaucratic capitalism or reimagine themselves as flexible subjects capable of accommodating themselves to any humiliation. This school of self-abstraction would come undone after *Miller v. California*.

Without the immediate threat of censorship, transgressive editors were forced to create their own controversies. Editors of visual pornography such as Al Goldstein of *Screw* magazine and Larry Flynt of *Hustler* magazine adopted combative personae while publishing increasingly graphic material. No longer compelled to edit for upstanding citizens, editors gained notoriety pursuing popular audiences. *Playboy* fell from cultural prominence, and the class politics of pornography shifted toward the disruptive and carnivalesque exuberance of working-class revolt.[7] Once the shared enemy of censorship no longer bound them together, the unstable alliance between PMC liberalism and hardcore obscenity dissolved.

This process was only accelerated by shifts in labor law and gender politics. As more women entered formal employment, feminists and civil rights activists reframed unwelcome sexual advances in the workplace as both a form of systemic violence against women and a type of illegal discrimination on the basis of sex.[8] Sexual harassment law prohibited many of the behaviors characteristic of the midcentury office playboy. Once employer-sanctioned hedonism could no longer serve as a prime motivator for enthusiastic worker participation, the PMC embraced a more ascetic spirit of capitalism. Leading managers abandoned Hefner for Ram Dass, promoting themselves as visionaries working selflessly with their teams for a better future.[9] Gender discrimination and sexual abuses continued in factories, shops, and offices, but they could no longer be excused as exercises in "the scientific management of the libido."[10]

The role of transgressive editors has shifted accordingly. While editors of textual pornography now seem far tamer by comparison to visual editors like Flynt and Goldstein, they still sometimes make efforts to revive the thrill of obscenity. For example, publishers of splatterpunk horror novels in the tradition of EC Comics release unexpurgated editions of old books with paratexts assuring readers that what they were reading was deemed too gruesome and unsavory by the previous editors. By presenting their books as "uncut" and "uncensored," extreme authors cash in on the allure of the forbidden.[11] Editors once blue-penciled questionable passages to remain within the law. Now, editors restore cuts in order to reanimate the obscenity effect.

For the most part, though, transgressive editors are on the decline. Thanks to the concentration and financialization of the publishing industry, relatively few editors break into public consciousness as causes célèbres. Inventing new audiences becomes difficult when every book has to be justified as a proven financial success based on existing sales. Editorial whimsy, risk-taking, and self-aggrandizement prove prohibitively costly now that trade book publishing is dominated by a dwindling number of multinational corporations who are legally responsible to shareholders to maximize profit.[12] Periodical editors retained their authority longer than their book publishing counterparts, only to see their own industry begin to fold as sales and advertising revenue plummeted in the digital era.

In this new media environment, transgressive literature is abandoning print publishing entirely. Most authors of erotica self-publish their novels as e-books. However, for all of the rhetoric about escaping cultural gatekeepers, the flight from legacy media has only displaced the locus of corporate influence from publishers owned by media conglomerates to online platforms that disavow any editorial responsibility for the content they disseminate. Section 230 of the Communication Decency Act—a law enacted in 1996 to regulate online pornography—holds that "no provider or user of an interactive computer service shall be treated as the publisher or speaker of any information provided by another information content provider."[13] Online platforms have used (or abused) this law to avoid liability for a range of crimes committed by their users, including obscenity.[14] Thanks to their lobbying efforts, tech companies have managed to undo a legal regime of editorial punishment that began with *Rex v. Curll* in 1727, if only in online spaces.

These platforms do of course make editorial choices whenever users violate their exhaustive, opaque, and ever-shifting terms of service. Erotica authors who make most of their sales on e-book platforms such as Amazon Kindle complain that their livelihoods are constantly threatened by black-boxed algorithms that deprioritize their books from search engine results, remove them from recommendation pages, and sometimes ban them from the site entirely based on mysterious criteria.[15] Editors have not gone away—they have simply become anonymous and unquestionable. While this may seem like a dream from the perspective of the outlaw editors of the midcentury period who fought hard to protect their editorial prerogative from regulatory interference, the new conditions of editorial labor under platform capitalism have proven to be abject and immiserated. When erotica authors complained about their disappearing porn, what seemed like the automatic responses of machines may have actually been the invisible work of overstressed and underpaid content moderators.[16] Increasingly, prohibitions against obscenity, un-simulated violence, child pornography, and other explicit material are enforced by low-paid workers who can develop post-traumatic stress syndrome from spending hours each day monitoring the most extreme content imaginable.[17] The outlaw editor used to be a public figure, an indispensable ally in the fight against censorship who had the cool determination to ignore the censors and make hard decisions about what was right for his readers. Now, the secret editors who draw the line between illicit and licit are disposable, outsourced employees who sometimes self-medicate or fantasize about self-harm to numb themselves.

Nevertheless, this predicament is not the main focus of media attention when it comes to censorship debates. Despite the absence of any strong legal challenge to individual First Amendment rights, a new generation of self-described victims have painted themselves as martyrs for free speech: the right-wing fringe group known as the alt-right. While the old right launched purity crusades to police public morals, the new right claims to break taboos, challenge censors, and speak the unspeakable. An anthology of fiction prefaced by Milo Yiannopoulos bears the title *Forbidden Thoughts* (2016) and warns its readers on the dust jacket that "you are not allowed to read this book."[18] Although this makes for good jacket copy, as I write this it is still perfectly legal to purchase *Forbidden Thoughts*, which is available at an affordable price in paperback and audiobook formats on Amazon.com.

Angela Nagle argues that the alt-right is the ultimate consequence of the mainstreaming of transgression I have examined throughout this book. According to Nagle, Dionysian excess is a transhistorical drive running from the Marquis de Sade to internet pornography, one which has been unleashed by well-meaning liberals only to destroy them.[19] Echoing the ideas of Fredric Wertham, she contends that transgression begins by challenging standards of decency and ends by overturning the egalitarian norms of liberal democracy to make way for fascism.[20] Over the course of this rather hasty argument, she opposes countercultural rebellion to middle-class conformity in a simplified way that ignores how the transgressive style was articulated through the postwar culture of work. We can easily dismiss Nagle's ahistorical claims in part because the author herself has moved far to the nationalist right with no help from de Sade.

Passing over these faults, Catherine Liu works to ground Nagle's ideas in class analysis, arguing that the alt-right is a reaction to the "culturalist pieties and neglect of economic policies" that characterize what she calls "professional-managerial class liberalism."[21] In Liu's estimation, the alt-right has turned the PMC's "fetishism of transgression" against it, shocking the middle-class faction as punishment for its political sins.[22] Although it is true that the alt-right presents itself in opposition to PMC liberalism, this analysis does not go far enough to account for the alt-right's own class position. Taking up the language of the cultural studies tradition she decries, Liu places the alt-right somewhere at the "margins," and they quickly come to look like nothing more than fascist versions of the culture-jamming outsiders and punk bricoleurs that first burst onto the academic scene with Dick Hebdige's *Subculture*.[23] To better understand the alt-right, we have to see them not as a threat external to the PMC but, rather, as the exacerbation of a tendency within the PMC.

Classing the alt-right is difficult because it is a political movement with no clear membership criteria, one composed of online users who have a strong reason to remain anonymous. Nevertheless, white nationalist Richard Spencer gave us a hint to how the movement sees itself when he described the average members of the cause as thirtysomething "tech professionals."[24] This is perhaps an aspirational picture of the alt-right, whose most visible members do not appear quite so successful and well-adjusted as Spencer suggests. Although the alt-right includes many long-term unemployed and working-class members, its most prominent spokesmen started out as would-be members of the PMC before stumbling onto a downwardly mobile class trajectory.[25] The alt-right's vanguard leaders all share the same experience of receiving the cultural training and educational credentials required to enter into the PMC but ultimately falling short of securing within it permanent positions. These white nationalists and antifeminists are not populist challengers to PMC liberalism—they are failed PMC aspirants who have kept themselves afloat by turning reactionary politics into a new hustle.

Far from being anarchic outsiders, the alt-right recombines and repurposes many of the elements of managing obscenity I have discussed in this study. The alt-right's mass base of support emerged out of shocking websites including Something Awful, an online forum dedicated to nihilistic, gross-out humor, and 4chan, an imageboard that began as a sharing site for Japanese cartoon pornography.[26] These platforms were populated primarily by young white men who looked to online culture as an escape from their lonely and unfulfilling lives. They bonded over offensive memes, often excluding women from their conversations. Many of them adopted troll personae out of frustration or malice and lashed out at others in targeted harassment campaigns that sometimes ruined the lives of their victims. Like the readers of midcentury pornography, the trolls who would become the alt-right developed a hardboiled, masculinist ethos that condemned outrage, sentimentality, and other excessive emotions as signs of weakness, effeminacy, and low intelligence.[27] When they were not expressing this emotional style as a form of hyperrationalism, they articulated it through a mordant irony that treated even the most serious of topics as absurd.

Following in the footsteps of the postwar rat race, these misanthropic internet users gamified their everyday lives. On Something Awful, one user wrote a popular account of how a series of company errors left him managing a department with no employees and no job duties. For years, the anonymous poster claimed, he surfed the internet instead of working, cleverly dodging employee meetings and job reviews while still receiving a paycheck. The point of these musings, Dale Beran suggests, was that "life is a joke."[28] In keeping with this spirit, the denizens of these forums drew inspiration from film and fiction narratives about alienated white-collar workers performing pointless tasks in unreal bureaucracies—*American Psycho* (2000), *Fight Club* (1999), *The Matrix* (1999).[29]

Similar attitudes governed the seduction advice that sometimes spilled onto these platforms: "game theory" or "pickup artistry." Like the playboys of the 1950s, pickup artists saw sex as a technical problem to be solved through repeatable strategies or "algorithms."[30] Pickup artistry adopted the jargon of military and business strategy—they call nonconsensually touching a woman to invade her personal space "kino," short for "kinesthetics"—and justified its practices with ideas borrowed from neurolinguistic programming (NLP), a fringe self-help movement from the 1970s.[31] *Dilbert* creator Scott Adams summed up NLP's operating assumptions when he described the brain as a "moist computer" that could be recoded to do what you want it to do through subliminal linguistic cues.[32]

Pickup artists also explained their exploits using concepts cribbed from popularizations of evolutionary psychology, a discourse that naturalized cold war ideas about social hierarchy, market competition, and gender essentialism using just-so stories involving apes and lobsters. Ultimately, evolutionary psychology comported well with their view of the world as an arbitrary but cutthroat game with winners and losers, alphas and betas.[33] Drawing these ideas together, pickup guru Mystery told his readers that they should learn to see "human beings as beautiful, elegant biological machines embedded with sophisticated behavioral systems designed to align with others to maximize their chances for survival and replication."[34] This erotic ideology ratifies relative inequalities among men—who are ranked based on sexual success—while reifying absolute inequalities between men and women.[35] According to the pickup artists, men are capable of becoming rational agents when it comes to love and sex, but women in these scenarios tend to remain trapped in their biologically hardwired emotional programming. Repeating a truism we have seen before in obscene discourse, Mystery argues that women are "creatures of sentiment."[36] The technical jargon and management-speak surrounding sex confirm men's masculinity while degrading women.

These discourses have a formative as well as ideological function. By objectifying women as animals who respond to social and biological signals in predictable—even instinctual—ways, pickup artistry serves as a distancing mechanism aimed at helping men overcome their anxieties and treat sex as a numbers game, an abstraction. Pickup artists use controlled forms of transgression as a training technique to reach this uncaring state. Through deliberate violations of everyday norms—groping, insulting, snubbing, and shocking women—they practice self-control or "inner game."[37] Pickup artists reason that if they can learn to move past the potential humiliation involved in breaking social decorum or violating personal boundaries, they will be all the better prepared to suppress their fear of rejection when it comes time to proposition a woman. Repetition of the same seduction algorithms with many different women also help bring about this desired effect. By treating women as interchangeable, pickup artists sever any embarrassing and inconvenient attachments to particular women that might get in the way of their ultimate goal of maximizing their number of erotic encounters.[38] Pickup artists think of their craft as gaming, which can only be perfected through countless replays. Needless to say, this attitude breaks any feeling of immediacy surrounding sexuality. Unable to live in the moment, seduction devotees tend to imagine sex in either a retrospective or anticipatory mode, an achievement unlocked or an enticement to be pursued.[39] Everything they do is organized around banishing intimacy from the bedroom, a move that would have been familiar to many of the emotionally distant postwar provocateurs we have already met.

Although popular journalism often presents pickup subculture as a strange deviation from the norm, scholars have observed that pickup artistry only reflects and exaggerates a broader trend in advice columns in men's magazines and other forms of self-help discourse that explain how to optimize and control sexuality through managerial techniques. Pickup artistry frames sex and seduction as an entrepreneurial project that must be approached with all the self-denying diligence of the Protestant work ethic.[40] As in the middle-class sexual revolution of the 1950s and 1960s, sex becomes a form of mental labor performed using strict professional codes.

Like the midcentury immoralists, postmillennial geeks built a training regimen around microbursts of transgression. But none of it worked. The cold cultural style of professional-managerial disaffection had already fallen in prominence to make way for a warm "middlebrow personalism," intended to give elites opportunities to resolve social antagonisms through sensitivity, empathy, and identification.[41] Emotional distance started to lose its cultural prestige, but, even more importantly, it fell precipitously in economic value. The postwar boom enabled white, college-educated men to translate their cultural capital into sizeable salaries, but after decades of economic stagnation, labor defeat, and financial crisis a generation of studious twentysomethings found themselves unable to live the American dream of a dead-end job. On boards like 4chan, they called themselves NEETs: Not in Education, Employment, or Training.[42] These young men's hopes for romantic satisfaction were equally frustrated. Screen time and social isolation left them unable to fulfill their often-unrealistic expectations about sex. Many of them began to identify as involuntary celibates, or "incels," and some even responded to their perceived plight by joining an ideological network devoted to male supremacy, "the manosphere."[43] This belief system inspired misogynist spree-killers like Elliot Rodger, the self-styled gentleman who killed six people out of vengeance against women he considered to be too irrational to make intelligent sexual and reproductive choices on their own. Toxic digital subcultures quickly turned these mass murders into another gamified pastime with its own ironic memes and score-keeping system.[44]

Potential recruits of the alt-right suffered from what might be called spoiled cultural capital. By immersing themselves in subcultures devoted to the erotic and the extreme, they developed a repertoire of disciplines designed to bring them romantic, financial, and personal success. When these self-improvement schemes failed them—or even stood in the way of realizing their goals—they were left only with a raging sense of entitlement. They had worked so hard on themselves without reaping any of the expected rewards. A vanguard of alt-right media personalities stepped in to resolve the contradiction between what they were trained to achieve and what they actually acquired.

Unsurprisingly, this has led many alt-right authors to spurn the PMC and its real or imagined liberalism. Borrowing all of the tropes of racist and anti-Semitic conspiracy theories, alt-right thinkers argue that this new class is a globalist elite of rootless cosmopolitans who are unbound by national loyalties, disconnected from the culture of white ethnic communities, and estranged from the biological fundamentals of race, sex, and innate hierarchy. One reactionary manifesto warns of "a ruling class whose only claim to legitimacy resides in its abstract manipulations (logico-symbolic) of the signs and values of the system already in place," a socioeconomic grouping consisting of "cold-blooded specialists," who wield a depersonalized "rationality detached from day-to-day realities."[45] By rejecting the PMC as a perversion of the natural order, these alt-right mouthpieces give their audience of déclassé white men an explanation for why they have not ascended into the upper-middle class. Much like Mencken, the white men of the alt-right see themselves as members of an aristocracy of inherited intellect, who have been cheated of their birthright by an absurd system rigged to favor the subrational masses. As these ideas filtered into the mainstream, they lent ideological cover to the capitalist project of proletarianizing credentialed workers, rolling back gains made in civil rights and welfare provisions, dismantling the public university system, and distracting from the more fundamental contradiction between the working class and the employing class.

Because the alt-right believes they have been deposed from their rightful places, they have leaned heavily into the culture of white male victimhood. Alt-right conspiracy theories depict white men as powerless to resist bodily violation by nefarious forces and feminizing pollutants. As Casey Ryan Kelly has argued, masochism has become crucial to reactionary forms of white masculinity from the manosphere to Trumpism.[46] By casting themselves as abject victims tortured by a global cabal of Jews, Muslims, feminists, people of color, and other marginalized groups, the alt-right seeks to downplay their own relative privilege while mobilizing support for sadistic counterviolence and, ultimately, genocide.

Despite turning their backs on PMC liberalism, the alt-right's constituents remain obsessed with pornography and see their capacity to resist the temptations of obscene content as a sign of superior self-control. Members of the movement who openly embrace Nazism point to outlaw editors such as Samuel Roth as proof that pornography has always been a Jewish conspiracy to weaken the Aryan race by encouraging degeneracy.[47] Even as they rail against immorality, though, these fascists betray their deep immersion in pornified culture: when alt-right trolls condemn interracial sex as a threat to white purity, they use the language and imagery of online pornography.[48] Nevertheless, popular white nationalists argue that refusing pornography is the first step on the path to overcoming weakness and becoming an Übermensch.[49]

Similar ideas pervade the manosphere. The NoFap trend blames pornography for modern men's sexual and social impotence. Echoing midcentury figures as disparate as Hefner and Marcuse, NoFap partisans argue that seduction forces men to strive for self-improvement to compete for women. They diverge from these figures, however, in arguing that virtual pornography disrupts this sexual meritocracy by rewarding men with erotic satisfaction that requires no effort to achieve.[50] They claim that porn-addicted men become unable to govern themselves, rendering them slovenly, listless, and feminized. To avoid this fate, *Vice* magazine editor turned right-wing gang-leader Gavin McInnes counsels his followers, the Proud Boys, that they should only masturbate alone to pornography once every thirty days. This elaborate erotic practice supposedly allows men to learn to master themselves, delay gratification, achieve greatness, and become more traditionally masculine.[51]

All of this might paint a picture of McInnes as an abstemious Comstock figure, but the author of *The Death of Cool* actually comes to look more like the midcentury organization man who once found covert pleasure in eroticizing normalcy. McInnes got his start as a "middle-class" punk before he cofounded *Vice*, which targeted the emerging hipster subculture.[52] At *Vice*, McInnes drew inspiration from what he called "hate literature," transgressive zines that reveled in shocking images and offensive writing.[53] McInnes considered himself a disciple of Jim Goad, who wrote and coedited *ANSWER Me!* along with Debbie Goad. In 1995, two booksellers in Bellingham, Washington, were tried and acquitted of obscenity after selling a copy of *ANSWER Me!* #4—the "Rape Issue"—which featured images of sexual violence designed to attack feminists and "traumatize the reader."[54] Impressed by Goad's vile provocations, McInnes emulated his writing style and later helped him get hired at *Taki's Magazine*.[55] Over the years, the reactionary ideology that was always implicit in McInnes's offensive humor has become more explicit. Now, McInnes's public persona is that of the unhinged square: he appeared on the popular *Joe Rogan Experience* podcast carrying a briefcase and dressed in precisely the same business attire as the rampage-killing, laid-off engineer played by Michael Douglas in *Falling Down* (1993). Even as McInnes brags about his sexual conquests, he counsels his followers to get married, move to the suburbs, raise children, and begin "venerating the housewife," all the while demanding that they force women back into subordinate domestic roles that now take on the fetishistic character of adult movie tropes.[56] Indeed, NoFap has already developed its own paradoxical subgenre of pornography: the actresses on screen pretend to reward men with sexual favors for not masturbating to pornography. Inadvertently following Foucault, McInnes suggests that strictly regulating sexuality along heteronormative lines offers an even greater impetus for perversion.[57]

Here I am not simply making the argument that pornography prompts privileged white men to view women as objects. Most pornographic platforms are not hotbeds of alt-right agitation. The problem here is not transgression itself but instead an anti-censorship discourse that claims that men should prove themselves to be rational by exercising their ability to see the obscene without succumbing it. Women become a temptation to be managed and overcome, a source of emotional and moral chaos that must be bound and disciplined. These old ideas about the dangers of sex take on a new urgency once they are filtered through the desperate performance ethos of neoliberal competition. In this community, adult-film stars are not merely seen as unclean: they are viewed as stumbling blocks to men's success. Whereas women used to appear in pornographic publications as symbols of achievement, they now serve as figures for personal and financial ruin.

We are in some sense back where we started: a new generation of young white men from PMC backgrounds think they can build character through carefully controlled engagements with obscenity. Of course, this is a repetition with a difference. While the editors examined in this study faced actual state censorship that carried with it the very real threat of jail time, alt-right hucksters now farcically claim to be censored whenever a school declines to host their speeches or an online platform refuses to publish their diatribes. Just as importantly, though, this movement organized around self-mastery faces an economic and political landscape in which they can no longer assume dominance. When the alt-right adherent dons on a fedora, pours whiskey into a tumbler, and proposes to have a frank public discussion about Nietzsche and sex, he is performing an outdated ritual of sophistication more likely to summon ridicule than admiration or prestige. Contrary to what Nagle implies, we cannot adequately understand transgression if we remove it from its historical context. The norm violations of previous decades did not function in the same way as they do now. The alt-right can dress up like their grandfathers and imitate their libertine indulgences, but they will only become desperate, even violent, when they fail to obtain the same cultural authority or economic security.

We can tell that this is all a sham from the fact that when obscenity is actually being prohibited, we rarely hear from the alt-right trolls. A serious look at how explicit speech is actually policed in the twenty-first century would call into question many of their cherished doctrines of libertarianism. Increasingly, obscenity censorship is carried out not by publishers or even platforms but by online payment processors like PayPal, who are wary of contravening *Miller v. California* but even more worried about the high rate of disputed purchase claims associated with online pornography, whose users do not always feel safe or comfortable admitting to making purchases from adult websites when the charges appear on their monthly statements.[58] In 2012, PayPal pushed the popular e-book platform Smashwords to remove all texts that included themes such as rape, incest, bestiality, and underage sex.[59] For its part, PayPal denied that it was making an editorial decision at all: it blamed unnamed banks and credit card companies for forcing it to restrict obscene speech.[60] Either way, when Smashwords complied it set off a firestorm among erotica authors. Remittance Girl, a popular author of erotic e-books, spoke out most forcefully against the decision:

> The publishers who published [Nabokov] did not sanction pedophilia. The publishers who published Yukio Mishima, or [de Sade], or Henry Miller did not sanction the morality in reality of what was contained fictionally in their novels. They sanctioned the prerogative of literature to fully explore humanity, no matter how dark the fictionalized explorations might be. They sanctioned the author's right to explore it and the reader's right to explore it in his or her turn.
> Smashwords, sir, is NO GROVE PRESS.[61]

Authors of extreme literature now feel acutely the absence of prominent editors who might champion their work in the face of legal or extralegal censorship. The dissolution of editorial responsibility in the post-pornographic era forces erotic authors to face no less arbitrary forms of silencing carried out by even more abstract and impersonal systems. The profit imperative rather than prudery now motivates obscenity enforcement.

To combat these new forms of speech restrictions, we must first abolish the obscene mystique. Genuine censorship struggles are ill served by the cool, masculine image of the sophisticated professional capable of rising above the feminized emotions and uncivilized urges experienced by naïve audiences. These debates about the limits of speech are also obscured by the distinctly middle-class notion that abjection must always be redeemed as socially valuable, morally instructive, or politically productive. Pornography does not need to teach empathy or dissolve class privileges to be worthy of legalization. More research will undoubtedly reveal greater complexities about deplatformed erotica, but most banned pornographic literature today seems to be written for audiences of women and queer men primarily interested in sexual pleasure rather than personal edification. Because they do not tap into the old mythology of anticensorship discourse, they often go ignored. Unlike the grandstanding media personalities of the alt-right, today's authors of extreme pornography never receive adulation and invitations to appear on television shows when they are silenced by Silicon Valley. If we want to make possible a greater range of erotic expression in literature, we will have to abandon the old myths promoted by transgressive editors and begin to wrest control of the book trade away from corporations owned and managed by the wealthy few.

Notes

Introduction: The Naked Editor

1. Ed Sanders, *Fug You: An Informal History of the Peace Eye Bookstore, the Fuck You Press, The Fugs, and Counterculture in the Lower East Side* (Philadelphia: Da Capo Press, 2011), 183–91.

2. Ibid., 163.

3. Ibid., 186.

4. Ibid., emphasis original.

5. Ibid.

6. Ibid., 214–15, 248.

7. I have proposed the editor function in response to Foucault's analysis of the "author function," which argues that texts "really began to have authors (other than mythical, 'sacralized' and 'sacralizing' figures) to the extent that authors became subject to punishment, that is, to the extent that discourses could be transgressive." Michel Foucault, "What is an Author?" in *The Foucault Reader*, ed. Paul Rabinow, trans. Josué V. Harari (New York: Pantheon, 1984), 108. However, in the US context editors have been held accountable more often than authors during obscenity trials. This study treats the category of "editor" as a discursive position rather than an occupational category. Many of the editors detailed in this project were also publishers, but, as we shall see, what binds them all together as editors is their ability to shape the reading practices of their audiences and speak on their behalf in legal or cultural controversies. Given this approach, I do not make hard and fast distinctions between periodical and trade book editors, especially given that several of the editors in this study fulfilled both roles. *Reading the Obscene* hopes to show that editing studies is a subfield in its own right that straddles periodical studies and book history. Andrew Piper applies the term "editor-function" to fictive editors (i.e., authors who claim that their works are found manuscripts). Andrew Piper, *Dreaming in Books: The Making of the Bibliographic Imagination in the Romantic Age* (Chicago: University of Chicago Press, 2009), 109. While I sometimes use "editor function" to refer to the editor as a figure or persona, I am also using it to denote a legal and authorial responsibility

that allows the editor to stand in for a press, its catalog, and its readers. Philip Lewis also uses this term to examine editorship through a Foucauldian lens, but within the context of academic journal publishing. Philip Lewis, "Notes on the Editor-Function," *Bulletin of the Midwest Modern Language Association* 12, no. 1 (Spring 1979): 20–31.

8. Sanders, *Fug You*, 184.

9. Ibid., 150.

10. Sanders quoted in Daniel Kane, *All Poets Welcome: The Lower East Side Poetry Scene in the 1960s* (Berkeley: University of California Press, 2003), 68.

11. Mary Rizzo, *Class Acts: Young Men and the Rise of Lifestyle* (Reno: University of Nevada Press, 2015), 41–42.

12. Sanders, *Fug You*, 349.

13. Following a similar line of analysis, Richard Ohmann suggests that on the cusp of the twentieth century, periodicals such as *Munsey's*, *Cosmopolitan*, and *Ladies' Home Journal* trained the emergent PMC to embrace consumption patterns, ways of living, and modes of comportment that signaled their "moral and intellectual superiority" over other classes. Richard Ohmann, *Selling Culture: Magazines, Markets, and Class at the Turn of the Century* (New York: Verso, 1996), 171–74. For the generation coming up under Mencken, however, moral probity and intellectual acumen increasingly came into sharp conflict.

14. Thanks to my anonymous reviewer for suggesting "sentimental education" as a formulation for this process.

15. Sanders, *Fug You*, 86.

16. Ibid.

17. Ibid.

18. *Fuck You / A Magazine of the Arts* 5, no. 2 (December 1962), cover, 2, https://rspull-supervert.netdna-ssl.com/images/bibliographic_bunker/fuck_you/fuck-you-press-pdfs/fuck-you.05.vol-02.pdf.

19. Sanders, *Fug You*, 250.

20. Ludwig Marcuse, *Obscene: The History of an Indignation*, trans. Karen Gershon (London: MacGibbon & Kee, 1962), 17. For a theoretical discussion of affect and pornography, see Susanna Paasonen, *Carnal Resonance: Affect and Online Pornography* (Cambridge, MA: MIT Press, 2011), 60.

21. Janice Radway, *Reading the Romance: Women, Patriarchy, and Popular Literature* (Chapel Hill: University of North Carolina Press, 1984), 30.

22. Many publishers tried to solve this problem by creating genre categories that promised to fulfill regular reader expectations, but, as Radway suggests, even the most preprogrammed examples of popular literature can elicit surprising and even subversive responses from readers. Ibid., 29, 45. While Radway explores this reception through

ethnographic methods, as a historical study *Reading the Obscene* can only see hints of reader resistance in the archive.

23. Here one might find some parallels between midcentury American editors and nineteenth-century German editors, who "defended their texts on grounds that they promoted *Bildung*, the cultivation of the emotions and intellect." Sarah L. Leonard, *Fragile Minds and Vulnerable Souls: The Matter of Obscenity in Nineteenth-Century Germany* (Philadelphia: University of Pennsylvania Press, 2015), 125.

24. Pierre Bourdieu, "The Production of Belief: Contribution to an Economy of Symbolic Goods," in *The Field of Cultural Production: Essays on Art and Literature*, ed. Randal Johnson, trans. Richard Nice (New York: Columbia University Press, 1993), 96. John Frow critiques this argument by suggesting that Bourdieu transforms artworks—with all of their inner tensions—into "non-contradictory expressive unities" that reflect in a straightforward manner a unified class logic. John Frow, *Cultural Studies and Cultural Value* (Oxford: Clarendon Press, 1995), 38–39.

25. Bourdieu, "Production of Belief," 95. For a systematic application of Bourdieusian theory to publishing, see John B. Thompson, *Merchants of Culture: The Publishing Business in the Twenty-First Century* (New York: Penguin, 2012).

26. Howard Becker, *Art Worlds* (Berkeley: University of California Press, 1982).

27. Ibid., 199–200.

28. Ibid., 200–201.

29. Ibid., 204.

30. Here I build upon recent work on extra-academic reading practices or "bad reading." See Merve Emre, *Paraliterary: The Making of Bad Readers in Postwar America* (Chicago: University of Chicago Press, 2017); Tyler Bradway, *Queer Experimental Literature: The Affective Politics of Bad Reading* (New York: Palgrave Macmillan, 2017).

31. Roger Escarpit briefly touches on this idea in *Sociology of Literature*, when he writes that publishers "influence the public by instigating new patterns and habits." Roger Escarpit, *Sociology of Literature*, trans. Ernest Pick (London: Frank Cass, 1971), 51.

32. See Gerard Genette, *Paratexts: Thresholds of Interpretation*, trans. Jane E. Lewin (Cambridge: Cambridge University Press, 1997).

33. Radway, *Reading the Romance*, 49–50.

34. On the formative function, see Joshua Landy, *How to Do Things with Fictions* (Oxford: Oxford University Press, 2012); Lee Konstantinou, *Cool Characters: Irony and American Fiction* (Cambridge, MA: Harvard University Press, 2016).

35. Linda Williams, *Screening Sex* (Durham, NC: Duke University Press, 2008), 18.

36. Georges Bataille, *Erotism: Death and Sensuality*, trans. Mary Dalwood (San Francisco: City Lights Books, 1986).

Chapter 1: Shocking the Middle Class

1. This study focuses primarily on the US context because the regulatory environment and class politics surrounding obscenity differed in other countries. Britain, for example, saw the liberalization of sex censorship during the same period, but, as Arthur Marwick observes, this was bound up in the self-assertion of a culturally insurgent working class. Arthur Marwick, *The Sixties: Cultural Revolution in Britain, France, Italy, and the United States, c. 1958–c.1974* (Oxford: Oxford University Press, 1998), 146. Readers interested in literature and obscenity law in other periods and national contexts should consult the following sources: Joan DeJean, *The Reinvention of Obscenity: Sex, Lies, and Tabloids in Early Modern France* (Chicago: University of Chicago Press, 2002); Kirsten Cather Fischer, *The Art of Censorship in Postwar Japan* (Honolulu: University of Hawai'i Press, 2012); Deana Heath, *Purifying Empire: Obscenity and the Politics of Moral Regulation in Britain, India and Australia* (Cambridge: Cambridge University Press, 2010); William Olmstead, *The Censorship Effect: Baudelaire, Flaubert, and the Formation of French Modernism* (Oxford: Oxford University Press, 2016); Marco Wan, *Masculinity and the Trials of Modern Fiction* (New York: Routledge, 2017).

2. Prior to *Rex v. Curll*, courts used obscenity to describe a breach of the peace such as the one committed by Sir Charles Sedley of Kent in 1663, when he and his friends stood on a balcony and flashed a crowd of onlookers while making a series of lewd propositions and indecent gestures, but in 1708 when judges took up the question of whether James Read's publication of the pornographic poem, *The Fifteen Plagues of a Maidenhead*, was obscene, they found that secular courts had no jurisdiction over obscenity in print form. Geoffrey R. Stone, "Origins of Obscenity," *New York University Review of Law and Social Change* 31 (2006), 720–22.

3. Pat Rogers and Paul Baines, "The Prosecutions of Edmund Curll, 1725–28," *Library* 5, no. 2 (2004): 176–94.

4. Edward de Grazia, *Censorship Landmarks* (New York: Bowker, 1969), 4, quoted in Stone, "Origins of Obscenity," 725.

5. Stone, "Origins of Obscenity," 725.

6. Rogers and Baines, "Prosecutions of Edmund Curll," 188.

7. Whitney Strub, *Obscenity Rules: Roth v. United States and the Long Struggle over Sexual Expression* (Lawrence: University Press of Kansas, 2013), 7.

8. Michael Millner, *Fever Reading: Affect and Reading Badly in the Early American Public Sphere* (Durham: University of New Hampshire Press, 2012), 71–72; Chris Forster, *Filthy Material: Modernism and the Media of Obscenity* (Oxford: Oxford University Press, 2019), 24–26.

9. Donna Dennis, *Licentious Gotham: Erotic Publishing and Its Prosecution in Nineteenth-Century New York* (Cambridge, MA: Harvard University Press, 2009), 31, 34.

10. Patricia Cline Cohen, Timothy J. Gilfoyle, and Helen Lefkowitz Horowitz, *The Flash Press: Sporting Male Weeklies in 1840s New York* (Chicago: University of Chicago Press, 2008), 84.

11. John McDowall quoted in Dennis, *Licentious Gotham*, 13.

12. Dennis, *Licentious Gotham*, 255.

13. For an extensive account of the flash press, see Cohen et al., *Flash Press*.

14. Ibid., 6–7.

15. Ibid., 57.

16. Dennis, *Licentious Gotham*, 67.

17. George Thompson quoted in Dennis, *Licentious Gotham*, 60.

18. Michael Millner, *Fever Reading*, 89–93.

19. Millner, *Fever Reading*, 72–73. Here, Millner draws heavily on Michael Warner's articulation of Jürgen Habermas's public sphere theory with queer theory. See also Michael Warner, "The Mass Public and the Mass Subject," in *Publics and Counterpublics* (New York: Zone Books, 2002), 164–68.

20. Millner, *Fever Reading*, 87.

21. Ibid., 81.

22. Ibid., 91–92.

23. Ibid., 93.

24. Gustav Lening quoted in Dennis, *Licentious Gotham*, 142.

25. Dennis, *Licentious Gotham*, 165, 148. Later publishers such as Samuel Roth carried on this tradition, sometimes listing the publication location of their books as "Cosmopoli," claiming to be from everywhere and nowhere. Jay A. Gertzman, *Bookleggers and Smuthounds: The Trade in Erotica, 1920–1940* (Philadelphia: University of Pennsylvania Press, 1999), 186, 229.

26. Dennis, *Licentious Gotham*, 164.

27. Judith Giesberg, *Sex and the Civil War: Soldiers, Pornography, and the Making of American Morality* (Chapel Hill: University of North Carolina Press, 2017).

28. For a complete account of Anthony Comstock's life and career, see Amy Werbel, *Lust on Trial: Censorship and the Rise of American Obscenity in the Age of Anthony Comstock* (New York: Columbia University Press, 2018).

29. Werbel, *Lust on Trial*, 75–74.

30. Giesberg, *Sex and the Civil War*, 3.

31. Edward de Grazia, *Girls Lean Back Everywhere: The Law of Obscenity and the Assault on Genius* (New York: Vintage, 1993), 5.

32. For a history of American free-love print culture, see Joanne E. Passet, *Sex Radicals and the Quest for Women's Equality* (Urbana: University of Illinois Press), 2003; Martin Henry Blatt, *Free Love and Anarchism: The Biography of Ezra Heywood* (Urbana: University of Illinois Press, 1989), 100–141.

33. Roderick Bradford, *D. M. Bennett: The Truth Seeker* (Amherst, NY: Prometheus, 2006), 110–83.

34. Werbel, *Lust on Trial*, 125–31. On the long history of the Hicklin test, see Stephen Gillers, "A Tendency to Deprave and Corrupt: The Transformation of American Obscenity Law from *Hicklin* to *Ulysses II*," *Washington University Law Review* 85 (2007): 225–38.

35. Paul S. Boyer, *Purity in Print: Book Censorship in America from the Gilded Age to the Computer Age* (Madison: University of Wisconsin Press, 2002), 276.

36. Josh Lambert, *Unclean Lips: Obscenity, Jews, and American Culture* (New York: New York University Press, 2014), 4–5.

37. Nicola Beisel, *Imperiled Innocents: Anthony Comstock and Family Reproduction in Victorian America* (Princeton, NJ: Princeton University Press, 1998), 4–7.

38. For a description of the professional-managerial class, see Barbara Ehrenreich and John Ehrenreich, "The Professional-Managerial Class," in *Between Capital and Labor*, ed. Pat Walker (Boston: South End Press, 1979), 5–45.

39. Mihaela Popescu, "Judicial Discourse as Feeling Rules: Obscenity Regulation and Inner Life Control, 1873–1956," *Law, Culture and the Humanities* 11, no. 2 (2015): 218–47.

40. Beisel, *Imperiled Innocents*, 49–75.

41. Dennis, *Licentious Gotham*, 95.

42. Bob Brown quoted in Gertzman, *Bookleggers and Smuthounds*, 67.

43. Gertzman, *Bookleggers and Smuthounds*, 55.

44. Liza Z. Sigel, *Governing Pleasures: Pornography and Social Change in England, 1815–1914* (New Brunswick, NJ: Rutgers University Press, 2002), 61. As Sarah Bull points out, this association between forbidden knowledge and erotic pleasure was very much an invention of publishing practices, which often marketed licit as well as illicit books as if they were part of the same censored archive or "secret museum." Sarah Bull, "Reading, Writing, and Publishing an Obscene Canon: The Archival Logic of the Secret Museum, c. 1860–c. 1900," *Book History* 20 (2017): 226–57.

45. Gertzman, *Bookleggers and Smuthounds*, 4.

46. Andrea Friedman, *Prurient Interests: Gender, Democracy, and Obscenity in New York City, 1909–1945* (New York: Columbia University Press, 2000), 7.

47. Ibid., 32.

48. United States v. Kennerley, 209 F. 119, 121 (S.D.N.Y. 1913).

49. Friedman, *Prurient Interests*, 177.

50. Ian Hunter, David Saunders, and Dugald Williamson, *On Pornography: Literature, Sexuality and Obscenity Law* (London: Macmillan, 1993), 208–11.

51. Ibid., 90.

52. Keep in mind that, as Nicos Poulantzas makes clear, the division between mental and manual labor is always a political and ideological distinction rather than a neutral

description of occupational categories or types of work. By maintaining their monopoly on the credible exercise of expert knowledge, the PMC contributes to the subjection of the proletarian workers by preventing them from accessing or acting on information about the production process. Nicos Poulantzas, *Classes in Contemporary Capitalism* (London: Verso, 1975), 224–70.

53. Boyer, *Purity in Print*, 71–72.

54. Morris Ernst and William Seagle, *To the Pure: A Study of Obscenity and the Censor* (New York: Viking Press, 1928), 4–8. See also Joseph Kelly, *Our Joyce: From Outcast to Icon* (Austin: University of Texas Press, 1998), 117–20.

55. Ernst and Seagle, *To the Pure*, 5.

56. Ibid., 9.

57. Paul Vanderham, *James Joyce and Censorship: The Trials of Ulysses* (London: Macmillan, 1998), 99.

58. Ibid., 99–100.

59. Brook Thomas, "*Ulysses* on Trial: Some Supplementary Reading," *Criticism* 33, no. 3 (1991), 381.

60. Loren Glass, "Redeeming Value: Obscenity and Anglo-American Modernism," *Critical Inquiry* 32, no. 2 (2006), 347.

61. Vanderham, *James Joyce and Censorship*, 102–3.

62. John Cowper Powys quoted in Kelly, *Our Joyce*, 120.

63. Ernst and Seagle, *To the Pure*, 59.

64. Ibid., 60.

65. Thomas, "*Ulysses* on Trial," 382.

66. Robert Spoo, "Judging Woolsey Judging Obscenity: Elitism, Aestheticism, and the Reasonable Libido in the *Ulysses* Customs Case," *James Joyce Quarterly* 50, no. 4 (2013), 1037. Merrill is frequently mistaken for the cofounder of Merrill Lynch. See Thomas, "*Ulysses* on Trial," 383–84.

67. Spoo, "Judging Woolsey," 139–40.

68. Friedman, for example, argues that the decision to shift the focus of obscenity trials from children to average readers turned the focus in censorship cases from the concerns of activist women to the deliberations of professional men. Friedman, *Prurient Interests*, 177–78.

69. Eric Larrabee, "The Cultural Context of Sex Censorship," *Law and Contemporary Problems* 20, no. 4 (1955), 673.

70. Ibid., 679.

71. Stephen Gillers, "Tendency to Deprave," 296.

72. Strub, *Obscenity Rules*, 75–78.

73. Roth v. U.S., 354 U.S. 476 (1957).

74. Refusing to commit to censorship or anti-censorship, liberals remained "ambivalent" about pornographic expression, which they treated as somehow different from other forms of speech. Whitney Strub, *Perversion for Profit: The Politics of Pornography and the Rise of the New Right* (New York: Columbia University Press, 2010), 45–48.

75. For a complete biography of Samuel Roth, see Jay A. Gertzman, *Samuel Roth, Infamous Modernist* (Gainesville: University of Florida Press, 2013).

76. Roth v. U.S., 354 U.S. 476 (1957).

77. "Roth v. United States," *Obscenity: The Complete Oral Arguments before the Supreme Court in the Major Obscenity Cases*, ed. Leon Friedman (New York: Chelsea House Publishers, 1970), 30.

78. Frederick Schauer, "Speech and 'Speech'—Obscenity and 'Obscenity': An Exercise in the Interpretation of Constitutional Language," *Georgetown Law Journal* 67, no. 4 (1979), 923. Molly McGarry suggests that Comstock performed a kind of spiritualist conjuring trick that "transformed ideas into bodies" by reimagining information about sexuality or reproductive health as a spectral invader materializing into the reader's private parlor through the medium of the postal system. Molly McGarry, "Spectral Sexualities: Nineteenth-Century Spiritualism, Moral Panics, and the Making of U.S. Obscenity Law," *Journal of Women's History* 12, no. 2 (2000), 22.

79. Schauer's argument is not a mere thought experiment: states including Texas and Alabama passed laws banning "obscene devices" such as dildos and artificial vaginas. See Reliable Consultants, Inc. v. Earle, 517 F.3d 738 (5th Cir. 2008); 1568 Montgomery Highway, Inc. v. City of Hoover, 45 So.3d 319, 321 (Ala. 2010). For a summary of recent obscene devices cases, see Jennifer Kinsley, "The Myth of Obsolete Obscenity," *Cardozo Arts and Entertainment Law Journal* 33 (2015), 627–28, 631–33.

80. Roth v. U.S., 354 U.S. 476 (1957).

81. Ginzburg v. United States, 383 U.S. 463 (1966).

82. James C. N. Paul and Murray L. Schwartz, *Federal Censorship: Obscenity in the Mail* (New York: Free Press of Glencoe, 1961), 217.

83. William B. Lockhart and Robert C. McClure, "Literature, the Law of Obscenity, and the Constitution," *Minnesota Law Review* 38, no. 4 (1954), 340–41.

84. The legal scholars' recommendations would be taken on board by the American Law Institute's Model Penal Code, and variable obscenity would become the mechanism for the Motion Picture Association of America's rating system. De Grazia, *Girls Lean Back*, 503; Jon Lewis, *Hollywood v. Hard Core: How the Struggle over Censorship Saved the Modern Film Industry* (New York: New York University Press, 2002), 140.

85. Ginzburg v. United States 383 U.S. 463 (1966).

86. Ibid.

87. Ibid.

88. Mishkin v. New York, 383 U.S. 502 (1966).

89. Strub, *Perversion for Profit*, 75.

90. De Grazia, *Girls Lean Back*, 503.

91. Merle Miller quoted in de Grazia, *Girls Lean Back*, 505. Something more than fashion-policing may have been going on in court here: Ginzburg later stated that he thought that his persecutors may have been motivated anti-Semitism. Ralph Ginzburg, "Playboy Interview: Ralph Ginzburg," *Playboy*, July 1966, 120.

92. Paul Bender quoted in de Grazia, *Girls Lean Back*, 505.

93. Charles Rembar used this strategy while defending the *Lady Chatterley's Lover* and *Tropic of Cancer* cases, and Edward de Grazia took the same position in the *Naked Lunch* case. Charles Rembar, *The End of Obscenity: The Trials of "Lady Chatterley," "Tropic of Cancer," and "Fanny Hill"* (New York: Random House, 1968), 123, 203; Michael Barry Goodman, *Contemporary Literary Censorship: The Case History of Burroughs' "Naked Lunch"* (Metuchen, NJ: Scarecrow Press, 1981), 230. Jacob W. Ehrlich in the *Howl* trial does not explicitly subscribe to the social-value test, but he does examine multiple witnesses on the work's "literary value" or "merit." J. W. Ehrlich, ed., *Howl of the Censor* (San Carlos: Nourse Publishing, 1961), 50–51.

94. Citing *Roth*, Judge Clayton W. Horn's decision seems to presage the Rembar and de Grazia obscenity defenses, arguing that "if the material has the slightest redeeming social importance it is not obscene because it is protected by the First and Fourteenth Amendments of the United States Constitution." Ehrlich, ed., *Howl of the Censor*, 126.

95. Loren Glass, *Counterculture Colophon: Grove Press, the "Evergreen Review," and the Incorporation of the Avant-Garde* (Stanford: Stanford University Press, 2013); Loren Glass, *Rebel Publisher: Grove Press and the Revolution of the Word* (New York: Seven Stories Press, 2018).

96. Grove Press, Inc. v. Christenberry, 175 F. Supp. 488 (S.D.N.Y. 1959).

97. Strub, *Perversion for Profit*, 70–79.

98. Michael Hemmingson, "Porno Kings (and Queens) of San Diego," *San Diego Reader*, June 30, 2005, https://www.sandiegoreader.com/news/2005/jun/30/feature-porno-kings-queens-san-diego/.

99. Strub, *Perversion for Profit*, 76–78.

100. Ibid., 293.

101. Ginzburg v. United States 383 U.S. 463 (1966).

102. Kinsey suggests that this is because college-educated men are more imaginative and less likely to engage in sex outside of marriage. Alfred C. Kinsey, Wardell B. Pomeroy, and Clyde E. Martin, *Sexual Behavior in the Human Male* (Bloomington: Indiana University Press, 1948), 363; Clive Barnes, *The Report of the Commission on Obscenity and Pornography* (New York: Bantam, 1970), 159.

103. Barbara Ehrenreich, *The Hearts of Men: American Dreams and the Flight from Commitment* (New York: Anchor Books, 1983), 46; Bill Osgerby, *Playboys in Paradise: Masculinity, Youth and Leisure-style in Modern America* (New York: Berg, 2001), 5.

104. Ehrenreich, *Hearts of Men*, 11.

105. H. L. Mencken, *In Defense of Women* (New York: Knopf, 1918), 32; Ehrenreich, *Hearts of Men*, 6–7.

106. Ehrenreich, *Hearts of Men*, 45–46.

107. Pierre Bourdieu, *Distinction: A Social Critique of the Judgement of Taste*, trans. Richard Nice (Cambridge, MA: Harvard University Press, 1984), quoted in Osgerby, *Playboys in Paradise*, 10.

108. Julie Berebitsky, *Sex and the Office: A History of Gender, Power, and Desire* (New Haven, CT: Yale University Press, 2012), 13–14.

109. Ehrenreich, *Hearts of Men*, 32–36.

110. David Riesman, Nathan Glazer, and Reuel Denney, *The Lonely Crowd: A Study of the Changing American Character* (New Haven, CT: Yale University Press, 2001), 19–24.

111. Ehrenreich, *Hearts of Men*, 33–34.

112. K. A. Cuordileone, *Manhood and American Political Culture in the Cold War* (New York: Routledge, 2005), 97–124.

113. Riesman et al., *Lonely Crowd*, 242.

114. Mencken, *In Defense of Women*, 33–34; Elizabeth Fraterrigo, *Playboy and the Making of the Good Life in Modern America* (New York: Oxford University Press, 2009), 114–19.

115. Endnotes Collective, "The Logic of Gender: On the Separation of Spheres and the Process of Abjection," *Endnotes* 3, https://endnotes.org.uk/issues/3/en/endnotes-the-logic-of-gender.

116. Ibid.

117. Ibid.

118. This account relies heavily on Phil Ford, *Dig: Sound and Music in Hip Culture* (New York: Oxford University Press, 2013), 157–61.

119. Erich Fromm, *The Sane Society* (New York: Holt, Rinehart & Winston, 1955), 111–20. For a more recent version of this argument, see Zygmunt Bauman, *Modernity and the Holocaust* (Ithaca, NY: Cornell University Press, 1989).

120. Ford, *Dig*, 133. See, for example, Dwight Macdonald, *The Root is Man* (New York: Autonomedia, 1995), 150; C. Wright Mills, "The Decline of the Left," in *Power, Politics, and People: The Collected Essays of C. Wright Mills*, ed. Irving Louis Horowitz (New York: Oxford University Press, 1963), 232.

121. The elision between the middle class and society as a whole was a problem endemic to midcentury social criticism. Richard H. Pells, *The Liberal Mind in a Conservative Age: American Intellectuals in the 1940s and 1950s* (Middletown, CT: Wesleyan

University Press, 1989), 183; Richard Ohmann, "The Shaping of a Canon: U.S. Fiction, 1960–1975," *Critical Inquiry* 10, no. 1 (1983): 199–223. This project is indebted to more recent work that clarifies the specific character and role of the midcentury middle classes such as Andrew Hoberek, *The Twilight of the Middle Class: Post–World War II American Fiction and White-Collar Work* (Princeton, NJ: Princeton University Press, 2005) and Stephen Schryer, *Fantasies of the New Class: Ideologies of Professionalism in Post–World War II American Fiction* (New York: Columbia University Press, 2011).

122. C. Wright Mills, *White Collar: The American Middle Classes* (New York: Oxford University Press, 1951), 110–11. Critiquing the "abstractification" and "alienation" required to administer a bureaucracy, Erich Fromm suggests that "the manager-bureaucrat must not feel, as far as his professional activity is concerned; he must manipulate people as though they were figures, or things." Fromm, *Sane Society*, 126.

123. Richard Edwards, *Contested Terrain: The Transformation of the Workplace in the Twentieth Century* (New York: Basic Books, 1979), 132. On the role of bureaucratic control in midcentury American culture, see Daniel Belgrad, *The Culture of Spontaneity: Improvisation and the Arts in Postwar America* (Chicago: University of Chicago Press, 1998), 3–5.

124. Edwards, *Contested Terrain*, 138–39, 145. For a contemporary critique of this phenomenon, see Daniel Bell, *The End of Ideology* (New York: Free Press of Glencoe, 1960), 222–62.

125. For another analysis of the "pornographic" possibilities of these administrative forms, see Mark Seltzer, *The Official World* (Durham, NC: Duke University Press, 2016), 11–13.

126. Edwards, *Contested Terrain*, 152.

127. Peter N. Stearns, *American Cool: Constructing a Twentieth-Century Emotional Style* (New York: New York University Press, 1994), 123.

128. Barbara Ehrenreich and John Ehrenreich point out that the major division within the professional-managerial class is between managers who have cozied up to the corporate world and professionals such as academics who still maintain some critical distance from capitalism. This conflict, however, does not make them members of a different class. In addition to performing many of the same social functions, these two groups often work for the same organizations, graduate from the same universities, travel in the same social circles, and share the same class experiences. Ehrenreich and Ehrenreich, "The Professional-Managerial Class," 28–30.

129. Alvin Gouldner, *The Future of Intellectuals and the Rise of the New Class: A Frame of Reference, Theses, Conjectures, Arguments, and an Historical Perspective on the Role of Intellectuals and Intelligentsia in the International Class Contest of the Modern Era* (London: Macmillan, 1979), 29.

130. Theodore Roszak, *The Making of a Counter Culture: Reflections on the Technocratic Society and Its Youthful Opposition* (Garden City, NY: Anchor Books, 1969), 205–38.

131. Ibid., 223.

132. Karl Marx, *Capital: Volume 1*, trans. Ben Fowkes (New York: Penguin Books, 1990), 150; Alfred Sohn-Rethel, *Intellectual and Manual Labour: A Critique of Epistemology* (London: Macmillan, 1978); Moishe Postone, *Time, Labor, and Social Domination: A Reinterpretation of Marx's Critical Theory* (Cambridge: Cambridge University Press, 1993), 123–85; Alberto Toscano, "The Open Secret of Real Abstraction," *Rethinking Marxism* 20, no. 2 (2008): 273–87; Alberto Toscano, "The Culture of Abstraction," *Theory, Culture and Society* 25, no. 4 (2008): 57–75.

133. Marx, *Capital*, 481–82.

134. Michael Bray, *Powers of the Mind: Mental and Manual Labor in the Contemporary Political Crisis* (Bielefeld, Germany: Transcript Verlag, 2019), 54.

135. For Marxist analyses of the split between the private and productive spheres, see Eli Zaretsky, *Capitalism, the Family, and Personal Life* (New York: Harper, 1976); Roswitha Scholz, "Patriarchy and Commodity Society: Gender without the Body," *Mediations* 27, nos. 1–2 (2014): 123–42.

136. Ford, *Dig*, 7.

137. Belgrad, *Culture of Spontaneity*, 5–6.

138. Norman O. Brown, *Life Against Death: The Psychoanalytical Meaning of History* (Middletown: Wesleyan University Press, 1959), 172–73. According to Brown, capitalism necessarily produced this attitude by subordinating life to an economy in which money acts as a fetish symbol for feces and encouraging an anal-sadistic character disposed toward calculation and acquisitiveness. Brown, *Life Against Death*, 234–304.

139. Ibid., 174–76.

140. Gay Talese, *Thy Neighbor's Wife* (New York: Doubleday, 1981), 179–80, 192.

141. Williamson initially called this endeavor Project Synergy and later, more informally, the Sandstone Retreat. Talese, *Thy Neighbor's Wife*, 194–95, 277–82.

142. Ibid., 186.

143. Eva Illouz, *Cold Intimacies: The Making of Emotional Capitalism* (Cambridge: Polity, 2007), 18–36. Fromm saw this as early as 1955, when he painted a picture of a perfectly transparent suburban world in which one's most intimate thoughts and experiences are immediately defused by being verbalized to chatty neighbors or mental-health professionals. Fromm, *Sane Society*, 157–69.

144. Sylvère Lotringer, *Overexposed: Perverting Perversions* (Los Angeles: Semiotext(e), 2007), 18–19, 25, 36–38.

145. Reinhold Martin, *The Organizational Complex: Architecture, Media, and Corporate Space* (Cambridge, MA: MIT Press, 2003), 9. I do not think it would be going too far to suggest that the pornographic push toward maximum visibility might be understood

as parallel to corporate architect's obsession with achieving full "transparency" through glass-curtain walls. Martin, *Organizational Complex*, 161.

146. Roszak, *Counter Culture*, 16.

147. Berebitsky, *Sex and the Office*, 16.

148. Ibid., 175.

149. Ibid., 163.

150. He writes that "sex is integrated into work and public relations and is thus made more susceptible to (controlled) satisfaction." Herbert Marcuse, *One-Dimensional Man: Studies in the Ideology of Advanced Industrial Society* (Boston: Beacon Press, 1964), 75.

151. Ibid.

152. Talese, *Thy Neighbor's Wife*, 261–65.

153. Stevi Jackson and Sue Scott, "Gut Reactions to Matters of the Heart: Reflections on Rationality, Irrationality and Sexuality," *Sociological Review* 45, no. 4 (1997), 558.

154. Ibid., 560.

155. Barbara Ehrenreich, *Fear of Falling: The Inner Life of the Middle Class* (New York: HarperPerennial, 1990), 29–34. Conservatives, of course, remained unconvinced by the purification rites of middle-class sex revolutionaries, and, by the 1970s, the right had developed an entire demonology surrounding what they called the "New Class," their term for liberal professionals who supposedly promoted civilizational decay by championing obscenity and other forms of "permissiveness." Ehrenreich, *Fear of Falling*, 167–82.

156. Walter Benjamin, "Toys and Play: Marginal Notes on a Monumental Work," in *Walter Benjamin: Selected Writings, Volume 2, Part 1: 1927–1930*, trans. Rodney Livingstone, et al., ed. Michael W. Jennings, Howard Eiland, and Gary Smith (Cambridge, MA: Belknap Press of Harvard University Press), 120.

157. Talese, *Thy Neighbor's Wife*, 330.

158. Helen DeWitt's satirical office novel *Lightning Rods* (2011) captured this erotic industrial complex by imagining a service for corporations designed to discourage sexual harassment and improve morale by providing male employees with the opportunity to copulate with the lower half of an anonymous woman, whose nude lower body is wheeled through an aperture in the bathroom wall while the rest of her remains hidden on the other side. These women are the lightning rods of the title, drawing and dissipating dangerous libidinal energy. Unsurprisingly, this extreme solution causes its share of problems, but few problems center on the feelings of lust, shame, degradation, and jealousy that one might expect. Instead, DeWitt spends the bulk of the novel walking readers through a series of managerial quandaries faced by the lightning rod's creator as he designs the delivery mechanism and staffs his company while ensuring its compliance with workplace regulations such as antidiscrimination laws. Helen DeWitt, *Lightning Rods* (New York:

New Directions, 2011). Sianne Ngai analyzes DeWitt's lightning rod system as a gimmick, a labor-saving device based on hyperexploited, feminized work. In many ways, Ngai's theory also explains why obscenity itself may sometimes seem like a gimmick: it can come off as a cheap and easy shock effect that nevertheless indicates the author is trying too hard. Sianne Ngai, *Theory of the Gimmick: Aesthetic Judgement and Capitalist Form* (Cambridge, MA: Harvard University Press, 2020), 3–4, 75–82. See also Jasper Bernes, "Character, Genre, Labor: The Office Novel after Deindustrialization," *Post45* 1, January 10, 2019, https://post45.org/2019/01/character-genre-labor-the-office-novel-after-deindustrialization/.

159. Susan Sontag, "The Pornographic Imagination," in *Styles of Radical Will* (New York: Picador, 1966), 52–53, 66–67.

160. Ibid., 54–55. As Marshall McLuhan would later intimate, "low definition" or "cool media" only enable greater audience investment or participation because they allow us to supply all the missing details. Marshall McLuhan, *Understanding Media: The Extensions of Man* (Cambridge, MA: MIT Press, 1994), 22–23.

161. Sontag, "The Pornographic Imagination," 37–38.

162. Lee C. Bollinger, *The Tolerant Society* (New York: Oxford University Press, 1986), 118. Bollinger tentatively suggests that there should be an exception to tolerance for obscenity, arguing that sexuality is a central aspect of the self that must be protected from pornographic influence. Bollinger, *Tolerant Society*, 184–5. This seems to be an ad hoc justification for existing law, and, as such, appears to be secondary to his overall argument about the nature of tolerance. Indeed, I would argue that obscenity's overpowering pull is precisely why it represents such a powerful test of self-denial.

163. The loyal selflessness of managers was central to labor law after the 1947 Taft-Hartley Act, which amended the National Labor Relations Act to exclude supervisory employees from bargaining with a labor organization on the basis that solidarity with a union would interfere with their faithful devotion to their employers: "A man can't serve two masters." Jean-Christian Vinel, *The Employee: A Political History* (Philadelphia: University of Pennsylvania Press, 2013), 2.

164. John Frow, *Cultural Studies*, 38.

165. Russell Lynes, "Highbrow, Lowbrow, Middlebrow," *Wilson Quarterly* 1, no.1 (1976), 151. On the changing class politics of taste see Tony Bennett, Mike Savage, Elizabeth Silva, Alan Warde, Modesto Gayo-Cal, and David Wright, *Culture, Class, Distinction* (New York: Routledge, 2009), 189; Richard A. Peterson, "Understanding Audience Segmentation: From Elite and Mass to Omnivore and Univore," *Poetics* 21, no. 4 (August 1992): 243–58.

166. By appealing to the "productivist ethic" of professional-managerial readers, problematic texts offer new opportunities for them to show that they can rework anything, no matter how lowbrow or artless, to fit their aesthetic: "Bad taste tends to be the

preserve of urban intellectuals (professional and pre-professional) for whom the line between work and leisure time is occupationally indistinct." Andrew Ross, *No Respect: Intellectuals and Popular Culture* (New York: Routledge, 1989), 156. Bourdieu might not be as opposed to these ideas as this formulation suggests: even he admits that the "obscene" can become chaste and refined when placed within the right context. Bourdieu, *Distinction*, 6. The difference between "commercial porn" and "quality eroticism," Bourdieu suggests, comes down to the class of the audience the publisher serves. Bourdieu, "Production of Belief," 95.

167. Hunter et al., *On Pornography*, 97–102.

168. Ibid., 124–28.

169. John Durham Peters, *Courting the Abyss: Free Speech and the Liberal Tradition* (Chicago: University of Chicago Press, 2005), 22.

170. Ibid., 23–24.

171. Ibid., 146.

172. Warner, "The Mass Public and the Mass Subject," 167. Thus, for example, the censor (usually a man) often appears as a pearl-clutching woman. During the US Senate hearings on comic books and juvenile delinquency, for example, Gaines testifies that "it would be just as difficult to explain the harmless thrill of a horror story to [a censor] as it would be to explain the sublimity of love to a frigid old maid." US Congress, Senate, Subcommittee to Investigate Juvenile Delinquency, *Juvenile Delinquency*, 83rd Congress, 2nd Session, 1954, 98.

173. Richard Yates, *Revolutionary Road* (New York: Dell, 1961), 75.

174. Ibid., 61.

Chapter 2: An Aristocracy of Smut

1. H. L. Mencken, "Puritanism as a Literary Force," in *A Book of Prefaces* (New York: Knopf, 1917), 277. Randolph Bourne responded to this passage bitterly in his review of the book it appeared in, arguing that "Mr. Mencken queerly shows himself as editor, bowing meekly under the puritan proscription, acting as censor.... If the Menckens are not going to run the risk, in the name of freedom, they are scarcely justified in trying to infect us with their caution." Randolph Bourne, "H. L. Mencken [Review Essay on *A Book of Prejudices*]," in *Critical Essays on H. L. Mencken*, ed. Douglas C. Stenerson (Boston: G. K. Hall, 1987), 44. For accounts of the "Hatrack" affair, see H. L. Mencken, *The Editor, The Bluenose, and the Prostitute: H. L. Mencken's History of the "Hatrack" Censorship Case*, ed. Carl Bode (Boulder, CO: Roberts Rinehart, 1988); Marion Elizabeth Rodgers, *Mencken: The American Iconoclast* (New York: Oxford University Press, 2005), 1–9; Neil Miller, *Banned in Boston: The Watch and Ward Society's Crusade against Books, Burlesque, and Social Evil* (Boston: Beacon, 2010), 87–96.

2. H. L. Mencken, "The 'Hatrack' Case," in *The Editor, The Bluenose, and the Prostitute: H. L. Mencken's History of the "Hatrack" Censorship Case*, ed. Carl Bode (Boulder, CO: Roberts Rinehart, 1988), 50.

3. Paul S. Boyer, *Purity in Print*, 176.

4. P. C. Kemeny, *The New England Watch and Ward Society* (New York: Oxford University Press, 2018), 250.

5. Rodgers, *Mencken*, 3.

6. Mencken, "The 'Hatrack' Case," 63.

7. Ibid., 64–65.

8. Ibid., 65.

9. Ibid., 66.

10. Terry Teachout, *The Skeptic: A Life of H. L. Mencken* (New York: HarperCollins, 2002), 227.

11. Ibid., 228.

12. Paul Boyer, *Purity in Print*, 178.

13. Charles Angoff, "Boston Twilight," *American Mercury*, December 1925, 439.

14. Ibid., 441.

15. Ibid., 443.

16. Ibid., 444.

17. Ibid., 444.

18. Sharon Hamilton, "'Intellectual in Its Looser Sense': Reading Mencken's *Smart Set*," in *Middlebrow Literary Cultures: The Battle of the Brows, 1920–1960*, eds. Erica Brown and Mary Grover (New York: Palgrave Macmillan, 2012), 133.

19. Frederick Lewis Allen, *Only Yesterday: An Informal History of the 1920s* (New York: Harper & Brothers, 1931), 228.

20. Erik Olin Wright, "Understanding Class: Towards an Integrated Analytical Approach," *New Left Review* 60 (2009), 104–6.

21. Peter Osborne, *The Politics of Time: Modernity and Avant-Garde* (New York: Verso, 1995), 14.

22. H. L. Mencken, editorial, *American Mercury*, October 1925, 159.

23. H. L. Mencken, *Notes on Democracy* (London: Jonathan Cape, 1927), 72–74.

24. Diane Chisholm, "Obscene Modernism: *Eros Noir* and the Profane Illumination of Djuna Barnes," *American Literature* 69, no. 1 (March 1997): 167–206; Rachel Potter, *Obscene Modernism: Literary Censorship and Experiment, 1900–1940* (Oxford: Oxford University Press, 2013).

25. For a critique of Mencken's generational politics from a procensorship perspective, see Rochelle Gurstein, *The Repeal of Reticence: America's Cultural and Legal Struggles*

over Free Speech, Obscenity, Sexual Liberation, and Modern Art (New York: Hill & Wang, 1996), 129–39.

26. Hamilton, "'Intellectual' in Its Looser Sense," 138–39.

27. H. L. Mencken, "A Word about *Smart Set*," in *Mencken on Mencken: A New Collection of Autobiographical Writings*, ed. S. T. Joshi (Baton Rouge: Louisiana State University, 2012), 111.

28. *Smart Set*, October 1914, 1.

29. Mencken suggested that "a subsidized magazine, conducted at a loss, is unsound in principle, and very apt to be led astray by all the current aesthetic crazes, to the dismay of the sort of readers we try to reach." Mencken, "A Word," 113.

30. Carl Richard Dolmetsch, *The Smart Set: A History and Anthology* (New York: Dial Press, 1966), 50.

31. David M. Earle, *Re-Covering Modernism: Pulps, Paperbacks, and the Prejudice of Form* (New York: Routledge, 2016), 20.

32. H. L. Mencken, *My Life as Author and Editor*, ed. Jonathan Yardley (New York: Vintage, 1992), 72–73.

33. Teachout, *The Skeptic*, 122.

34. Douglas C. Stenerson, *H. L. Mencken: Iconoclast from Baltimore* (Chicago: University of Chicago Press, 1971), 6.

35. Ibid., 7–9.

36. Ibid., 10.

37. Ibid., 9.

38. Ibid., 22.

39. Zechariah Chafee, "Freedom of Speech in War Time," *Harvard Law Review* 32, no. 8 (1919): 932–73; Alexander Meiklejohn, *Free Speech and Its Relation to Self-Government* (New York: Harper and Brothers, 1948).

40. Johannes Fabian, *Time and the Other: How Anthropology Makes Its Object* (New York: Columbia University Press, 1983), 31.

41. Ernest Hemingway, *The Sun Also Rises* (New York: Charles Scribner's Sons, [1926] 1927), 49.

42. D. H. Lawrence, "Pornography and Obscenity," in *Sex, Literature and Censorship*, ed. Harry T. Moore (New York: Viking, 1953), 64–67.

43. Ibid., 76.

44. Arthur Symons quoted in H. L. Mencken, "Joseph Conrad" in *A Book of Prefaces* (New York: Knopf, 1917), 19.

45. Ibid., 18.

46. Ibid., 20.

47. Edward Bullough, "'Psychical Distance' as a Factor in Art and an Aesthetic

Principle," in *Aesthetics: Lectures and Essays by Edward Bullough*, ed. Elizabeth M. Wilkinson (Stanford: Stanford University Press, 1957), 93.

48. Ibid., 101–2.
49. Ibid., 101.
50. Ibid., 102–4.
51. Ibid., 100–101.
52. H. L. Mencken, "Joseph Conrad," 35.
53. Ibid., 35.
54. Mencken, "Puritanism," 225.
55. Bullough, "'Psychical Distance' as a Factor," 103.
56. Walter Kendrick, *The Secret Museum: Pornography in Modern Culture* (New York: Viking, 1987), 11.
57. Kendrick, *Secret Museum*, 15. For more on this strategy in nineteenth century erotic print culture, see Bull, "Reading, Writing."
58. Willa Cather, "Coming, Eden Bower!," *Smart Set*, August 1920, 8.
59. Ibid.
60. Werbel, *Lust on Trial*, 198–203.
61. Ibid., 203–8.
62. Ibid., 206–7.
63. Ibid., 208–211.
64. Lynda Nead, *The Female Nude: Art, Obscenity and Sexuality* (New York: Routledge, 1992), 25.
65. James Woodress, *Willa Cather: A Literary Life* (Lincoln: University of Nebraska Press, 1987), 314.
66. Cather, "Coming, Eden Bower!," 8.
67. Allison Pease, *Modernism, Mass Culture, and the Aesthetics of Obscenity* (Cambridge: Cambridge University Press, 2000), 81.
68. Cather, "Coming, Eden Bower!," 8–9.
69. Ibid.
70. Ibid., 4.
71. Ibid., 10.
72. Ibid., 10.
73. Ibid., 3.
74. Mark McGurl, *The Novel Art: Elevations of American Fiction after Henry James* (Princeton, NJ: Princeton University Press, 2001), 9–19.
75. H. L. Mencken, "*Youth and the Bright Medusa*," in *H. L. Mencken's Smart Set Criticism*, ed. William H. Nolte (Washington, DC: Gateway Editions, 1987), 266.

76. Dorothy Parker, "Such a Pretty Little Picture," *Smart Set*, December 1922, 73–78.

77. F. Scott Fitzgerald, "Benediction," in *The Smart Set Anthology*, ed. Burton Rascoe and Groff Conklin (New York: Reynal and Hitchcock, 1934), 77–78.

78. H. L. Mencken, "Two Years Too Late," in *H. L. Mencken's* Smart Set *Criticism*, ed. William H. Nolte (Washington, DC: Gateway Editions, 1987), 286.

79. Ibid., 286.

80. Allen, *Only Yesterday*, 239.

81. H. L. Mencken, "Osculation Anatomized," *H. L. Mencken's* Smart Set *Criticism*, ed. William H. Nolte (Washington, DC: Gateway Editions, 1987), 144.

82. Ibid., 146. Mencken's mention of the instant photograph is significant here. Beginning in 1890, with the publication of Louis Brandeis and Samuel Warren's "The Right to Privacy," legal professionals struggled to undo the threat to the "inviolate personality" posed by the indiscriminate gaze of the camera lens. Robert E. Mensel, "'Kodakers Lying in Wait': Amateur Photography and the Right of Privacy in New York, 1885–1915," *American Quarterly* 43, no. 1 (1991): 24–45. These anxieties about photography's perceived tendency to reduce the intimate self to its fleshly exterior reverberated in the literary sphere as well, worrying critics that realism would damage the human character by looking upon it with a view "as impartial as a photographic plate." William R. Thayer quoted in Gurstein, *Repeal of Reticence*, 45–46.

83. Mencken, "Osculation Anatomized," 144.

84. James Branch Cabell, *Jurgen, A Comedy of Justice* (Mineola: Dover, 2011), 336–37.

85. Ibid., 28.

86. Ibid., 52–54.

87. Ibid., 196.

88. Stearns, *American Cool*, 171–72.

89. Ibid., 172–74.

90. Ibid., 174–78.

91. Ibid., 11.

92. Ibid., 191.

93. Paul de Man, "The Rhetoric of Temporality," in *Blindness and Insight: Essays in the Rhetoric of Contemporary Criticism* (Minneapolis: University of Minneapolis Press, 1983), 187–228.

94. Theodore Schroeder, *"Obscene" Literature and Constitutional Law: A Forensic Defense of Freedom of the Press* (New York: Privately Printed, 1911), 243–44. Similarly, Mencken argues for the mutability of morals by reminding us that "things that were crimes in the middle ages are quite respectable at present." H. L. Mencken, *The Philosophy of Friedrich Nietzsche* (New York: Transaction, 2004), 89.

95. Cabell, *Jurgen*, 261–70.

96. H. L. Mencken, "The Flood of Fiction," *Smart Set*, January 1920, 138.

97. Charles Taylor, *A Secular Age* (Cambridge, MA: The Belknap Press of Harvard University Press, 2007), 27–43.

98. Ibid., 37.

99. Schroeder, *"Obscene" Literature*, 14.

100. Ibid., 269.

101. Ibid., 103.

102. Ibid., 243–44.

103. Talal Asad, *Formations of the Secular: Christianity, Islam, Modernity* (Stanford: Stanford University Press, 2003), 11.

104. Saba Mahmood, "Secularism, Hermeneutics, and Empire: The Politics of Islamic Reformation," *Public Culture* 18, no. 2 (2006), 333. Although Christopher Hitchens takes exception to his authoritarian tendencies, he draws on Mencken's critique of religion and adopts his temporal schema: to enter into an age of Enlightenment, he writes, "We have first to transcend our prehistory, and escape the gnarled hands which reach out to drag us back to the catacombs and the reeking altars and the guilty pleasures of subjection and abjection." Christopher Hitchens, *God Is Not Great: How Religion Poisons Everything* (New York: Hachette, 2007), 283. Less reserved in his approval of Mencken, Richard Dawkins quotes him extensively. Richard Dawkins, *The God Delusion* (London: Bantam, 2006), 27, 228, 331.

105. Mahmood, "Secularism, Hermeneutics, and Empire," 345.

106. H. L. Mencken, "Footnote on Criticism," in *Prejudices: Third Series* (New York: Knopf, 1922), 91.

107. Ibid., 101.

108. Ibid., 84.

109. Walter J. Kingsley quoted in Emergency Committee Organized to Protest Against the Suppression of James Branch Cabell's *Jurgen*, *Jurgen and the Censor* (New York: Barrett H. Clark, 1920), 16.

110. Boyer, *Purity in Print*, 75.

111. Emergency Committee, *Jurgen and the Censor*, 17.

112. Boyer, *Purity in Print*, 76.

113. James Branch Cabell, *Taboo: A Legend Retold from the Dirghic of Sævius Nicanor, with Prolegomena, Notes, and a Preliminary Memoir* (New York: Robert M. McBride, 1921), 28.

114. Emergency Committee, *Jurgen and the Censor*, 53.

115. Cabell, *Jurgen*, viii.

116. Judge Charles C. Nott, *Jurgen and the Law: A Statement with Exhibits, Including the Court's Opinion, and the Brief for the Defendants on Motion to Direct an Acquittal*, ed. Guy Holt (New York: Robert M. McBride, 1923), 74.

117. Ernst and Seagle, *To the Pure*, 60.

118. Emergency Committee, *Jurgen and the Censor*, 53.

119. Ezra Pound chided his friend, "What is wrong with it, and with your work in general is that you have drifted into writing for your inferiors. . . . We have all sinned through trying to make the uneducated understand things. Certainly you will lose a great part of your public when you stop trying to civilize the waste places; and you will gain about fifteen readers." William H. A. Williams, *H. L. Mencken Revisited* (New York: Twayne, 1998), 88. Edmund Wilson leveled sharper criticism against him: "Mencken is the civilized consciousness of modern America . . . realizing the grossness of its manners and mind and crying out in horror and chagrin." Edmund Wilson, "H. L. Mencken," in *Critical Essays on H. L. Mencken*, ed. Douglas L. Stenerson (Boston: G. K. Hall, 1987), 71. Malcolm Cowley's *Smart Set* retrospective proved even more dismissive, sneering at Mencken's neglect of more serious European literature in favor of his "long crusade against rural Baptists," which he waged for the *Smart Set* audience of "people who like fiction with a little tang to it and relish a bit of subtlety now and then—in other words, for drugstore cowboys." Malcolm Cowley, *Think Back On Us . . . A Contemporary Chronicle of the 1930's*, ed. Henry Dan Piper (Carbondale: Southern Illinois University Press, 1967), 250.

120. Garry Wills, *Under God: Religion and American Politics* (New York: Simon and Schuster, 1990), 101–7.

121. Throughout his career, Mencken dismissed scientific findings as often as he upheld them. Mencken styled himself as a stubborn empiricist who claimed that only direct observation yields true facts. He denied the utility and accuracy of mathematical models, a position that leads him to discount fields ranging from astronomy to theoretical physics. See, for example, H. L. Mencken, "The Eternal Conundrum," *American Mercury*, February 1931, 252–53.

122. Chip Rhodes, *Structures of the Jazz Age: Mass Culture, Progressive Education, and Racial Discourse in American Modernism* (New York: Verso, 1998), 32.

123. Edward J. Larson, *Summer for the Gods: The Scopes Trial and America's Continuing Debate Over Science and Religion* (New York: Basic, 2006), 104.

124. H. L. Mencken, *A Religious Orgy in Tennessee: A Reporter's Account of the Scopes Monkey Trial* (New York: Melville House, 2006), 11–16.

125. Laura Weinrib, *The Taming of Free Speech: America's Civil Liberties Compromise* (Cambridge, MA: Harvard University Press, 2016), 7.

126. Ibid., 168–69.

127. Ibid., 40.

128. Ibid., 166.

129. Arthur Garfield Hays quoted in Weinrib, *Taming of Free Speech*, 167.

130. Weinrib, *Taming of Free Speech*, 172–73.

131. Mencken, *A Religious Orgy*, 11.

132. Ibid., 56.

133. Ibid.

134. H. L. Mencken, "The Sahara of the Bozart," in *A Mencken Chrestomathy*, ed. H. L. Mencken (New York: Knopf, 1949), 184–95.

135. Gertzman, *Bookleggers and Smuthounds*, 192–93. If all of this sounds strange, note that pornographic films are still cataloged and titled using anthropological terms such as "fetish" and "taboo."

136. Sigel, *Governing Pleasures*, 50–51.

137. Ibid., 62.

138. Ibid., 53.

139. Ibid., 50.

140. Ibid., 60.

141. Fabian, *Time*, 80–81.

142. H. L. Mencken, "Adolescence," *American Mercury*, November 1928, 380.

143. H. L. Mencken, "A City in Moronia," *American Mercury*, March 1929, 379–80.

144. Mencken, *A Religious Orgy*, 154–55.

145. H. L. Mencken, *Minority Report: H. L. Mencken's Notebooks* (New York: Knopf, 1956), 39.

146. Ibid., 39–41.

147. Mencken, *Nietzsche*, 197. For a discussion of Mencken's reception of Nietzsche, see Jennifer Ratner-Rosenhagen, *American Nietzsche: A History of an Icon and His Ideas* (Chicago: University of Chicago Press, 2011), 53–57, 113, 183–84.

148. See Corey Robin, "Nietzsche's Marginal Children: On Friedrich Hayek," *Nation*, May 27, 2013, https://www.thenation.com/article/nietzsches-marginal-children-friedrich-hayek/.

149. Mencken, *Nietzsche*, 172.

150. Ibid., 167.

151. Harry Braverman, *Labor and Monopoly Capital: The Degradation of Work in the Twentieth Century* (New York: Monthly Review, 1998), 77–83.

152. Ibid., 125. See also Georg Lukács, "Reification and the Consciousness of the Proletariat," in *History and Class Consciousness: Studies in Marxist Dialectics*, trans. Rodney Livingston (Cambridge, MA: MIT Press, 1971), 90.

153. Sigfried Giedion, *Mechanization Takes Command: A Contribution to Anonymous History* (Minneapolis: University of Minnesota Press, 2013), 24–30, 102–13.

154. H. L. Mencken, "Confidences," *Smart Set*, January 1923, 139.

155. Mencken, "Confidences," 139.

156. Mencken, *Nietzsche*, 102.

157. David R. Roediger and Elizabeth D. Esch, *The Production of Difference: Race and the Management of Labor in U.S. History* (New York: Oxford University Press, 2012), 14, 139–69.

158. Mencken, *Nietzsche*, 167.

159. Ibid., 165.

160. H. L. Mencken, "On Eugenics," *Chicago Sunday Tribune*, May 15, 1927.

161. See Anson Rabinbach, *The Human Motor: Energy, Fatigue, and the Origins of Modernity* (New York: Basic Books, 1990).

162. Edward A. Martin, *H. L. Mencken and the Debunkers* (Athens: University of Georgia Press, 1984), 6.

163. See Antonio Gramsci, *Selections from the Prison Notebooks of Antonio Gramsci*, ed. and trans. Quintin Hoare and Geoffrey Nowell Smith (New York: International Publishers, 1971), 301–6.

164. Jennifer Burns, *Goddess of the Market: Ayn Rand and the American Right* (Oxford: Oxford University Press, 2009), 33, 48; James R. Lewis, "Diabolical Authority: Anton LaVey, The Satanic Bible and the Satanist 'Tradition,'" *Marburg Journal of Religion* 7, no. 1 (2002): 8–9; Blanche Barton, *The Secret Life of a Satanist: The Authorized Biography of Anton LaVey*, rev. ed. (Port Townsend, WA: Feral House, 2014), 107.

165. Alex Amend, "Daily Caller News Foundation reporter cancels scheduled appearance at influential white nationalist gathering," Southern Poverty Law Center, September 14, 2018, https://www.splcenter.org/hatewatch/2018/09/14/daily-caller-news-foundation-reporter-cancels-scheduled-appearance-influential-white; Richard Spencer, @richardbspencer, "@joshtpm1930s? No, tomorrow belongs to us," https://m.youtube.com/watch?v=29Mg6Gfh9Co, Twitter, March 18, 2017, 5:44 p.m., https://twitter.com/RichardBSpencer/status/843216482838355968?ref_src=twsrc%5Etfw%7Ctwcamp%5Etweetembed%7Ctwterm%5E843216482838355968&ref_url.

Chapter 3: Decrypting EC Comics

1. For a history of EC Comics, the comic book panic, and the emergence of the Comics Code, see David Hajdu, *The Ten-Cent Plague: The Great Comic-Book Scare and How It Changed America* (New York: Farrar, Straus & Giroux, 2008).

2. Ibid., 114–15.

3. Whitney Strub, "Slouching Towards *Roth*: Obscenity and the Supreme Court, 1945–1957," *Journal of Supreme Court History* 38, no. 2 (2013): 124–26.

4. Hajdu, *Ten-Cent Plague*, 220–21.

5. Ibid., 221.

6. Ibid., 222.

7. Ibid., 223.

8. Ibid., 245–73.

9. Ibid., 284–285.

10. Ibid., 286–93. On the Motion Picture Production Code or Hays Code, see Lewis, *Hollywood v. Hard Core*, 7–8, 86–134.

11. To read the 1954 Comics Magazine Association of America Codes Code, see Amy Kiste Nyberg, *Seal of Approval: The History of the Comics Code* (Jackson: University Press of Mississippi, 1998), 166–69.

12. Hajdu, *Ten-Cent Plague*, 319–23. Despite its redundancy, the phrase "EC Comics" is commonly used by fans, scholars, and the publisher itself. See, for example, Qiana Whitted, *EC Comics: Race, Shock, and Social Protest* (New Brunswick, NJ: Rutgers University Press, 2019).

13. Hajdu, *Ten-Cent Plague*, 312–13.

14. Strub, *Perversion for Profit*, 14.

15. "The Vault-Keeper's Corner," *The Vault of Horror* 33 (Oct.–Nov. 1953), in *The EC Archives: The Vault of Horror Volume 4* (Milwaukie, OR: Dark Horse Books, 2015), 132.

16. James Gilbert, *A Cycle of Outrage: America's Reaction to the Juvenile Delinquent in the 1950s* (New York: Oxford University Press, 1986), 3.

17. US Congress, Senate, Subcommittee, *Juvenile Delinquency*, 86.

18. Bart Beaty, *Fredric Wertham and the Critique of Mass Culture* (Jackson: University Press of Mississippi, 2005), 131.

19. David Riesman et al., *The Lonely Crowd*, 25.

20. Ibid., 13–24.

21. Fredric Wertham, *Seduction of the Innocent* (New York: Amereon House, 1954), 226.

22. Fredric Wertham, "The Catathymic Crisis: A Clinical Entity," *Archives of Neurology & Psychiatry* 37, no. 4 (1937): 976.

23. Wertham, *Seduction*, 118.

24. Gilbert, *Cycle*, 96.

25. Wertham, *Seduction*, 68.

26. Gilbert, *Cycle*, 98–99.

27. Judith Crist, "Horror in the Nursery," *Collier's*, March 27, 1948, 22.

28. Wertham, *Seduction*, 92.

29. Ibid., 91.

30. Leslie Fiedler, "The Middle Against Both Ends," in *Arguing Comics: Literary Masters on a Popular Medium*, eds. Jeet Heer and Kent Worcester (Jackson: University Press of Mississippi, 2004), 131.

31. Fiedler, "Middle," 131.

32. Ibid., 132.

33. Janice Radway, *A Feeling for Books: The Book-of-the-Month-Club, Literary Taste, and Middle-Class Desire* (Chapel Hill: University of North Carolina Press, 1997), 283.

34. Radway, *Feeling for Books*, 296.

35. Beaty, *Fredric Wertham*, 68; Nyberg, *Seal*, 50–51.

36. Wertham, *Seduction*, 68.

37. Walter Berns, *Freedom, Virtue and the First Amendment* (Chicago: Henry Regnery Co., [1957] 1965), 10.

38. Ibid., 255–56.

39. Walter Berns, "Pornography vs. Democracy: The Case for Censorship," *Public Interest* 22 (1971), 15.

40. Berns, *Freedom*, 72.

41. Berns, "Pornography vs. Democracy," 13.

42. Fred Turner, *The Democratic Surround: Multimedia and American Liberalism from World War II to the Psychedelic Sixties* (Chicago: University of Chicago Press, 2013).

43. Wertham, *Seduction*, 2.

44. Carol Tilley, "Seducing the Innocent: Fredric Wertham and the Falsifications That Helped Condemn Comics," *Information & Culture* 47, no. 4 (2012): 383–413.

45. John Petrie and Jay Lynch, "Subversion of the Innocent," *Blab!* 2 (Summer 1987): 51–55. "Comix" refers to the alternative comics that were sold in head shops and record stores without the oversight of the Comics Code Authority. Many of them were characterized by explicit sex, raunchy humor, and psychedelic themes. For an overview of underground comix, see Patrick Rosenkranz, *Rebel Visions: The Underground Comix Revolution, 1963–1975* (Seattle: Fantagraphics, 2008).

46. Frank Jacobs, *The Mad World of William M. Gaines* (New York: Lyle Stuart, 1972), 26.

47. William Gaines, "The William Gaines Interview," interview by Dwight Decker and Gary Groth, *The Comics Journal Library 10, The EC Artists Part 2* (Washington: Fantagraphics, 2016), 16.

48. Gaines, "Gaines Interview," 17.

49. Ibid., 17.

50. Gene Kannenberg Jr., "Graphic Text, Graphic Context: Interpreting Custom Fonts and Hands in Contemporary Comics," in *Illuminating Letters: Typography and Literary Interpretation*, eds. Paul C. Gutjahr and Megan L. Benton (Amherst: University of Massachusetts Press, 2001), 183. When Dwight Decker told Gaines that fans thought that "Leroy lettering gave the horror books and even the science-fiction books a rather stranger, rather inhuman look, because it was so mechanical," Gaines admitted that that may be so but noted that he used Leroy lettering because he inherited it, along with the business, from his father. Gaines, "Gaines Interview," 23.

51. Jacobs, *Mad World*, 80.

52. Ray Bradbury, "Skeleton," in *The October Country* (New York: Knopf, 1970), 79.

53. Al Feldstein and Ray Bradbury, "Jellyfish," in *The Living Mummy and Other Stories* (Seattle: Fantagraphics Books, 2016), 47.

54. Ibid., 53.

55. Ibid., 51.

56. Irving Howe, "Notes on Mass Culture," in *Arguing Comics: Literary Masters on a Popular Medium*, eds. Jeet Heer and Kent Worcester (Jackson: University Press of Mississippi, 2004), 44.

57. Riesman et al., *Lonely Crowd*, 93–94.

58. Ibid., 99.

59. Digby Diehl, *Tales from the Crypt: The Official Archives* (New York: St. Martin's, 1996), 43.

60. Riesman et al., *Lonely Crowd*, 100–101.

61. George Evans, "The George Evans Interview," interview by John Garcia, *The Comics Journal Library 10, The EC Artists Part 2* (Washington: Fantagraphics, 2016), 122.

62. US Congress, Senate, Subcommittee, *Juvenile Delinquency*, 102.

63. Carl Wessler, "Concerto for Violin and Werewolf" in *'Tain't the Meat . . . It's the Humanity! And Other Stories Illustrated by Jack Davis*, ed. Gary Groth (Seattle: Fantagraphics Books, 2013), 158.

64. Ibid., 158.

65. Wally Wood, "Deadlock!," *Weird Fantasy* 17 (Jan.–Feb. 1951), in *The EC Archives: Weird Fantasy Volume 1* (Milwaukie, OR: Dark Horse, 2014), 171.

66. Ibid., 172.

67. Peter Galison, "The Ontology of the Enemy: Norbert Wiener and the Cybernetic Vision," *Critical Inquiry* 21, no. 1 (1994): 230.

68. Norbert Wiener quoted in Galison, "Enemy," 256.

69. Ibid., 231–32.

70. Marianna Torgovnick, *The War Complex: World War II in Our Time* (Chicago: University of Chicago Press, 2005), 7.

71. Torgovnick, *War Complex*, 9.

72. Frances Ferguson, *Pornography, the Theory: What Utilitarianism Did to Action* (Chicago: University of Chicago Press, 2004), xiv–xvi.

73. Ibid., 1.

74. Ibid., 30, 109–10.

75. Gaines, "Gaines Interview," 19.

76. Ibid., 19.

77. William Gaines, "On Censorship," interview by Steve Ringgenberg, *The Comics Journal Library 8, The EC Artists Part 1* (Washington: Fantagraphics, 2013), 68.

78. Hajdu, *Ten-Cent Plague*, 240.

79. "Foul Play!," *The Haunt of Fear* 19 (May–June 1953), in *The EC Archives: The Haunt of Fear Volume 4* (Milwaukie, OR: Dark Horse, 2017), 43.

80. Evans, "Evans Interview," 122.

81. Gahan Wilson, "Notes from the Underground Part II," *Blab!* 2, Summer 1987, 63.

82. Al Feldstein, "Fare Tonight, Followed by Increasing Clottyness," in *'Tain't the Meat . . . It's the Humanity! And Other Stories Illustrated by Jack Davis*, ed. Gary Groth (Seattle: Fantagraphic Books, 2013), 103.

83. Gaines, "On Censorship," 71.

84. Even in Harvey Kurtzman's war stories, we find a Fordist humanism in which soldiers find they are interchangeable with their enemies in the mass production of war matériel and dead bodies.

85. William Gaines and Al Feldstein, "In Each and Every Package," in *The High Cost of Dying and Other Stories*, ed. Gary Groth (Seattle: Fantagraphics Books, 2016), 125.

86. Ibid., 126.

87. Hajdu, *Ten-Cent Plague*, 255.

88. US Congress, Senate, Subcommittee, *Juvenile Delinquency*, 103.

89. US Congress, Senate, Subcommittee, *Juvenile Delinquency*, 103.

90. Al Feldstein, "The Al Feldstein Interview," *The Comics Journal Library 10, The EC Artists Part 2* (Washington: Fantagraphics, 2016), 65.

91. Feldstein, "Feldstein Interview," 65.

92. Jacobs, *Mad World*, 110.

93. Feldstein, "Feldstein Interview," 64.

94. Linda Williams, *Hard Core: Power, Pleasure, and the "Frenzy of the Visible"* (Berkeley: University of California Press, 1999), 94.

95. Walter Benjamin, "On Some Motifs on Baudelaire" in *Illuminations*, ed. Hannah Arendt, trans. Harry Zohn (New York: Schocken Books, 1968), 155–200.

96. As Mark Seltzer puts it, "The comic-book genre provides the iterative model of an unremitting and systemic violence—a Cold War violence suspended and preemptive." Seltzer, *Official World*, 23.

97. Orit Halpern, *Beautiful Data: A History of Vision and Reason since 1945* (Durham, NC: Duke University Press, 2014), 62.

98. Ibid., 79–144.

99. William Gaines and Al Feldstein, "Judgment Day!" in *Judgment Day And Other Stories*, ed. Gary Groth (Seattle: Fantagraphics Books, 2014), 35.

100. EC's more didactic comics—known as preachies—take a more nuanced and complex approach to race. See Whitted, *EC Comics*.

101. Hajdu, *Ten-Cent Plague*, 323.

102. Ray Bradbury, "There Will Come Soft Rains," *Weird Fantasy* 17, January–February 1950, 26.

103. Gershon Legman, *Love and Death: A Study in Censorship* (New York: Hacker Art Books, 1963), 32.

104. Sharon Ghamari-Tabrizi, *The Worlds of Herman Kahn: The Intuitive Science of Thermonuclear War* (Cambridge, MA: Harvard University Press, 2005), 147.

105. Ghamari-Tabrizi, *Herman Kahn*, 162.

106. Robert Warshow, "Paul, the Horror Comics, and Dr. Wertham," in *Arguing Comics: Literary Masters on a Popular Medium*, eds. Jeet Heer and Kent Worcester (Jackson: University Press of Mississippi, 2004), 70.

107. Jared Gardner, *Projections: Comics and the History of Twenty-First-Century Storytelling* (Stanford: Stanford University Press, 2012), 73. This is why the most stylized artists at EC—Ingels and Davis—were typically assigned the most gruesome stories, while artists who did not foreground their cartooning abilities (artists like Jack Kamen and Johnny Craig) were relegated to the suspense thrillers.

108. Paul Mavrides, "Notes from the Underground Part II," *Blab!* 2, Summer 1987, 82.

109. For a formalist analysis of *Mad Magazine*, see Ziva Ben-Porat, "Method in *Madness*: Notes on the Structure of Parody, Based on MAD TV Satires," *Poetics Today* 1, no. 1/2 (1979): 245–72.

110. US Congress, Senate, Subcommittee, *Juvenile Delinquency*, 100.

111. William Gaines and Al Feldstein, "The Flying Saucer Invasion," in *Child of Tomorrow and Other Stories by Al Feldstein*, ed. Gary Groth (Seattle: Fantagraphics Books, 2013), 22.

112. Feldstein liked the idea so much he wrote a similar story about aliens from Jupiter who take over the planet by landing immediately after a War-of-the-Worlds style broadcast. The people of Earth assume the Jupiterians are just another media stunt, allowing them to take control without resistance. See Al Feldstein, "Panic!," in *Child of Tomorrow and Other Stories by Al Feldstein*, ed. Gary Groth (Seattle: Fantagraphics Books, 2013), 49–56.

113. Feldstein, "Feldstein Interview," 59, 61–62.

114. Jacobs, *Mad World*, 80.

115. "Are You a Red Dupe?," *The Tales from the Crypt* 43 (Aug.–Sept. 1954), in *The EC Archives: Tales from the Crypt Volume 5* (Milwaukie, OR: Dark Horse Books, 2014), 80.

116. Ibid., 80.

117. Jacobs, *Mad World*, 105.

118. Hajdu, *Ten-Cent Plague*, 253, 260.

119. Gaines, "Gaines Interview," 29.

120. G. B. Aydelott, "Problems of Taking Over: The Human Relations Practitioner—An Enlightened View," in *Management for Tomorrow*, ed. Nicholas A. Glaskowsky, Jr. (Stanford: Stanford University Graduate School of Business, 1958), 22.

121. Charles Winnick, "Teenagers, Satire, and *Mad*," *Merrill-Palmer Quarterly of Behavior and Development* 8, no. 3 (1962): 190.

122. Ibid., 192–93.

123. Mike Benton, *Horror Comics: The Illustrated History* (Dallas: Taylor, 1991), 23.

124. Warshow, "Paul," 70.

125. *The National E. C. Fan-Addict Club Bulletin* 2, March 1954, 2.

126. Ibid., 2.

127. "The Vault-Keeper's Corner," 132.

128. William Gaines, "The 'Publisher of the Issue,' William M. Gaines, Alias Melvin," *Mad* 1, no. 5, June–July 1953, 1.

129. Ibid., 1.

130. Seltzer, *Official World*, 6.

131. Ibid., 4.

132. Ibid., 6–13.

133. Jacobs, *Mad World*, 169.

134. Ibid., 170.

135. Charles Trueheart, "The Aging of *Mad*," *Washington Post*, December 14, 1991, https://www.washingtonpost.com/archive/lifestyle/1991/12/14/the-aging-of-mad/891789e4-95ae-4c43-8bd7-b1abd0f7ea68/?utm_term=.a1648f1cedc3.

136. Seltzer, *Official World*, 6–7.

137. "Kamen's Kalamity!," in *The Tales from the Crypt* 1.31 (Aug.–Sept. 1952), in *The EC Archives: Tales from the Crypt Volume 3* (York, PA: Gemstone, 2008), 100.

138. Larry Stark, *EC's Number One Fan: The Historic 1950s Fanzine Writings of Larry Stark* (Bartlett, TN: Boardman Books, 2016). For a history of EC fandom, see Thommy Burns, "The Madness of it All," *The Comics Journal Library* 10, The EC Artists Part 2 (Washington: Fantagraphics, 2016), 256–73.

139. Winnick, "*Mad*," 199.

140. See Seltzer, *Official World*, 164–65.

141. Erving Goffman, *Behavior in Public Places: Notes on the Social Organization of Gatherings* (New York: Free Press, 1963), 69.

142. Goffman, *Behavior*, 75.

143. Bob Levin, "The Horror! The Horror!: Graham Ingels and the Art of Real Yuch,"

Comics Journal, May 13, 2016, http://www.tcj.com/the-horror-the-horror-graham-ingels-and-the-art-of-real-yuch/.

144. Bret Easton Ellis, *American Psycho* (New York: Vintage, 1991), 206.

145. Bret Easton Ellis, "A Tale of Two Brets," *Amazon*, https://www.amazon.com/gp/feature.html?ie=UTF8&docId=571852.

146. Levin, "The Horror! The Horror!"

147. On the influence of EC on Crumb and underground comix, see Hajdu, *Ten-Cent Plague*, 332–34.

148. According to Gaines, "We used to have the college kids, but now I think they read *Playboy* and *Penthouse* . . . But then they come back to us." Trueheart, "Aging of *Mad*," n.p.

Chapter 4: Reading *Playboy* for the Science Fiction

1. Norman Mailer, *The Presidential Papers* (New York: G. P. Putnam's Sons, 1963), 260.

2. Ray Bradbury, "Fahrenheit 451," *Playboy*, March 1954, 47.

3. Ibid., 49.

4. Ray Bradbury, "Fahrenheit 451," *Playboy*, October 1954, 44.

5. Steven Watts, *Mr. Playboy: Hugh Hefner and the American Dream* (Hoboken, NJ: John Wiley & Sons, 2008), 82–83, 200. Perhaps just as importantly, though, *Playboy*'s status as an adult men's magazine threatened to scare off companies uncomfortable with the idea that their advertisements might be printed next to potentially obscene materials. Russell Miller, *Bunny: The Real Story of Playboy* (London: Michael Joseph, 1984), 64.

6. Kendrick, *The Secret Museum*, 203.

7. Thomas R. Adams and Nicolas Barker, "A New Model for the Study of the Book," in *The Book History Reader*, eds. David Finkelstein and Alistair McCleery (New York: Routledge, 2006), 59.

8. It is true that, as Jacques Derrida points out, the repeatability of messages means that the potential absence of an addressee is a precondition for all writing and, indeed, in all media. While this remains a latent possibility in speech, private manuscripts, and the mail, it becomes an inevitability in publishing. Jacques Derrida, "Signature Event Context," in *Margins of Philosophy*, trans. Alan Bass (Chicago: University of Chicago Press, 1982), 315–18.

9. Kendrick, *Secret Museum*, 13.

10. Joe Westmoreland, "The White Album," in *Queer 13: Lesbian and Gay Writers Recall Seventh Grade*, ed. Clifford Chase (New York: William Morrow, 1998), 221.

11. Bradbury, "Fahrenheit 451," *Playboy*, March 1954, 46.

12. Ibid., 44.

13. Evan Brier, *A Novel Marketplace: Mass Culture, the Book Trade, and Postwar American Fiction* (Philadelphia: University of of Pennsylvania Press, 2010), 55.

14. Drawing on Walter Ong, Havelock Ellis, and the *Phaedrus*, Susan Spencer argues that *Fahrenheit 451* elevates literate culture over oral culture, pointing to the fact that the postapocalyptic society of readers plan to write down all of the books they have memorized someday. Susan Spencer, "The Post-Apocalyptic Library: Oral and Literate Culture in *Fahrenheit 451* and *A Canticle for Leibowitz*," in *Ray Bradbury*, ed. Harold Bloom (New York: Infobase Publishing, 2018), 133. Here, however, I would argue that Faber and Montag's closed society and the private dialogues between Montag and Clarisse suggest that what the novel opposes about mass media is not its secondary orality but, instead, its indiscriminate dispersion.

15. Susan Gunelius, *Building Brand Value the Playboy Way* (New York: Palgrave Macmillan, 2009), 173.

16. Hugh Hefner, "The Playboy Philosophy: Part Two," *Playboy*, January 1963, 52.

17. Watts, *Mr. Playboy*, 222.

18. Anna Gough-Yates, *Understanding Women's Magazines: Publishing, Markets and Readerships* (London: Routledge, 2003), 125.

19. Watts, *Mr. Playboy*, 103.

20. Frank Brady, *Hefner* (New York: Macmillan, 1974), 82.

21. Theodore Peterson, "Magazine Publishing in the U.S.," *International Communication Gazette* 6, no. 2 (1960), 107.

22. David Abrahamson, *Magazine-Made America: The Cultural Transformation of the Postwar Periodical* (Cresskill, NJ: Hampton Press, 1996), 50.

23. "Editorial," *Playboy*, December 1953, 2.

24. In many ways, the Madison Avenue playboy acted as a precursor to the Silicon Valley hippie and other neoliberal subjects. See Thomas Frank, *The Conquest of Cool: Business Culture, Counterculture, and the Rise of Hip Consumerism* (Chicago: University of Chicago Press, 1997); Richard Barbrook and Andy Cameron, "The Californian Ideology," *Science as Culture* 6, no. 1 (1996): 44–72; Fred Turner, *From Counterculture to Cyberculture: Stewart Brand, the Whole Earth Network, and the Rise of Digital Utopianism* (Chicago: University of Chicago Press, 2006); Michel Foucault, *The Birth of Biopolitics: Lectures at the Collège de France, 1978–79*, ed. Michel Senellart, trans. Graham Burchell (New York: Palgrave Macmillan, 2004). On *Playboy* and post-Fordist labor, see Paul B. Preciado, *Pornotopia: An Essay on Playboy's Architecture and Biopolitics* (New York: Zone Books, 2014), 53–54. On *Playboy's* class composition and consumerist ethos, see Osgerby, *Playboys in Paradise*; Mark Jancovich, "The Politics of Playboy: Lifestyle, Sexuality and Nonconformity in American Cold War Culture," in *Historicizing Lifestyle: Mediating Taste, Consumption and Identity from the 1900s to 1970s*, eds. David Bell and Joanne Hollows (Burlington, VT: Ashgate, 2006), 70–88; and Fraterrigo, *Playboy*.

25. Adrian Johns, *The Nature of the Book: Print and Knowledge in the Making* (Chicago: University of Chicago Press, 1998); D. F. McKenzie, *Bibliography and the Sociology of Texts* (Cambridge: Cambridge University Press, 1999); Robert Darnton, "What is the History of Books?," *Daedalus* 111, no. 3 (1982): 65–83.

26. Darnton, "What is the History?," 68.

27. Watts, *Mr. Playboy*, 154.

28. Arthur C. Clarke, "Machina Ex Deux," *Playboy*, July 1961, 102.

29. Thomas Hine writes that Hefner "was perhaps not so cool himself, but he made a very successful business by seeking to be the cause of cool in others." Thomas Hine, "Cold War Cool," in *The Birth of the Cool: California Art, Design, and Culture at Midcentury*, ed. Elizabeth Armstrong (Newport Beach, CA: Prestel, 2007), 204. Nevertheless, as we have seen, it is difficult to make the distinction between Hefner and his business. Hefner himself may or may not be cool, but the figure of Hefner in *Playboy* during this period was cool.

30. Dick Pountain and David Robins, *Cool Rules: Anatomy of an Attitude* (London: Reaktion Books, 2000); Alan Liu, *The Laws of Cool: Knowledge Work and the Culture of Information* (Chicago: University of Chicago Press, 2004).

31. Helmut Lethen, *Cool Conduct: The Culture of Distance in Weimar Germany*, trans. Don Reneau (Berkeley: University of California Press, 2002), 74.

32. John DeWitt, *Cool Cars, High Art: The Rise of Kustom Kulture* (Jackson: University Press of Mississippi, 2002), 16.

33. Liu, *Laws of Cool*, 238.

34. Peter N. Stearns, *American Cool: Constructing a Twentieth-Century Emotional Style* (New York: New York University Press, 1994), 123.

35. Lethen, *Cool Conduct*, 18.

36. Watts, *Mr. Playboy*, 198. Charles Beaumont registers how exhausting this predicament might be in "You Can't Have Them All," a *Playboy* story about a man who plugs information about the woman of his dreams into an advanced calculator—"Procurer One"—and sets out to seduce 563 women across the globe who fit his specifications according to the machine. Although he makes this task easier with the help of a powerful aphrodisiac, he ends the story a nervous wreck, sapped of all energy and horrified at the prospect that if he rests even for a brief period he might fall behind because more women who fit the desired profile will turn eighteen, making his quest for erotic completism eternal. Charles Beaumont, "You Can't Have Them All," *Playboy*, August 1956, 16.

37. Shel Silverstein, "Shel Silverstein's History of *Playboy*," *Playboy*, March 1964, 59.

38. For a complete overview of the relationship between Playboy and the Bond phenomenon, see Claire Hines, *The Playboy and James Bond: 007, Ian Fleming, and* Playboy *Magazine* (Manchester: Manchester University Press, 2018).

39. "Playbill," *Playboy*, March 1960, 3.

40. On James Bond's professionalism, see Edward P. Comentale, "Fleming's Company Man: James Bond and the Management of Modernism," in *Ian Fleming and James Bond: The Cultural Politics of 007*, ed. Edward P. Comentale, Stephen Watt, and Skip Willman (Bloomington: Indiana University Press, 2005), 3–23. See also Hines, *The Playboy*, 66–70.

41. We see anxiety about this theme in *Playboy*'s interview with Sean Connery, who seems to lapse into the tough-guy responses of 007 even as he complains that he is more than just the actor who plays James Bond. "Playboy Interview: Sean Connery," *Playboy*, November 1965, 78. See also Hines, *The Playboy*, 64–65.

42. Ian Fleming, "On Her Majesty's Secret Service," *Playboy*, June 1963, 163.

43. Ian Fleming, "Playboy Interview: Ian Fleming," *Playboy*, December 1964, 100.

44. Ian Fleming, "You Only Live Twice," *Playboy*, June 1964, 178. When Fleming introduced a collection of essays from famous authors on the seven deadly sins, he wrote, "Only Sloth in its extreme form of *accidia*, which is a form of spiritual suicide and a refusal of joy, so brilliantly examined by Evelyn Waugh, has my wholehearted condemnation, perhaps because in moments of despair I have seen its face." Ian Fleming, "Foreword," in *The Seven Deadly Sins* (Pleasantville, NY: Akadine Press, 2002), ix. For a psychoanalytic reading of accidie in Fleming, see Laurence Rickels, *SPECTRE* (Fort Wayne, IN: Anti-Oedipus Press, 2013).

45. Ian Fleming, "On Her Majesty's Secret Service," *Playboy*, April 1963, 74.

46. Perhaps due to the editor's racial liberalism, Fleming's anti-Asian racism is more muted in the *Playboy* version. The book attributes Blofeld's command over his men to the "automatic ant-like subservience to discipline and authority of the Japanese." Ian Fleming, *You Only Live Twice* (New York: Signet, 1964), 128. The serialized narrative omits this observation and refers only to their "disciplined seriousness." Ian Fleming, "You Only Live Twice," 102. On the Orientalist stereotype and emotionlessness, see Xine Yao, "Black-Asian Counterintimacies: Reading Sui Sin Far in Jamaica," *J19: The Journal of Nineteenth-Century Americanists* 6, no. 1 (2018): 199–200.

47. Patrick O'Donnell explores this dimension in his reading of Bond and Hefner, who both represent for him the figure of the "cyborg-aristocrat." Patrick O'Donnell, "James Bond, Cyborg-Aristocrat," in *Ian Fleming and James Bond: The Cultural Politics of 007*, ed. Edward P. Comentale, Stephen Watt, and Skip Willman (Bloomington: Indiana University Press, 2005), 56–59.

48. Watts, *Mr. Playboy*, 60.

49. Leslie Fiedler, "Literati of the Four-Letter Word," *Playboy*, June 1961, 85.

50. Fiedler, "Literati," 126.

51. Eva Illouz, *Cold Intimacies*, 18–19.

52. Ibid., 29.

53. See Michel Foucault, *The History of Sexuality: Volume 1: An Introduction*, trans. Robert Hurley (New York: Vintage, 1978), 21–22.

54. Mike Ashley, *Transformations: The Story of the Science Fiction Magazines from 1950 to 1970* (Liverpool: Liverpool University Press, 2005), 158.

55. Ashley, *Transformations*, 70.

56. Ray Russell, "Horror and Fantasy Writer," *New York Times*, March 22, 1999.

57. Ray Russell, "Preface," *The Playboy Book of Science Fiction and Fantasy*, ed. Ray Russell (Chicago: Playboy Press, 1966), viii.

58. Ursula K. Le Guin, "The Golden Age," *New Yorker*, June 4 and 11, 2012, 77.

59. Ibid., 77.

60. Darko Suvin, "On the Poetics of the Science Fiction Genre," *College English* 34, no. 3 (1972), 372.

61. Suvin, "Science Fiction," 374. See also Rey Chow, "When Reflexivity Becomes Porn: Mutations of a Modernist Theoretical Practice," in *Entanglements, or, Transmedial Thinking about Capture* (Durham, NC: Duke University Press, 2012), 13–30.

62. Liu, *Laws of Cool*, 201.

63. ELSA is presumably kin to ELIZA, the natural language computer program, so named because, like Eliza Doolittle in *Pygmalion* and *My Fair Lady*, it could be taught. See Ernest Havemann, "Computers: Their Scope Today," *Playboy*, October 1967, 209.

64. Stan Dryer, "The Fully Automated Love Life of Henry Keanridge," *Playboy*, July 1968, 151.

65. Arthur C. Clarke, Letter to A.C. Spectorsky, June 27, 1963, *Playboy* Collection, 1960–1969, Cushing Memorial Library and Archives, Texas A&M University Libraries, College Station, TX.

66. Rollo May, *Love and Will* (New York: W. W. Norton, 1969), 43.

67. Ibid., 44.

68. Ibid., 46–47.

69. Ibid., 43.

70. Gayle Rubin, "The Traffic in Women: Notes on the 'Political Economy' of Sex," in *The Second Wave Reader*, ed. Linda Nicholson (New York: Routledge, 1997), 27–62; Eve Kosofsky Sedgwick, *Between Men: English Literature and Male Homosocial Desire* (New York: Columbia University Press, 1985).

71. Williams, *Hard Core*, 80. See also Barbara Ehrenreich, *The Hearts of Men*.

72. Hugh Hefner, "The Playboy Philosophy," *Playboy*, December 1962, 170.

73. Bradbury, "Fahrenheit 451," *Playboy*, March 1954, 41.

74. Ibid., 8.

75. Ibid., 8.

76. Ibid., 10.
77. Ibid., 10.
78. Ibid., 42.
79. Ibid., 42
80. "Playboy's Office Playmate," *Playboy*, July 1955, 27.
81. "A Holiday Evening with Janet Pilgrim," *Playboy*, December 1955, 29–33.
82. Watts, *Mr. Playboy*, 118.
83. "Right Number," *Playboy*, April 1962, 73.
84. Bradbury, "Fahrenheit 451," *Playboy*, April 1954, 24.
85. "Mid-Winter Thaw," *Playboy*, February 1960, 59.
86. Marshall McLuhan, *Understanding Media*, 25.
87. See "Miss November," *Playboy*, November 1955, 30–33; "Playboy's Girl Friday," *Playboy*, September 1957, 39–41; "Playboy's TV Playmate," *Playboy*, March 1956, 35–37; and "Girls Who Wear Glasses," *Playboy*, January 1959, 39–41.
88. "Type Casting," *Playboy*, April 1959, 35.
89. According to Friedrich A. Kittler, "Only as long as women remained excluded from discursive technologies could they exist as the other of words and printed matter." Friedrich A. Kittler, *Gramophone, Film, Typewriter*, trans. Geoffrey Winthrop-Young and Michael Wutz (Stanford: Stanford University Press, 1999), 214. With *Playboy*, however, it becomes clear that even after the epochal shift that Kittler identifies with 1900, some media networks remained what Kittler would call "a sexually closed feedback loop." Ibid., 184.
90. "What Sort of Man Reads Playboy?," *Playboy*, February 1958, 89.
91. See Illouz, *Cold Intimacies*, 19.
92. Carrie Pitzulo, *Bachelors and Bunnies: The Sexual Politics of "Playboy"* (Chicago: University of Chicago Press, 2011), 73. See also Illouz, *Cold Intimacies*, 26.
93. Pitzulo, *Bachelors and Bunnies*, 74–75.
94. "Playbill," *Playboy*, June 1957, 2.
95. Watts, *Mr. Playboy*, 449.
96. Significantly, Modleski's project was inspired by a *Playboy* list of the "worst chick flicks." Tania Modleski, "Clint Eastwood and Male Weepies," *American Literary History* 22, no. 1, 136.
97. Patricia Vettel-Becker, *Shooting from the Hip: Photography, Masculinity, and Postwar America* (Minneapolis: University of Minnesota Press, 2005), 102.
98. Diana Lurie, "An Empire Built on Sex," *Life*, October 29, 1965, 71.
99. Ibid., 71.
100. Mark Rose, *Authors and Owners: The Invention of Copyright* (Cambridge, MA: Harvard University Press, 1993), 88–89.
101. Lord Blackstone quoted in Rose, *Authors and Owners*, 89.

102. Gloria Steinem, "A Bunny's Tale, Part One," *Show*, May 1963, 90–115; Gloria Steinem, "A Bunny's Tale, Part Two," *Show*, June 1963, 66–116.

103. Steinem, "A Bunny's Tale, Part Two," 66.

104. Ibid., 110.

105. Steinem, "A Bunny's Tale, Part One," 68, 114.

106. Ibid., 114–15.

107. Ibid., 114.

108. Steinem, "A Bunny's Tale, Part Two," 114.

109. Steinem, "A Bunny's Tale, Part One," 115.

110. Feona Attwood, "Reading Porn: The Paradigm Shift in Pornography Research," *Sexualities* 5, no. 1 (2002), 91–92.

111. Rae Langton, "Speech Acts and Unspeakable Acts," in *Sexual Solipsism: Philosophical Essays on Pornography and Objectification* (Oxford: Oxford University Press, 2009), 25–63.

112. Here it is important to note that Langton's argument is not simply that women's speech acts are unpersuasive—that would be "perlocutionary frustration"—but rather that they do not register as speech acts at all. Ibid., 48.

113. Ibid., 44–46.

114. Jules Archer, "Don't Hate Yourself in the Morning," *Playboy*, August 1955, 21.

115. Rona Jaffe, *The Best of Everything* (New York: Penguin, 2005 [1958]), vii.

116. *Playboy's Penthouse*, episode 1, directed by Don Rushton and Carl Tubbs, aired October 24, 1959, on WBKB-TV.

117. Ibid.

118. Ibid.

119. Philip Wylie, "The Womanization of America," *Playboy*, September 1958, 51–77.

120. Jennifer Saul, "Pornography, Speech Acts and Context," *Proceedings of the Aristotelian Society* 106, no. 1 (2006): 229–48.

121. Judith Butler, *Excitable Speech: A Politics of the Performative* (New York: Routledge, 1997), 66.

122. Frederik Pohl, "The Fiend," *Playboy*, April 1964, 108.

123. Ibid., 108.

124. Ibid., 108.

125. Osgerby, *Playboys in Paradise*, 151.

126. Bruce Clarke, *Posthuman Metamorphosis: Narratives and Systems* (New York: Fordham University Press, 2008), 133.

127. Ibid., 130.

128. Jerome McGann, *The Textual Condition* (Princeton, NJ: Princeton University Press, 1991), 7–8.

129. George Langelaan, "The Fly," *Playboy*, June 1957, 67–68.

130. Bradbury, "Fahrenheit 451," *Playboy*, March 1954, 50.

131. Boris Kachka, *Hothouse: The Art of Survival and the Survival of Art at America's Most Celebrated Publishing House, Farrar, Straus & Giroux* (New York: Simon & Schuster, 2013), 48.

132. Harlan Ellison, "On Getting a *Playboy* Bounce," in *The Write Book: An Illustrated Treasury of Tips, Tactics, and Tirades*, ed. Bob Perlongo (Glenbrook, CT: Art Direction, 2002), 209.

133. Harlan Ellison, "Pretty Maggie Moneyeyes," in *Deathbird Stories* (London: Pan Books, 1997), 125.

134. "Swedish Accents," *Playboy*, November 1972, 171.

135. Jamie Hutchinson, "Culture, Communication, and an Information Age Madonna," *IEEE Professional Communication Society Newsletter* 45, no. 3 (2001), 1.

136. Ibid.

137. Ibid., 5. *Playboy* would eventually drop any attempts to restrict the image's circulation. Eileen Kent, vice president of new media at Playboy, told *Wired*, "We decided we should exploit this, because it is a phenomenon." Janelle Brown, "Playmate Meets Geeks Who Made Her a Net Star," *Wired*, May 20, 1997, https://www.wired.com/1997/05/playmate-meets-geeks-who-made-her-a-net-star/.

138. Brown, "Playmate Meets Geeks."

139. Linda Kinstler, "Finding Lena, The Patron Saint of JPEGS," *Wired*, January 31, 2019, https://www.wired.com/story/finding-lena-the-patron-saint-of-jpegs/.

140. Hutchinson, "Culture, Communication," 6.

141. Hicks suggests that "the *Playboy* thing gets our attention, but really what it's about is this world-building that's gone on in computing from the beginning—it's about building worlds for certain people and not for others." Kinstler, "Finding Lena."

142. See, for example, the Nature Research family of journals' directive to authors. "A Note on the Lena Image," *Nature Nanotechnology* 13, no. 1087 (2018).

Chapter 5: Mad Ones, Mad Men

1. Bill Morgan, *I Celebrate Myself: The Somewhat Private Life of Allen Ginsberg* (New York: Penguin, 2006), 138.

2. Morgan, *I Celebrate Myself*, 138; National Opinion Research Center, *National Opinion Research Center Fiftieth Anniversary Report: America by Number* (Chicago: NORC, 1991), 3.

3. National Opinion Research Center, *America by Number*, 10.

4. Allen Ginsberg, "Subliminal," in *Journals: Early Fifties Early Sixties*, ed. Gordon Ball (New York: Grove Press, 1977), 154.

5. Allen Ginsberg, "America," in *Howl and Other Poems* (San Francisco: City Lights Books, 1956), 43.

6. Sarah E. Igo argues that mass society was constituted through new techniques for capturing social statistics about reportedly average Americans. Sarah E. Igo, *The Averaged American: Surveys, Citizens, and the Making of a Mass Public* (Cambridge, MA: Harvard University Press, 2007), 5.

7. Allen Ginsberg, "Allen Ginsberg – Montreal 1969 – (Q & A – 2 – continues)," *Allen Ginsberg Project*, March 15, 2016, https://allenginsberg.org/2016/03/allen-ginsberg-montreal-1969-q-a-2/.

8. Steven Watson, *The Birth of the Beat Generation: Visionaries, Rebels, and Hipsters, 1944–1960* (New York: Pantheon Books, 1995), 119.

9. Allen Ginsberg, "Poetry, Violence, and the Trembling Lams, or, Independence Day Manifesto," in *Deliberate Prose: Selected Essays, 1952–1995*, ed. Bill Morgan (New York: HarperCollins, 2000), 3–5; Allen Ginsberg, "Demonstration or Spectacle As Example, As Communication, or, How to Make a March/Spectacle," in *Deliberate Prose: Selected Essays, 1952–1995*, ed. Bill Morgan (New York: HarperCollins, 2000), 9–13.

10. Oliver Harris, "Minute Particulars of the Counter-Culture: *Time*, *Life*, and the Photo-poetics of Allen Ginsberg," *Comparative American Studies* 10, no. 1 (2012), 9.

11. Allen Ginsberg, "Howl," in *Howl and Other Poems* (San Francisco: City Lights Books, 1956), 14.

12. Morgan, *I Celebrate Myself*, 183–85.

13. Ibid., 196.

14. Ibid., 195.

15. Jane Kramer, *Allen Ginsberg in America* (New York: Vintage, 1970), 43.

16. James Breslin, "The Origins of 'Howl' and 'Kaddish,'" in *On the Poetry of Allen Ginsberg*, ed. Lewis Hyde (Ann Arbor: University of Michigan Press, 1984), 406.

17. Dick from Towne-Oller and Associates, Inc., to Allen Ginsberg, June, Edith, and Hazel, April 13, 1955, Box 5, Folder 36, Allen Ginsberg Papers, M0733, Stanford University Special Collections, Palo Alto, CA.

18. Allen Ginsberg to Jack Kerouac, April 22, 1955, in *Jack Kerouac and Allen Ginsberg: The Letters*, ed. Bill Morgan (New York: Viking, 2010), 284.

19. Breslin, "The Origins of 'Howl,'" 406.

20. Thomas Frank, *Conquest of Cool*, 42.

21. Ibid., 43–44.

22. Ibid., 57.

23. Ibid., 93.

24. Ibid., 114. "Mad men," which collapses "Madison Avenue" with "admen," seems to have been used infrequently during the midcentury period, but the phrase has grown

in popularity thanks to the AMC television series about a 1960s advertising agency, *Mad Men*. Thomas Frank, "Ad Absurdum and the Conquest of Cool: Canned Flattery for Corporate America," *Salon.com*, December 22, 2013, https://www.salon.com/2013/12/22/ad_absurdum_and_the_conquest_of_cool_canned_flattery_for_corporate_america/.

25. Rizzo, *Class Acts*, 4–5, 71–75.

26. Jonah Raskin, *American Scream: Allen Ginsberg's* Howl *and the Making of the Beat Generation* (Berkeley: University of California Press, 2006), 175–76.

27. Allen Ginsberg to Richard Eberhart, May 18, 1966, in *Howl: Original Draft Facsimile, Transcript and Variant Versions, Fully Annotated by Author, with Contemporaneous Correspondence, Account of First Public Reading, Legal Skirmishes, Precursor Texts, and Bibliography*, ed. Barry Miles (New York: HarperPerennial, 2006), 152.

28. Allen Ginsberg and Gregory Corso, "From *The Literary Revolution in America*," *Howl: Original Draft Facsimile, Transcript and Variant Versions, Fully Annotated by Author, with Contemporaneous Correspondence, Account of First Public Reading, Leagl Skirmishes, Precursor Texts, and Bibliography*, ed. Barry Miles (New York: HarperPerennial, 2006), 165.

29. Michel de Certeau, *The Practice of Everyday Life*, trans. Steven Rendall (Berkeley: University of California Press, 1984), 176.

30. Belgrad, *The Culture of Spontaneity*, 203–4.

31. Carolyn Marvin observes that "popular and specialist notions of literacy alike conceive of the human body as physically and socially detached from literate practice.... A mark of literate competence is skill in disguising or erasing the contribution of one's body to the process of textual production and practice." Carolyn Marvin, "The Body of the Text: Literacy's Corporeal Constant," *Quarterly Journal of Speech* 80, no. 2 (1994), 129.

32. Belgrad, *Culture of Spontaneity*, 198.

33. Radway, *Feeling for Books*, 283.

34. Michael Szalay, *Hip Figures: A Literary History of the Democratic Party* (Stanford: Stanford University Press, 2012), 2012, 22–23.

35. Allen Ginsberg, "Reintroduction to Carl Solomon," in *Howl: Original Draft Facsimile, Transcript and Variant Versions, Fully Annotated by Author, with Contemporaneous Correspondence, Account of First Public Reading, Legal Skirmishes, Precursor Texts, and Bibliography*, ed. Barry Miles (New York: HarperPerennial, 2006), 111.

36. Appeals to cultural politics as a vehicle for change became endemic to the New Left, the counterculture, and, ultimately, the PMC during this period. See Seann McCann and Michael Szalay, "Do You Believe in Magic? Literary Thinking after the New Left," *Yale Journal of Criticism* 18, no. 2 (2005): 425–68; Schryer, *Fantasies*.

37. Jasper Bernes, *The Work of Art in the Age of Deindustrialization* (Stanford: Stanford University Press, 2017), 17–19; Luc Boltanski and Eve Chiapello, *The New Spirit of Capitalism*, trans. Gregory Elliott (New York: Verso, 2007).

38. Stephen P. Waring, *Taylorism Transformed: Scientific Management Theory since 1945* (Chapel Hill: University of North Carolina Press, 1991), 104–31.

39. William H. Whyte, *The Organization Man* (Garden City, NY: Doubleday, 1956), 61–62.

40. Alfred J. Marrow, *Behind the Executive Mask: Greater Managerial Competence through Deeper Self-Understanding* (New York: American Management Association, 1964), 32–33.

41. Robert Kaiser, "Let It Go," *Playboy*, July 1969, 80, 84.

42. Waring, *Taylorism Transformed*, 124.

43. Ginsberg and Corso, "From *The Literary Revolution in America*," 165.

44. Raskin, *American Scream*, 78.

45. Douglas Kahn, *Noise, Water, Meat: A History of Sound in the Arts* (Cambridge, MA: MIT Press, 1999), 331–34.

46. Antonin Artaud, "An Affective Athleticism," in *The Theatre and Its Double*, trans. Mary Carolien Richards (New York: Grove Press, 1958), 133.

47. Ibid., 135.

48. Rachel Blau Duplessis, "Manhood and Its Poetic Projects: The Construction of Masculinity in the Counter-cultural Poetry of the U.S. 1950s," *Jacket* 31 (2006), 66, 39. http://jacketmagazine.com/31/duplessis-manhood.html. Michael Davidson calls this "compulsory homosociality." Michael Davidson, *Guys Like Us: Citing Masculinity in Cold War Poetics* (Chicago: University of Chicago, 2004), 30–31.

49. Kahn, *Noise, Water, Meat*, 295–321; William S. Burroughs, *Naked Lunch* (New York: Grove Press, 1962), 17–18.

50. William S. Burroughs, *Queer* (New York: Penguin Books, 2010), 33. Reading this passage Tyler Bradway points out that "the ambivalence about sociality in Burroughs' fiction stems from the homophobic restrictions that limit the possibility of manifesting queer relationality within and against a rigid heteronormative society." Bradway, *Queer Experimental Literature*, 31.

51. Oliver Harris, *William S. Burroughs and the Secret of Fascination* (Carbondale, IL: Southern Illinois University Press, 2003), 66.

52. Allen Ginsberg, "Introduction," in *Junky* (New York: Penguin, 1977), vii. Burroughs was equally repulsed by Solomon's handling of *Queer*: "Furthechrissakes a girl's gotta draw the line somewhere or publishers will swarm all over her sticking their nasty old biographical prefaces up her ass." William S. Burroughs to Allen Ginsberg, April 22, 1952, in *The Letters of William S. Burroughs*, ed. Oliver Harris (New York: Viking, 1993), 119–20. As this example suggests, homosexual panic subtends at least some of the Beat anxieties about editorship. Working as his editor, Solomon reminds Kerouac of his subordinate position at Ace Books by recasting him as a rent boy—"Here writers

are trade and editors are aunties." Carl Solomon to Jack Kerouac, December 13, 1951, Box 14, Folder 13, Jack Kerouac Papers, Columbia University Rare Book & Manuscript Library, Columbia University, New York. This kind of line must have disturbed Kerouac, who sometimes saw "the writer was the masculine possessor of the sacred orgasm / literary text, and the editor, who insisted on revision, was the emasculating agent of repression." James Penner, *Pinks, Pansies, and Punks: The Rhetoric of Masculinity in American Literary Culture* (Bloomington: Indiana University Press, 2011), 126. When working with Grove Press on the publication of *The Subterraneans*, Kerouac hissed to Joyce Johnson that he refused to be "castrated" by "liverish pale fag editors." Jack Kerouac and Joyce Johnson, *Doors Wide Open: A Beat Love Affair in Letters, 1957–1958* (New York: Viking, 2000), 12.

53. Ginsberg's discourse on angels resembles the one laid out by Michel Serres, *Angels: A Modern Myth*, trans. Francis Cowper (Paris: Flammarion, 1995).

54. Ginsberg, "Howl," 13. As Anne Hartman points out, angels in Ginsberg almost always serve as code for "male lover." Anne Hartman, "Confessional Counterpublics in Frank O'Hara and Allen Ginsberg," *Journal of Modern Literature* 28, no. 4 (2005), 52.

55. Tim Dean, *Unlimited Intimacy: Reflections on the Culture of Barebacking* (Chicago: University of Chicago Press, 2009), 45–46; Ginsberg, "Howl," 13.

56. John Durham Peters explores a similar complex of fantasies surrounding perfect forms of exchange that he calls "the dream of communication." *Speaking into the Air: A History of the Idea of Communication* (Chicago: University of Chicago Press, 1999), 1.

57. Morgan, *I Celebrate Myself*, 203–9.

58. Ibid., 209.

59. Allen Ginsberg to Lawrence Ferlinghetti, February 10, 1961, in *I Greet You at the Beginning of a Great Career: The Selected Correspondence of Lawrence Ferlinghetti and Allen Ginsberg*, ed. Bill Morgan (San Francisco: City Lights Books, 2015), 109.

60. Maria Damon, *The Dark End of the Street: Margins in American Vanguard Poetry Culture* (Minneapolis: University of Minnesota Press, 1993), 169–70.

61. On the editor as the "primary mediating force," see Tim Groenland, *The Art of Editing: Raymond Carver and David Foster Wallace* (New York: Bloomsbury, 2019), 4–16.

62. On *Howl*'s legal travails, see Morgan, *I Celebrate Myself*, 218, 236, 242, 250. Raskin, *American Scream*, 212–26. For a sourcebook of court transcripts, documents, and information about the trial, see *Howl on Trial: The Battle for Free Expression*, ed. Bill Morgan and Nancy J. Peters (San Francisco: City Lights Books, 2006).

63. As William Eskridge observes, "the postwar antihomosexual campaign sought not only to deny homosexuals any public space (i.e., the prewar philosophy) but also to pry them out of their closets and expose and punish them." William N. Eskridge, Jr., *Gaylaw: Challenging the Apartheid of the Closet* (Cambridge, MA: Harvard University

Press, 1999), 58. See also Margot Canaday, *The Straight State: Sexuality and Citizenship in Twentieth-Century America* (Princeton, NJ: Princeton University Press, 2009), 3. Meanwhile, the ACLU often refused to intervene to protect gay rights during the 1950s. Although the ACLU did support due process for homosexual defendants, and many of its members acted as allies to the homophile movement (including Ferlinghetti's attorney, Albert Bendich), it also affirmed the constitutionality of laws that prohibited homosexual acts and allowed employers to discriminate against homosexuals. John D'Emilio, *Sexual Politics, Sexual Communities: The Making of a Homosexual Minority in the United States 1940–1970* (Chicago: University of Chicago Press, 1983), 112.

64. Joyce Murdoch and Deb Price, *Courting Justice: Gay Men and Lesbians v. the Supreme Court* (New York: Basic Books, 2001), 29.

65. Eric Julber, "You Can't Print It!," *One*, October 1954, 6.

66. Murdoch and Price, *Courting Justice*, 29–47.

67. Brother Grundy, "Lord Samuel and Lord Montagu," *One*, October 1954, 19.

68. Murdoch and Price, *Courting Justice*, 43–44.

69. Strub, *Perversion for Profit*, 37.

70. Dal McIntire, "Tangents," *One*, May 1957, 10–13.

71. Eskridge, *Gaylaw*, 95.

72. Ehrlich, ed., *Howl of the Censor*, 7.

73. Simon Garfield, *Just My Type: A Book about Fonts* (New York: Penguin, 2011), 63. See also Owen Williams, "Berthold Wolpe and His Typeface Albertus," *Letter Arts Review* 20, no. 1 (2005): 16–23.

74. Sigmund Freud, "Psycho-analytic Notes on an Autobiographical Account of a Case of Paranoia (Dementia Paranoides)," in *The Standard Edition of the Complete Psychological Works of Sigmund Freud*, trans. James Strachey (London: Hogarth Press, 1958), 63.

75. Ibid., 62.

76. Guy Hocquenghem, *Homosexual Desire*, trans. Daniella Dangoor (Durham, NC: Duke University Press, 1993), 55.

77. Eve Kosofsky Sedgwick, "Paranoid Reading and Reparative Reading, or, You're So Paranoid, You Probably Think This Essay Is About You," in *Touching Feeling: Affect, Pedagogy, Performativity* (Durham, NC: Duke University Press, 2003), 123–50.

78. See Paul Ricoeur, *Freud and Philosophy: An Essay on Interpretation*, trans. Denis Savage (New Haven, CT: Yale University Press, 1970), 32–33.

79. William Hogan, "Ferlinghetti Defends Publication," *Howl on Trial: The Battle for Free Expression*, ed. Bill Morgan and Nancy J. Peters (San Francisco: City Lights Books, 2006), 107.

80. Ibid., 107–8.

81. Ibid., 109.

82. Ibid., 108.

83. In a similar vein, Duncan and Professor Ruth Witt-Diamant hear in "Howl" a misunderstood "voice of desire" that emerges from "elements of suffering and dismay." Ibid., 109.

84. Ibid., 109.

85. Rachel Blau Duplessis, "Manhood and Its Poetic Projects," 31; Cuordileone, *Manhood and American Politics*, 104. On the class politics of contemporary anxieties about the death of the individual, see Hoberek, *Twilight*.

86. Timothy Melley, *Empire of Conspiracy: The Culture of Paranoia in Postwar America* (Ithaca, NY: Cornell University Press, 2000), 47–63.

87. Ibid., 10.

88. Ibid., 32.

89. Bradway, *Queer Experimental Literature*, 2.

90. Allen Ginsberg to John Hollander, September 7, 1958, in *The Letters of Allen Ginsberg*, ed. Bill Morgan (Philadelphia: Da Capo Press, 2008), 216.

91. William Carlos Williams, "Howl for Carl Solomon," in *Howl and Other Poems* (San Francisco: City Lights Books, 1956), 8.

92. This strategy appears throughout the most popular queer magazines of the 1950s, physique magazines. F. Valentine Hooven III, *Beefcake: The Muscle Magazines of America, 1950–1970* (Cologne: Taschen, 1994), 74. Constantly threatened by censorship, physique editors promulgated homoerotic photographs and illustrations by casting them as artist's references, bodybuilding models, or Greco-Roman heroes. Thomas Waugh, *Hard to Imagine: Gay Male Eroticism in Photography and Film from Their Beginnings to Stonewall* (New York: Columbia University Press, 1996), 219. Through accompanying captions, articles, and other paratexts, these magazines aestheticized young men roughhousing in posing pouches, allowing them to be read not as sexual but instead as playful, noble, healthy, or rebellious. Bob Mizer, editor of *Physique Pictorial*, used images of scantily clad men as a platform to discuss everything from racism to the death penalty, spinning out his libertarian viewpoint in long, tangential legends that allegorized homosexuality while eroticizing politics. However, as Christopher Nealon contends, physique editorial discourse went beyond closeting to project an imagined community in which male homosexuality pervaded the social. Christopher Nealon, *Foundlings: Lesbian and Gay Historical Emotion before Stonewall* (Durham, NC: Duke University Press, 2001), 113. By diagnosing and promoting a kind of adhesive love, physique magazines made the case for the broader political importance of queer, masculine sexuality—homosocial value.

93. A similar strategy would later be deployed in *Attorney General v. A Book Named "Naked Lunch,"* in which Norman Mailer and other defense witnesses turned homosexuality and drug usage into mere metaphors of depravity and woe while likening the

entire work to the hellscapes of Hieronymous Bosch. Frederick Whiting, "Monstrosity on Trial: The Case of 'Naked Lunch,'" *Twentieth Century Literature* 52, no. 2 (2006), 47.

94. Ehrlich, ed., *Howl of the Censor*, 72.

95. Ezra Pound, *The Cantos of Ezra Pound* (New York: New Directions, 1996), 62. This focus on Pound seems in keeping with the preface, as well. Perhaps to distance Ginsberg's work from charges of obscenity, the preface resituates *Howl* inside high modernism, a movement holding irreproachable social and aesthetic value in postwar intellectual culture. Despite his lengthy correspondence with Ginsberg, Williams misdates the author's career, implying that Ginsberg began to write poetry in the boom years of modernism during World War I, well before he was even born. Williams, "Howl for Carl Solomon," 7. Witnesses Leo Lowenthal and Herbert Blau both follow Williams in their testimony, associating it with works and movements following what Lowenthal called the "great upheaval" of the war. Ehrlich, ed., *Howl of the Censor*, 60. For Blau, who picks up on the poem's brief reference to the movement, the poem is an example of Dadaism, "a kind of art of furious negation." Ibid., 68.

96. T. S. Eliot, *After Strange Gods: A Primer of Modern Heresy* (London: Faber & Faber, 1934), 47. Beat criticism and commentary has long dwelled on the biographical connections between Ginsberg and the inhabitants of *Howl*, a fact that would not have gotten past contemporary audiences. Upon hearing Ginsberg intone the first lines of his poem, Frank O'Hara is said to have turned to his neighbor and asked, archly, "I wonder who Allen has in mind?" Marjorie Perloff, "A Lion in Our Living Room: *Collected Poems 1947–1980* by Allen Ginsberg," *American Poetry Review* 14, no. 2 (1985), 35.

97. On paranoia as a strong theory, see Sedgwick, "Paranoid Reading," 133–35.

98. Susan Sontag, "Against Interpretation," in *Against Interpretation and Other Essays* (New York: Farrar, Straus & Giroux, 1966), 6.

99. Ibid.

100. Ibid, 7, 13–14.

101. Leo Lowenthal, *Literature and the Image of Man: Sociological Studies of the European Drama and Novel, 1600–1900* (Boston: Beacon Press, 1957), iii, 188–89.

102. Ehrlich, ed., *Howl of the Censor*, 60.

103. Ginsberg, "Poetry, Violence," 4.

104. Ehrlich, ed., *Howl of the Censor*, 119.

105. Ibid., 106–7.

106. Marc Stein, *Sexual Injustice: Supreme Court Decisions from Griswold to Roe* (Chapel Hill: University of North Carolina Press, 2010), 2–4.

107. Ehrlich, ed., *Howl of the Censor*, 92.

108. Jacob W. Ehrlich, *A Life in My Hands: An Autobiography* (New York: G. P. Putnam's Sons, 1965), 332. Jon Hamm, who played a more subdued Ehrlich in the 2010 film *Howl*, later observed that his star role as *Mad Men*'s Don Draper had a lot in common with

Ehrlich. Although Hamm emphasized their shared rhetorical abilities, this comparison also points to Ehrlich's elusive nature. Ruthe Stein, "Jon Hamm Talks about Playing Jake Ehrlich," *SFGate*, September 19, 2010, https://www.sfgate.com/entertainment/article/Jon-Hamm-talks-about-playing-Jake-Ehrlich-3252603.php.

109. Ehrlich, *Life*, 292–93. Ehrlich begins to look like what Abigail Cheever calls a "real phony," a character of the 1950s whose outward dissembling or "phony mask" turns out to be hiding not an interior self but the absence of any authentic identity at all. Abigail Cheever, *Real Phonies: Cultures of Authenticity in Post–World War II America* (Athens: University of Georgia Press, 2010), 6.

110. Michael Trask, *Camp Sites: Sex, Politics, and Academic Style in Postwar America* (Stanford: Stanford University Press, 2013), 1.

111. Ibid., 3–5.

112. Andrea Most, *Theatrical Liberalism: Jews and Popular Entertainment in America* (New York: New York University Press, 2013), 7.

113. Milner S. Ball, "The Play's the Thing: An Unscientific Reflection on Courts under the Rubric of Theater," *Stanford Law Review* 28, no. 1 (1975), 109–10.

114. Emphasis deleted. Paul Goodman, *Growing Up Absurd: Problems of Youth in the Organized Society* (New York: New York Review Books, [1960] 2012), 145.

115. Ibid., 152–53.

116. Paolo Virno, *A Grammar of the Multitude*, trans. Isabella Bertoletti, James Cascaito, and Andrea Casson (New York: Semiotext(e), 2004), 86–88.

117. Ibid., 53–63.

118. Albert Bendich, "Poetry on Trial," *Seattle University Law Review* 37, no. 1 (2013), 6.

119. Michael Schumacher, *Dharma Lion: A Critical Biography of Allen Ginsberg* (New York: St. Martin's Press, 1992), 254. Later, McIntosh would pin his failure on "lack of public support by decent people," claiming that "there was no one behind me. . . . I felt lost." Joel E. Black, "Ferlinghetti on Trial: The *Howl* Court Case and Juvenile Delinquency," *Boom: A Journal of California* 2, no. 4 (2012), 40.

120. Ehrlich, ed., *Howl of the Censor*, 111.

121. Christopher Lowen Agee, *The Streets of San Francisco: Policing and the Creation of a Cosmopolitan Liberal Politics, 1950–1972* (Chicago: University of Chicago Press, 2014), 119.

122. Richard Rorty, *Contingency, Irony, and Solidarity* (New York: Cambridge, 1989).

123. Canaday, *The Straight State*.

124. Frank D. McConnell, "William Burroughs and the Literature of Addiction," *Massachusetts Review* 8, no. 4 (1967), 665. Despite his aggressive attacks on *Naked Lunch* in court, the prosecutor who cross-examined Ginsberg would later admit that he agreed that it was free speech covered by the First Amendment. Michael Goodman, *Contemporary Literary Censorship*, 246.

125. Jacob Brackman, *The Put-On: Modern Fooling and Modern Mistrust* (Chicago: Henry Regnery, 1971), 90–93. See Ford, *Dig*, 130–31.

126. Goodman, *Growing Up Absurd*, 256.

127. Arlie Russell Hochschild, *The Managed Heart: Commercialization of Human Feeling* (Berkeley: University of California Press, 2012), 129.

128. Ginsberg, "America," 41.

129. Ibid., 43.

130. Sianne Ngai, *Our Aesthetic Categories: Zany, Cute, Interesting* (Cambridge, MA: Harvard University Press, 2015), 174–232.

131. Jasper Bernes, *The Work of Art*, 65.

132. Hochschild, *Managed Heart*, 33.

133. Allen Ginsberg to Lawrence Ferlinghetti, April 3, 1957, in *I Greet You at the Beginning of a Great Career: The Selected Correspondence of Lawrence Ferlinghetti and Allen Ginsberg*, ed. Bill Morgan (San Francisco: City Lights Books, 2015), 23.

134. Allen Ginsberg to Lawrence Ferlinghetti, April 15, 1958, in *I Greet You at the Beginning of a Great Career: The Selected Correspondence of Lawrence Ferlinghetti and Allen Ginsberg*, ed. Bill Morgan (San Francisco: City Lights Books, 2015), 56.

135. Allen Ginsberg to Lawrence Ferlinghetti, last week of May 1958, in *I Greet You at the Beginning of a Great Career: The Selected Correspondence of Lawrence Ferlinghetti and Allen Ginsberg*, ed. Bill Morgan (San Francisco: City Lights Books, 2015), 59.

136. On the importance of correspondence and other forms of private communication to Beats, see Harris, *William S. Burroughs*, and Hartman, "Confessional Counterpublics."

137. Allen Ginsberg, "The Art of Poetry," interview with Tom Clark, *Paris Review*, Spring 1966, in *Allen Ginsberg: Spontaneous Mind: Selected Interviews 1958–1996*, ed. David Carter (New York: HarperCollins, 2001), 41–42.

138. Ibid., 41–42.

139. Ibid., 42.

140. Ibid., 43.

141. Eve Kosofsky Sedgwick, *Epistemology of the Closet* (Berkeley: University of California Press, 1990).

Chapter 6: White-Collar Masochism

1. On how publication remediates texts, see McGann, *The Textual Condition*, and McKenzie, *Bibliography*.

2. Glass, *Counterculture Colophon*, 130–31.

3. Barney Rosset, *Rosset: My Life in Publishing and How I Fought Censorship* (New York: OR Books, 2017), 101.

4. "'Evergreen' Digs into Underground Appeal, Finds 'Sold Out' Types Really Dig Its Copy," *Advertising Age*, July 25, 1966, 107.

5. Glass, *Counterculture Colophon*, 131.

6. *Advertising Age*, "'Evergreen' Digs," 107.

7. Stephen Schryer, "*Counterculture Colophon: Grove Press, the* Evergreen Review, *and the Incorporation of the Avant-Garde* Review," *ALH Online Review* Series I (January 5, 2015), 3.

8. Rosset, *Rosset*, 28–30.

9. Rosset, *Rosset*, 154–55.

10. Laura Lederer, "Women Have Seized the Executive Offices of Grove Press Because . . ." in *Take Back the Night: Women on Pornography*, ed. Laura Lederer (New York: William Morrow, 1980), 267–71.

11. Barney Rosset, "Barney Rosset and the Art of Combat Publishing: An Interview," interview by John Oakes, *Review of Contemporary Fiction* 10, no. 3 (1990), 31.

12. Barney Rosset, "On Publishing," *Review of Contemporary Fiction* 10, no. 3 (1990), 58.

13. Rosset, "Barney Rosset," 56.

14. Gilbert Sorrentino, "Working at Grove: An Interview with Gilbert Sorrentino," interview by S. E. Gontarski, *Review of Contemporary Fiction* 10, no. 3 (1990), 105.

15. Leo Bersani, "Is the Rectum a Grave?" in *Is the Rectum a Grave? and Other Essays* (Chicago: University of Chicago Press, 2010), 25.

16. Janet Halley, *Split Decisions: How and Why to Take a Break from Feminism* (Princeton, NJ: Princeton University Press, 2008), 161. Similar notions can be found in authors such as varied as Georges Bataille and Gilles Deleuze, despite their significant terminological and conceptual differences. Kadji Amin offers another critique of this line of thought, suggesting that "the pleasure of white self-annihilation is a highly scripted fantasy scenario" resting on a series of racialized assumptions and tropes. Kadji Amin, *Disturbing Attachments: Genet, Modern Pederasty, and Queer History* (Durham, NC: Duke University Press, 2017), 97.

17. Samuel Beckett, "Texts for Nothing" in *Stories and Texts for Nothing* (New York: Grove Press, 1967), 85.

18. Susan Sontag, "One Culture and the New Sensibility," in *Against Interpretation and Other Essays* (New York: Farrar, Straus & Giroux, 1966), 297. For a broader survey of this sensibility, see George Cotkin, *Feast of Excess: A Cultural History of the New Sensibility* (New York: Oxford University Press, 2016).

19. Mark Greif, *The Age of the Crisis of Man: Thought and Fiction in America, 1933–1973* (Princeton, NJ: Princeton University Press, 2015), 279. Greif defines antihumanism as "a principled removal of the level of explanation of phenomena from single rational human

actors and their explicit self-understandings to sub- and superpersonal aggregations." More than just a conceptual turn, however, antihumanism casts the death of the liberal subject as a sublime experience, whether it is described as jouissance, schizophrenia, or desubjectification. Greif, *The Age*, 285–86.

20. French antihumanism broke onto the intellectual scene in the US in the late 1960s and early 1970s, with landmark events including the 1966 John Hopkins conference "The Languages of Criticism and the Sciences of Man," the 1966 *Yale French Studies* "Structuralism" special issue, Jacques Derrida's 1968 "The Ends of Man" lecture, and the 1970 translation of Michel Foucault's *The Order of Things*. François Cusset, *French Theory: How Foucault, Derrida, Deleuze, & Co. Transformed the Intellectual Life of the United States*, trans. Jeff Fort (Minneapolis: University of Minnesota Press, 2008), 17–32.

21. In other words, eroticized self-mortification serves the very same function as hip identifications with Black people in bondage: "It allows the professional or manager to transcend, in an act of self-liberation, the class conflict he is paid to mediate." Szalay, *Hip Figures*, 185.

22. Serge Guilbaut, *How New York Stole the Idea of Modern Art: Abstract Expressionism, Freedom, and the Cold War*, trans. Arthur Goldhammer (Chicago: University of Chicago Press, 1983).

23. Editors of *Partisan Review*, "Our Country and Our Culture," in *A Partisan Century: Political Writings from "Partisan Review,"* ed. Edith Kurzweil (New York: Columbia University Press, 1996), 118.

24. Donald E. Pease, "Moby Dick and the Cold War," in *The American Renaissance Reconsidered*, ed. Walter Benn Michaels and Donald E. Pease, 113–55 (Baltimore: Johns Hopkins University Press, 1985), 127; Mark Jancovich, *The Cultural Politics of the New Criticism* (Cambridge: Cambridge University Press, 1993), 37.

25. Leerom Medovoi, *Rebels: Youth and the Cold War Origins of Identity* (Durham, NC: Duke University Press, 2005).

26. Hoberek, *Twilight of the Middle Class*, 8.

27. Harry Clor, *Obscenity and Public Morality: Censorship in a Liberal Society* (Chicago: University Press of Chicago, 1969), 225.

28. Ibid., 238; 241–42.

29. Irvin Kristol, "Pornography, Obscenity, and the Case for Censorship," *New York Times*, March 28, 1971, 24; Catharine A. MacKinnon, *Toward a Feminist Theory of the State* (Cambridge, MA: Harvard University Press, 1989), 209–11.

30. Susan Sontag, "The Pornographic Imagination," in *Styles of Radical Will* (New York: Farrar, Straus & Giroux, 1966), 51.

31. Ibid., 44.

32. Ibid., 36.

33. Leslie Fiedler, "The New Mutants," in *The New Fiedler Reader* (New York: Prometheus, 1999), 204.

34. Foucault, "What is an Author?," 120.

35. Gilles Deleuze and Félix Guattari, *Anti-Oedipus: Capitalism and Schizophrenia*, trans. Robert Hurley, Mark Seem, and Helen R. Lane (Minneapolis: University of Minnesota Press, 1983), 9, 71, 133; Gilles Deleuze and Félix Guattari, *A Thousand Plateaus: Capitalism and Schizophrenia*, trans. Brian Massumi (Minneapolis: University of Minnesota Press, 1987), 134, 150, 173. Deleuze and Guattari also cite Lawrence, Miller, and the Beats as examples of "men who know how to . . . traverse the desert of the body without organs." Deleuze and Guattari, *Anti-Oedipus*, 133.

36. Leo Bersani, *Homos* (Cambridge, MA: Harvard University Press, 1996), 158.

37. On de Sade's monumental influence on twentieth-century thought and culture, see Alyce Mahon, *The Marquis de Sade and the Avant-Garde* (Princeton, NJ: Princeton University Press, 2020).

38. Glass, *Counterculture Colophon*, 128.

39. Roland Barthes, "Objective Literature: Alain Robbe-Grillet," *Evergreen Review* 5 (1958): 13–126; Maurice Blanchot, "Where Now? Who Now?," *Evergreen Review* 2 (1959): 222–29.

40. Eli Zaretsky, *Capitalism, the Family, and Personal Life* (New York: Harper, 1976), 74.

41. Schauer, "Speech and 'Speech,'" 922–23.

42. Henry Miller, *Tropic of Cancer* (New York: Grove Press, 1961), 2.

43. Ibid., 242.

44. Ibid., 144.

45. Kate Millett, *Sexual Politics* (New York: Doubleday, 1970), 300.

46. Steven Marcus, *The Other Victorians: A Study of Sexuality and Pornography in Mid-Nineteenth-Century England* (New York: Basic Books, 1964), 274.

47. Lionel Trilling, *The Liberal Imagination: Essays on Literature and Society* (New York: New York Review Books, 1950), xx–xxi.

48. John Crowe Ransom, "Criticism, Inc.," in *Praising It New: The Best of the New Criticism*, ed. Garrick Davis (Athens, OH: Ohio University Press, 2008), 60.

49. See Richard M. Weaver, *Ideas Have Consequences* (Chicago: University of Chicago Press, 1948), 27.

50. George Orwell, "Inside the Whale," in *Henry Miller: Three Decades of Criticism*, ed. Edward Mitchell (New York: New York University Press, 1971), 12–14.

51. Henry Miller, "Obscenity and the Law of Reflection," in *Henry Miller on Writing* (New York: New Directions, 1964), 186–87.

52. See Benjamin Noys, *Malign Velocities: Accelerationism and Capitalism* (Winchester, UK: Zero Books, 2014), xii.

53. Miller, "Obscenity," 188.
54. Miller, *Cancer*, 246.
55. Ibid.
56. Ibid., 258.
57. Ibid.
58. Fiedler, "The New Mutants," 192–99.
59. Margot Weiss, *Techniques of Pleasure: BDSM and the Circuits of Sexuality* (Durham, NC: Duke University Press, 2011), 146.
60. Michael O'Donoghue and Frank Springer, "Buddy Can You Spare a Fin?" *Evergreen Review* 9, no. 36 (1965), 17.
61. Ibid.
62. Ibid.
63. Ibid.
64. Earl Shorris quoted in John Anthony Moretta, *The Hippies: A 1960s History* (Jefferson, NC: McFarland, 2017), 130.
65. Lauren Berlant, *The Female Complaint: The Unfinished Business of Sentimentality in American Culture* (Durham, NC: Duke University Press, 2008), 100.
66. Ibid., 6.
67. Ibid., 3.
68. Claire Sisco King, "It Cuts Both Ways: *Fight Club*, Masculinity, and Abject Hegemony," *Communication and Cultural/Critical Studies* 6, no. 4 (2009), 370–71.
69. Ehrenreich and Ehrenreich, "The Professional-Managerial Class," 45; Catherine Liu, *American Idyll: Academic Antielitism as Cultural Critique* (Iowa City: University of Iowa Press, 2011), 183.
70. Robert D. Johnston, *The Radical Middle Class: Populist Democracy and the Question of Capitalism in Progressive Era Portland, Oregon* (Princeton, NJ: Princeton University Press, 2003), 3–17.
71. William S. Burroughs, "Revolt!," interview with Jeff Schiro, in *Burroughs Live: The Collected Interviews of William S. Burroughs*, ed. Sylvère Lotringer (New York: Semioxtext(e), 2001), 111.
72. Braverman, *Labor and Monopoly Capital*, 282.
73. Van Gosse, *Where the Boys Are: Cuba, Cold War America, and the Making of the New Left* (London: Verso, 1993), 55.
74. LeRoi Jones, "Cuba Libre" in *Evergreen Review Reader: 1957–1967*, ed. Barney Rosset (New York: Grove Press, 1968), 346.
75. Régis Debray, *Revolution in the Revolution?: Armed Struggle and Political Struggle in Latin America* (New York: Grove Press, 1967), 110–11.

76. Tom Wolfe, "Radical Chic: That Party at Lenny's," *New York Magazine,* June 8, 1970, 26–56.

77. Jean-Paul Sartre, "Preface," in Frantz Fanon, *The Wretched of the Earth*, trans. Constance Farrington (New York: Grove Press, 1963), 9–10.

78. On theories of subjectivation, see Jodi Dean, *Crowds and Party* (New York: Verso, 2016).

79. Joshua Bloom and Waldo E. Martin, Jr., *Black against Empire: The History and Politics of the Black Panther Party* (Berkeley: University of California Press, 2013), 21, 66; Nikhil Pal Singh, "The Black Panthers and the 'Undeveloped Country' of the Left," in *The Black Panther Party Reconsidered*, ed. Charles E. Jones (Baltimore: Black Classic Press, 2005), 57–105.

80. Bloom and Martin, *Black against Empire*, 232.

81. David Hilliard and Lewis Cole, *This Side of Glory: The Autobiography of David Hilliard and the Story of the Black Panther Party* (Boston: Little, Brown, 1993), 151–52.

82. William S. Burroughs, *The Ticket That Exploded* (New York: Grove Press, 1967), 219. For the relationship between Burroughs's interest in Napoleon Hill and his fascination with deindividualization, see Konstantinou, *Cool Characters*, 132.

83. Burroughs, *Ticket*, 221.

84. Gouldner, *The Future of Intellectuals*, 64; Ehrenreich and Ehrenreich, "The Professional-Managerial Class," 19; Schryer, *Fantasies*, 11. For a history of the communication and control techniques that managers used to secure the consent of their employees, see Waring, *Taylorism Transformed*.

85. D. H. Lawrence, *Lady Chatterley's Lover* (New York: Grove Press, 1959), 72.

86. On intimate communication, see Illouz, *Cold Intimacies*.

87. Simone de Beauvoir, "Must We Burn Sade?," trans. Annette Michelson, in *The Marquis de Sade: 120 Days of Sodom and Other Writings*, trans. Austryn Wainhouse and Richard Seaver (New York: Grove Press, 1966), 21–23, 26–32, 60–61. For a publishing history of the Grove editions of de Sade, see Amy S. Wyngaard, "Translating Sade: The Grove Press Editions, 1953–1968," *Romanic Review* 104, nos. 3–4 (2013): 313–31.

88. Henry Miller, *Tropic of Capricorn* (New York: Grove Press, 1961), 28–29.

89. S. E. Gontarski, "Preface," in *The Grove Press Reader, 1951–2001*, ed. S. E. Gontarski (New York: Grove Press, 2001), xiv.

90. Sorrentino, "Working at Grove," 101; Gontarski, "Preface," xii.

91. Sorrentino, "Working at Grove," 102.

92. Gontarski, "Preface," xii.

93. Richard Ellis, "Disseminating Desire: Grove Press and 'The End[s] of Obscenity'" in *Perspectives on Pornography: Sexuality in Film and Literature*, ed. Gary Day and Clive Bloom (London: Macmillan, 1988), 35–36.

94. *Obscene*, directed by Daniel O'Connor and Neil Ortenberg (2007; New York: Arthouse Films, 2010), DVD.

95. Burroughs, *Naked Lunch*, 21; A. C. Spectorsky, *The Exurbanites* (New York: J. B. Lipincott, 1955), 7.

96. Michael Foucault, *Discipline and Punish: The Birth of the Prison*, trans. Alan Sheridan (New York: Vintage, 1977), 200–203.

97. Burroughs, *Naked Lunch*, 23–24.

98. See Bersani, *Homos*, 95–96.

99. Elizabeth Freeman, *Time Binds: Queer Temporalities, Queer History* (Durham, NC: Duke University Press, 2010), 143.

100. Jack Halberstam, *The Queer Art of Failure* (Durham, NC: Duke University Press, 2011), 130–31.

101. Andrew Marzoni, "Henry Miller and Deleuze's 'Strange Anglo-American Literature'" in *Understanding Deleuze, Understanding Modernism*, ed. Paul Ardoin, S. E. Gontarski, and Laci Mattison (New York: Bloomsbury, 2014), 193.

102. Miller, *Cancer*, 11.

103. Frances Ferguson, "Sade and the Pornographic Legacy," *Representations* 36 (1991), 3.

104. Marquis de Sade, "Philosophy in the Bedroom," in *Justine, Philosophy in the Bedroom, and Other Writings*, trans. Richard Seaver and Austryn Wainhouse (New York: Grove Press, 1965), 185.

105. LeRoi Jones, "The Death of Horatio Alger," in *Tales* (New York: Grove Press, 1967). Miller demonstrates a similar antipathy toward the Alger myth. In *Tropic of Capricorn*, the vice president of the Cosmodemonic Telegraph Company encourages Miller's literary double to write an Alger narrative about the messengers working under him. Appalled at this suggestion, Miller concocts a plan to write an anti-Alger story: "I will give you Horatio Alger as he looks the day after the Apocalypse, when all the stink has cleared away." Miller, *Capricorn*, 31.

106. Barbara Ehrenreich and John Ehrenreich, "The New Left and the Professional-Managerial Class," *Radical America* 11, no. 3 (1977), 8–10.

107. Ibid., 10–11.

108. James William Gibson, *The Perfect War: Technowar in Vietnam* (New York: Atlantic Monthly Press, 2000), 14, 79. Theodore Roszak asserts that "McNamara's career is almost a paradigm of our new elitist managerialism." Roszak, *Making of a Counter Culture*, 12.

109. Gibson, *Perfect War*, 79–80, 112.

110. Ibid., 80.

111. Ibid., 319.

112. Ibid., viii, 80, 177.

113. Ibid., viii, 123.

114. Ehrenreich and Ehrenreich, "The New Left and the Professional-Managerial Class," 12.

115. None of this should be taken to suggest that antiwar protests were exclusively middle-class phenomena. On the overlooked importance of working-class organizations and individuals in the antiwar movement, see Penny W. Lewis, *Hardhats, Hippies, and Hawks: The Vietnam Antiwar Movement as Myth and Memory* (Ithaca, NY: Cornell University Press, 2013).

116. On the right to agitation, see Weinrib, *Taming of Free Speech*.

117. Trask, *Camp Sites*, 91.

118. Seth Rosenfeld, *Subversives: The FBI's War on Student Radicals, and Reagan's Rise to Power* (New York: Farrar, Straus & Giroux, 2012), 243; David Allyn, *Make Love, Not War: The Sexual Revolution: An Unfettered History* (London: Routledge, 2000), 46.

119. Mario Savio quoted in Rosenfeld, *Subversives*, 245.

120. *Cohen v. California*, 403 U.S. 15 (1971).

121. Trask, *Camp Sites*, 88.

122. Hal Draper, *Berkeley: The New Student Revolt* (New York: Grove Press, 1965), 141–42; Rosenfeld, *Subversives*, 244.

123. Draper, *Berkeley*, 142.

124. Rosenfeld, *Subversives*, 244.

125. Jim Prickett, "A License to Kill," *Spider* 4, March 15, 1965, http://www.freedomarchives.org/Documents/Finder/DOC55_scans/55.FSM.Spider.Periodical.pdf.

126. Ibid.

127. Watts, *Mr. Playboy*, 212–15.

128. Stephen E. Kerchner, *Revel with a Cause: Liberal Satire in Postwar America* (Chicago: University of Chicago Press, 2006), 117. Roszak suggests reading *Mad* as a child was a common formative experience among members in the counterculture. Roszak, *Making of a Counter Culture*, 24.

129. Robert Anton Wilson, "Don't Go Away, *Mad*," *fact* 2, no. 6 (1965), 39.

130. Rosenfeld, *Subversives*, 222. Using language reminiscent of Moloch, Hal Draper describes the "mass university" as "an overpowering, over-towering, impersonal alien machine in which [the student] is nothing but a cog going through preprogrammed motions—the 'IBM' syndrome." Draper, *Berkeley*, 153. See also Steven Lubar, "'Do Not Fold, Spindle or Mutilate': A Cultural History of the Punch Card," *Journal of American Culture* 15, no. 4 (1992): 43–55.

131. Sylvia Shin Huey Chong, *The Oriental Obscene: Violence and Racial Fantasies in the Vietnam Era* (Durham, NC: Duke University Press, 2011), 10, 115. Note that the

photographs of the My Lai massacre were not published until the year after the event, which took place in 1968. Ibid., 29.

132. Robin Morgan, "Goodbye to All That," in *Going Too Far: The Personal Chronicle of a Feminist* (New York: Random House, 1978), 122.

133. Ibid., 123.

134. Ibid., 125.

135. Laura Lederer, "Women Have Seized," 268.

136. Ellen Smith Mendocino, "A Feminist Takes on the Evergreen," *Rat Subterranean News*, April 17, 1970, 6.

137. Glass, *Rebel Publisher*, 196.

138. Lederer, "Women Have Seized," 271.

139. Robin Morgan, "The Politics of Sadomasochistic Fantasies," in *Going Too Far: The Personal Chronicle of a Feminist* (New York: Random House, 1978), 236.

140. Alice Echols, *Daring to Be Bad: Radical Feminism in America 1967-1975* (Minneapolis: University of Minnesota Press, 1989), 204-10.

141. Glass, *Counterculture Colophon*, 202-15.

142. Robin Morgan, "Rights of Passage" in *Going Too Far: The Personal Chronicle of a Feminist* (New York: Random House, 1978), 13.

143. See Strub, *Perversion for Profit*, 237. For examples of the role of Grove authors in cultural feminist discourse, see Robin Morgan, *The Demon Lover: The Roots of Terrorism* (New York: Washington Square, 2001), 107, 115, 119.

144. Robin Morgan, "Lesbian and Feminism: Synonyms or Contradictions?" in *Going Too Far: The Personal Chronicle of a Feminist* (New York: Random House, 1978), 180-81.

145. Glass, *Rebel Publisher*, 215.

146. Chris Kraus, *After Kathy Acker: A Literary Biography* (South Pasadena, CA: Semiotext(e), 2017), 196-97.

147. Kraus, *After Kathy Acker*, 240-41. When Jordan quit Grove to edit at Pantheon Books for Random House, Acker followed him to publish two books there, but she returned to Grove when he left the position. Kraus, *After Kathy Acker*, 242.

148. Glass, *Rebel Publisher*, 215.

149. Timothy Melley, *Empire of Conspiracy*, 33. Suzette Henke, "Oedipus Meets Sacher-Masoch: Kathy Acker's Pornographic (Anti)Ethical Aesthetic," *Contemporary Women's Writing* 2, no. 2 (2008), 97.

150. See, especially, Chris Kraus, *I Love Dick* (New York: Semiotext(e), 1997); Chris Kraus, *Aliens and Anorexia* (New York: Semiotext(e), 2000).

151. Kathy Acker, *Don Quixote, Which Was a Dream* (New York: Grove Press, 1986), 158.

152. Szalay, *Hip Figures*, 183-87.

Afterword: Transgression in the Post-Pornographic Era

1. Neil A. Lewis, "A Prosecution Tests the Definition of Obscenity," *New York Times*, September 28, 2007, http://www.nytimes.com/2007/09/28/us/28obscene.html?_r=0.

2. Paula Reed Ward, "Afraid of Public Trial, Author to Plead Guilty in Online Obscenity Case," *Pittsburgh Post-Gazette*, May 16, 2008, http://www.post-gazette.com/frontpage/2008/05/17/Afraid-of-public-trial-author-to-plead-guilty-in-online-obscenity-case/stories/200805170216.

3. Defendant Fletcher's Memorandum in Support of Motion to Declare Obscenity Statute Unconstitutional as Applied to Text or, in the Alternative, to Dismiss Indictment for Failure to Allege a Crime at 65–66, United States v. Fletcher, No. 2:06-cr-00329-JFC (W.D. Pa. Apr. 26, 2007), 14.

4. Motion to Dismiss, 33. For a legal discussion of the *Fletcher* case, see Ryen Rasmus, "The Auto-Authentication of the Page: Purely Written Speech and the Doctrine of Obscenity," *William and Mary Bill of Rights Journal* 20 (2011): 253–85.

5. Kendrick, *Secret Museum*, 209.

6. Jean Baudrillard, *The Ecstasy of Communication*, trans. Bernard Schütze and Caroline Schütze, ed. Sylvère Lotringer (New York: Semiotext(e), 1988), 11–28; Lotringer, *Overexposed*, 13–31.

7. Laura Kipnis, *Bound and Gagged: Pornography and the Politics of Fantasy in America* (Durham, NC: Duke University Press, 1999), 122–60.

8. Carrie N. Baker, *The Women's Movement against Sexual Harassment* (Cambridge: Cambridge University Press, 2008), 177–91.

9. Boltanski and Chiapello, *New Spirit of Capitalism*, 78, 90–91, 111–21.

10. Marcuse, *One-Dimensional Man*, 75.

11. Edward Lee, "Afterword," *Header* (Portland, OR: Deadite Press, 2012), loc. 1600 of 1678, Kindle.

12. Thompson, *Merchants of Culture*, 103; Dan N. Sinykin, "The Conglomerate Era: Publishing, Authorship, and Literary Form, 1965–2007," *Contemporary Literature* 58, no. 4 (2017), 471–72. André Schiffrin calls this "market censorship." André Schiffrin, *The Business of Books: How International Conglomerates Took Over Publishing and Changed the Way We Read* (New York: Verso, 2000), 103–28. Evan Brier sees countervailing tendencies to the decline of the editor in this era, including the rise of editorial imprints and the emergence of a discourse that presents the editor as safeguarding the literary from corporate corruption. Evan Brier, "The Editor as Hero: The Novel, the Media Conglomerate, and the Editorial Critique," *American Literary History* 30, no. 1 (2018): 85–107.

13. Communication Decency Act of 1996, 47 U.S.C. § 230. For a detailed account of Section 230 and its relationship to obscenity law, see Jeff Kosseff, *The Twenty-Six Words That Created the Internet* (Ithaca, NY: Cornell University Press, 2019).

14. Section 230 is frequently invoked by tech companies whenever they want to absolve themselves of any wrongdoing: because they are not considered publishers of information provided by third-party users, eBay is not responsible for the products it sells, and Airbnb is not responsible for the rooms it rents. Christopher Zara, "The Most Important Tech Law Has A Problem," *Wired*, January 3, 2017, https://www.wired.com/2017/01/the-most-important-law-in-tech-has-a-problem/; Julia Carrie Wong, "How a Failed Attempt to Get Porn off the Internet Protects Airbnb from the Law," *Guardian*, June 29, 2016, https://www.theguardian.com/technology/2016/jun/29/airbnb-lawsuit-san-francisco-regulation-internet-porn. Danielle K. Citron and Mary Anne Franks have presented a critique of what they see as overextended interpretations of Section 230. Danielle Keats Citron and Mary Anne Franks, "The Internet as a Speech Machine and Other Myths Confounding Section 230 Reform," *Boston University School of Law, Public Law Research Paper* 20–8, February 7, 2020, last modified June 23, 2020, http://dx.doi.org/10.2139/ssrn.3532691.

15. Samantha Cole, "Amazon Is Burying Sexy Books, Sending Erotic Novel Authors to the 'No-Rank Dungeon,'" *Vice*, March 29, 2018, https://www.vice.com/en_us/article/bjpjn4/amazon-erotica-best-seller-rankings-removed.

16. Mary L. Gray and Siddharth Suri, *Ghost Work: How to Stop Silicon Valley from Building a New Global Underclass* (New York: Houghton Mifflin, 2019), ix–xxi. See also Casey Newton, "The Trauma Floor: The Secret Lives of Facebook Moderators in America," *The Verge*, February 25, 2019, https://www.theverge.com/2019/2/25/18229714/cognizant-facebook-content-moderator-interviews-trauma-working-conditions-arizona.

17. Sarah T. Roberts, *Behind the Screen: Content Moderation in the Shadows of Social Media* (New Haven, CT: Yale University Press, 2019), 116–23, 213–14.

18. *Forbidden Thoughts*, ed. Jason Rennie (USA: Superversive Press, 2016).

19. Angela Nagle, *Kill All Normies: Online Culture Wars from 4chan to Tumblr to Trump and the Alt-Right* (Winchester, UK: Zero Books, 2017), 28–39.

20. Ibid., 115–16.

21. Catherine Liu, "Dialectic of Dark Enlightenments: The Alt-Right's Place in the Culture Industry," *Los Angeles Review of Books*, July 30, 2017, https://lareviewofbooks.org/article/dialectic-of-dark-enlightenments-the-alt-rights-place-in-the-culture-industry/.

22. Ibid.

23. Ibid.

24. George Hawley, *Making Sense of the Alt-Right* (New York: Columbia University Press, 2017), 77–78.

25. Spencer dropped out of his PhD program. Hawley, *Making Sense*, 53. Greg Johnson received his doctoral degree before leaving academia. "Greg Johnson," *Southern Poverty Law Center*, https://www.splcenter.org/fighting-hate/extremist-files/individual/greg-johnson. Nick Land resigned from his lecturer position at the University of Warwick.

Olivia Goldhill, "The Neo-Fascist Philosophy That Underpins Both the Alt-Right and Silicon Valley Technophiles," *Quartz*, June 18, 2017, https://qz.com/1007144/the-neo fascist-philosophy-that-underpins-both-the-alt-right-and-silicon-valley-technophiles/. Mike Cernovich obtained a law degree, but his career was derailed after sexual assault allegations. Dale Beran, *It Came from Something Awful: How a Toxic Troll Army Accidentally Memed Donald Trump into Office* (New York: All Points Books, 2019), 147. Milo Yiannopoulos went to an expensive private grammar school but quit one college before being expelled from another. Milo Yiannopoulos, "I Dropped out of Manchester and Cambridge But It's Honestly Fine," *The Tab*, February 13, 2015, https://thetab.com/2015/02/13/dropped-manchester-cambridge-honestly-fine-30198; "Milo Yiannopoulos Invited to Talk in Canterbury at His Old School," *BBC*, November 16, 2020, https://www.bbc.com/news/uk-england-kent-38006442. Others, like Jason Kessler, finished their university educations but never quite made it into the respectable middle class. Beran, *It Came*, 228.

26. See Beran, *It Came*.

27. Whitney Phillips, *This Is Why We Can't Have Nice Things: Mapping the Relationship Between Online Trolling and Mainstream Culture* (Cambridge, MA: MIT Press, 2015), 35, 124–28.

28. Dale Beran, *It Came*, 45.

29. Nagle, *Kill All Normies*, 113–15.

30. Joseph M. Reagle, Jr., *Hacking Life: Systematized Living and Its Discontents* (Cambridge, MA: MIT Press, 2019), 107.

31. Andrew Stephen King, "Feminism's Flip Side: A Cultural History of the Pickup Artist," *Sexuality & Culture* 22 (2018): 303–8.

32. Reagle, *Hacking Life*, 111.

33. Alexandra Minna Stern, *Proud Boys and the White Ethnostate: How the Alt-Right Is Warping the American Imagination* (Boston: Beacon Press, 2019), 71–92.

34. Reagle, *Hacking Life*, 110.

35. On pickup artistry's evolutionary discourse and how it contributes to rape culture, see Amanda Denes, "Biology as Consent: Problematizing the Scientific Approach to Seducing Women's Bodies," *Women's Studies International Forum* 34, no. 5 (2011): 411–19.

36. Ran Almog and Danny Kaplan, "The Nerd and His Discontent: The Seduction Community and the Logic of the Game as a Geeky Solution to the Challenges of Young Masculinity," *Men and Masculinities* 20, no. 1 (2015): 37. See also Nagle, *Kill All Normies*, 113.

37. Almog and Kaplan, "The Nerd and His Discontent," 36.

38. Ibid.

39. Rachel O'Neill, "The Work of Seduction: Intimacy and Subjectivity in the London 'Seduction Community,'" *Sociological Research Online* 20, no. 4 (2015): paragraph 4.12.

40. Ibid., paragraphs 4.1–4.6

41. See Radway, *Feeling for Books*, 283.

42. Beran, *It Came*, 115.

43. Alice E. Marwick and Robyn Caplan, "Drinking Male Tears: Language, the Manosphere, and Networked Harassment," *Feminist Media Studies* 18, no. 4 (2018), 545–47.

44. Beran, *It Came*, 118. On the longer history of the relationship between mass murder, capitalism, and the competitive logic of social Darwinism, see Franco "Bifo" Berardi, *Heroes: Mass Murder and Suicide* (New York: Verso, 2015), 41.

45. Alain de Benoist and Charles Champetier, *Manifesto for a European Renaissance* (London: Arktos, 2012), 36. See also Paul Edward Gottfried, *After Liberalism: Mass Democracy in the Managerial State* (Princeton, NJ: Princeton University Press, 1999).

46. Casey Ryan Kelly, *Apocalypse Man: The Death Drive and the Rhetoric of White Masculine Victimhood* (Columbus: Ohio State University Press, 2020), 5–9, 145–46.

47. *The Daily Stormer*, for example, ran an article on Roth. For a broader discussion of antipornography and anti-Semitic ideology, see Kristoff Kerl, "'Oppression by Orgasm': Pornography and Antisemitism in Far-Right Discourses in the United States since the 1970s," *Studies in American Jewish Literature* 39, no. 1 (2020): 117–38. On obscenity and Jewish culture in the US, see Lambert, *Unclean Lips*.

48. Dale Beran, *It Came*, 124.

49. The Golden One, a white nationalist bodybuilder, tells his viewers that "the masculine energy you spend on porn should be used [on] more productive endeavors" such as weight-lifting and other "glorious" pursuits. The Golden One, "Why I Hate Porn and Why You Should Stop Watching It," *YouTube*, June 14, 2017, https://www.youtube.com/watch?v=guck9gUOIls.

50. Marlene Hartmann, "The Totalizing Meritocracy of Heterosex: Subjectivity in NoFap," *Sexualities* 24, no. 3 (2021), 15.

51. Gavin McInnes Clips, "STOP WATCHING PORN," *YouTube*, May 14, 2019, https://www.youtube.com/watch?v=KZ62oybdTKc.

52. Gavin McInnes, *The Death of Cool: From Teenage Rebellion to the Hangover of Adulthood* (New York: Scribner, 2012), 36.

53. Ibid., 89–90.

54. Jim Goad, *Shit Magnet: One Man's Miraculous Ability to Absorb the World's Guilt* (Port Townsend, WA: Feral House, 2002), 135–66.

55. McInnes, *Death of Cool*, 218.

56. The Elders, "Proud Boys: Who Are They?" *Proud Boy Magazine*, August 24, 2017, https://officialproudboys.com/proud-boys/whoaretheproudboys/.

57. Foucault, *History of Sexuality*, 45.

58. Whitney Mallet, "How Banks Make It Hard for Sexy Startups," *Fast Company*, November 16, 2016, https://www.fastcompany.com/3065256/banking-discrimination-porn-sex-toys.

59. Alistair Barr, "Exclusive: PayPal Backtracks on 'Obscene' Ebook Policy," *Reuters*, March 13, 2012, https://www.reuters.com/article/us-paypal/exclusive-paypal-backtracks-on-obscene-e-book-policy-idUSBRE82C11C20120313.

60. Ironically, the free flow of finances is also the greatest beneficiary of First Amendment jurisprudence under the Roberts court. Cold war liberals treated words and images as abstract communications, divorced from bodily realities and political deliberations, and now the same detached perspective considers money as speech in cases such as *Citizens United v. FEC* and *Janus v. AFSCME*. Zephyr Teachout, "Facts in Exile: Corruption and Abstraction in *Citizens United v. Federal Elections Commission*," *Loyola University of Chicago Law Journal*, 42, no. 2 (2011): 295–326. A counter-rights revolution has turned the constitutional protections won during the Warren years against the liberal project they were enacted to protect. Jefferson Deckers, *The Other Rights Revolution: Conservative Lawyers and the Remaking of American Government* (New York: Oxford University Press, 2016). However, right-wing jurists are only drawing on antidemocratic potentials already contained within free speech libertarianism. Susan Sontag may have been more prescient than she could have realized when she observed that the pornographic imagination treated everything as fungible, but she did not account for the fact that under the present system some have more capital to spend than others. Susan Sontag, "The Pornographic Imagination," 52–53, 66–67.

61. Remittance Girl, "Two Legs Bad: An Open Letter to Mark Coker #smashwords #censorship #erotica," February 25, 2012, *Remittance Girl*, http://remittancegirl.com/discussions/two-legs-bad-an-open-letter-to-mark-coker-smashwords-censorship-erotica/.

Index

abstraction, 4, 7–8, 11–13, 16, 18, 29–38, 46, 68, 73, 77, 142, 146, 157, 160–62, 172, 181, 186–88, 202n78, 253n60
Acker, Kathy, 178–79
Adams, Scott, 186
Adorno, Theodor, and Max Horkheimer, 81
advertising, 6, 43, 44, 105, 128–32, 167, 182
Albee, Edward, 159
Alger, Horatio, 82, 170–71, 246n105
Alighieri, Dante, 144–45
alt-right, 70, 183–85, 187–91
Amazon.com, 183
American Civil Liberties Union (ACLU), 62–63, 139, 236n58
American Mercury, 40–42, 45, 65
Anderson, Margaret, 19
Anderson, Sherwood, 42
angels, 137–38
anthropology, 64–66
antihumanism, 156–59, 161, 179, 241n19, 242n20
Appalachia, 65
Artaud, Antonin, 136, 160
Asbury, Herbert, 40
Atkinson, Ti-Grace, 177
Attorney General v. A Book Named "Naked Lunch," 24, 144, 151, 203n93, 237n93, 239n124. *See also* Burroughs, William S.

Baraka, Amiri, 6, 165, 167, 171
Bataille, Georges, 10, 159, 241n16
Baudrillard, Jean, 180
Beaumont, Charles, 111, 226n36
Beauvoir, Simone de, 167
Becker, Howard, 8–9
Beckett, Samuel, 154, 156, 159, 167, 170, 178
Bendich, Albert, 139, 150, 236n58
Benjamin, Walter, 10, 35, 89
Bennett, D. M., 14–15
Berg, Jean de, 159
Berlant, Lauren, 163–64
Berkeley Free Speech Movement, 173–75
Bernays, Edward, 43
Bersani, Leo, 156, 159
Black, Hugo, 23
Black Mask, 45
Blackness, 68–69, 74–75, 89–90, 102, 107, 129, 162–63, 166, 172, 174, 242n21
Black Panther Party, 166
Blake, William, 152
Bond, James, 108–9, 174, 227n41
Borges, Jorge Luis, 154
Bourdieu, Pierre, 8–9, 36, 197n24, 208n166
Bradbury, Ray, 80–81, 90, 101–3, 111, 116
Braverman, Harry, 67, 164–65
Brennan, William J., Jr., 23–25
Brown, Norman O., 32, 135, 206n138
Buckley, William F., 4
Bullough, Edward, 47–48
bureaucracy, 27, 30, 32, 36, 38–39, 96, 129, 135, 142, 175, 181, 205n122. *See also* offices
Burroughs, William S., 24, 128, 130,

136–37, 144, 151, 154, 159, 164, 166–67, 169, 178–79, 203n93, 234n50, 234n52, 239n124, 245n82

Cabell, James Branch, 42, 55–58, 60–61
California v. Ferlinghetti, 24, 132–33, 138–51, 238n95, 238n108
Caragianes, Felix, 40–41
Castro, Fidel, 101, 154, 165
Cather, Willa, 42, 49–53, 63
censorship, 1–3, 6–10, 12, 14–15, 17, 20–26, 33, 36–37, 40–41, 45–50, 57–61, 70, 71–78, 90, 93–94, 99–100, 101–2, 119–20, 125, 138–40, 150–51, 154, 158–59, 173–74, 180–83. See also *California v. Ferlinghetti*; obscenity
Cerf, Bennett, 18
Chafee, Zechariah, 45
Chase, J. Frank, 40–42
City Lights Books, 24, 139, 141, 142–43. See also *California v. Ferlinghetti*; Ferlinghetti, Lawrence; Ginsberg, Allen
civilized minority, 33, 42–45, 52, 54, 61, 62, 66–67, 69, 70, 103
Claflin, Tennessee, 14
Clarke, Arthur C., 106, 111, 113
class, 27, 30, 31–32, 42–43, 52–53, 66–68, 76–77, 132, 155, 158; classlessness, 76–77, 134, 156, 163, 165, 177–78, 187; downward mobility, 15, 70, 170–71, 184–85; obscenity and, 13, 15–20, 23, 25; upward mobility, 5, 52, 66, 81–82, 106. See also labor; professional-managerial class; proletariat
Cohen, Paul Robert, 173
Comfort, Alex, 60
Comics Code, 72, 90
communication, 21, 32–33, 46, 84, 106, 110, 116–17, 122–24, 133, 137–38, 167–68, 235n56. See also media
Communications Decency Act, 182
communism, 19, 27, 30, 62, 78, 93–94, 96, 129, 148, 155, 157, 164, 174
Comstock, Anthony, 14–15, 50

Comstock Act, 14
Conrad, Joseph, 43, 47–48
coolness, 16, 30, 56, 104, 106–13, 117, 125–26, 160, 174–75, 190, 192, 208n160, 226n29. See also distance; emotions
Craig, Johnny, 95, 97, 222n107
Crime SuspenStories, 72, 85, 87–88, 91
Crumb, R., 99
Crypt-Keeper, the, 86, 98
cybernetics, 73, 83–85, 89, 227n47

Davis, Jack, 85–86
Day, Dorothy, 4
Debray, Régis, 165
Deleuze, Gilles, and Felix Guattari, 159, 241n16, 243n35
desensitization, 10, 91
DeWitt, Helen, 207n158
Dexedrine, 79, 87, 108
distance, 16, 27, 29, 37, 58, 69, 104, 131, 163, 205n128; aesthetic distance, 47–48; emotional distance, 11, 26, 79, 107, 126, 187; overcoming distance, 133, 135–138, 161–62; temporal distance, 44, 47, 54; and secularism, 58–59. See also coolness; emotions
Doherty, Clifford, and Shenfield, 129–30
Douglas, William O., 23
Doyle Dane Bernbach, 131
Dreiser, Theodore, 42, 43
Dryer, Stan, 113
Duncan, Robert, 138, 237n83
Dworkin, Andrea, 119

EC Comics (Entertaining Comics), 4–5, 79, 82, 88–89, 91–94, 97–99, 175, 182; censorship of, 71–73. See also Craig, Johnny; *Crime SuspenStories*; Davis, Jack; fan-addicts; Feldstein, Al; Gaines, William; *Haunt of Fear, The*; Ingels, Graham; Kurtzman, Harvey; *Mad* magazine; Norris, Shirley; *Panic*; Stuart, Lyle; *Tales from the Crypt*; *Weird Fantasy*; *Weird Science*
editorship, 2–3, 4–5, 7–10, 11–15, 17–18,

21–26, 46, 73, 105, 118–19, 121, 122, 125–26, 137–38, 144, 154–56, 168, 180–83, 192–93, 195n7; theorized as editor function, 2, 118–19, 125–26, 195n7
Ehrenreich, Barbara, 26, 164, 171–72, 205n128
Ehrlich, Jacob W., 139, 140–41, 146–50, 152, 203n93, 203n94, 238n108, 239n109
Eliot, T. S., 145
Ellis, Bret Easton, 98, 195
Ellison, Harlan, 111, 126
emotional labor, 28, 151–52
emotions, 6–7, 13, 27, 74; detachment, 16, 47, 88, 91, 98, 107, 109–10, 113, 122, 126, 152, 160, 175, 181; emotional self-control, 15, 26, 30–31, 37, 39, 56–57, 63, 104, 107; feminized, 53, 70, 117–18, 121, 185–86, 190–92; managing emotions, 30–31, 107, 110, 135; and reading, 76–77, 79, 86, 132–34, 136. *See also* coolness; distance; emotional labor; sentimentalism
Ernst, Morris, 18–20, 25, 61
eroticism, 7, 22, 29, 32, 35, 49, 54, 57, 63, 113, 142, 146, 156–57, 167–68, 178, 182, 191–92. *See also* sexuality; sexual revolution
Esquire, 26, 56, 175
Evans, George, 82
Evergreen Review, 154–55, 159, 160, 162–63, 165, 176–77

family, 26–29, 39, 53, 73–74, 96, 99, 151
fan-addicts, 73, 79, 82, 89–92, 95, 98–99
Fanon, Frantz, 154, 166
Feldstein, Al, 5; as an author, 82, 88, 93, 222n112; editorship of, 73, 79–81, 87, 88, 93
femininity, 7, 26–27, 53, 118, 126, 136, 143, 163–64, 178–79. *See also* Playmates (*Playboy*); secretaries; wives
feminism, 14, 119–22, 155, 159, 176–79
Ferber, Edna, 163
Ferlinghetti, Lawrence, 24, 132; editorship of, 137–38, 152; legal defense, 141–43, 150. *See also California v. Ferlinghetti*; City Lights Books; Ginsberg, Allen
Fiedler, Leslie, 76, 110–12, 115, 159, 162
Fight Club (1999), 164, 185
Filthy Speech Movement, 173–74
First Amendment, 12, 21, 24, 38, 70, 77, 120, 140, 180, 183
Fitzgerald, F. Scott, 53–54
Fletcher, Karen. See *United States v. Fletcher*
Flynt, Larry, 181–82
Ford, Henry, 43, 68–70
Fordism, 28, 69, 107. *See also* Ford, Henry; management science; Taylorism
Forsén, Lena. See "Lenna"
Foucault, Michel, 110, 159, 169, 190, 195n7, 242n20
Freeman, Elizabeth, 169
Freudian psychoanalysis, 75, 84, 110, 141, 206n138
Fromm, Erich, 30, 205n122, 206n143

Gaines, William, 5, 86–87, 98; editorship of, 73, 79–80, 88, 92–93, 96–97, 100; and censorship, 71–72, 90, 93–94; and fan-addicts, 99; testimony at Juvenile Delinquency hearings, 72, 82, 85, 87–88; and office culture, 95–97
game theory, 83–84, 172, 185
gay physique magazines, 237n92
Genet, Jean, 159, 178
gender. See femininity; masculinity
George Fine Market Research, 130
Gilbreth, Frank, 68
Ginsberg, Allen, 5, 6, 238n96; and advertising, 128, 130; campiness of, 151; and class, 134, 151; disaffection with the publishing industry, 136–37, 152–53; and emotional labor, 151–52; as an employee of market research and public opinion firms, 128–32; and gender, 136; and Lawrence

Ferlinghetti, 137–38, 142–44; *Howl and Other Poems*, 24, 129, 132–52, 238n96; reading practices of, 132–33, 135–37, 146; and queer sexuality, 130, 136–37, 143, 235n54; testimony of, 151, 239n124. *See also* Burroughs, William S.; *California v. Ferlinghetti*; Ferlinghetti, Lawrence; Kerouac, Jack
Ginzburg v. United States, 23–24
Goad, Jim, 190
Goethe, Johann Wolfgang von, 42
Goffman, Erving, 98
Goldstein, Al, 169, 181–82
Goodman, Paul, 149, 151
Gouldner, Alvin, 30–31
Griswold v. Connecticut, 147
Grove Press, 5, 44, 153, 154; and antihumanism, 157, 159, 179; censorship trials of, 24; editorial policies of, 168–69; and masochism, 156, 170–71, 177–78; occupation of, 155, 176–77; and radical politics, 154, 165–66; readership of, 155–56, 162–63

Haines, William, 13–14
Hand, Augustus, 20–21
Hand, Learned, 17, 44
Harlan, John Marshall II, 23
Harman, Moses, 14
Haunt of Fear, The, 85–86, 88–89
Hays Code, 72
Hazlitt, William, 61
Heap, Jane, 19
Hefner, Hugh, 5, 101, 174; coolness of, 38, 106–7, 109–11, 226n29, 227n47; editorship of, 9, 100, 103–6, 125–26; and gender, 26, 118, 121–22, 176; and obscenity, 102; and Playmates, 116–19, 136; and science fiction, 111; sentimentality of, 117–18; and white-collar labor, 26–27, 108, 152, 181, 189
Hemingway, Ernest, 46
Heywood, Ezra, 14
Holmes, Oliver Wendell, Jr., 37
Holmes, John Clellon, 129

homosexuality, 2, 26, 102–3, 114, 123, 125, 139, 143–44, 147, 237n92, 237n93
Horn, Clayton W., 139, 140, 146, 148, 203n94
horror, 4–5, 71

Ingels, Graham, 88, 98, 222n107
International Business Machines (IBM), 38, 94, 109, 119, 131, 162, 175, 247n130
intimacy, 31, 113–14, 135, 137, 147, 151, 187
Ionesco, Eugène, 167
Islam, 59

Jaffe, Rona, 121–22
Joyce, James, 51, 110. *See also United States v. One Book Called "Ulysses" by James Joyce*

Kamen, Jack, 88, 97
Kant, Immanuel, 42, 47, 51
Kerouac, Jack, 101, 128, 131, 144, 234n52
Kinsey, Alfred, 25, 111, 114, 203n102
Knopf, Alfred A., 41
Kraus, Chris, 179
Kurtzman, Harvey, 221n84

labor, 26–27, 29–32, 62, 67–70, 92, 96–98, 107–9, 118–19, 122–23, 125, 134–35, 149, 151–52, 158, 160–62, 164–65, 181, 183, 207n158, 208n163; mental versus manual labor, 17–18, 21, 52–53, 187, 200n52; reproductive labor 27–29, 31. *See also* emotional labor
Langelaan, George, 123–25
Langton, Rae, 120
Lawrence, D. H., 46, 110; *Lady Chatterley's Lover*, 24, 154, 155, 167, 169, 173, 203n93
lawyers, 7, 16–17, 19–20, 24, 41, 60, 62–63, 139, 140–41, 148–51, 180
Le Guin, Ursula K., 111–12
"Lenna," 126–27
Levertov, Denise, 132
Lewis, Sinclair, 56, 164

liberalism, 37–38, 45, 78, 148–50, 163, 174, 181, 184–85, 188–89
Little Review, 19
Lotringer, Sylvère, 180
Lowenthal, Leo, 146, 238n95
lumpenproletariat, 161, 166
Lynd, Robert S., and Helen Merrell Lynd, 65–66

Madison Avenue, 39, 130, 131, 232n24
Macauley, Robie, 111
MacKinnon, Catharine, 119–20, 122, 159
Maddox, Cynthia, 118
Mad magazine, 5, 72, 92, 162, 175
Mailer, Norman, 101, 110, 237n93
management science, 68, 107, 110, 112–13, 134–35. See also Fordism; Taylorism
Mansfield, Jayne, 102
market research, 117, 128–30, 154–55
Marx, Karl, 31
Marxism, 31, 157, 159, 164–65
masculinity 2–4, 7, 26–29, 39, 114, 121–23, 126, 143, 162, 186, 189
masochism, 96, 156, 162, 166, 169–71, 177–79, 189
Matheson, Richard, 111
Matrix, The (1999), 185
May, Rollo, 114
McHugh, Vincent, 145
McInnes, Gavin, 189–90
McIntosh, Ralph, 150, 239n119
Mead, Margaret, 65
media, 6, 73–74, 76, 92, 103, 105, 114, 116–17, 122–27, 129, 136–38, 167, 229n89, 235n61
Meiklejohn, Alexander, 45
Memoirs v. Massachusetts, 24
Mencken, Henry Louis, 4, 71; alt-right and, 70, 188; class and, 42–45, 52–53, 66–70, 196n13; as a critic, 47–48, 67, 73, 209n1; editorship of, 9, 18, 44–43, 53, 209n1, 211n29, 215n119; gender and, 26, 28; "Hatrack" obscenity trial and 40–42; puritanism and, 41–43, 46, 48, 55, 57–59; race and, 43, 68–70;

Scopes trial and, 61–66; sexuality and, 46–48, 54–55; temporality and, 43, 46, 51–52, 63, 65, 213n94, 214n104; the *Smart Set* and, 42, 44–43; the *American Mercury* and, 40–42. See also civilized minority
Mendocino, Ellen Smith, 176–77
middlebrow, 36, 61, 76–77, 86, 91, 97–98, 99, 129, 134, 163, 181, 187
Miller, Henry, 24, 154, 159, 160–62, 164, 168–71, 179, 192, 243n35, 246n105
Miller v. California, 25, 180
Millett, Kate, 160–61
Mills, C. Wright, 30, 158
Milton, John, 37
Minh, Ho Chi, 154
Mishkin v. New York, 23
Mizer, Bob, 237n92
monsters, 73, 76, 82–84, 93, 97–98, 124
Morgan, Robin, 176–78
Murao, Shigeyoshi "Shig," 139
Murrow, Edward R., 33
Mystery (pickup artist), 186

Nabokov, Vladimir, 101, 192
Nagle, Angela, 184, 191
Nathan, George Jean, 42, 45
National Opinion Research Center, 129–30
neoconservatism, 77–78, 159, 180
New Criticism, 157, 161
New England Watch and Ward Society, 40
New Left, 79, 164, 171–76
New York Intellectuals, 157, 161
New York Society for the Enforcement of Criminal Law, 50
New York Society for the Suppression of Vice (NYSSV), 28–29, 45
Nietzsche, Friedrich, 44, 67–69, 189, 191
Norris, Shirley, 71–72
nudism, 75

Obelisk Press, 161
obscenity, 4–8; as an aesthetic category,

37, 47–48, 50–51, 110, 157, 161–62, 175, 177–78, 179; as a class concept, 4–5, 8, 10, 15–20, 23, 25–26, 33, 36–37, 44, 46, 61, 173, 181, 208n166; and editors, 3, 10, 11, 22–24, 54, 79, 106, 182; as an emotional complex, 6–7, 92, 126; indeterminacy of, 5–7, 58–59, 102; as a legal category, 2, 7, 11–15, 17–26, 40–42, 45, 50, 57, 63, 102–3, 132, 139–51, 154, 160, 173–74, 180, 182; and moral character, 75, 78, 158–59; and online platforms, 181–82, 185, 191–92; as transgressive, 10, 32, 99–100, 180–82, 184–91; and queer sexuality, 139–40; and violence, 71. See also *California v. Ferlinghetti*; *Ginzburg v. United States*; *Memoirs v. Massachusetts*; *Miller v. California*; *Mishkin v. New York*; *One, Inc. v. Oleson*; *Redrup v. New York*; *Regina v. Hicklin*; *Rex v. Curll*; *Roth v. United States*; *United States v. Fletcher*; *United States v. Kennerley*; *United States v. One Book Called "Ulysses" by James Joyce*; *Winters v. New York*

offices, 27–28, 30, 33–34, 38, 71–72, 85, 95–98, 108, 113, 116, 117, 121, 130–31, 177, 181, 185

O'Hara, Frank, 6, 238n96

Olson, Charles, 3

One, Inc. v. Oleson, 139–40

organization man, 39, 94, 135, 143, 157, 158, 190

Orientalism, 109, 175, 227n46

Orlovsky, Peter, 130–31

Paine, Thomas, 13

Panic, 71–72, 93–94

paranoia, 94, 129, 132, 140–47, 149

Parisienne, 45

Parker, Dorothy, 53

Patchen, Kenneth, 142

PayPal, 191–92

pickup artistry, 185–87

Pilgrim, Janet, 116, 124

Pinter, Harold, 167

Playboy, 5, 26, 33, 44, 56, 135, 169, 174, 177, 181, 224n5; and gender, 118–22; and labor, 108–9, 152, 225n24, 226n36; readership of, 100, 101, 103–6, 114, 117, 125–27, 136, 185–86; and science fiction, 101–2, 104, 111–13, 126. See also Hefner, Hugh; Playmates

Playmates (*Playboy*), 101, 105, 106, 113–14, 116–19, 122–23, 125–27, 136

Pohl, Frederik, 122–23

police, 1–3, 23, 40–44, 71–72, 138–41, 166, 174, 178

pornography, 6, 9, 11–16, 88, 154, 157, 162, 181–82; and abstraction, 13, 29, 35–38, 85, 159, 161, 181; and anthropology, 64; audience for, 13, 15–16, 25–26, 102–3, 185; censorship of, 14–15, 21–22, 24–25, 73, 150, 180, 182, 191–93; critique of, 78, 119–22, 158–59, 167–68, 177–78, 184, 189–90; origins of, 48–49

post-Fordism, 39, 149, 152, 181

Pound, Ezra, 3, 76, 145, 215n119, 238n95

privacy, 12–13, 30–31, 37–39, 73–74, 82, 103–5, 135, 147, 149–52, 158, 160, 162, 168, 174, 202n78, 206n143, 213n82, 224n8

professional-managerial class, 4–5, 17–18, 52–53, 62, 158, 181, 200n52, 233n36; and abstraction, 29–32; cultural capital of, 10, 15, 17–20, 23, 36, 43, 102, 170, 196n13; and gender, 26–28; reading habits of, 17, 31, 42–43, 45–46, 53, 76–77, 97–98, 102, 106, 134, 155; resistance against, 130, 156, 164–71, 171–76, 179, 184–85, 188; and self-control, 7–8, 11, 34–35, 71, 189, 191; self-loathing of, 164–65; sexuality of, 27–29, 32–37; theatricality of, 132–33, 149. See also class

proletariat, 3, 15, 52–53, 67–69, 123, 158, 165, 181, 188, 200n52

public opinion, 128–30

publishing, 22–25, 101–3, 152–53. *See also* editorship
puritanism, 18, 40–41, 43, 46, 48, 55, 57–58, 69, 209n1; the new puritanism, 114

race. *See* Blackness; orientalism; whiteness
Radway, Janice, 7, 9, 76, 196n22
Rand, Ayn, 32, 70, 101
Rat Subterranean News, 176
reading, 3, 4–5, 13, 163, 180, 233n31; and editorship, 7, 9, 25–26, 79–80, 142, 144, 182, 195n7; and mediation, 103, 105, 116, 123–24, 133, 138; and moral uplift, 73, 76–77, 97–98, 134; paranoid, 94, 132, 140–47; reparative, 133–36, 142, 146; as a training exercise, 7–8, 10, 34–36, 46, 79, 81–82, 89, 104, 181, 247n128
Reáge, Pauline, 159, 171
Redrup v. New York, 24–25
Regina v. Hicklin, 15, 17, 18, 20, 21
Remittance Girl, 192
Rex v. Curll, 12, 182
Riesman, David, 27–28, 74, 81–82, 143, 147–48, 158
Rodger, Elliot, 188
Rosen, Lew, 15
Rosset, Barney, 5; and class, 155–56, 177; editorship of, 9, 154–56, 168–69, 178; and masochism, 156; and obscenity, 24, 160; protest of, 176–77
Roszak, Theodore, 31, 33
Roth, Samuel, 21, 189, 199n25. *See also Roth v. United States*
Roth v. United States, 21–25, 33, 139, 150
Rubin, Gayle, 114
Russell, Ray, 111

Sade, Donatien Alphonse François, Marquis de, 13, 64, 84–85, 154, 159, 167–168, 169, 171, 178
Sanders, Ed, 1–6, 176
Satanism, 70

Saul, Jennifer, 122
Savio, Mario, 173, 175
Schorer, Mark, 145, 173
Schroeder, Theodore, 43–44, 57–58
science fiction, 83–84, 89–90, 92, 101–2, 104, 111–13, 126
Seagle, William, 18, 41, 61
secretaries, 71, 97, 106, 116, 121, 124–25
Sedgwick, Eve Kosofsky, 114, 141–42, 145, 153
self-help, 32, 42, 107, 117, 166–67, 186–87
Semiotext(e), 179, 180
sensitivity, 131, 135, 143, 149
sentimentalism, 26, 76, 88, 99, 117–18, 163–64, 185
sexuality, 3, 4, 8, 10, 26–29, 32–39, 54, 56, 104, 110, 114, 139–40, 144–45, 151, 167–68, 187, 190
sexual revolution, 4, 26–27, 32–33, 35, 187
sex work, 22, 33–34, 40, 126, 160–61
Shea, Robert, 111
Silverstein, Shel, 108
Smart Set, 42, 44–45, 49–56, 68, 215n119
Smashwords, 192
Solomon, Carl, 134, 136, 137, 145, 234n52
Song of Songs, 144–45
Sontag, Susan, 35–36, 145–46, 156–57, 159, 160, 253n60
Sorrentino, Gilbert, 155
Spectorsky, A. C., 105, 111, 113, 121
Speiser, Lawrence, 139
Spencer, Richard, 70
Spicer, Jack, 138
Spider magazine, 174
Steinem, Gloria, 119
Stewart, Potter, 23
Stoicism, 37
Straus, Roger, 126
Stuart, Lyle, 71–72, 87
Superman, 74

Talese, Gay, 32
Tales from the Crypt, 5, 72, 82–83, 86, 91, 99
Taylor, Charles, 58

Taylorism, 34, 67–68, 107
temporality, 43, 45, 47–48, 51–57, 66, 69–70, 169–70
Tennessee v. John Thomas Scopes, 61–63, 66
Towne-Oller and Associates, 130–31
transgression, 5, 8, 10, 35, 43, 48, 85, 99–100, 157, 164, 166, 180–87, 190–91, 195n7
trauma, 38, 74, 84, 143, 161, 175, 183

underground comix, 79, 99
United States Civil War, 14, 64
United States v. Fletcher, 180
United States v. Kennerley, 17
United States v. One Book Called "Ulysses" by James Joyce, 18–20

Vietnam War, 171–73, 174, 175, 246n108, 247n115
violence, 5, 71–72, 74, 78, 88–89, 92, 142, 166–68, 175, 180, 181, 183, 189, 190, 221n96

Waisbrooker, Lois, 14
Warren, Earl, 22–23

Weird Fantasy, 83, 90
Weird Science, 83
Wertham, Fredric, 72–79, 85–87, 91–94, 184
whiteness, 68–69, 241n16
Whitman, Walt, 137, 143
Williams, Linda, 10, 89
Williams, William Carlos, 143–45, 238n95
Williamson, John, 32
Wilson, Edmund, 110, 215n119
Wilson, Robert Anton, 111, 175
Wilson, Sloan, 38, 158, 167
Winters v. New York, 85
wives, 26–29, 39, 55, 80, 87, 97, 109, 112, 115–16, 124, 125, 147, 190
Wood, Wallace, 83–84
Woodhull, Victoria, 14
Woolsey, John M., 20–21
World War I, 238n95
World War II, 83–84
Wright, Erik Olin, 43

X, Malcolm, 154, 166

Yates, Richard, 38–39
Yiannopoulos, Milo, 183

Michael Dango, *Crisis Style: The Aesthetics of Repair*

Mary Esteve, *Incremental Realism: Postwar American Fiction, Happiness, and Welfare-State Liberalism*

Dorothy J. Hale, *The Novel and the New Ethics*

Christine Hong, *A Violent Peace: Race, U.S. Militarism, and Cultures of Democratization in Cold War Asia and the Pacific*

Sarah Brouillette, *UNESCO and the Fate of the Literary*

Sophie Seita, *Provisional Avant-Gardes: Little Magazine Communities from Dada to Digital*

Guy Davidson, *Categorically Famous: Literary Celebrity and Sexual Liberation in 1960s America*

Joseph Jonghyun Jeon, *Vicious Circuits: Korea's IMF Cinema and the End of the American Century*

Lytle Shaw, *Narrowcast: Poetry and Audio Research*

Stephen Schryer, *Maximum Feasible Participation: American Literature and the War on Poverty*

Margaret Ronda, *Remainders: American Poetry at Nature's End*

Jasper Bernes, *The Work of Art in the Age of Deindustrialization*

Annie McClanahan, *Dead Pledges: Debt, Crisis, and Twenty-First-Century Culture*

The authorized representative in the EU for product safety and compliance is:
Mare Nostrum Group
B.V Doelen 72
4831 GR Breda
The Netherlands

www.ingramcontent.com/pod-product-compliance
Lightning Source LLC
Chambersburg PA
CBHW030613230426
43661CB00053B/1968